Also by Beatrice Trum Hunter

THE NATURAL FOODS PRIMER

THE NATURAL FOODS COOKBOOK

GARDENING WITHOUT POISONS

CONSUMER BEWARE!

◆ ◆ ◆ ◆

YOUR FOOD AND WHAT'S BEEN DONE TO IT

by Beatrice Trum Hunter

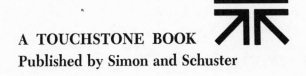

A TOUCHSTONE BOOK
Published by Simon and Schuster

First Touchstone paperback printing 1972

SBN 671-20797-0 Casebound edition
SBN 671-21232-X Touchstone paperback edition
Library of Congress Catalog Card Number: 75-139632
Designed by Irving Perkins
Manufactured in the United States of America

To Ruth Desmond, President,
Federation of Homemakers

CONTENTS

◆ ◆ ◆ ◆

Abbreviations Defined

ADA:	American Dental Association
AEC:	Atomic Energy Commission
AFDOUS:	Association of Food and Drug Officials of the United States
AMA:	American Medical Association
BBC:	British Broadcasting Corporation
BHA:	butylated hydroxyanisole
BHT:	butylated hydroxytoluene
CBS:	Columbia Broadcasting System
CRS:	Chinese Restaurant Syndrome
CSM:	corn, soy, milk (food blend)
EFA:	essential fatty acids
FAO/WHO:	Food and Agricultural Organization of the World Health Organization
FDA:	Food and Drug Administration
FDLI:	Food and Drug Law Institute
FDS:	federal definitions and standards
FPC:	fish protein concentrate
FSI:	federal standards of identity
GMA:	Grocery Manufacturers of America
GRAS:	Generally Recognized as Safe
HEW:	Health, Education and Welfare
MDR:	minimum daily requirements
MSG:	monosodium glutamate
NAM:	National Association of Manufacturers
NAS-NRC:	National Academy of Sciences—National Research Council
NBC:	National Broadcasting Company
NCI:	National Cancer Institute
NDGA:	nordihydroguaiaretic acid

NPK:	nitrogen, phosphorus, potash
ppb:	parts per billion
ppm:	parts per million
PSE:	pale, soft, exudative (of pork)
RDA:	Recommended Daily Allowances
USDA:	United States Department of Agriculture
USDI:	United States Department of the Interior
USGPO:	United States Government Printing Office
USPHS:	United States Public Health Service
WARF:	Wisconsin Alumni Research Foundation

FOREWORD

◆ ◆ ◆ ◆

"LET THE buyer beware!" has always been sensible advice in the free market place. Today this admonition is especially meaningful for food consumers—in other words, for everyone.

The 1960's was a decade marked by growing awareness of a rapid deterioration of environmental quality. Although air and water received ample publicity, soil and food were neglected. Our basic foodstuffs, how they are grown, modified, and processed, relate to the overall quality of life.

Although scientists had warned of the perils and declining quality in our food at Congressional hearings during the 1950's, they went unheeded. Meanwhile the hazards have escalated. Often with government sanction and encouragement, short-term self-defeating agricultural practices have been recommended, while long-term ecological consequences have been ignored. Results are reflected in problems such as nitrate and mercury poisonings in food chains, water eutrophication, and world-wide pesticidal contamination of all life forms. Also with government sanction, the use of food additives has been allowed to proliferate, despite repeated warnings by scientists that such substances may pose subtle hazards, suspected but at present incompletely understood. In the 1950's, experts were concerned mainly with toxic and carcinogenic properties of food additives as dangers to people eating them; by the 1970's, they are also concerned with possible teratogenic and mutagenic effects on the quality of life for future generations.

This book, begun in 1965, has been completed in 1970. During this period, many of the subjects discussed in the book have become front-page news items: the curbing of persistent pesticides

11

and certain herbicides; the banning of cyclamates; the proposed review of the GRAS list; the elimination of MSG from baby foods; the startling inadequacies of the American diet, regardless of income; and the nutritional inadequacies of many commercial breakfast cereals, to name a few.

During this period, the uninformed, inarticulate, and unorganized consumer has begun to show a glimmer of understanding that all is not well with basic foodstuffs. More people are trying to buy poison-free foods; others are growing their own, even on city rooftops.

During this period, "consumerism" has begun to flourish in some quarters, and some small blessings can be counted. Some supermarkets and other food stores have begun to assist consumers by unit pricing, dating of perishable foods, and deciphering of coded dates. The number of package sizes has been reduced, and some fractional quantities have been replaced by more uniform net quantities. But the grave, momentous problems of perils in foods and deteriorating quality remain with us.

Early in 1970 E. B. Weiss, a columnist in *Advertising Age,* wrote that the return to natural foods is a consumer revolt against the "plastic" society. He predicted that natural foods will become the most dynamically expanding segment of the food industry during the 1970's, with such foods available at hotels and restaurants, in hospitals and supermarkets, at roadside stands, and on airplanes.

As this book goes to press, new Congressional hearings on the safety of food additives are scheduled for the fall of 1970 by Senator Gaylord Nelson. Testimony will be given, no doubt, on many subjects discussed in this book. Will the newly publicized facts remain unheeded as they were in the 1950's? Or will they serve to shake us from complacency? Will we, as consumers convinced of the urgency of the problems, begin to demand quality in our environment? If we do, we shall make certain that the foodstuffs are grown and handled in ways that will make them nutritious and safe.

BEATRICE TRUM HUNTER

September 1970

"The shopper, really informed and looking for a plain food with nothing added or taken away, is like Diogenes with a lantern unable to find an honest man."

MRS. IONE DENNIS STARKEY,
homemaker, before Congressional hearings
on color additives, 1960

PART I

◆ ◆ ◆ ◆

PRIMER FOR THE CONSUMER

1

The Food Revolution

WHAT HAS happened to that 40-ounce container, the average human stomach? And what is likely to happen to it if our sometimes disastrous food revolution goes on apace?

A food-industry executive, John W. Vassos of the Pet Milk Company, once viewed the human stomach as a merchandising problem. At a Congressional hearing he said: "There is extreme competition for space in the human stomach." At this point Senator Harrison A. Williams, Jr., noted wryly: "You are not only in competition with food. You are in competition with liquids. Just to mention one relatively inoffensive liquid—beer; that takes up some part of the stomach space, does it not?"[1]

In other words, competition for those precious 40 ounces puts the consumer in the position of being a valuable pawn, with each eager competitor trying his best to fill the stomach with as much of his own merchandise as possible.

The paradox is that daily new food items are being displayed on shelves and counters, but annual food consumption in America has *decreased* nearly 200 pounds per person over the last half century.[2] Weight-conscious Americans now consume 400 fewer calories daily. This means that the giants of the food industry must exert high-pressure persuasion to convert the consumer to new creations, new product names, more "convenience" foods.

It is true that every new food item introduced must be *made to seem* an improvement. Alluring new packaging, new sales gim-

17

micks, new slogans, new "wonder" foods, once perishable items
made to keep "forever," foods dehydrated, homogenized, vacuum-
packed, frozen, condensed—the colorful pageant goes on and on.
But where does it leave the consumer, who once upon a time
bought food that was just plain food, and learned to market with
the seasons, to recognize farm freshness in vegetables, quality in
meat, tree ripeness in fruit, and many other old-fashioned virtues
that have nearly disappeared from today's food basket?

Thanks to the efficiency of the food industry, we now have an
unparalleled selection of food products in almost unimaginable
variety, at all times of the year, and at costs that are distinctly
moderate compared with costs in many other countries. But upon
closer scrutiny, all too often the vast variety of new food products
turns out to be a bewildering array with superficial, meaningless
product differentiations.

THE BILLION-DOLLAR PERSUADERS

It costs money to launch a new food item. As much as $10 million
may be allotted for an advertising budget. As a matter of fact,
advertising mogul David Ogilvy believes that a budget under $2
million a year fails to achieve national acceptance for a new
product.[3]

There is an added problem for food producers; only one of
every ten new creations will pass the Food and Drug Administration (FDA) safety standards. Despite the fact that only about 500
of all new food products introduced annually will survive, the
food industry continues to market some two dozen new items
daily.[4]

In the 1960's, food manufacturers had spent over a billion dollars
annually in advertising.[5] Trailing slightly were the food retailers
with a $700 million advertising budget;[6] then came wholesalers
with only about $100 million.[7] Ultimately, consumers pay, through
higher food costs. Among the first major proposals made at the
1969 White House Conference on Food, Nutrition, and Health was
a call for mandatory limitations on food advertising. At the time of
the Conference, for every $10 spent on food, $.26 was for advertising.[8]

Study of a highly processed food—especially one with a large promotional budget—may show it to be far more costly than the original basic commodity. For instance, the cost of a dry breakfast cereal may be many times more per pound than that of the grains from which it is processed.[9] A recent survey by the Co-operative Extension Service at Cornell University showed that the cost per pound of corn chips was $1.03; of potato chips, $1.04; of corn puffs with cheese flavoring, $1.56 and of popcorn, $2.08.

THE BURGEONING SUPERMARKET

The explosive development of that unique institution, the supermarket, has paralleled the phenomenal growth in food advertising. Both have been fashioned to fulfill each other's needs, and have become active participants in speeding up the food revolution.

A century ago, when our country was mainly rural, a store sold fewer than 100 different food items, consisting mainly of dried staples and produce from nearby farms. Meals were eaten at home, prepared daily from basic ingredients. Perishables were eaten as quickly as possible, or converted into butter, cheese, sausage, and other items that kept longer.[10]

Today, with a population that is more than 90 per cent urban, eating habits and food technology have undergone radical changes. Practically all urban residents eat at least one meal a day away from home, representing a yearly expenditure in restaurants of more than $22 billion. There is also an increased use of "convenience foods" in commercial catering, delicatessens, hospitals, schools, and other institutions through vending machines. The operation of automatic food dispensers has reached more than $200 million annually.

When the first supermarkets opened in the early 1930's they did less than 5 per cent of the total retail-food business. By the 1950's, after the rationing of World War II ended, and building materials became available, supermarkets mushroomed across the United States. By 1955 they had captured more than half the retail-food sales dollar and they have continued to thrive.[11] Of the $80 billion spent yearly in retail food stores, several of the largest chains each do up to $5 billion, with the remainder going to many intermediate-size chains and to about 15,000 small independent supermarkets. Although only 12 per cent of all grocery stores are supermarkets, they account for 75 per cent of all food sales.[12]

Food processing has become inextricably intertwined with segments of other giant industries, including chemicals, drugs, packaging, advertising, retailing, and merchandising. Meanwhile, the supermarket has undergone a subtle change. Today it is primarily a seller of shelf space to brand advertisers, and only secondarily a seller of foods. Economist Irston R. Barnes has dubbed it "a display depot."[13]

Row upon row of self-service shelves are used as a potent and highly effective advertising tool. The average supermarket, stocking some 7,000 to 9,000 different items, with some up to 20,000, becomes an arena where forces do constant battle, struggling to achieve and maintain prominent display space.[14]

The average American has been found to be an eye-to-waist-level shopper.[15] Moving a product 18 inches higher on a display rack can increase its sale. The layout of a supermarket is planned so that the high-profit items will be noticed. Many are placed on the aisle to which the shopper has first access.[16]

The food broker's responsibility to his clients includes efforts to obtain the best display space for their wares. The more space a package requires on the shelf, the louder it screams Buy Me! This need is filled by the giant, jumbo, king, economy, and family-sized packages, which occupy more shelf space without necessarily providing greater economy to the consumer.

"A good deal of what is called product research today is a sales-promotion expenditure undertaken to provide what the trade calls a profitable 'product mix,'" says Vance Packard in *The Waste Makers*.[17] A judicious product mix is, among other things, a combination of brands designed to commandeer for the advertiser the greatest possible shelf space in the supermarket. This results in a multiplicity of brands; the so-called new product may be simply a new packaging gimmick.

As the battle for shelf space has intensified, sales-promotion expenditures have skyrocketed. The food industry pours money into premiums, trading stamps, cents-off campaigns, deals, give-aways, contests, and tie-in sales. There have been attractive offers —and some outright bribes—to supermarket operators for special shelf space or display privileges. They include gifts, advertising allowances, extra money or goods for store display, free freezer equipment, or loans. Fees are paid for handling coupons, or handing out premiums, obtaining window-display space, hanging banners along the ceiling, or having clerks wear promotional buttons. Ultimately, the cost of such merchandising must be absorbed by the consumer in the retail price of food.

IMPULSE BUYING

Analysts have found that the average supermarket shopper does not arrive with a list of exactly what she needs. She—or he—can be lured into impulse buying by eye-catching packages in plastic and glass. So easily is the shopper manipulated that items called in the trade "self-gratifying"—that is, luxury foods or exotic products more expensive than basic foodstuffs—frequently run as high as 90 per cent of all purchases.

To their delight, the experts have found that more and more men shop in supermarkets, and that often they are bigger and better impulse buyers than their more budget-conscious female counterparts. The unplanned purchase is the supermarket's bonanza, and welcome indeed is the gullible male who will succumb to colorful displays and the impact of massive choice.

Customer-hypnosis is never ending: soft background music, pleasant lighting, free cheese cubes, pickles and other snacks, a soft-drink bar, electric fans wafting baking smells from glass-sided ovens, aerosprays filled with coffee or chocolate aromas.[18]

EYE BLINKS, ANYONE?

You may not know it, but a hidden motion-picture camera may record your eye-blink rate as you progress through the supermarket. It knows when you are tense and wary, when you are relaxed and susceptible. It sometimes records shoppers in such a state of trance that they do not recognize neighbors or friends, so hypnotized are they by the offerings on the shelves. Understandably, eyelids often blink nervously as the customer, wondering whether there is enough money to pay the tab, wheels an over-loaded cart to the check-out counter.

An even neater trick was an advertising technique introduced in a New Jersey motion picture theater in 1957. The words DRINK COCA-COLA and EAT POPCORN were flashed intermittently on the screen during the feature film, but with a light intensity so low that viewers were not consciously aware of it, and for periods so brief—1/3,000 of a second—that it was recorded only on the subconscious mind. It worked! Over a six-week period, some 50,000 movie patrons were subjected unknowingly to this experiment. Coca-Cola sales rose 18 per cent; popcorn skyrocketed by 57 per cent.[19] Once the secret was revealed, moral indignation and revulsion brought the whole matter of "subliminal advertising" before the Code Review Board of the National Association of Radio and Television Broadcasters. Members were directed to forbid use of subliminal techniques in spite of pleas from James Vicary, the innovator, that such advertising was "very innocent . . . a relatively weak form of reminder advertising."[20]

A NEW MODEL ORANGE EVERY YEAR!

"The citrus industry might consider the development of a yearly model, as in the automobile industry. Each year's crop could be presented as the current, improved model."[21] This was the advice given by Dr. Ernest Dichter, a leading motivational expert, to the citrus-growing combines.

After a "probe in depth," candy was discovered to be a reward symbol. One manufacturer responded with this slogan: "To make that tough job easier . . . you deserve candy."[22] His sales doubled in the test area.

Even the prosaic prune underwent a probe, and prune sellers were advised that their fruit had unpleasant associations with such things as constipation, devitalization, dried-out spinsters, and old age. The prune was promptly revamped as a California wonder fruit—juicy, inclined more to a purple hue than to a brown. The prunes remained unchanged, but they had acquired a new personality.[23]

WHAT PRICE FOR THE PRETTY PACKAGE?

The average family in the United States spends at least $200 of its yearly budget just for the package, which is eventually thrown away.[24] Often the streamlined modern package is a neat tool for deception. Orange stripes on a plastic bag can make carrots look brighter. Stalks of celery (lovely to look at through the top of the package) may be rotting and discolored at the concealed end. Lush strawberries on top of the plastic-wrapped box may hide the moldy or unripe. Packaged potatoes, onions, oranges, apples often present their best faces, while the unusable ones are nested below. Fat can be tucked under packaged bacon, and prewrapped center-cut pork chops have been known to cover up cheaper rib chops beneath.

Admittedly, it is tough for the conscientious consumer to penetrate the façade of modern packaging. Some packages have to be turned over and over and practically examined with a magnifying glass to find the small print designating the net weight. FDA regulations require that this designation be placed prominently on the main display panel of the package. But in many cases it is harder to read than a telephone book and more difficult to decipher because of the odd fractional ounces and pounds that are used. Yet the same package may have its advertising message in bold, clear type.

In a survey conducted in May 1963 by the National Bureau of Standards more than 80 per cent of all prepackaged foods were found to be under the specified weight.[25] A representative area of one state was chosen, covering 14 chain and independent supermarkets. The study was made to update an earlier one in the same area. Recent conditions were found to be even worse. Judging by the frequency with which short-weight foods are seized by federal and state authorities, the situation is widespread. A resolution unanimously adopted by more than 500 state and local weights-and-measures officials called on manufacturers, packers, and advertising agencies to recognize their moral obligations, as well as the legal requirements for honest labeling. At the same time, the consumer was urged to stop buying odd-sized packages. It was hoped that this would encourage manufacturers to return to the practice of using common multiples of ounces and pounds.

But what happens when *all* manufacturers of a particular item present odd-sized packages? In 1961 Helen Ewing Nelson, consumer counselor for the State of California, found that a large wholesale grocer listed 17 different sizes of salad and cooking oil items, of which 16 were standard measures. Three years later, the same wholesaler listed 39 oil items, of which more than half were odd sizes.[26] Similarly, all sizes of frozen vegetables, initially sold in one-pound boxes, were reduced gradually to 14 ounces, ten ounces, and even nine ounces. Yet the difference in the box size was practically imperceptible. The once standard No. 2 can (containing about 20 ounces) has been replaced by the No. 303 (about 16 ounces).

Protracted Congressional hearings, led by Senator Philip A. Hart, from 1963 to 1966 ended with the passage of the Fair Packaging and Labeling Act. Witness after witness cited packaging malpractices in a wide range of processed foods and other supermarket items, as well as other consumer goods. *Advertising Age* admitted: "Individual sizes and shapes, we suspect, have been created to the point where they no longer serve any useful purpose, even as merchandising devices. A little standardization might help everyone."[27]

THE INDUSTRY CLOSES RANKS

A different sort of warning to industry was sounded in *Packaging:* "If we don't smother all this talk about how the consumer is being deceived and cheated, our whole economy will emerge *sell shocked.*"[28] By then, after more than a year of hearings, a second round was scheduled. With a truth-in-packaging bill in the offing, the food industry began to close ranks for an assault. The power wielded by this group should not be underestimated.

Over 100 separate national trade associations of food processors worked closely with allied industries (packaging supplies, equipment such as bottles, boxes, glass, paperboard, and packaging machinery). Many trade associations of food brokers, wholesalers, retailers, and supermarket chains joined the battle. There were also groups representing soft drinks, paper products and household supplies, as well as the U.S. Chamber of Commerce and the National Association of Manufacturers. In addition to these giants, thousands of smaller groups worked at state and local levels, among them the Grocery Manufacturers of America (GMA).

GMA, acting as spokesman for the entire food industry, made its position clear to the country's news media. Before the second truth-in-packaging hearing began in March 1963, Paul S. Willis, GMA head, addressed the annual meeting of the Television Bureau of Advertising, informing his audience that GMA representatives had already met with 16 top management people from national magazines, to "discuss . . . the facts of life covering advertising-media relationships.

"We suggested to the publishers that the day was here when their editorial department and business department might better understand their interdependency relationships, as they affect the operating results of their company and as their operations may affect the advertiser—their bread and butter. We invited them to consider publishing some favorable articles about the food industry."

Mr. Willis went on to list the accomplishments of meetings with top management people from national magazines. Then, regretfully, the president of GMA reported that he could not say "similar nice things about the relationship of our advertisers with television." Pointedly, he reminded his audience that television stations received "about 65 per cent of their advertising revenue from GMA members," who, he continued, "have seen some television newscasts bellowing out stories . . . critical of this industry." Although he denied any pressure to limit media from using materials "of their own choice," he ended with the question: What can you do additionally that will influence your advertiser in spending his advertising dollars?[29]

The Willis speech was denounced in an editorial in *Sponsor* as "containing some of the most outrageous and shocking statements ever delivered at an industry meeting." And: "Worse still, it betrays evidence of a type of mentality and type of thinking which, unless checked soon and hard and fast, can easily destroy the whole structure of the American free press and free broadcasting by revealing the disgraceful fact that last year a GMA committee put the arm on 16 supposedly powerful publishers. The magazines got the message. In the past year a flood of puffy, public-relations-type food articles have appeared, the proudest names in the mass magazine field . . . all knuckled under."[30]

THE BIG BLACKOUT

Arm-twisting tactics were effective, and there was a virtual blackout on radio and television coverage for the entire 1963 truth-in-packaging hearings. In discussing the formidable pressures to kill the bill, Senator Philip A. Hart charged: "The industries that oppose it represent minimum yearly sales of $100 billion—or approximately one sixth of the gross national product. And money is power. Millions of sheets of paper have been consumed in press releases and reports. . . . One group of business home economists was told to get out and work against the bill or they might lose their jobs. There are editorial services in Washington, supported by business, that send out editorials against truth-in-packaging which are used by hundreds of small newspapers across the nation; papers that rely on canned editorials. . . . What national forum do we have? Two large-circulation magazines retained writers to do stories on truth-in-packaging, but the stories somehow have never seen print."[31]

Several scheduled appearances of Senator Hart to discuss truth-in-packaging were canceled. The Senator reported: "Off the record, I was told advertisers had objected. Matter of fact, as I was preparing this talk, our office received a call from an educational television station which is considering a series aimed at informing consumers on how to buy wisely. The station man was somewhat interested in background in truth-in-packaging. But he was more interested in what strength—and shape—the opposition took. 'Frankly,' he said, 'we are not yet sure we can survive such a series.' As he explained, 'Educational television may not have to depend directly on advertisers for financial life, but the largest contributors to the foundations which feed money to them are the major industries.' "[32]

The 1965 legislative year began with the food industry's having its trade groups well organized and news media favorably disposed to its image. The following year the GMA had organized a special committee to fight the truth-in-packaging bill. The National Association of Manufacturers (NAM) briefed Congressmen on the bill. Six Congressmen were taken on a tour of a Baltimore plant. Some machines bore special placards saying that their operations would cease if a certain section of the bill passed. One candy manufacturer announced that if the bill became law, romance would vanish from Valentine packages and holes would not be permitted in Life Savers.

The bill was enacted in 1966, but was termed by *The New York Times* as "little more than a shadow" of the original draft. Instead of prohibiting misleading labels, the new act merely provided that ingredients and package sizes be clearly displayed. The crucial provision for readily calculable weights and measures was eliminated. Instead, there was a plea for voluntary reform by industry.

"FOOD IS A BARGAIN"—OR IS IT?

The food industry, the U.S. Department of Agriculture (USDA), and agricultural officials at the state level, as well as mass media, have joined together in a repeated chanting of the slogan "Food is a Bargain." Is it?

Supermarkets are no longer designed to pass along to consumers the economies made possible through mass buying. Originally, they operated on a slim 12 per cent markup but, with the explosion in advertising, wasteful packaging, and the battle for shelf space, markups have risen, on the average, to nearly 20 per cent.[33]

Twenty years ago, a little more than half of every dollar spent by the consumer for domestically produced food went to the farmer. Since then, although the farmer has been more productive, he has not benefited from the higher prices of the food he produces. In fact, he receives 15 per cent less profit from the farm-food market basket than he did 20 years ago. At the same time, consumers pay higher retail prices for this food. The spread between these two—the marketing margin—has widened. Processing and marketing costs have risen 43 per cent.[34]

CAN WE AFFORD CHEAP FOOD?

The revolution in food has brought about many alterations in the American diet. We now have the dubious honor of ranking highest in consumption of refined carbohydrates and sugars as well as empty calories, which sustain neither life nor growth.

Nutritionally desirable foods such as fresh meats, vegetables, fruits, eggs, and fish are represented far less frequently in popular food advertising than are the starchy and sugary products. Even when nutritionally desirable foods are bought, they are likely to be frozen, canned, or dried. Neither the processor nor consumer seems to consider such vital factors as favorable enzymes, which are present in fresh foods but destroyed by certain processing. Denatured foodstuffs, which should be used sparingly, if at all, are being used in a routine way.

Our intake of saturated, hydrogenated, and dairy fats is the world's highest. We lead in eating factory-processed foods (baked, boxed, canned, precooked, preserved, and frozen), containing thousands of chemical preservatives and additives.

The consumer seems to be willing to accept nutritional information from radio announcers or actors trained to deliver convincing television commercials. These "experts" may sell products in huge quantities and at the highest profits for their clients, but they and their writers and producers are often totally ignorant of nutrition. The consumer is influenced by this highly developed art of persuasion and finds it difficult to distinguish good nutritional information from absurdities.

Children are especially easy targets. When two children were given $5 each and turned loose in a supermarket for a shopping spree, this is what they bought:[35]

girl (eight years old)		boy (seven years old)	
cheese wedge	.59	synthetic fruit drink	.10
fizzies	.19	bubble gum	.05
maraschino cherries	.34	truck	.98
cheese curls	.49	bow and arrow	.98
pony-tail holders	.39	rifle	1.29
" " "	.39	ice cream	.89
cigars for father	.39	ice-cream cones	.23
" " "	.39	cookies	.49
macaroni salad	.39	Father's Day card	.05
candy bars	.50		$5.06
watermelon	.45		
cucumbers	.10		
drink mix	.10		
popsicles	.29		
	$5.00		

As for the mature adult, columnist Harriet Van Horne observed: "So many times lately I have watched young mothers trundling their little ones around the supermarket, carefully choosing the foods that offer nothing to the blood, bones, teeth, or spirit of man. The roughage poured daily into Rover's dish is infinitely richer in minerals and proteins. I wince as these women stroll past the dark, crusty loaves of honest French bread, seizing instead the deathly white, gummy loaves, each sliced and packaged like some obscene marshmallow. . . . Their children, I note with sadness, are always pale, with dead, stringy hair. . . . There appears to be a shocking ignorance of what the human body needs for good health. It is not necessary to be prosperous to eat well. One can be poor and have a sleek pelt."[36]

WILL THE CONSUMER REBEL?

Carla S. Williams, an FDA official, warned the food industry:

Gentlemen, the consumer is angry. The housewife is on the warpath. There is a revolution astirring. The American housewife feels exploited. She is insulted. She is hurt at being treated as a grocery-cart goon. Unfortunately, for the time being, a . . . voice . . . from the "wilderness of Madison Avenue" . . . will have you believe that how good? how much? how honest? do not really matter to the matron in the marketplace . . . that she is an irrational, emotion-motivated giddy "butterfly" type of buyer. . . . To use *their* words . . . she searches for status-symbol satisfaction as she chooses the most expensively wrapped product . . . selects the TV-touted brand rather than the best buy for her budget . . . that a blistering badinage of ballyhoo sold her that product and that *rationality* and *good buying sense* had not a whit to do with it! The Food and Drug Administration's Consultants and I . . . judging purely from what *we* hear the consumer say . . . just don't think this is so! . . . for questions which [we are asked] . . . reflect a rising resistance and very sharp retort to the motivational researchists, the Madison Avenue manipulators, the mores and maneuvers which dominate the marketplace today.[37]

2

Unholy Alliance—
Science and
the Food Industry

"THE GOOD IN YOUR FOOD" was the disarming title of a pamphlet handed out in 1960, tucked into the shopping bag along with groceries, sales slips, and trading stamps, in supermarkets across the country. The pamphlet articles, by people with authoritative titles, attempted to counteract a recently published book, *The Poisons in Your Food*, by William Longgood. Leading up to this, there had been the much publicized tainted-cranberries case, contaminated milk, seizures of stilbestrol-pelleted caponettes, and the growing problem of pesticide residues in foodstuffs. The pamphlet was aimed at reassuring the consumer, who had begun to question and resist the tide of additives, artificial flavorings and colorings, chemical substitutes, and the general corruption of his food supply.

All is well, the writers announced. The food industry, at a meeting of the Super Market Institute, had been warned that such public reassurance was necessary. As one official expressed it:

"Our entire economy and way of life is based on faith. If faith in the wholesomeness of our food is undermined, it can have a serious effect on the health of our nation. It can seriously affect the public's confidence in government, agriculture, science and education, as well as in manufacturers, processors and distributors of food."[1]

It is not difficult to identify the cause served by groups with such names as the Manufacturing Chemists' Association, the National Agricultural Chemicals Association, or similar trade organizations, interested in selling the food industry their preservatives, emulsifiers, stabilizers, dyes, and the like. But too often the voice of the food industry comes from a mouthpiece behind an impressive but misleading façade.

It may be argued that some industry-sponsored projects and support are worthwhile, and so they are. But food industry-supported projects are misinterpreted as unbiased, independent research. Frequently they are not. The general public is unaware, for example, that some seemingly "independent" nutritional research quoted may have been sponsored by segments of the food industry. Naturally, it would be against the food processors' own interests to support research that would be apt to demonstrate either the shortcomings of overrefined products or hazards associated with processing practices. Research projects chosen by such groups are likely to reflect areas of concern to industry.

A number of organizations have been formed which act as propaganda agencies for their own particular interests. Such giants in the food field include the American Dairy Association, National Dairy Council, American Meat Institute, National Livestock and Meat Board, Cereal Institute, Wheat Flour Institute, the recently formed Wheat and Wheat Foods Foundation, and the Sugar Research Foundation, Inc.

THE SUGAR-COATED PROPAGANDA PILL

The sugar interests will serve as a typical example. Although the medical community has repeatedly condemned the excessive consumption of refined sugar as detrimental to health, the propaganda for its use is ever louder and more persuasive.

During World War II the National Confectioners' Association created a Council on Candy as a Food in the War Effort. Prominent citizens, desiring to make patriotic gestures but with little knowledge of nutrition, were persuaded to speak favorably of candy on a nationwide broadcast. As a result, parents and friends sent tons of confections to loved ones in the armed services to "fortify energy" and "boost morale."[2]

Dr. Melvin E. Page, a Florida dentist interested in preventive dentistry, presented a paper before the American Dental Association (ADA) concerning the general effects of sugar on the body. Although this organization ordinarily publishes papers presented at its national meetings in its official *Journal,* this particular paper remained unpublished. Upon inquiry, Dr. Page was told that there was little general interest in the subject.[3]

The Sugar Research Foundation was incorporated in 1943 by 77 producers and processors of cane and beet sugar in the United States and other sugar-producing countries.[4] Since then, its membership has doubled. The foundation also entered the field of food science. After the group was well established, the reason for its interest in food research was stated in its publication, *Sugar Molecule:*

"The purpose of our dental caries research is to find out how tooth decay may be controlled effectively without restriction of sugar intake."[5]

One of the projects supported for more than ten years by the Sugar Research Foundation was the work of a biochemist, James H. Shaw, and his associates. Working at the Harvard School of Dental Medicine with $57,000 in grants from the Foundation, they explored the effect of sugar on experimental animals. Using rats on sugar-rich diets, and control rats on sugar-free diets, the relationship of sugar to dental decay was demonstrated clearly. Shaw and his group concluded: "We should cut down on our sugar consumption, particularly candy. We should be careful about sugars in forms that remain in the mouth because of their physical properties."[6]

With these clear, unqualified statements, Shaw reported that the work of his group was terminated because *the Sugar Research Foundation had withdrawn further support from the project.* The findings, although published, were not publicized.[7]

In addition to nutritional research, the sugar interests have spent large sums on advertising, featuring such slogans as "For health and to maintain one's correct weight, one should eat sugar and the good things contained in it," "Sugar for quick energy," and "Nature's miracle food."[8]

Such nutritional nonsense has been deplored by medical groups. Dr. Ogden C. Johnson, a spokesman for the Department of Foods and Nutrition, AMA, wrote: "Often the physician has not been able to keep pace with the tremendous advances in nutritional knowledge . . . [as a result] most changes in food habits within the U.S. are brought about by advertising and promotion, and not by the persuasive statements of physicians and nutritionists."[9]

At a convention of carbonated-beverage bottlers, the audience was told by the organization's committee on research and public relations that "soft-drink producers are recruiting scientists to battle the increasing number of dentists who contend that sugar-containing beverages damage teeth."[10]

At present, the largest users of sugar in the United States are the baking industry, the two major cola-drink processors, and seven of the largest national food-processing advertisers. Inexpensive processing converts sugar at seven to ten cents a pound into cake mixes, cookies, ice cream, frozen coffee cakes, cake toppings, and other sugary luxuries at 30 cents to $1 a pound. Far higher prices are set for candies, "breakfast drinks," and soft-drink powders. The Sugar Research Foundation has urged canners to use about 60 per cent more sugar in processing fruits "to gain maximum consumer acceptance." Although many consumers may prefer water-packed fruits to those in heavy syrups, both the sugar interests and the canners find the current practice quite profitable.[11]

THE NUTRITION FOUNDATION, INC.

The Nutrition Foundation, created in 1941, is supported by the largest food processors and refiners in America. The listing of its Board of Trustees reads like "Who's Who" of the industry.*

*Founder members of the Nutrition Foundation included American Can, American Sugar Refining, Beechnut, California Packing, Campbell Soup, Coca-Cola, Container Corp., Continental Can, Corn Products Refining, General Foods, General Mills, H. J. Heinz, Libby McNeill & Libby, National Biscuit, National Dairy Products, Owens-Illinois Glass, Pillsbury Flour Mills, Quaker Oats, Safeway, Standard Brands, Swift, and United Fruit.

The first director of the Foundation's program for aiding research and dissemination of information about nutrition was Dr. Charles Glen King. In 1932, as a young chemist, he had isolated ascorbic acid in its pure form. Synthetic vitamins, such as Dr. King's discovery, have been a boon to the food refiners who can "fortify" foods impoverished by overprocessing.

The sugar interests collected more than $4 million for research, and the Nutrition Foundation disbursed the money in grants to medical and dental schools. While it may be true that the Nutrition Foundation has supported valuable basic and applied research at many schools, the Foundation has reserved the right to control the choice of the projects.

Between 1942 and 1951, 77 different companies donated a total of $4,158,400 to the Nutrition Foundation, of which $2,272,560 was appropriated for 196 grants to 69 universities, $379,619 for "educational projects," and $739,665 for "direct education" and administrative activities.[12]

"MORE THAN VOCAL SUPPORT"

Between 1950 and 1956 the Department of Nutrition at Harvard University received $113,000 from the Nutrition Foundation. During the same period, other donors to this department included the Sugar Research Foundation, Kellogg, National Biscuit, Wheat Flour Institute, pharmaceutical companies such as Merck and Upjohn, and chemical companies such as Du Pont. Additional sums were contributed by other food processors, refiners, soft-drink manufacturers, and chemical interests. Funds were earmarked for projects under the direction of the chairman of the Department of Nutrition, Dr. Fredrick J. Stare.

Dr. Stare had been a prime force in organizing the Nutrition

Sustaining members included Abbott's Dairies, American Home Foods, American Lecithin, Bowman Dairy, Continental Foods, Crosse & Blackwell, Curtiss Candy, William Davies, R. B. Davis, Drackett, Flako, Gerber, Golden State, Hansen Lab., Knox Gelatine, McCormick, Minnesota Valley Canning, National Sugar Refining, Nut & Chocolate, E. Prichard, Red Star Yeast, Stouffer, Weston, and Zinsmaster.

Donations were also received from American Maize Products, A&P, Hawaiian Pineapple, Eli Lilly, Merck, Penick & Ford, and A. E. Staley.

Foundation, and has served as editor of its publication, *Nutrition Reviews*, which now reaches more than 5,000 universities, government agencies, libraries, and private organizations and individuals in the United States and Latin America.

Since its inception, the Department of Nutrition at Harvard University has received increased financial assistance from the Nutrition Foundation,* as well as from individual segments of the food industry. In 1963, *Medical Tribune* reported that Dr. Stare's Department of Nutrition received about $200,000 yearly from the food industry.[13]

Dr. Stare has become a highly vocal spokesman. Through his prolific writings in medical journals, his associations with a great school of medicine, and his membership on policy-making committees in scientific organizations, he wields a powerful influence among scientists, especially in the medical profession. As reported

---

* The Nutrition Foundation's annual reports list Dr. Stare as the recipient of the following grants from the Nutrition Foundation: for *Nutrition Reviews*, $48,000, and an additional grant of $5,900 for its Spanish edition (1945); $62,000 for *Nutrition Reviews* and for critical review of literature (1946); $76,000 for *Nutrition Reviews* (1947), $96,000 (1948) and $148,000 (1949); $7,500 in yearly grants for fellowship fund for advanced training of physicians and dieticians in clinical nutrition (1945, 1946) and $12,500 (1947, 1948, 1949); $17,865 in yearly grants for research and education in community nutrition (1946, 1947, 1948, 1949); $600 in yearly grants for nutritional research equipment (1946, 1949); $10,000 for basic research studies in nutrition and health (1947), and for the same studies $19,000 (1948) and $46,000 (1949); $9,000 for three years for study of nutrition and health with special reference to hypertension (1956); $15,000 for three years for research in nutrition education in primary and secondary schools (1951), with renewal of grant-in-aid for $5,000 (1954); $7,500 in yearly grants for basic research in geriatrics (1952, 1953, 1954, 1955, 1956, 1957, 1958), $10,000 for same studies (1959–60), and $5,000 in yearly grants for the same study (1962–63); $27,000 for three years for study of nutrition and health (1952); renewals of grant-in-aid for $9,000 in yearly grants (1955, 1956), and renewal for $27,000 (1957), $18,000 (1959–60), and $24,000 (1962–63); $45,000 for study of dietary role of fats (1957); $10,000 (1959–60), $5,000 (1961); $8,000 in yearly grants for studies of nutrition education in early childhood and adolescence (1957, 1958).

The Nutrition Foundation's annual reports list Harvard University's School of Nutrition as recipient of grants from the Nutrition Foundation as follows: new and renewed grants-in-aid, $15,000 (1952), $9,600 (1954), $30,000 and $5,000 (1955), $27,000, $9,000, $10,000, and $4,800 (1956), $24,000 and $9,600 (1957), $15,000, $9,000, $5,480, $5,000, $5,000, and $4,800 (1958), $20,000, $15,000, and $13,400 (1959–60), $20,000, $13,400, and $7,200 (1961), and $20,000, $16,000, and $4,800 (1962–63).

in *Medical Tribune,* Dr. Stare "maintains close contact with the food industry by accepting invitations to talk to various trade associations from time to time, and he generously helps magazine and newspaper writers unravel the technicalities of his specialty."[14]

In current FDA hearings on proposed food supplement regulations, Dr. Stare has been listed by at least six major trade organizations and food processing companies as a witness in their behalf, including The Cereal Institute, Inc., Corn Products Company, The Pharmaceutical Manufacturers Association, National Biscuit Company, Kellogg Company, and The Sugar Association.

Through Dr. Stare's syndicated column,* now appearing in 123 newspapers throughout the country and purported to be read by approximately 19 million,[15] plus his frequent radio and television appearances, he is able to mold the thinking of a large segment of the lay public as well. Some typical statements from his columns reflect his views:

"There is no convincing evidence that in the average American diet decreasing the intake of sweets will lessen tooth decay."[16]

"Sugar is a quick energy food and pleasant to take. Sugar does not contain any appreciable amounts of vitamins and minerals,

---

* During the hearings before the Consumers Subcommittee of the Senate Commerce Committee, Dr. Stare submitted prepared remarks on breakfast cereals on Aug. 4, 1970. He stated that he serves "as a consultant for a number of trade associations and food companies in almost all areas of the food industry including the cereal industry." He appeared at the hearing "at the request of the Kellogg Company and the National Biscuit Company." On Aug. 15, 1970, C. M. Gitt, of the *Gazette & Daily* of York, Pennsylvania, announced editorially that Dr. Stare's syndicated column would be dropped. "We do not feel that the column has served or can do so for the purposes we intend for our readers. What we want is the thinking and knowledge and facts on the subjects of diet, nutrition and food from a person who is an unquestionable expert in the field and who is independent and without inhibiting ties in regard to all other considerations, so that he can provide such consumer-oriented information straightforwardly and directly to the point without any limitations. . . . We have learned . . . that Dr. Stare reported, in response to Congressional questioning, that roughly four per cent of his department's million-dollar-a-year research budget, some $40,000 annually, is provided by the cereal industry. . . . We of the *Gazette & Daily* regret that we have not been able to present the kind of unquestionable information on nutrition and diet that we thought that we had been giving our readers. . . . We apologize . . . for presenting the views of one who was not as unattached as we thought or wanted him to be."

furnishing calories only. Even people on a severe reduction diet can afford to put a teaspoonful of sugar in their tea or coffee three or four times a day."[17]

"Those who speak with disdain of the empty calories of sugar and fat or of processed foods as though they were a blight are also doing a fair share of exaggeration. The empty calories of sugar and fat have always been important to any normal, well-balanced, nutritious diet and add taste, zest and pleasure to a meal."[18]

In writing of the protein requirements of teenagers, Dr. Stare suggests that protein for snacks can be taken from all sources, and thus the quality of any one source is not important, since it forms part of the total diet. He wrote:

"Contrary to opinions held by some people, frankfurters and luncheon meats are good food and furnish high-quality protein."[19]

"The nutritive qualities of canned* evaporated milk are every bit as good as those of fresh pasteurized milk."[20]

"Nutritious snacks include: nuts, cheese and crackers, a glass of milk, ice cream, potato or corn chips, cookies—and with these foods a soft drink or a glass of beer to give zest and enjoyment to snack time."[21]

As an after-school teenage snack, Dr. Stare has recommended Coke. For a summer menu, he included a mid-afternoon "iced tea, lemon- or limeade or Coke."[22]

A General Foods Corporation official expressed his favorable impression of the work at the Department of Nutrition at Harvard, and said that he felt that its "contributions to a basic knowledge of nutrition and to nutrition research deserve more than vocal support."[23]

Harvard received more than verbal kudos. General Foods granted the Department of Nutrition at Harvard $1,026,000 to expand its nutritional work. The University announced it to be a "momentous" gift, and the largest ever made by a business corporation for the capital purposes of Harvard.

Elsewhere the situation is similar. Columbia University, for example, received (1957–58) a $15,000 grant from the Nutrition Foundation at the inception of the Institute of Nutrition Sciences.[24] Additional grants have been made by the Nutrition Foundation to

---

* Dr. Stare was elected as a board member of Continental Can Company in April 1964 (*The New York Times*, Apr. 29, 1964).

support the Institute's research studies. The Institute was planned by Dr. Charles Glen King, who at the time was professor of chemistry at Columbia University and became a scientific director of the Institute (1943–55). He also has served as executive director (1955–61), and president (1961–63) of the Nutrition Foundation. Later (1963–66), he was associate director of the Institute of Nutritional Sciences.

Dr. King's dual contact with a university and industry have reaped financial blessings on the former and prestige for the latter. The Institute announced a $5 million grant from a food corporation, a number of research studies supported by the Nutrition Foundation,* and a scholarship fund financed largely by the food industry.

A different type of university-industry relationship has been mutually beneficial at the University of Wisconsin. The Wisconsin Alumni Research Foundation (WARF) was established as early as 1925. It was the direct result of an irradiation process to produce synthetic vitamin D perfected by Dr. Harry Steenbock, a staff biochemist. WARF serves as a patent management agent for the university and its staff. When a scientist assigns a discovery to WARF, he receives a royalty of about 15 per cent on the net

---

* The Nutrition Foundation's annual reports list Dr. King as recipient of the following grants from the Nutrition Foundation: $33,000 to study the effects of environment on nutritional requirements and cell respiration; $7,000 for food composition (1945); $10,000 and an additional grant of $40,000 for cell respiration (1946); $24,000, and an additional grant of $40,000 for the same study (1947); $38,000 for the same study (1949); $14,000 for functions of vitamins B and C, and an additional grant of $52,000 for the same study (1949); $14,000 for the same study (1950); $14,000 for the study of vitamin C and niacin (1952); $12,000 to Dr. King and R. R. Bricker for study of the functional role of vitamin C and related nutrients (1954); $9,000 renewal of the grant-in-aid for the above study (1955); yearly grants of $10,000 for renewal of grant-in-aid for the above study (1956, 1957, 1958); $4,000 for renewal of grant-in-aid for the above study (1959–60).

The Nutrition Foundation's annual reports list Columbia University as recipient of the following grants from the Nutrition Foundation: $3,400 new grant-in-aid (1952); $16,800 new grant-in-aid (1957). Columbia University's Institute of Nutrition Sciences started operations (1957–58) with a $15,000 grant from the Nutrition Foundation. Subsequently, a number of the Institute's research studies have been supported by the Nutrition Foundation: $20,000 and $11,400 renewal of grants-in-aid (1959–60); $12,000 renewal of grant-in-aid (1961); and $9,000 renewal of grant-in-aid (1962).

proceeds. WARF undertakes to obtain the patent and to market the product. The remainder of the profit is put into investments, from which WARF makes gifts and grants to the university. Since its inception, this arrangement has brought in more than $37 million in grants to the university.[25]

Ever since the synthesis of vitamin D, dairies have been "fortifying" fluid and evaporated milk. Not to be outdone, other food processors began fortifying breakfast cereals, bread, macaroni, margarine, ice cream, prepared vegetables for infants, and, at times, even hot dogs! In October 1930, Consumers' Research warned of the dangers of excessive intake of vitamin D (hypercalcemia), especially by infants.[26] Since then, other warnings have been sounded in professional literature, but for several decades the FDA failed to take any action. Finally, the agency requested a review by joint committees of the AMA and the American Academy of Pediatrics. Upon their recommendations, the FDA ordered a reduction of vitamin D fortification of foodstuffs. But in July 1968, the FDA *withdrew* its proposal to remove vitamin D from the "Generally Recognized As Safe" (GRAS) list, although it *should* have been removed from the list.

WARF has been paid for research on pharmaceuticals, pesticides, and food additives. When the sugar interests became alarmed at the surging popularity of artificial sweeteners in foodstuffs, which cut deeply into their own sales, the Sugar Research Foundation contracted with WARF to investigate its competitor's product.

RESEARCH AND "PUBLIC INFORMATION"

The annual reports of the Nutrition Foundation reflect the largesse bestowed upon universities and colleges. In the first ten years of the Foundation's existence, more than $2 million was granted for research and training in 64 universities and medical centers in the United States and Canada. The generosity was extended to other areas appreciated by such institutions, especially building programs. By 1962, the annual Foundation expenditures were up to more than $8 million, with three quarters of a million dollars for public relations and "public information."

By 1960, the Nutrition Foundation had embarked on a broadened program of public information, after a year of careful planning. During the following year, nutritional material in daily newspapers in the United States and Canada appeared with acknowledged assistance from the Nutrition Foundation. In 1961, there were 6,460 column inches of space and 1,754 "informational" stories on nutrition, amounting to "41 full-size newspaper pages."[27]

In addition, in trade and consumer magazines there were 188 feature articles and some 1,540 column inches of editorial material, equal to about 51 *Time*-size pages. The Nutrition Foundation estimated that the total readership of consumer magazine articles during 1961 could be estimated at some 40 million.

Articles were placed in business publications "to acquaint food and related industries with the work done by the Foundation." Radio and television information and scripts were "reviewed" for accuracy, while the official imprimatur could be found at the end of popular articles: "This article has been read and approved by the Committee on Nutrition Education of the Nutrition Foundation."[28]

A project, Dial-a-Dietician, begun in Detroit in 1958 was given initial financial assistance by the Nutrition Foundation in other cities. A person may call a publicized phone number and receive a prompt answer about food and nutrition.[29] It will be an answer that the food industry wants the consumer to hear, and it will assure him of the safety and wholesomeness of his food supply.

Promptly after publication of William Longgood's *The Poisons in Your Food*, a scathing review of it appeared in *Science* (April 1960) by Dr. William J. Darby, a prominent nutritionist. Dr. Darby has conducted research supported by funds from the Nutrition Foundation,* as well as by grants from manufacturers of synthetic vitamins, drugs, and chemicals. Dr. Darby's review was promptly reprinted by a chemical trade association, and distributed widely to newspaper editors throughout the country. The Nutrition Foundation sent the review, and an additional unfavorable one written by its then executive director, Dr. Charles Glen

---

* The Nutrition Foundation's annual reports list Dr. Darby as recipient of the following grants from the Nutrition Foundation: yearly grants of $10,000 for studies of malnutrition in a specific area (1949, 1950); renewal of grant-in-aid for same study, $17,500 (1952) and $5,000 (1954).

King, along with a printed letter, to librarians.[30] How many librarians were aware of the fact that the mailing piece was sent out from a food-industry organization?

Librarians have been further "enlightened" through the efforts of the National Dairy Council. During National Library Week in 1964, for example, the Council sent to librarians, as well as to schools and physicians, a list of nutritional books it considered reliable. In Topeka, Kan., the local chapter of the Council offered assistance to the public library to arrange a display of books deemed nutritionally sound.

When publication of Rachel Carson's *Silent Spring* threatened to upset the pesticide industry, the Nutrition Foundation, jointly with the Manufacturing Chemists' Association, put together a "Fact Kit" on the subject of *Silent Spring*.[31] The kit consisted of a defense of chemical pesticides, prepared by the New York State College of Agriculture; a printed letter signed by the Nutrition Foundation's president, Dr. Charles Glen King, who termed the book unscientific and written by a "professional journalist—not a scientist in the field of her discussion"; and reprinted book reviews, all derogatory, including those written by Drs. Stare and Darby. The kit was widely distributed. Included on the mailing lists were university people in many fields, researchers and other staff members of state agricultural experiment stations, the membership of the American Public Health Association, leaders of women's organizations, librarians, visiting nurses, and various state, county, and municipal officials. The kit was sent to tree wardens in Connecticut, to a mayor of a small New Jersey borough, and even to a local Audubon Society chapter.

In Connecticut, recommended books on the subject of nutrition are listed by the State Board of Health and issued to librarians. Although *Silent Spring* touches upon the problems of pesticide residues in foodstuffs, basically the book deals with pesticides in relation to ecology and total environmental pollution. Is it possible that Dr. Stare's unfavorable review, appearing in the Nutrition Foundation's *Nutrition Reviews*, influenced the decision to have *Silent Spring* placed on Connecticut's "not recommended" list of nutritional books? This action aroused public indignation, including a protest by Connecticut Senator Abraham S. Ribicoff.[32]

Food-industry propaganda also penetrates magazines and newspapers. Food editors are feted at industry-sponsored luncheons that display new products. At the same time editors are reminded of the safety, wholesomeness, and fine nutritional qualities of processed foods.

The interested consumer should study the feature departments of the popular magazines, questioning why so many recipes use inordinately large quantities of refined sugars, and why margarine, refined flour, white rice, and other denatured foods predominate.

Pressures from the food industry do not end with recipes and columns. Subtle influences now reach into organizations once esteemed for their complete independence.

NATIONAL ACADEMY OF SCIENCES–
NATIONAL RESEARCH COUNCIL (NAS-NRC)

More than a century ago, the National Academy of Sciences was established as a private nonprofit organization "dedicated to the furtherance of science and to its use for the general welfare."[33] In 1916 industry gained entry when the Academy organized the National Research Council. Although the Council consisted of eminent scientists, it acted as a liaison between government agencies and industry.

Industry, given a toehold, began to expand its influence. In 1941, under the auspices of NAS-NRC, a Committee on Food and Nutrition was created, later known as the Food and Nutrition Board. This group consists of twenty-four members chosen from three groups: (1) scientists from universities, (2) research organizations, and (3) industry.[34] The Nutrition Foundation organized its ambitious program of research grants the following year. The year 1940 marked another milestone for the food industry, when enrichment was made possible by chemists' ability to prepare certain synthetic nutrients that could be incorporated into refined foods. The Williams-Waterman Fund was established that year, named for Robert R. Williams and Robert E. Waterman, discoverers of an inexpensive method of manufacturing synthetic thiamin (vitamin B_1), which was to play a role in the "enrichment" program of flour and cereal.

The Food Protection Committee of the Food and Nutrition Board was organized in 1950, according to its official report, "at the request and with the financial support of the food and chemical industries." This Committee "consults at frequent intervals with members . . . representing these supporters."[35]

At various times Drs. Stare, Darby, and King have served as officers and members of various committees of the Food and Nutrition Board. The Nutrition Foundation,* food processors, and chemical and pesticide industries are all well represented. The membership reflects the technique of interlocking directorates, in which the same individuals and groups are listed, in organizations which control the nutritional fate of the nation. For example, Robert R. Williams, of the Williams-Waterman Fund, served as chairman of the committee on cereals of the Food and Nutrition Board from 1940 to 1957, while Dr. Darby served as chairman of the Food Protection Committee, at times when it has been requested by the FDA to review such subjects as chemical food additives, pesticide residues in foodstuffs, and the safety of nonnutritive sweeteners in foods.

The charter of the NAS-NRC provides that the organization act as official adviser to the U.S. government. Since it often reviews problems, and operates on government funds, it has become linked in the public mind with the government. In recent years, some of its recommendations have affected the health and welfare of every individual throughout the land.

As an example, take the case of chlordane, a pesticide widely used on many fruit and vegetable crops. Limits of 3 parts per million (ppm.) had been established in 1963 as a tolerance level by the FDA. Later the agency attempted to revise this tolerance downward to zero. The proposal was protested by the manufacturer, who requested a review by the NAS-NRC. On the basis of this Committee's recommendation (Feb. 21, 1965), the FDA reversed its proposed new tolerance of zero, and retained the previous tolerance of 3 ppm. (Apr. 6, 1965).

The Food and Nutrition Board has also established food calorie

---

* The Nutrition Foundation's annual reports list the Food and Nutrition Board, NAS-NRC, as recipient of grants-in-aid for the following educational projects: $10,000 and an additional grant of $20,000 for war emergency (1947), $7,500 in yearly grants (1951 through 1958), $4,000 for work of the Committee on Fats in Human Nutrition (1957), $15,000 for educational projects (1959–60), $7,500 (1961), and $22,500 (1962).

allowances that have become standards for food planning and diet evaluation. Amounts of nutrients described as "adequate to maintain good nutrition in healthy persons" are revised from time to time "according to newer knowledge of nutritional needs," and purportedly are intended to "cover individual variations among most normal persons as they live in the U. S. under usual environmental stress."[36]

These Recommended Daily Allowances (RDA) have come under sharp criticism. Food composition varies considerably, so that the use of "food tables" to gather statistics is an unreliable guide. *Vitamin values in food tables may vary as much as 100 per cent. Also, no provision is made to cover nutritive losses in food during storage, preparation, and cooking.* There is a tendency to overestimate the vitamin intake in diets, which in reality may be lower than figures reveal. The same data may receive widely divergent interpretation by different nutritional workers.[37]

The RDA are considered by some nutritionists and nutrition-minded physicians as being far too low. For example, the recommended daily dietary allowance (revised 1964) suggests 70 grams of protein for a man, and 58 for a woman.[38] Some authorities feel that to maintain optimum health, *twice* these amounts is desirable. The low vitamin C recommendation barely surmounts the scurvy threshold.

The following statement was issued originally by the FDA, and quoted by Dr. E. V. Askey, a past president of The American Medical Association (AMA): "Americans have to go out of their way nutritionally speaking, to avoid being well nourished."[39] Food processors and their apologists have quoted this *ad nauseam.* Is the statement confirmed by the facts? Results of nationwide nutrition surveys, made during the relatively prosperous years from 1947 through 1955, gave incontrovertible proof that a great many Americans, of all ages, and at all social and economic levels, were subsisting on diets falling substantially short—even at the low RDA standards—in one or more essential nutrients.[40] Later surveys, from 1956 through 1963, and again in 1965, reflect similar conditions.[41] And this in the land of plenty.

The FDA has also established minimum daily requirements (MDR) for various nutrients, in the labeling of foods and pharmaceutical preparations for special dietary use. Bare minimums to prevent deficiency diseases, MDR are generally even lower than

RDA.[42] Under this plan, the fortification program of adding synthetic vitamins A and D to denatured foods has been given continued support by the Food and Nutrition Board. This, too, reflects a general pattern of justification for foods robbed of essential elements.

Within the NAS-NRC is another group related to food production, the Committee on Pest Control and Wildlife Relationships. Within this committee are 43 "supporting agencies," 19 of which are chemical corporations that comprise the major force of this industry. In addition, there are at least four trade organizations, including the National Agricultural Chemicals Association. Reports issued by the Committee on Pest Control and Wildlife Management in 1962 bear close resemblance to industry's own viewpoint. In analyzing the composition of the Committee and its subcommittees, Dr. Frank B. Egler, an ecologist, noted:

> The problem of industries' influence on scientists who are on their payrolls as consultants, through research grants and otherwise, is a prickly one. It has been brought up in connection with these reports. My surprise is not that such influence exists, but that other scientists are so naïve and unsophisticated as to refuse to believe it. The reader should at least know of such connections in appraising the final conclusions. In short, these two [reports] cannot be judged as scientific contributions. They are written in the style of a trained public relations official of industry, out to placate some segments of the public that were causing trouble. With different title and cover pages, they would serve admirably for publication and distribution by a manufacturers' trade association. Indeed, they are being much quoted in such places.[43]

In November 1966 the USDA asked the NAS-NRC to appoint a special Committee on Persistent Pesticides to review the problem. As the National Audubon Society commented, the Committee should have been an ecological board, since the pest-control problem and pesticide pollution are both ecological problems. But only two of the eleven members were so oriented. "Eight others, including the chairman, had backgrounds and philosophical commitments close to the agricultural community; two were from the chemical industry. Even though all these men were highly qualified and respected specialists, most of them were ecologically incompetent."

The Committee heard testimony from more than eighty witnesses. Analyzing the compilation of this testimony, the National

Audubon Society described it as "a case where we suffer from the democratic notion that majority opinion is right *per se,* with public relations substituting for education. This stumbling block is evident in the makeup of the persons interviewed by the committee: nineteen more or less ecologically oriented witnesses were exactly counterbalanced by nineteen industry spokesmen whose job has been to produce and sell the technology that has gotten us into trouble. The other testimony came from three people in food processing, fourteen in public health (as yet an unecological field), and twenty-eight from agriculture, men who planned and directed our commitment to DDT!"[44]

The Committee failed to recommend a ban on DDT, and instead recommended more research. This recommendation, noted the National Audubon Society, is always a good way to put off action.

THE FOOD INDUSTRY AND GOVERNMENT

Government agencies, too, are likely to respond to industry pressure. Charges have been made that the FDA, directly responsible for consumer welfare, frequently makes decisions favoring industry. The consumer, lacking organization and funds, has no way to counterbalance these pressures. This becomes apparent at public hearings in Congress as well as at open meetings such as those held jointly by the FDA and the Food and Drug Law Institute (FDLI). This group, originally called the Food Law Institute, was formed in 1949, shortly before the Delaney Hearings, by the food, drug, cosmetic, and allied industries concerned with public laws governing their activities. The late Charles Wesley Dunn, one of the founders and prime movers of the FDLI, played an important role in drafting the 1958 Food Additives Act that was an outgrowth of the Delaney Hearings. (The legal loopholes created in this legislation will be discussed in Chapter 4.)

The FDLI is composed in large part of major industry members.* It also includes "public members" drawn largely from food-

* Industry supporters of the Food and Drug Law Institute, Inc., in 1966: Anchor-Hocking Glass, Anheuser-Busch, Atlas Chemical, Bacardi, California Packing, Coca-Cola, Consolidated Foods, Continental Can, Corn

law officials. Officers of the FDLI are from industry members, while trustees include persons from industry and the "public." Among the "public trustees" who served in 1966 were Drs. Darby and King, as well as the president of the Nutrition Foundation, Inc. The FDLI wields subtle but enormous and varied influence. It supports courses of instruction in food, drug, cosmetics, and related laws at leading law schools throughout the country to prepare persons "to give sound advice to industry and government," with courses providing industry and government lawyers and administrators with "sound knowledge of the problems involved," so that "existing laws be understood and observed and that amendments to it be carefully considered and adopted only when sound and in the public interest."[45] *Hence the FDLI plays an important role in the drafting and interpretation of all legislation dealing with consumer protection in the areas of food, drugs and cosmetics.*

The FDLI sponsors conferences, lectures, and seminars to advance understanding of food and drug laws.[46] It publishes legal research books and issues a journal. It acts as a liaison group with domestic and international bar associations and with universities and governmental agencies here and abroad. Its resources, skills, and technical knowledge are used at public hearings.

Regarding the influence of the chemical industry on faculty members of agricultural colleges, universities, and employees of experimental agricultural stations, Leonard Wickenden, an industrial chemist, testified at a Congressional hearing:

I have upon my desk an advertisement published by the National Fertilizer Association. I think it is fair to call it a typical advertisement. From beginning to end it is extremely biased. Its by-line reveals that it was written by a distinguished professor on the staff of one of our more important agricultural colleges. If some of the pro-

---

Industries Research Foundation, Corn Products, Distillation Products, Duffy-Mott, Fries & Fries, General Foods, General Mills, Gerber, Glidden, A&P, Griffith Lab., Heinz, Hershey, Hoffmann-LaRoche, Huntingdon Research, International Milling, Kellogg, Kraft, Libby, McNeill & Libby, Eli Lilly, Lipton, McCormick, Monsanto, Morton, Mueller, National Biscuit, Nestlé, Owens-Illinois, Pepsi, Pet Milk, Pfizer, Pillsbury, Procter & Gamble, Quaker Oats, Ralston Purina, Schenley, Schering, Seagram, Seeman, Seven-Up, S&H, Seymour Foods, Standard Brands, Swift, United Fruit, U.S. Brewers Association, and Hiram Walker.

fessors in our agricultural colleges are employees of the National Fertilizer Association, or of any of its members, can we be quite confident that their teaching is entirely unbiased? If some of the members of the staffs of our state experiment stations are receiving compensation in any form from the same source, can we be fully satisfied that all their research work is wholly in the interests of the farmers and to no slightest degree in the interests of manufacturers of fertilizers, poison sprays, or other materials or equipment used in agriculture?[47]

To determine the role of diet in producing heart disease, the National Heart Institute, USPHS, launched a project involving 500,000 Americans. The pilot study planned to supply much of the food to the participants. Dr. Fredrick J. Stare was appointed deputy chairman of the committee organizing the project. He announced that the plan had strong Congressional backing, and also was supported by the food industry. *The New York Times* reported that the aim of the project was "to find out whether America should change its eating habits and, if so, *how this can be done with as little disruption of the food industry* as possible" (emphasis mine).[48] The chief biochemist appointed as economic head of the diet-heart studies was a representative of one of the large meat packers.

Government agencies responsible for consumer welfare sometimes appoint committees to review problems. But what happens when members of such committees are affiliated with the very industries whose business will be affected? One committee formed to evaluate food safety was composed in part of food-industry members. Another committee studying pesticide residues included two members directly associated with the pesticide industry. Can we expect unbiased evaluations from such committees?

Harlan Cleveland and Harold D. Lasswell in *Ethics and Bigness* noted that "business firms and their managers are acting more and more in ways that tend to blur the division between public and private."[49] This is evidenced in many ways. The USDA has contracted with the National Canners' Association for the Association to study changes that pesticide residues undergo during commercial processing of fruits and vegetables.[50] The National Cancer Institute (NCI) farmed out to General Foods an investigation of the potential carcinogenicity of deep-fat cooking in food products. Birdseye, now part of the General Foods Corporation, produces quick-frozen fried potatoes. How can the public expect an unbiased report with such a potential conflict of interests? What's good for General Foods may not be best for the nation.

Now and then, a courageous individual scientist attempts to speak out. Dr. Wilhelm C. Hueper, an internationally esteemed cancer specialist, pathologist and toxicologist, accepted an invitation to appear before the Congressional hearings on chemicals in foods. Strong attempts were made to prevent him from giving testimony that affirmed the hazards of chemical additives and pesticide residues in foods and other consumer goods. Afterwards, he was reprimanded by his superior for showing "bad judgment."[51]

As Chief of the Environmental Cancer Section of the NCI, Dr. Hueper denounced "extra-governmental influences, more concerned with the practical economic implications of the results of such activities than with proper public protection of the health of the American public. As a result of these selfish and, in my opinion, irresponsible influences, the work of the Environmental Cancer Section has been obstructed."[52] Repeatedly, he was prevented by higher officials from addressing professional groups, and participating in various national and international science congresses. Prolonged clearance delays made it impossible for him to participate in the preparation of a handbook on toxicology. He dropped other work he had prepared for publication rather than place his name on an "arbitrarily perverted version" of it.

One of Dr. Hueper's papers, "Consumer Goods and Cancer Hazards," included a discussion of harmful substances in foods. An official of the FDA commented on this paper: "We think it advisable that our agencies bear in mind the great public concern about cancer. Our experience indicates that remarks by a scientist intended for a scientific audience may be picked up by lay press writers and used to confuse and alarm the public."[53] There may be some truth in this, but does it justify the suppression of information vital to the health and welfare of consumers?

The food industry, through its spokesmen, has not only propagandized its viewpoint, but has engaged in vituperative battle with any and all who dare question some of its practices. Edward J. Ryan, D.D.S., former editor of *Dental Digest*, noted:

> Anyone who speaks up against food adulteration in any of the many forms is subject to "name calling." The most common epithets are "food faddist" or "food fakir." If you object to spraying foods with

poisonous chemicals, picking fruits green and then applying a dye, or injecting or administering antibiotics to poultry and dairy herds, to removing minerals and vitamins from natural foods, to adding chemical adulterants to preserve foods from normal chemical changes, you are offending . . . some of our largest and most influential corporations. . . . We can be certain that the public relations counsellors will go to work to change the situation—even if that requires a bit of character assassination directed against those who are in the opposition."[54]

3

Taste, Flavor and Freshness —Where Did They Go?

THE FUTURE FABRICATED FOODS

The British chemists W. O. Kermack and P. Eggleton made a prediction several decades ago: "The chemistry of nature is being supplemented and even replaced by the chemistry of man."[1] The Russians have already perfected a synthetic caviar, which *Soviet Life* declares is "absolutely indistinguishable from the natural variety . . . it takes a microscope to see the difference." The only trouble is that "fish cannot be hatched from the synthetic."[2]

Gourmets who have relished snails may be in for a surprise. When snails were in short supply after World War II, French chefs improvised with waste rubber reduced to a powder, mixed to a paste, molded into snail shape, and soaked in a liquid. These "snails" were inserted into real snail shells and served with garlic butter. Many Frenchmen were fooled.

Food technologists promise us a future filled with fabricated peas made from a blend of starch, flavoring, color, and a binder to hold the mixture together. The simulated meats, poultry, and fish will be made from "spun" vegetable proteins, binders, fats, colors, flavors, and "nutrients"![3]

We are already well along on this road to synthetic foods. A case

in point is the use of synthetic vitamin C, or ascorbic acid. When
frozen concentrated orange juice was introduced it was backed up
by a promotional campaign exceeding $3 million. The juice was
considered to be high in quality, and many Americans preferred it
to whole fresh oranges. The retail price of frozen juice concentrates was stabilized at a higher level than that of oranges. When
the consumer began to lose faith in the quality of orange products
and to become unhappy about the price rise, the unforeseen occurred. Severe freezes in Florida reduced the citrus crops. Less
orange-juice concentrate was frozen, and prices rose. The combined
circumstances were fortuitous for the launching of orange drinks
in which scarce oranges could be used sparingly.

In 1963 a large company introduced a new frozen concentrated
orange-juice breakfast drink. It was presented as having all the
good qualities of orange juice, at a much lower price. The basic
falsity of these claims was exposed by Mrs. Carol Malstrom, a
homemaker, who testified before the Congressional Hearing on
Packaging and Labeling Legislation that she received a free sample
of the new orange drink. It was presented as containing no added
preservative. But she testified that when she read the small print
on the paper cap of the drink, she discovered that it was composed
of orange concentrate, water, sugar, citric acid, orange oil, artificial
coloring, and sodium benzoate—a preservative.[4]

Federal and state governments seized "pure orange juice" commonly adulterated and misbranded. In some instances, these
products contained as little as 20 per cent orange juice, the
remainder consisting of colored and flavored water.[5] A chaotic
market place made things worse. Lacking government standards,
the shopper faced the fruit-juice drink, nectar, -ade, and punch
with no indication of how much actual fruit the various products
contained.

Another homemaker, Mrs. Ruth T. Robinson, testified: "When I
was in Union Station . . . waiting for a train, an employee came
to service the vending machine beside me. A sign on [it] said
'Orangeade—real juice, sugar added, no water added—10¢.' But
here is the label that came off the can used to fill the machine. It
reads: 'Contents: water, concentrated orange juice, sugar, dextrose, orange oil, citric acid, vitamin C, U.S. certified artificial
color.' "[6]

At this point, the sale of orange juice and orange drinks was sharply challenged by "instant breakfast drinks," created by large food processors, and launched with ballyhoo. These new products were highly contrived laboratory inventions, mainly sugar, citric acid, and gum arabic, thickened with a cheap cellulose filler questionable as a food additive and containing two synthetic vitamins, artificial color and flavor, and a preservative. The consumer was persuaded that these "instant breakfast drinks," cheaper than orange juice, were its equal in value. Sales of the synthetic drinks mounted, and consumption of orange juice declined. The alarmed Florida Citrus Commission attempted to regain its market through advertising. An ad ridiculed: "Imitation juice products which have a list of the funniest sounding chemicals" (on their labels), and: "Mother nature provides her children with genuine Florida orange juice. Don't let chemical imitations persuade you to do less for yours."[7]

The citrus-fruit-juice industry has felt the sting of substitutes. This billion-dollar-a-year business is now made up of only 70 per cent real fruit juices, 25 per cent substitutes which combine natural and synthetic ingredients, and 5 per cent complete synthetics. The synthetics are growing; the real juice is shrinking both in sales and quality. The latest abomination is the addition of "flavor essence" from citrus peel which "gives a five- to ten-fold increase of fresh-fruit flavor and aroma to frozen citrus products."[8] USDA has developed the process, despite the fact that citrus-peel oils are suspected carcinogens.

The Florida Citrus Commission spent $56,000 to have three nutritionists—including Dr. Fredrick J. Stare—prepare a report which it hoped would point up the nutritive values of citrus juices, and which it could use in advertising to counteract the synthetic drinks. The choice of Stare was surprising in view of his earlier statement that "those who proclaim that 'natural vitamins' are better than 'synthetic vitamins' are just plain stupid."[9]

The recommendations of the committee were disappointing to the Commission, and played directly into the hands of the synthetic processors. The report downgraded the importance of natural vitamin C, and all three members adhered to the view that this vitamin, when created in the test tube, is as effective as any natural vitamin found in foods.[10]

NATURAL VERSUS SYNTHETIC

Although synthetic and natural ascorbic acid may be *chemically* identical, there are findings which point to subtle but vital *biological* differences. These may not be well understood at present, but they seem to exist. Many experimental reports show that ascorbic acid consumed in its natural medium (citrus juices, leafy greens, rose hips, green walnuts, green onion tops) is *better utilized* under certain circumstances (e.g., scurvy) than the synthetic form.[11]

In animal experiments, synthetic ascorbic acid failed to cure scurvy in a litter of puppies, whereas fresh orange juice resulted in "spectacular recovery."[12] Russian investigators reported natural vitamin C more effective in preventing scurvy and hemorrhage in guinea pigs than the synthetic product.[13]

Other researchers reported a higher level of storage of ascorbic acid in organs of experimental guinea pigs supplied with natural sources of vitamin C than in those supplied with synthetic ascorbic acid,[14] while others found better storage of ascorbic acid in the tissues of guinea pigs when it was administered as a food than when given in its crystalline (synthetic) form.[15]

Although vitamin C was found to play an important role in enhancing resistance to poliomyelitis infection in experiments on monkeys, optimal results were obtained with natural vitamin C and less favorable ones with synthetic ascorbic acid.[16]

Similar results have been noted in studies with human beings. In Germany, prisoners suffering from scurvy in a war camp failed to respond to synthetic vitamin C treatment, but were cured by quantities of green onions. (This was later confirmed with experimental animals.)[17] A similar report indicated the failure of synthetic vitamin C to cure gum inflammations in Norway among troops in World War II, whereas a quick cure was effected with fresh green leaves.[18]

In another experiment, treating 29 humans with scurvy, three failed to be cured in the manner that would be expected if synthetic ascorbic acid and vitamin C were absolutely identical. The scorbutic symptoms disappeared only after the three individuals were given lemon juice.[19]

Dentists[20] affirm that, aside from nutrient content, it does make a difference whether we get ascorbic acid naturally or synthetically. Dr. Theron G. Randolph, an allergist, reported his medical experience:

> A *synthetically derived* substance may cause a reaction in a chemically susceptible person when the same material of *natural origin* is tolerated, despite the two substances having identical *chemical* structures. This point is illustrated by the frequency of clinical reactions to synthetic vitamins—especially vitamins B_1 and C—when these naturally occurring vitamins are tolerated. There is also other evidence indicating that the biological activity of synthetic and natural vitamins is not identical." (Emphasis mine.) [21]

We stand at the crossroads, and a choice is being made upon which our very survival may depend. Are we to assume, with brash arrogance, that we can dispense with biological processes and ignore the nourishment derived from soil and sea? The food processors and their spokesmen are pushing us in a doubtful direction.

"Synthetic foods," warns the editor of the *British Medical Journal,* "are rarely, if ever, of exactly the same composition as the original." [22] Nevertheless, attempts are being made to create artificial food from petroleum, atmospheric nitrogen, natural gas, and even sewage and sludge. [23] Are we sure that these synthetic products will contain all vital elements for our biological needs?

Dr. Paul B. Dunbar, former FDA Commissioner, said: "What new disease may grow out of the use of synthetic foods, no man can tell. But when man starts competing with nature in the blending of food elements, he should be sure that his formula does not bear the skull and crossbones." [24]

"PECULIAR" FLAVORS

The flavor, or lack of it, in our foods sometimes depends on how a crop is grown. Variations in the mineral content of soil may account for a great range in composition, as well as taste. For example, the calcium in growing cabbages has been measured as low as 17 per cent and as high as 60 per cent; iron in crops may range from 20 per cent to 94 per cent; and magnesium, 15 per cent to 43 per cent. [25]

On occasion, the disappearance of characteristic aroma and

taste, or superimposed off-flavors in produce has been traced to pesticides. Officials in the USDA have admitted that a kerosenelike oil, used against weeds in fields of young carrots, gave the carrots a tinge of kerosene flavor.[26] Similarly, in England, a visiting German scientist, Dr. Werner Schuphan, noted a strange "phenol-like" taste in all English carrots he ate. He concluded that British consumers had grown so accustomed to the flavor that they were not so acutely aware of it as a foreigner. Upon investigation, this scientist discovered that the root of carrots has a great ability to store fat-soluble insecticides by dissolving them in the essential carrot oil. These materials were found to enter the plant, derange the carbohydrate metabolism as well as nitrogen balance, and result in a poor taste and loss of aroma in the carrot.[27]

Peculiar flavors noted in potatoes have been traced to an oil solvent used in a DDT emulsion. Potatoes, treated at certain periods in their development, or with inappropriate combinations (DDT and lindane), develop a foreign taste and odor.

Under certain circumstances, crops treated with insecticides have not developed off-flavors in the raw commodities, but when cooked they show such a loss of flavor that they become unusable. This has been especially true of cabbage. Also, off-flavors in canned vegetables have been traced to pesticidal treatment of the crops. Lindane residue in the soil is held to be responsible for poor taste in onions, potatoes, and carrots. Chlordane, applied to foliage, affects onions; in the soil, this pesticide affects potatoes. The canned foods most sensitive and likely to develop off-flavors from pesticide residues are pumpkin, sauerkraut and beets.[28]

The effects of metals used in food canning were studied by researchers. Iron and tin from the containers were found in the canned foodstuffs, and these contaminants increased after prolonged storage.[29] When canned food was fed experimentally to human beings, tin and major portions of the iron were found to be excreted in the feces.[30]

PASS THE SALT, PLEASE

The practice of salting food may have come down through the years as a habit, but the present food revolution has escalated salt's use to astronomical proportions. What is the truth about salt in the modern American diet? Cookbooks still call for it in generous quantities, and salt shakers are omnipresent on kitchen shelves and dining tables. "For absolutely sumptuous flavors," advised a writer, use salt with a "heavy hand."[31] For healthy people, the writer continued, everything should be salted, and the free use of salt is basic to health, civilization, and the national economy. Despite such gibberish, physicians, recognizing the harmfulness of too much sodium, are more and more placing patients on salt-restricted diets.

Salt is extremely useful to the food industry. It acts as a preservative. It can mask the flavor of odorous foods. It can help inhibit the growth of molds and bacteria. It bleaches and "improves" food color. It can prevent discoloration. It is a processing aid in peeling, sorting, and floating. It is useful in drying and freezing foods. It whets the appetite to consume *more* processed foods and beverages. And, being one of the cheapest commodities, every ounce of salt used in place of food is a saving for the processors.

Brining, pickling, curing, and salting are processes which produce especially high salt content in foods. For example, a cured ham is about 20 times more salty than fresh pork, and potato chips have about 340 times as much sodium as that found naturally in raw potatoes of the same weight.[32]

Ready-processed and prepared, and ready-to-serve foods also have objectionably high levels of sodium. The salt on pretzels, popcorn, and crackers can add more weight to the body than the snacks themselves. The list of highly salted items is long and varied.

Sodium compounds are added to certain canned and frozen vegetables, relishes, canned soups and fish, and quick-cooking cereal. Without consumer awareness, other canning and freezing practices add additional salt to foods. Often salt water is used as a rinse for produce just prior to canning. It is also used to separate peas or lima beans before canning or freezing. Ocean and fresh-water frozen fish may have additional sodium because of processing methods.

A number of food additives in common use also contain sodium. For example, baking powder and baking soda, as well as *sodium* propionate (a mold retarder), may be present in bakery goods; *sodium* nitrate and *sodium* nitrite (preservatives) are used in processed meats; mono*sodium* glutamate is in hundreds of processed foods; and a wide array of other food additives are sodium compounds, even including sodium additives in salt!

Additional sodium may be ingested from unsuspected sources such as soft drinks, sparkling water, and desserts. Drugs such as pain relievers, antacids, and many over-the-counter medicines contain a high proportion of sodium.

The sodium content is high in certain foods even when no additional salt is added. Many farmers provide livestock with salt licks in order to hasten weight gains or increase milk production. Animals, encouraged to use salt licks, may retain abnormal amounts of sodium which is then consumed by the person who eats the meat or drinks the milk from the animals. Fluid cow's milk may have more than three times as much sodium as human milk.

In some parts of the country drinking water may naturally have a high sodium content. Water softeners used in homes or municipalities, as well as sodium fluoride, may be additional sources of sodium. Chemicals used to "salt" the roads, carried by rain or melting snow, sometimes contaminate private and public water supplies, thus adding more sodium to the diet.

Consequently, it is not surprising to learn that many Americans consume up to twenty times as much salt as the body needs or can use.[33] The salt habit is started young, as will be seen later (Chapter 13).

Excessive salt intake is involved in many serious health conditions, including high blood pressure, obesity, heart disease, atherosclerosis, and tooth decay. There are some indications that excess salt may be involved in problems such as loss of hair, insomnia, tension, and many other ailments. Physicians have become more aware of these problems. Today many people are on low-sodium diets. Unfortunately, some conditions are irreversible. For these reasons, it is prudent to reduce drastically or eliminate sources of sodium other than those normally found in natural foods. Much is accomplished by *eliminating all processed foods* from the diet. It should be remembered that "sodium-free" and "salt-free" are not synonymous. Special dietary foods labeled "low sodium" may be unreliable. Commercial salt substitutes should be avoided.

THE SUBSTITUTE SALT SHAKER

Fresh protein foods, as well as fresh fruits and vegetables, do not contain objectionable amounts of sodium. Herbs, flavorsome and low in sodium, are a good substitute for the salt shaker. Onion, chive, garlic, mushroom, lemon, and lime are useful salt substitutes for those wishing or needing to reduce sodium intake. Fish normally relatively low in sodium include salt-water varieties such as albacore, tuna, pollack, yellowtail, rockfish, Spanish mackerel, halibut, and shad. Fresh-water varieties include lake herring, buffalo fish, yellow pike, mullet, and whitefish.

Many persons cling to the myth that adding salt to food is natural. They usually cite the example of animals who seek salt licks. This myth was exploded by A. R. Patton, a chemist, who studied salt licks in the mountains of Montana. He found that the one chemical property that all salt licks had in common was a *complete absence of sodium chloride!* He suggested that the interest of the animals drawn to the mud in so-called salt licks might be a craving for some mineral ingredient, but not salt.[34] Anyhow, no medical or physiological evidence exists at present that the human body needs more salt than is contained naturally in foods.

THE "FLAVOR ENHANCER": MONOSODIUM GLUTAMATE (MSG)

MSG has had a long history of use in food preparation and serving in the Orient. Extracted from seaweed or soybean, it was used to impart a meaty flavor to dishes in which meat, scarce or costly, was used sparingly.

The composition of the MSG now added to more than 10,000 different processed food items in America differs from the Oriental product. It is manufactured from wheat or corn gluten or from sugar-beet by-products. At present, more than 40 million pounds of MSG are sold annually to add to American foodstuffs.[35]

When first introduced, it was put in canned soups. By now, it is virtually impossible to avoid MSG in processed foods. MSG is found commonly in heat-and-serve convenience foods; meats, stews, and meat tenderizers; canned and frozen vegetables; seafoods, fish fillets, clam chowder, codfish cakes, and canned tuna; poultry and chicken à la king; almost all canned soups and soup mixes; seasonings; mayonnaise, French dressing, and salad dressing; imitation maple syrup; potato chips; crackers; and tobacco.

Nutritionist Dr. Jean Mayer claimed that MSG was added to baby foods "to disguise the fact that there was less meat and more starch" in these products than formerly. He added, "The MSG was a risk added to a disadvantage."[36] MSG was also added to some vegetable and meat mixtures of commercially processed baby foods to make them more palatable to mothers who sampled them. Experimental evidence raised doubts about the safety of this additive in baby foods, and pending further study, in October 1969 some processors voluntarily stopped adding it to their baby-food products.[37]

MSG has even been put into animal feed, since it induces cattle, swine, poultry and sheep to eat more.[38]

Why has the food industry displayed such enthusiasm for MSG? It is a material described as being "much used to step up the indifferent or undistinguished flavor of many canned and processed foods."[39] Frozen-food processors discovered that MSG acted as a color and flavor preserver.[40] A trade release noted that MSG prevented or retarded the development of "warmed over" off-flavors that develop normally during storage. Canners were told that MSG "helps to maintain the fresh-cooked quality of canned food despite packing operations, long storage, and reheating by the housewife" and that it "restores flavor to your products" and "protects flavor lost through over- or under-cooking."[41] MSG also appears to have an antioxidant quality, since it was advertised to "suppress oxidized flavor which may develop during storage."[42] Food technologists demonstrated its antioxidant effect on hams, bacon, pork sausage, and fatty fish, as well as "acceptability of MSG in frankfurters."[43]

Federal legislation specifically prohibits the addition of any material to food which causes "damage or inferiority" to be "concealed in any manner" or which can make a food "appear better or of greater value than it is." This prohibition is precise and without qualifications. Nonetheless, the FDA permits wide latitude in the use of MSG, a substance which helps disguise inferior food quality.

In addition, food processors, restaurants—from the greasy-spoon diner to the posh establishment—use MSG extensively. Restaurateurs have been urged to use it "to hold the flavor" and overcome "steam-table fatigue" for meats. "Hamburgers or meat patties that cannot be made to order," the chef was advised, "are better if kept on a steam table in a pan that includes MSG in the juices; if stews and creamed chipped beef remain on the steam table, a liberal shake of MSG in small additions of gravy or milk will restore the product's flavor or desirable texture."[44]

MSG has been glamorized for the general public as a "flavor enhancer" which brings out the natural flavor of food.[45] It is packaged and sold under several brand names in food stores. The housewife is encouraged to sprinkle it on raw or cooked meats and vegetables before cooking or freezing them in her own kitchen. MSG frequently appears either by its generic or trade names under ingredient listings of printed recipes in magazines and newspapers. On occasion, it is introduced into the home in "flavor packets" tucked into purchased cellophane-wrapped vegetables such as spinach.

Three of MSG's components—namely wheat, corn, and sugar-beet by-products—are common allergens. For those who need to limit or eliminate these substances from their diets, the widespread use of MSG makes this extremely difficult. Even a careful reading of labels will not help. For instance, although the addition of MSG must appear in the ingredient listings of all canned vegetables, *this substance may be added to mayonnaise, French dressing, and salad dressing without label declaration.*[46]

Since MSG's use is sanctioned by federal regulation, it might be assumed that the safety of this material is well established. This is not the case.

As early as 1955, *Consumers' Research Bulletin* printed a report of a physician who had traced a serious allergy, affecting a woman and her son, to MSG. Within a half hour after eating meals of excellent food prepared at home, as well as meals eaten at fine restaurants, they developed acute distress resembling gall-bladder trouble. Their symptoms included epigastric fullness, belching, distention and marked upper-abdominal discomfort. The reactions were traced to MSG.[47]

More recently, additional information has been publicized. Dr. Robert Ho Man Kwok, senior research investigator at the National Biomedical Research Foundation, described a strange syndrome that he personally experiences in restaurants serving Northern Chinese food. About fifteen to twenty minutes after eating, he develops "numbness at the back of the neck, gradually radiating to both arms and the back, general weakness and palpitation." Dr. Kwok added that some of his Chinese friends, both medical and nonmedical, also complained of similar symptoms after eating Chinese food. He speculated that it might be caused by some ingredient in the soy sauce, the high sodium content of the food, and/or the generous use of monosodium glutamate seasoning in many Chinese restaurants.[48]

Dr. Kwok's description elicited other reports of what came to be dubbed the "Chinese Restaurant Syndrome" (CRS). Many physicians confirmed similar experiences. In addition to the symptoms Dr. Kwok described, some included "profuse, cold sweat," "tightness on both sides of the head . . . felt as though, at any second, the sides of my head would burst," "pounding, throbbing sensation in the head, viselike."[49]

Interest in the subject continued. Medical researchers followed up the lead. Dr. Herbert H. Schaumburg, assistant professor of neurology, and Dr. Robert Byck, assistant professor of pharmacology, both at Albert Einstein college of medicine, found MSG related to the CRS symptoms. They acknowledged that the syndrome has been well known to allergists and Chinese restaurateurs.

The researchers ate Chinese food three times daily at a cooperating Chinese restaurant. The search was narrowed to soups. Upon sampling the individual ingredients, "the dagger of suspicion pointed at monosodium glutamate." The researchers found that as little as 1½ grams, or about one quarter of a teaspoon, of MSG can produce symptoms in some subjects. They also found that MSG "can produce undesirable effects in the amounts used in the preparation of widely consumed foods."[50]

Independently of these experiments, a team of four students in the department of pharmacology at New York University school of medicine also investigated the CRS. By feeding MSG in tomato juice or diluted in broth to sensitive persons, symptoms of the CRS were faithfully reproduced.

The nation's largest producer of MSG conceded that it is possible that MSG can produce "certain unpleasant but short-lived symptoms in a relatively few individuals under unusual circumstances." To test this possibility, the company announced plans to conduct a thorough, independent scientific study.[51]

Even those not particularly sensitive to MSG should be aware of its description as "one of the more concentrated sources of sodium." Because of this characteristic, it "could not be permitted in diets in which sodium intake must be kept low."[52]

To determine whether MSG causes more than transitory symptoms, laboratory experiments were conducted, and large amounts were injected into animals. It caused brain damage in newborn mice. As adults, the MSG-treated animals showed stunted skeletal development, marked obesity and female sterility. The researcher, Dr. John W. Olney, of the Washington University school of medicine in St. Louis, said that he believed that pregnant women should not use MSG until further data are available.[53]

Although the FDA requested the AMA's Council on Foods and Nutrition to review the subject of MSG in baby foods, before the review was completed, Dr. Olney reported further findings. Brain lesions had occurred in every species of experimental animals tested thus far, including mice, rats, and rabbits. The next species tested was a primate: the rhesus monkey. Dr. Olney and his associate, Lawrence G. Sharpe, reported that brain lesions occurred in infant rhesus monkeys treated with a relatively high dose of MSG, administered subcutaneously. Nerve-cell deaths occurred in seven of the nine baby animals with about five times the amount of MSG to be expected in a 4½-ounce jar of some baby foods. The researchers commented: "The lack of symptoms in the primate during the time when a small percentage of its brain cells were being destroyed is evidence of a subtle process of brain damage in the developmental period, which could easily go unrecognized were it to occur in the human infant under routine circumstances."[54]

As a result, the FDA announced its intention of reviewing MSG, which has been on the GRAS list (Generally Recognized As Safe).[55] It should never have been put on that list, since it was already known and reported in a medical journal that MSG had caused eye damage in newborn mice.

"FLAT" AND "WARMED OVER"

In a survey conducted by National Family Opinion of 5,000 typical homemakers, the leading complaint against frozen processed dishes was that they lacked taste and flavor, were judged "flat," like "warmed over leftovers," and "not so tasty as advertised."[56]

Other typical comments made by groups evaluating convenience foods confirm these results. Frozen entrées were judged of mediocre quality and "all in all . . . hardly . . . worthwhile." Most frozen beefsteaks would not "pass for a steak at any self-respecting dinner table."[57] Trade reports have indicated that the various types of so-called frozen steaks are often made from low-quality meat cuts, texture was often described as "tough, gristly or rubbery," and flavor as "stale."[58] Surveyors found that hens were used for canned chicken and turkey, as well as for frozen chicken and turkey pies. Meat pies were found to "contain little meat and plenty of extenders," while frozen and canned chow mein had "lots of liquid and little meat."[59]

Three-course frozen meals were sampled but "none would be mistaken for good home cooking."[60] Frozen dinners were described as "not . . . examples of culinary art at its best . . . none up to the quality of fine restaurant or expertly home-cooked fare."[61] The declining quality of frozen fruit pies over the last few years "is well known to the trade," what with lower weights and fruit fillings, but more chemical additives, designed for longer life in the freezer, and artificially induced flavor, color, and appearance.[62] Dry soup mixes were judged "not what mother used to make," and some "with more salt than meat in the mix."[63]

PLANNING TO EAT OUT?

"The appalling, tasteless food served in most American restaurants . . . today is surely tolerated only because we don't know any better," comments the writer William Vogt.[64]

"Staples of highway dining," noted *The New York Times*, "are the plastic hamburger, the asbestos French fry, apple mucilage pie, peas and limas plucked back in the Eisenhower years, and cardboard bread, all brought back from beyond the grave through the miracle of food freezing. From Secaucus to Key West, 'half Southern fried chicken' is available in brown, glove-like rubber casings of the chicken. 'Seafood platters' come similarly packaged in rubber batter; unpackaged, the shrimp taste like scallops, which taste like the flounder, which taste like catsup."[65]

What with labor shortages and a constant drive for economic short cuts, the quality of food in restaurants has gone into a steady decline. Inadequate sanitation, refrigeration, and kitchen practices combine to make the food tasteless, poorly prepared, low in nutrients, and sometimes hazardous. Some restaurants now substitute nondairy products for coffee cream, margarine for drawn butter, and hydrogenated shortenings for vegetable oils. Canned or frozen peas or orange juice may be listed on the menu as "fresh." White salmon may be substituted for trout, scallops plus artificial pink coloring for lobster, shark meat for lake sturgeon, and other less expensive items for costly ones.

Rancid oils may be used over and over for quick frying. Salads may be cut long in advance and have lost their vitamin C, and foods held for long periods of time on steam tables have lost many nutrients. Potatoes may be peeled in advance and soaked in a bleach to maintain their whiteness and prevent spoilage.

Even many of the "gourmet" restaurants are no longer preparing foods from basic ingredients, although they don't advertise these short cuts. "Some of the most expensive restaurants in New York are among my best customers," boasts a distributor of frozen, precooked meals.[66] "It would probably drive some customers away if they knew the entrées were preprepared." Some customers would be disgruntled about the price of the meal, if they knew they were eating a glorified version of a TV dinner. For example, in an elegant Manhattan restaurant, waiters serve handsome chicken à la Kiev, for more than six dollars. The restaurant buys the dish, fully prepared and frozen, from a San Francisco factory at about one dollar per portion.

Hotel restaurants, catering to large numbers, may now have their eggs cracked, greens chopped, radishes cleaned, celery cut, fat trimmed from meat, and other labor-saving services performed at the purveyors' plants, before the foods arrive for use.

Several large restaurant chains use menus on which entrées are frozen, prepared items. Even charcoal-broiled steaks and chops are cut, seared almost black, and frozen, for later use.

John Steinbeck, traveling through the country, remarked that "in eating places along the roads the food has been clean, tasteless, colorless, and of a complete sameness." He wondered if our taste buds are so atrophied that we find tasteless foods not only *acceptable* but *desirable*.[67]

Hospital food also reflects lowered standards. Jane Hartman, a dietician, wrote: "The vegetables served in all too many hospitals would be spurned by a starving rabbit. Soggy, steam-battered and devitalized by over-cooking, they have little value and less appeal for patients."[68]

A physiotherapist in a modern hospital wrote: "White bread, packaged cereals, canned foods predominate on the menus. Vegetables, when fresh, are boiled and reboiled. Salads are at a minimum. The menu today was pork chop, mashed potatoes (reconstituted), stuffing, biscuits, cake, beverage. Colas are frequently given to those who have gas. The lollipop give-away is popular with the doctors in the emergency room and laboratories."[69]

The automatic-vending-machine industry promotes a school-lunch program. The candy-bar machine in some school corridors is updated to include cookies, puddings, coffee, ice cream, and pastries, as well as cold sandwiches. The vending industry was warned through its trade magazine that it faces a battle trying to promote these foodstuffs with school authorities, who "view vending as a threat both to insuring that children eat nutritional lunches and to teaching children the value of good nutrition,"[70] largely because of the inclusion of soft drinks and candy.

"LOOK NICE . . . TASTE NICE" . . . WHAT ELSE?

"Will [the food industry] . . . continue to concentrate on taste, eye appeal, convenience, economy, shelf life and quantity? Or will [it] consider a new dimension of food—quality?" asked a concerned Congressman, Representative David King.[71] At present, nutrition seems to be the last value considered by food technologists.

With modern techniques, the food chemist can simulate almost any flavor or texture of food. According to Professor John Yudkin, a British nutritionist, this ability creates "a dietary hazard of greatest importance." Dr. Yudkin notes that we demand of the processor items which "look nice, taste nice, and have a pleasant texture. Since we demand nothing more, and since [the food technologist] can provide us quite readily with these qualities of palatability, quite apart from the qualities of nutritional value, *this is what we frequently get.*"[72] The chemicals that provide taste and texture are usually nutritionally valueless, while protein, vitamins, and minerals are relatively tasteless.

As an example of the danger, Dr. Yudkin noted how the use of refined sugar has replaced fruit in our patterns of eating. Yet sugar provides only calories, which are already abundant in our diets. Dr. Yudkin suggested that "we may soon be eating pies, hamburgers, and sausages with every quality of the meat they should contain, except the nutritional value."[73]

Dr. Frederick Kilander, dean of the graduate school of Wagner College, reported in 1964 that a study, extending over nearly three decades, revealed that "two out of three Americans cannot select a well-balanced diet in a cafeteria, even when cost is no object." The same is true for the homemaker doing her weekly food shopping. The American food supply may be "unsurpassed in volume, variety and nutritional value," but it is no guarantee that a shopper will choose what is good for him just because it is available.[74]

VANISHING VITAMINS

The following is from a report to the Surgeon General of the USPHS, made by a committee of experts who commented on the nutritional quality of market food:

The newer types of food processing, packaging and storage provide many opportunities for the addition, removal, modification and interaction of substances which are physiologically important. For example, high temperatures may destroy heat-labile [sensitive] vitamins and amino acids, and they may also affect the availability of calcium or other mineral components. Efforts to compensate for such losses by supplementation may lead to imbalances and excesses in the total diet. Blending and reprocessing of products may bring about changes of possible health significance which would not otherwise be encountered.[75]

This is an astonishing statement. The USPHS, a governmental agency, is criticizing the processes that are officially sanctioned and encouraged by other governmental agencies, the FDA and the USDA.

Vitamins available in America's food have declined steadily. Changed eating habits, and a shift away from the consumption of fresh deep-yellow and dark-green vegetables are blamed.[76] The decline in vitamins is also related to changes in the raising and processing of food. Varieties of fruits and vegetables raised for commercial markets are selected on the basis of what will ship and store well, rather than for their vitamin content. Processing, which involves the use of certain chemical additives, and pesticides destroy vitamins. Faulty handling, long exposure to air, and poor methods of cooking may deplete them still further.

As an example of vitamin loss, examine the highly unstable vitamin C. Freshly mashed potatoes retain about 66 per cent of this vitamin, but only about 25 per cent of the original vitamin is retained in potatoes reconstituted from dehydrated flakes.[77] This loss is so serious that, in buying dehydrated mashed potatoes for distribution the USDA requires "fortification" of 50 milligrams per ounce of vitamin C in the finished product.[78]

Researchers in the USDA found that vine-ripened tomatoes grown out of doors in sunlight are twice as rich in vitamin C as their greenhouse counterparts grown in wintertime.[79] Some varieties of apples are sevenfold richer in vitamin C than others, yet they never reach the American consumer. In a review of data on several thousand samples of oranges, their vitamin C content ranged from less than 20 milligrams per 100 grams in one orange to more than 80 milligrams per 100 grams in another. Tree-ripened fruits have more vitamin C than those picked immature. Commercial chilled orange juice loses up to 57 per cent of the vitamin C contained in a freshly squeezed orange. These are common practices responsible for vitamin losses.[80]

Canned foods, as well as fresh, lose nutrients during long storage. The loss is accelerated by high temperatures. Canned vegetables stored at 65° F. lose up to 15 per cent of their thiamin within a year; stored at 80° F., the loss is about 25 per cent. Vitamin C loss in canned fruits and vegetables approximates that of thiamin, with 10 per cent loss at 65° F., and up to 25 per cent loss at 80° F., within a year. Thiamin in canned meats may be reduced as much as 30 per cent in only six months when stored at 70° F.[81]

FOODS "JUST LIKE NEW"

"By 1975, few American will know what natural food tastes like," warned William Vogt in 1960:

> Today, only one-eighth live on farms, and along with a few exurbanites and gardeners, know how good fresh picked sweet corn and strawberries can be. By 1975, there may be only one-fourteenth of our population left on the land. One economist, considered by many to be an authority, puts the estimate as low as two million! The rest of us will be eating canned, frozen, dried and dried-out victuals, or foods that have been preserved by radiation or bactericidal chemicals.[82]

The problems of transporting, distributing, and storing foodstuffs far from their source of origin have long been a challenge to the food industry. The ultimate goal has been to find means of preservation requiring no refrigeration, thus bestowing indefinite shelf life on foodstuffs.

With our present advanced technology, fresh foods can be supplemented with processed ones in which important nutrients can be kept largely intact, *provided methods used are the least destructive.* Freezing, for example, when done properly, can preserve vital enzymes, vitamins, and minerals, as well as flavors, in many foods. This technique offers advantages both to the consumer and to the food industry.

PUTTING FOODS TO SLEEP

In addition to mechanical freezing of food, a relatively new process has been developed. Using liquid nitrogen, a colorless, odorless, and nonreacting gas, food can be quick-frozen faster.

The nitrogen displaces oxygen in the air, thus reducing deterioration in the food by oxidation. The fast freezing forms extremely small ice crystals; in mechanical deep-freezing, the crystals are larger and accompanied by ice needles. The faster freezing results in better texture, flavor, and appearance of the food and in the retention of most nutrients.

Nitrogen has also entered the field of fresh-food transport. An electronically controlled liquid-nitrogen cylinder continuously pumps the gas into a refrigerated trailer truck in transit. On a five-day cross-country truck trip, or even a three-week ocean voyage, produce in a controlled nitrogen atmosphere has not deteriorated. The technique offers the possibility of shipping ripened produce and also of extending markets for highly perishable foods. Using this technique, shippers found that they could truck a load of strawberries cross-country with no spoilage, and do it more cheaply than by overnight air freight. Nitrogen-controlled shipments of fresh meat and fish have also shown promise.[83]

To reduce the waste of wilted lettuce caused by long shipping distances, it may be packaged with material that keeps out humidity. Also, to slow down the respiration rate of lettuce, inert nitrogen may be injected into the railroad car or truck trailer that transports the lettuce, thus extending the life of this vegetable.[84]

Freeze-drying is another process that offers possibilities of retaining nutrients. It is likely to prove cheaper than deep-freezing, because of the ease of distributing and storing freeze-dry foods. The process is one of the gentlest techniques known, and it causes far less damage to flavor, texture, and color than conventional heat drying. At the same time, nutritive values are conserved. The food is frozen and then placed in a vacuum cabinet, where air pressure is reduced. Ice crystals in the food are transformed to vapor. The ice level recedes with the food itself, and the natural salts, sugars, and protein in the food are dried in a natural position rather than being drawn out to the surface as in more conventional drying processes. There is little shrinking or shriveling, and the food is rehydrated by soaking.[85]

Food processed by methods just cited should be considered only *supplementary* to fresh food, i.e. to fill a secondary need. These techniques demonstrate that processing *per se* need not cause drastic reduction of nutritional values, nor need it be hazardous to the consumer. Even using present technological knowledge—without considering other possibilities yet unexplored—far better practices could be developed. Instead of the present arrangement of the supermarket, we could have huge walk-in refrigerators to hold fresh foodstuffs, supplemented by greatly expanded deep-freezer cabinets. To do this, both the consumer and the food industry must recognize that the only worth-while foods are those which are perishable.

But instead of turning in this direction, processors have toyed with some methods that ignore the twin problems of food losses and human hazards. Containers of food have been exposed to short bursts of high-speed electrons. Such treated foods have been kept at room temperature for several years without apparent deterioration. Or, experimentally, ultrasonic waves have preserved fruit-juice concentrates in hermetically sealed containers, which require no additional processing. Ultraviolet light has been used to kill microbial growths in many foods. Such techniques may serve the processor, but not the consumer.

PROCESSED BY "IONIZING ENERGY"

"Huge saving seen in food preservation by radiation: could save country millions annually."[86]

"The gateway to a new era for a new food industry and a better way of life for America and the rest of the world."[87]

"This is the first truly new process for preserving food that the world has received in one hundred and fifty years."[88]

These headlines are typical of the fanfare that accompanied government attempts to develop a means of preserving foodstuffs by ionizing radiation. No fewer than nine federal agencies have been involved, but the most aggressive promotion has been launched and perpetuated jointly by the U.S. Army and the Atomic Energy Commission (AEC). To date, more than $25 million has been spent for research on a project fraught with danger for the consumer.[89]

At first, U.S. Army officials promoted the irradiation processing for shipping foods to front-line troops. Hopes were high for *permanent* preservation. Research was urged on university laboratories and private research foundations, as well as government laboratories. A $7,500,000 Ionizing Radiation Center at Stockton, California, was built by the U.S. Army to serve as a pilot plant, long before basic knowledge had been gathered.

Various experimental tests have revealed extensive damage to animals fed irradiated food.[90] Early trials failed when the laboratory animals dropped dead from no apparent cause. As far back as 1948, experimental rats fed on irradiated foods showed impairment or loss of fertility, increased mortality in litters, abnormal eyes, hemorrhages, and hearts with enlarged left ventricles, which frequently resulted in death. In other tests, offspring of rats fed irradiated chicken and beans were born blind, and had a shortened life span. Dogs fed irradiated eggs produced fewer litters or became sterile. Mice developed enlarged hearts and breast cancer. Many test animals exhibited marked symptoms of vitamin deficiencies.

At first, researchers lacked information concerning the effect of irradiated foods on biological processes. As trials were continued, it became apparent that Vitamin K, a primary factor in blood clotting, was destroyed completely in high-dosage irradiated foods, which accounted for hemorrhages of body tissues.[91] In human beings, deficiency of this vitamin is suspected as an important factor in the development of coronary thrombosis.

The pilot project at Stockton was a fiasco. A food-trade journal described attendant promotion by "well-paid experts who, like race track touts, offered 'cold sterilization' as the horse to bet on in the Preservation Sweepstakes." The Stockton project was dubbed the "million dollar blunder," and plans to ionize food were canceled.[92]

The U.S. Army and the AEC decided to revamp their approach. Instead of attempting to achieve permanent preservation, they began to aim at extending the shelf life of foods. By reducing the amount of radiation and combining the process with pasteurization, they salvaged the project.[93]

The U.S. Army and the AEC enlisted aid from the Interdepartmental Commission on Irradiation and Preservation of Foods. "By sheer weight of numbers and of bureaucrats with university degrees," a journalist noted, "the officials helped to dispel the [unpleasant] facts."[94] As a result, a Congressional grant of $10 million was made to continue research and development of low-dose irradiation processing of perishable foods to extend their shelf life.

But irradiated foods developed off-flavors and off-tastes, suspected by scientists to be caused by subtle changes in the chemical structure of the food. Irradiated beef, which turned pink, was described as smelling "oily, sweet, fragrant, spicy, burnt, rancid, metallic, etherish, and sulphurous." Its taste was like "wet dog hair" or "burnt chicken feathers." Treated cured meat turned brown, and pork and chicken became pink. Cereals darkened; cheddar cheese and salmon were bleached. Whites of eggs became watery. Irradiated milk was described by a dairy scientist as tasting "more bitter than gall."[95]

Fruits and vegetables also suffered notable changes,[96] and lost their firmness. Grapes developed off-flavors and odors. Lemons showed a marked loss of both citric and ascorbic acids. Pears turned muddy green and mealy, and had a flat flavor. Beets turned black. Tomatoes decreased in firmness, and were easily bruised when handled during harvesting, packing and shipping. Apples, avocados, nectarines, olives, oranges, peaches, pears, plums, and grapes all softened and shriveled, with losses of color and flavor. Irradiated potatoes, lemons, and peaches were more likely to rot than untreated ones. Figs and strawberries, among all fresh produce tested, were the only ones that did not suffer adverse effects in appearance or flavor.[97]

When analyzed, these unfavorable characteristics were accompanied by extensive alteration and destruction of nutritional elements in the foods. Various research studies have produced fragmentary information. Estimated losses of vitamin B complex in certain foods are high. For example, 66 per cent of thiamin is destroyed in treated beef, and 92 to 98 per cent in treated pork, with lower losses for other fractions of this vitamin.[98]

In some foods vitamin E losses are 10 to 30 per cent. Gamma rays destroy vitamin C, and ionizing rays destroy vitamin A, as well as pyridoxine and B_{12} from the vitamin B complex. At least six important amino acids are reduced, with a change in pattern and a lowering of the quality of protein.[99] Irradiation reduces milk protein even more than heat sterilization does. There is also destruction of fats and enzymes.[100]

A physician attached to the U.S. Army's own scientific advisory board, Dr. Walter J. Nungester, having examined the experimental findings up to 1960, advised caution. He testified that knowledge was far from conclusive, and what was known raised enough danger signals for the U.S. Army to proceed slowly before launching any program of feeding irradiated foods to troops. He emphasized the great need for further checking.[101]

Not only is the destruction of essential elements in irradiated foods extensive, but the alterations are accompanied by the formation of new chemical compounds not yet understood. These substances are suspected of being either acutely or chronically toxic, as well as carcinogenic.[102] At the cellular level at least two types of chemical changes have been noted in irradiated foods (in the carbon chains, and in the steroids).[103] These alterations have been termed "potentialities for biological activity which are, as yet, only a field for speculation."[104] In addition, ionizing energy is a potential cancer inciter when applied to living organisms even at very low levels.

The food industry has displayed a cautious wait-and-see attitude during the U.S. Army–AEC promotion of ionizing radiation. Although the industry recognizes the enormous significance of the project, especially if "perfected" at government expense, technical problems of practical concern remain unsolved. These include altered appearance of the food, flavor, and taste, as well as lowered marketability of irradiated items. The present process is more expensive than other processing and preservation methods; it also creates special problems. Botulism, for example, destroyed by heat pasteurization of foods, is *not* killed by low levels of radiation. Irradiation does *not* inactivate meat enzymes; certain meats, even if treated, would need additional processing with heat or chemicals to prevent deterioration. Under U.S. Army sponsorship, however, the meat industry has displayed some interest in developing methods of disguising off-flavors of meat. Food technologists have experimented with sauces and spices to cloak unpalatability.

The fishing industry has been tempted by the possibility of irradiation-pasteurization of fish on board ship within a few hours after the catch. When treated, such fish can be stored for several weeks and allow the trawler to stay at sea for long periods.

Refrigerated shrimp, which normally spoils in about two weeks, is reported, when treated, to resist spoilage up to seven weeks. Cooked crabs, usually kept up to a week, when treated remain edible for as long as a month.

The fresh-produce industry has been offered similar advantages, with the U.S. Army suggesting truck-mounted trailers designed for irradiating harvested fruits right in the fields or orchards. However, the fresh fruit and vegetable industry is not enthusiastic and has labeled as "science fiction" the U.S. Army's report that fresh foods stay "just like new."[105]

The meat industry has been wooed by governmental announcements that the U.S. Defense Department will guarantee the purchase of large amounts of irradiated meats. Despite this bait, the meat packers have remained wary. The entire food industry has an uneasy feeling that the consumer will regard irradiated foods suspiciously and associate them with the idea of radioactive contamination.

At present, no irradiated foods are being sold to the consuming public. But the U.S. Army and AEC push onward aggressively. Several years ago they predicted that many irradiated foods would be on the shelves by now.[106] Their timing may have been inaccurate, but they still strive to achieve their goal. They have sought approval for irradiation of a great many foodstuffs, including oranges, dehydrated vegetables, strawberries, ham, pork, onions, chicken, beef, shrimp, hamburgers, pork sausage, clams, crabs, papayas, mangoes, turkey, frankfurters, bananas, figs, oysters, luncheon meats, lamb, duck, sweet cherries, apricots, nectarines, and prunes. These petitions have been filed by the U.S. Army or the AEC, but not by any of the industries that would be involved.

THE FDA'S POLICY REGARDING
IRRADIATED FOODS

The irradiation of foods, categorized as a food additive, is under the FDA's jurisdiction. As early as 1963, this agency approved a petition by the U.S. Army to feed troops with treated canned bacon, and white potatoes irradiated to inhibit sprouts. Later that same year, for insect control, the FDA sanctioned the irradiation of wheat, wheat products and flour in shipments abroad. However, since then, the FDA has taken a closer look at data submitted, and, as a result of a review of independent findings, the agency has changed its position. The FDA denied the U.S. Army–AEC's petition to irradiate strawberries (January 1968); rejected its petition for irradiated canned ham (June 1968); and withdrew its approval for irradiated bacon (July 1968),[107] although this item had already been served on twelve military bases for two years. These three actions seemed to jeopardize the whole U.S. Army–AEC program. What made the FDA reverse itself?

In the case of the irradiated strawberries, the FDA ruled that data submitted were no longer sufficient. Independent studies at Cornell University showed that sugar, exposed to sufficient radiation, breaks down and can transmit the lethal effect of radiation to living plant cells, and, possibly, to other forms of life. Although it has been well established that radiation affects living cells *directly*, this new evidence shows that the chemical substances formed can affect plant cells almost as if they were irradiated directly. The effects were produced by stable substances that acted long after the exposure of the original substance to radiation had ceased. The experiments also showed that at *low* dosages of radiation, cell growth was stimulated rather than stopped. The trials, extended to fruit flies, showed adverse effects on the living cells, with stunted growth and chromosome damage. All living cells contain sugar, the report emphasized, and "humans may suffer similar consequences from long-term consumption of irradiated foods."[108]

Another study with irradiated sugar was made at the medical school at the University of Michigan, testing the effect of sucrose solution irradiated several months previously by cobalt-60 on samples of human white blood corpuscles. The sugar solutions were found to be extremely toxic to the cells. Attempts to assess the extent of damage to individual chromosomes proved impossible because so few of the cells divided normally, and the damage to these cells was already severe. The scientists emphasized that the results were not proof that an irradiated food would, after being eaten, damage the cells of a human consumer, but that these possibilities "must not be lightly brushed aside now that mass consumption of irradiated foods is being seriously considered."[109]

In the case of irradiated canned ham, the FDA reversed its former position because the data submitted failed to establish that the proposed use of gamma radiation would be safe. The agency also announced that all previous clearances of food preserved by irradiation would have to be re-evaluated to make certain that the data justified approval. In notifying the U.S. Army that its data were unconvincing, the FDA termed the material submitted as "poorly executed studies," "incomplete," and with "inadequate evaluation of results."[110] At the same time, the FDA cited a UCLA study on rats fed irradiated bacon and fruit compote which revealed that "the feeding of a diet containing irradiated bacon at the 1x level [minimum level of radiation producing sterilization] was associated with the reduction of 22 per cent in weaned progeny and a 23 per cent reduction in liveborn progeny."[111] Other adverse effects included increased mortality rates in rats fed a diet of bacon irradiated at the 2x level. "There was consistently reported a slight but persistent depression of body weight observed both in dogs and mice that were fed irradiated diets." The FDA also expressed concern over the tumor-causing potential of irradiated foods. Rats fed a diet of irradiated bacon and fruit developed more tumors than a control group of animals. "One study of rats reported three carcinomas of the pituitary gland among 52 animals on irradiated pork diet versus none in the 26 animals on the control diet. Since this is a rarely occurring type of tumor, this could be very significant."[112]

The FDA also mentioned a "possibility that irradiation of food produces a factor or factors in the treated food that are antagonistic to the essential nutrients in the untreated portion of the diet when the two portions are mixed."[113]

In the case of the FDA's withdrawal of approval for irradiated bacon, which had already been served to the armed services, the agency once again, upon closer scrutiny, found that the U.S. Army–AEC's data were unsatisfactory.

Understandably, the FDA's actions have caused a storm of protest from the U.S. Army–AEC. These groups, in turn, have combined their forces with many Congressmen to press for wholesale irradiation of foodstuffs. The Congressmen see in future food-irradiation plants a means of introducing new, potentially prosperous industries into the economies of their constituents back home. This is particularly attractive if the federal government develops the process and pays for its cost.

The FDA's re-evaluation of data appears to jeopardize the entire irradiation program envisaged by the U.S. Army–AEC, at the very time when they appeared to be gaining some interest from industry, which previously had shown a singular lack of enthusiasm. By 1967, four independent companies signed contracts with the AEC to build and operate the first commercial processing plant for irradiating foods, in Allentown, Pennsylvania. The AEC agreed to furnish federal funds for source material, and the U.S. Army's radiation laboratories were to have offered technical assistance. The deal was made financially attractive, with a guaranteed purchase of 150,000 pounds of irradiated bacon yearly, 300,000 pounds of irradiated meat for the first three years, and the promise of chicken and seafood included in the program.[114] Now, in view of the FDA's actions, these plans may be shelved or killed.

Statements elsewhere strengthened the FDA's policy. The World Health Organization issued a report on irradiated food, urging extreme caution before launching any wholesale program.[115] The British Ministry of Health prepared draft regulations which would have the effect of placing a complete ban in the United Kingdom on the irradiation of food and food products intended for human consumption, and on the sale of food subjected to irradiation.

The potential hazards for human beings consuming irradiated foods over a lifetime are still largely unknown, and what *is* known suggests major hazards. Cancer specialists have stated repeatedly that carcinogenic action may be triggered but remain latent for 10, 20, 30, or even 40 years as a "biological timebomb."

4

The Race Between
Toxicologist and Undertaker

"CHEMICALS NO menace, expert declares additives to food helpful, never dangerous."[1]

"Better foods through additives."[2]

"Food additives aid nutrition."[3]

"Food additives: despite furor, most are safe, necessary and beneficial."[4]

These are typical headlines, aimed at you, the American consumer, to quell your growing uncertainties. You are assured that additives such as salt, vinegar, sugar, and spices have been used for centuries.[5] So they have. But no one points out that these materials bear no relationship to the newer ones, created by chemists, which are highly complex, and foreign to the normal metabolism of the body.

Chemists engaged in food manipulation are often misnamed food scientists. They may have little or no knowledge of the physiology and pathology of the body. Nor do they grasp the significance and complexities of living processes. Biological adaptations evolve slowly, and the human body is incapable of making radical changes within the brief period of a lifetime. As Dr. Edward Mellanby expressed it, in a lecture on the chemical manipulation of food: "Medical science often cannot give adequate answers to questions of toxicological action, not only as regards new compositions but even in the case of substances long in use. Indeed, to the medical man unpleasant surprises are constantly being revealed, in the case both of drugs and of chemicals used in food preparations."[6]

Many chemical food additives may be technologically desirable for the food industry, but biologically disastrous for the body. As noted by Dr. William E. Smith, in a letter to Representative James J. Delaney: "The human digestive tract provides an endless and understandably attractive outlet for products of ingenuity; but the health and power of the nation depend in large part on its food, and it is to our peril if the human digestive tract is legislated into the role of a sewer for the disposal of chemicals."[7]

Dr. Smith warned again: "In this problem of chemical food additives and pesticides, our country has gotten into a race to see whether the toxicologist can keep ahead of the undertaker."[8]

"THE CONFUSERS"

During the Delaney Congressional Hearings on Chemical Additives in Foods, the chemical and food-processing industries, concerned with the public anxieties produced by the shocking information divulged, raised sizable funds to counteract unfavorable publicity. Dr. Roy Newton, vice-president in charge of research for Swift and Company, attempted to address an interindustry conference of both groups, to plead for caution in using chemical additives in foods. He was prevented from addressing the gathering, but later presented his views before the Delaney hearings.

Dr. Newton had wished to warn the chemical and food industries that many of their members did not have "a full realization of the delicacy of balance of chemical reactions within the human body and the ease with which foreign substances can throw this delicate mechanism out of balance." He had wanted to tell the industries that fund raising to counteract unfavorable publicity "may eventually affect public opinion to such an extent that the FDA will be prevented from carrying out its responsibility in protecting the public. If this . . . should come to pass, there will undoubtedly be a surge of new chemical substances incorporated in food without adequate pretesting."[9]

Propaganda emanating from the industries, Dr. Newton charged, was based on many unsound premises, and indicated "a planned objective of confusion." One of the "confusers" he cited "is that even table salt is poisonous under some conditions. It is well established that one can cram enough table salt down his throat to kill him, but is there any doubt . . . that table salt used by the normal individual in the manner which it has been used for thousands of years represents any hazard? Conversely, is there any doubt in anyone's mind that it is possible to incorporate in food products small amounts of chemical substances which, without being obvious to the consumer, would either kill him or impair his health when consumed over a long period of time?"[10] This was the *real* issue, and the *only* issue, he said.

Dr. Newton urged pretesting of new and unusual substances proposed for food. Then he made some remarkably clear predictions of "confusers" that industry would use in attempts to repudiate pretesting: "Many . . . will object to the long test period . . . to the levels that are included in the test . . . to the interpretation of results . . . to delegating authority to a government body to serve as a referee on the adequacy of such tests."[11]

Dr. Newton's question was: "Should such pretesting be compulsory?" His own answer was: "There are many who will laud the ethical standard of the chemical industry and the food industry in an attempt to show that they are reliable and intelligent enough to make all the tests required without compulsory action. A moment's reflection on the part of anyone should convince him that this is not true."[12]

Dr. Newton's predictions were fulfilled. The "confuser" arguments and tactics have been used. Repeatedly, the consumer is assured that safeguards are maintained, and that government agencies as well as industry keep close surveillance.[13] Meantime, the race continues, sharper than ever, between the toxicologist and the undertaker.

When the Hearings on Chemical Additives in Foods were held in the 1950's, it was admitted that some 700 chemicals were being added to American foodstuffs. Grave doubt existed of the safety of at least 150 of them. Since then, the total number of chemical additives in foods has soared.[14] Official estimates now reach up to 10,000! To list and describe fully all food and color additives that have received government sanction now requires a directory of five volumes, and there is no exact knowledge of the number in present use. All that can be said is that they are constantly increasing. Industry continually petitions for the inclusion of new additives, and the FDA has never attempted to close the floodgates. At no point has this agency suggested any restriction or reduction of the list. It is true that the agency has favored a host of additives. *Accidental* additives, along with the known *intentional* ones, increase the total number.

The former FDA Commissioner James L. Goddard had a somewhat more critical attitude toward food additives than George Larrick, his predecessor. Addressing the Food Protection Committee, NAS-NRC, in December 1966, Dr. Goddard admitted: "In a number of cases the additives proposed have only an economic benefit to the food producer and no benefit at all to the person who eats the final product."[15]

WHAT HARM CAN
CHEMICAL FOOD ADDITIVES DO?

Analyzing a chemical additive in food is not merely a problem of exploring its possible acute harmfulness. Yet past testing techniques have been developed largely for the study of *direct* toxic effects. Scientists are becoming aware of the need to study the untoward results—those which are slight, unnoticed, delayed, and indirect. These are the subtle effects on the human system at the basic cellular level, resulting from hundreds, even thousands of substances biologically foreign to the body, consumed daily in common foodstuffs, over many years, or even during an entire lifetime. The problem is complicated by the need to examine chemical food additives in relation to additional chemical and physical factors, such as polluted air and water, pesticide residue, tobacco, drugs, alcohol, radiation, and other environmental elements.[16]

Some additives produce chemical changes in the food itself by altering its biological structure. Others, which produce derangements in the human system, are so insidious that they do not become apparent until long after the original exposure. Because of this, they may not even be suspected as the original instigator of trouble.

The fundamental biological mechanism of the body may be affected in ways scarcely appreciated at present. One of the earliest signs of harm may be the enlargement of vital organs, accompanied by microscopic changes that can be detected by a trained pathologist. Frequently, the enlarged liver, kidneys, and spleen of experimental animals are signs of damage. The increased size of these organs may be caused by stresses placed upon them to detoxify strange materials.

Many chemical food additives interfere with the normal functioning of vitamins and enzymes, which work closely together in the body. Vitamins play an important role in releasing energy for all physiological processes, including cell repair. Closely associated with them are the enzymes, which are the effective agents of the whole life-process. As long as each cell lives, it is continually being broken down and rebuilt. Energy is needed for this repair process. In a vitamin deficiency, where energy liberation is interfered with by the introduction of chemical food additives or other substances, the rebuilding process slows down or ceases; the cells die. When enough cells sicken and die, the body dies.[17]

Injury or deterioration of the cells is recognized by physicians aware of vitamin- and enzyme-deficiency symptoms. Patients are easily fatigued, show such symptoms as weakness, constipation, loss of appetite, headache, disturbance of sleep, excessive irritability, depression, inability to concentrate, queer feelings in the fingers and toes, burning tongue, gas, and many other odd bodily sensations. These symptoms may be classified vaguely as nervousness, neurasthenia or imagination, when in reality they may stem from impairment of the vitamin-enzyme system of the body.

Medical authorities and researchers have suggested that losses or deficiencies of enzymes lead to many diseases. Commonly used chemical food additives such as sulphur dioxide, sodium nitrate, food dyes, certain hormones used to stimulate plant and animal growth, antibiotics used in food production, fluorides used in processing water, and pesticides are all acknowledged enzyme destroyers. Adverse effects can occur even when the chemicals are present in exceedingly small amounts. For example, as little as 0.4 ppm of DDT inhibits a vital enzyme in human blood. Many chemical additives permitted in foods are present in amounts that adversely affect the body's enzymes. Some contaminants are harmful to animal life in amounts measured as parts per billion.

Catalase is one important enzyme found almost universally in living cells, not only in human beings, but also in animals, plants, and even in bacteria. This particular enzyme plays many vital roles. It is intimately related to cell respiration, and buffers the cell from toxic substances, infection, virus, radiation, and cancer. The normal cell maintains a specific balance of catalase and hydrogen peroxide. Catalase controls the hydrogen peroxide at a very low level, and converts it into oxygen and water. However, many substances, including some chemical food additives, destroy catalase. When this happens, the level of peroxide rises. This, in turn, results in the electron-transport system of the cell slowing down or stopping altogether. Cellular abnormalities may then develop, and the cell becomes predisposed to tumor formation and cancer.

Dr. R. A. Holman, a physician especially concerned with the catalase-peroxide balance, stated:

> It is obvious . . . that if this fundamental biological mechanism is interfered with for a long enough time by physical and chemical agents present in our environment, whether in food, drink, drugs, or in the air we breathe, then we shall see in races so exposed a progressive increase in the incidence of cancer. By contrast, in those primitive communities where such agents are not used or encouraged, the incidence will remain at a very low level. In my opinion most of the chemicals added to food and drink for preservation or coloring could and should be abolished."[18]

"THE GOVERNMENT WOULDN'T ALLOW IT!"

"If anything were harmful, the government wouldn't allow it." How many Americans reassure themselves with this comforting thought? Unfortunately, both the past record and the present situation show this to be false. There is no assurance of the safety of chemical additives merely because they have been approved by federal agencies. The toxic as well as the carcinogenic nature of a number of once-approved chemical food additives, now condemned, were discovered *not* by government agencies, but by private investigators. Some substances, approved officially, were later banned by the same agency. Synthetic coal-tar dyes (Butter Yellow dye and Red dye No. 1, to name but two), a synthetic flavoring (safrole), a weed killer (Aminotriazole), a pesticide (Aramite), artificial sweeteners (cyclamates), and a hormone (stilbestrol) have all been shown as cancer-inciters in test animals, but only *after* they had been in widespread use. Even when one of these substances produced tumors in experimental animals, the FDA permitted continued public exposure to it while more extensive studies of its carcinogenic potency were being conducted. Subsequent tests showed that the chemical had exceptionally strong carcinogenic qualities. However, it was not banned altogether; the tolerance was merely lowered.

No assurance of safety can be given simply because chemical food additives have been used for a long time. A flour bleach (agene) was used for 30 years before its harmfulness was established; an artificial sweetener (Dulcin), for 50 years; and a widely used synthetic flavoring (coumarin), for 70 years.

"We have had some very narrow escapes because of the use of additives that had no place in food," admitted George P. Larrick, the former FDA Commissioner. "It is inconceivable that this country should continue to expose itself indefinitely to the risks inherent in the present scheme of food control,"[19] he said. (Nevertheless, the great proliferation of food additives occurred during George Larrick's administration.) He referred, in part, to the fact that the toxic, as well as the cancer-inciting, properties of some substances were discovered only after studies of human injuries. Several deaths occurred before it was recognized that a salt substitute (lithium chloride) could be fatal. Recently a number of deaths in Canada and in the United States led to an investigation of an additive (a cobalt salt) used to improve the foamy appearance of beer. This additive had been approved as "safe" by the FDA in 1961, and had also been cleared by the Canadian Food and Drug Directorate. Used within the prescribed amounts sanctioned by law, this additive was responsible for fatal heart attacks of 50 to 100 heavy beer drinkers before it was banned by both governments.

There were some near misses when a highly dangerous anti-browning agent (thiourea) was introduced for processing peaches, and a chemical (hydrofluoric acid) for processing beer. Both chemicals were withdrawn before actual fatalities occurred.

Other food additives long sanctioned as "safe" by the FDA are being questioned. Mineral oil has been found to interfere with vitamin absorption in the body. Synthetic vitamin D, long added to "fortify" certain food, appears related to hypercalcemia in infants.

U.S. CERTIFIED COLORS— NO ASSURANCE OF SAFETY!

The label U.S. Certified Colors has been regarded by the uninformed as a seal of safety. Not true. In the past, the FDA approved coal-tar and other chemical dyes that were later shown to induce cancer. Only after long public exposure to these materials, some have been decertified, or "delisted" (Sudan I, Butter Yellow, Red No. 32, Orange No. 1 and 2, Yellow No. 1, 3, and 4, and Red No. 1 and 4). Even the terms "decertified" and "delisted" may be misleading. *This does not mean that they have been banned from use, but merely that they are no longer certified.* These dyes may still be found in foodstuffs resting in warehouses and on store shelves and in foods shipped *within* states, where federal agencies have no control.

The case of Red dye No. 1 is typical of many past errors in official judgment. This particular dye was used widely in foods, with official acceptance of its "safety." After many years, more thorough tests were conducted, in which 250 experimental rats were fed diets containing varying amounts of this coal-tar dye; 116 died, and many suffered liver damage and malignant tumors. Similar damaging results were observed in experimental mice and dogs.[20] Despite the cancer-inciting property of the dye, the FDA's ruling was described in *Chemical Week*[21] as a "reasonable approach," in that it allowed industry to use up its supplies on hand.

Coal-tar dyes have been described as "chemically completely unnatural . . . exceedingly complex, imperfectly researched, contain[ing] impurities of uncertain properties, and . . . quite unrelated to the familiar bright natural colors seen in undyed fruits and vegetables."[22] Of 82 food dyes permitted in 22 countries, only one is permitted in all. No universal agreement exists regarding the safety of these materials. A large percentage of food dyes available in the early 1950's have since been banned in foods.

Despite this poor record, about 90 per cent of all dyes used in foods today are synthetic.[23]

HOW ADEQUATE ARE ANIMAL TESTS?

Thorough testing, which is costly and time-consuming, has never been done for many additives now in use. Dr. Wilhelm C. Hueper, a cancerologist, listed nearly 40 categories of food additives and contaminants classified as carcinogens present in our food.[24]

Even with carefully devised animal tests, it is difficult to extrapolate results in terms of human beings. Animals do not necessarily react to substances in the same manner as people. For example, beta-naphthylamine, one of the most active human-cancer-inciting chemicals, in repeated tests failed to induce tumors in animals. Many years passed before a species was found whose response to this substance was like man's.[25]

The Joint FAO/WHO Conference on Food Additives has cautioned that absolute proof of nontoxicity cannot be established through animal tests because of special conditions of human life and individual human idiosyncrasies.[26] Experimental animals are tested in a thoroughly controlled environment, impossible with human beings. The old, the ill, the allergic, or the very young human being may be far more sensitive to substances than the well-fed rat, with a diet balanced in all known nutrients, and isolated from other chemicals in the environment. Pharmacologically, the fetus or newborn child is an entirely different organism from the adult.

HOW ADEQUATE ARE LABORATORY TESTS?

Laboratory analyses of chemical food additives are also inadequate. Dr. Arnold J. Lehman, former director of the Pharmacological and Toxicological Divisions of the FDA, admitted a present lack of precise knowledge regarding the ultimate fate of chemicals in the body. For a long time, he reported, toxicologists thought that the body was able to call upon some special mechanism to detoxify poisonous substances absorbed in the body. Experts had also believed that the toxic substances were broken down into less toxic compounds. More recent findings demonstrate the error of both beliefs. Special mechanisms do *not* exist. Toxic substances are subject to the metabolic influences that function normally in the body. Absorbed products are not necessarily less harmful than the original materials; in some cases, the toxicity of the breakdown compound has been found *more* poisonous than the original.[27]

Valid toxicologic studies for chemical food additives are complicated further by a mechanism known as synergism. The toxicity of one chemical can be strengthened considerably in interaction with another one that may be present. During a given meal the consumer may eat a number of chemical additives, and it is impossible to know the potential harm in the infinite variety of possible chance combinations that may occur. Such instances have been found in synergistic effects created by combinations, not only among food additives, but with pesticides, drugs, alcohol, and other substances. One important example is the consumption of alcohol before exposure to carbon tetrachloride fumes. Another is the sometimes fatal combination of alcohol and barbiturates.

Dr. Irving Selikoff, professor of environmental medicine at Mount Sinai school of medicine, stated: "We may eventually see diseases that we don't even begin to understand at this time. Also, the sum total of these various low-level contaminants—each in itself not very important—may be to generally shorten life." Dr. Selikoff expressed concern about the ever-increasing "total body burden of environmental contaminants."[28]

Some substances are known as "weak" carcinogens or co-carcinogens, which normally are not cancer-inciting. In combination with other materials, however, they *can* become active carcinogens. Some chemical food additives are in this category. Because of the many possibilities for synergism, valid results from toxicity tests are unlikely.

Toxicity tests do not necessarily show cancer-inciting properties of a chemical. As a rule, the smallest effective carcinogenic dose is lower than the toxicity threshold. Frequently, it is even within a "nontoxic" level of the smallest acute or chronic toxic dose of a chemical. In addition, there is no direct relationship between the relative toxic potency of a chemical and its carcinogenic power. Benzene, for instance, is highly toxic to the blood-forming tissue, but has only a relatively mild cancer-inciting effect. On the other hand, beta-naphthylamine, which has a very low degree of toxicity for man, is one of the most potent of human carcinogens. In fact, there seems to be an antagonism between toxic and carcinogenic properties of chemicals. Highly toxic chemicals are rather apt to kill cells outright than merely injure them, or modify them biologically. Because of this immediate destruction, the cells do not survive long enough to become abnormal and cancerous.[29] These facts are important, because *the tests that are made for chemical food additives are based on toxicity. The carcinogenic quality of the chemical is not likely to be revealed.* At times, it has been found only inadvertently.

The toxic effect of chemicals has been linked to some birth defects. Dr. Wilhelm C. Hueper noted: "It is likely that at least some of the cancers observed at birth or in infants and children are attributable to an exposure of the maternal organism, before or during lactation, to carcinogenic agents which passed through the placental barrier or were secreted in the milk."[30] Toxic chemical food additives are being viewed as one of the chief culprits in the alarming rise in numbers of birth defects.

Not only is the new generation likely to be affected by these additives, but also those yet unconceived may be threatened. The late Professor Hermann J. Muller, eminent geneticist, reminded the public that new mutagenic agents in the body may be "induced by one of the many novel practices of our day," including, among others, the use of chemical food additives. Concerning these suspect materials, he added that none of them have been adequately tested for their ability to produce mutations. "It is obvious that unless people . . . reach a firm decision not to pass along their burden to posterity, the genetic quality of future generations must inevitably undergo decline."[31]

Many chemicals, including food additives and pesticides, produce the same biological effects as atomic radiation, and are known as radiomimetic chemicals, because they mimic similar effects. Warning that "by far the most mutagenic agents known to man are chemicals, not radiation," Dr. Richard Caldecott added: "and in this regard, food additives rather than fallout at present levels may present a greater danger."[32]

The launching of a chemical food additive without adequate

prior testing, and testing based largely on industry-sponsored research, is well demonstrated in the astonishing case of two antioxidants, BHT and BHA. The developments are worthy of detailed study.

BHT AND BHA—THOSE "FRESHNESS PRESERVERS"

Natural antioxidants, which delay rancidity, are lost during the factory processing of refined oils and fats. An attempt is made to restore the antioxidation qualities by the addition of fat-stabilizing substances. Most of these added materials with antioxidant properties are known to be toxic to some degree. They are also considered by some authorities as possible cancer-inciters.[33]

BHT (butylated hydroxytoluene) and BHA (butylated hydroxyanisole) are petroleum products that have come into widespread use as antioxidants in foods. At first they were used with fats, but later they were incorporated so extensively in other items that today you can scarcely find in your shopping basket any factory-processed food or food packaging material that does not contain one or both of these chemicals. BHT/BHA manufacturers suggest their use in animal fats such as lard, beef tallow, bacon, chicken fat, butter, cream, shortenings, and grease; fried foods such as potato chips, doughnuts, and processed meats and fish; baked goods such as crackers, pastries, cakes, candies, and cookies; vegetable fats such as shortenings, margarine, peanut butter, and salad oils and dressing; ground grain meals and grain germs; a miscellany of other food items, including nutmeats, raisins, milk, candied fruit, whipped topping mixes, imitation fruit drinks, breakfast foods, extracts, essential oils, spices, and pet foods; food-packaging paper and containers, such as cartons for milk; containers for cottage cheese, ice cream, potato chips, cereals, cookies, and pastries; wrappers for breads, butter, and cheeses; rubber gaskets that seal food jars; and household wax paper. They are also found in some beverages, chewing gum, cosmetics, drugs, and animal feeds.

According to one of the large manufacturers, these antioxidants prevent "rancidity of lard; discoloration of meat; off-flavor in milk; bitterness in citrus oils; loss of potency in vitamin A; brittleness in chewing gum; unpleasant flavor and odor in paraffin wax."[34] The company has claimed that it is quite common to store fat treated with an antioxidant, under favorable conditions, and have the fat "remain 'sweet' for more than two years." Within four years of its introduction on the market, this company's antioxidant was used to treat over a billion pounds of lard.

These antioxidants were also recognized as useful in animal feeds. Another large manufacturer suggested that livestock feed processors use the antioxidants in numerous ways: to stabilize vitamins in animal fats used to "fortify" feed; to increase feed efficiency; to improve palatability of feed because of improved taste and appearance; for dust control; to heighten the color of feed; for ease in pelleting feed; to reduce fire hazards; and to increase the ease of handling and shipping feed in bulk.[35]

The consumer and farmer would *assume* that materials in such widespread use had undergone thorough prior testing, which established their safety beyond doubt. Curious to know what tests were used to establish the safety of BHT and BHA, individuals in co-operation with Consumers' Research wrote to the FDA in the early 1960's. As the story developed, *Consumer Bulletin* publicized it,[36] and forced two federal agencies to disclose information to which the public should have had free access, but didn't.

Although four references were supplied by the FDA, one of them could not be found in libraries. It was a report published by the American Meat Institute. When contacted directly, the Institute stated that copies of the report were unavailable.

The FDA wrote that the report, unpublished, had been submitted to the Bureau of Meat Inspection, USDA, when approval was requested for BHA as an antioxidant with food fats. The FDA stated that it could not make its own copy of the paper available, and admitted that the report should not have been listed among references on the subject.

When contacted, the Meat Inspection Division, USDA, wrote that BHT and BHA were tested by animal-feeding experiments. The agency gave assurance that: " . . . the toxicity studies were not conducted by a governmental agency but by private companies . . . under the direction of this division . . . [and results are in our files but] not available for distribution since furnished us in confidence."

Thus, the "safety" of two widely used chemical food additives was not based on independent research but on data supplied by an industry desiring to market products made with them. Two tax-supported federal agencies had denied individuals the right of access to information. Right or wrong, the conclusion that may be drawn is that the information is inadequate or damaging.

Another disturbing question was whether at any time the secret report was available to authors of other papers who cited it, or whether abstracts or secondhand reports about its contents had to be used. As Consumers' Research pointed out, with an ever-increasing number of chemical additives in foods, it becomes urgent that all experimental work purported to assure their safety be exposed to review by experts, as well as open to public scrutiny. Government officials should not give weight to data supplied in confidence and not freely available to all. A policy of free access would *not* mean public disclosure of "trade secrets" of manufacturing methods. It would require that the exact formulation be known of any chemical product being considered or already in use as a food additive or adjunct. It also implies that tests that have been used to establish its safety are readily accessible at all times.

TESTING OF THE ANTIOXIDANTS

The sole paper on BHT that the FDA sent to individuals who requested information was a study published in 1955[37] and financed by three chemical manufacturers of this antioxidant. Four species of test animals were fed BHT in various dosages. Amounts were determined for single doses that would kill the animals, and lower levels tolerated in repeated feedings for a period of two years. In the latter tests some animals died, but their deaths seemed unrelated to the amounts of BHT which they were fed. Some control animals, without BHT in their diet, also died. With this conflicting evidence the researchers "believed" that BHT had not caused the deaths, and they concluded that this antioxidant "could be used without any public health hazard." *Apparently on this inconclusive result the federal regulatory agencies approved the use of BHT in foods.*

Actually, earlier studies had been conducted elsewhere that *had* raised doubts by researchers about the safety of BHT. Those studies *should have* appeared on the government's list of material sent to interested individuals. Various experiments had demonstrated damaging effects of BHT in test animals, including metabolic stress,[38] depression of the growth rate,[39] loss of weight,[40] increase of liver weight,[41] damage to the liver,[42] increase of serum-cholesterol,[43] baldness,[44] and fetal abnormalities such as a failure to develop normal eyes in offspring.[45] Experimental tests in Romania, in the 1950's, using rats fed BHT in their diets, revealed such metabolic stress in the animals that upon further investigation undertaken by the Romanian Hygiene and Public Health Institute, recommendation was made that BHT should be banned from use in food.[46]

In 1959, Australian investigators W. D. Brown, A. R. Johnson, and M. W. O'Halloran found that BHT, fed at the normal testing dose in combination with lard, "significantly reduced the initial growth rate and mature weight of male rats." This inhibition of growth was judged "a direct toxic effect of BHT." The antioxidant "produced a significant increase in the weight of the liver relative to the body weight. The mean absolute weight of the liver was also increased." The researchers concluded that "if the conventional NTD [normal testing dose] be accepted . . . BHT . . . produced deleterious deviations from normal cellular behavior which *casts doubt on the advisability of permitting this antioxidant in foodstuffs for human consumption.*" The researchers suggested the probability that the detoxification of these phenols occurs in the liver, and the changes of this organ "represent an attempt . . . to meet the stresses placed upon it by the ingestion of these unphysiological substances . . . the toxic effect found in the animals fed BHT at the NTD . . . form *a prima facie case against the use of BHT in human diets.*" (Emphasis mine.)[47]

Since 1959, many fragmentary pieces of experimental research on BHT and BHA have been conducted, using various species of animals. They have been done, interestingly enough, not in America, where these antioxidants proliferate in foods and other consumer goods, but in Europe, Australia and New Zealand. To date, no thorough, systematic studies exist. Clear-cut satisfactory evidence of safety is lacking; most researchers agree that evaluation is difficult and further studies are needed.

Despite these studies, the FDA has permitted wide latitude in the use of antioxidants. In August 1966, the agency proposed to forgo requiring any label declaration of antioxidants used in fatty emulsifiers that are food components, deeming such antioxidants merely as "incidental additives." The proposal was opposed vigorously by some allergists, as well as by some state officials. For example, George H. Akau, Food Commissioner and Analyst, Honolulu, protested:

> If label exemptions of ingredient statements continue to be made, the American consumer cannot be an "intelligent voter," because no repetitious reading of food labeling will ever disclose the presence of antioxidants . . . and myriad other food additives which some members of the food industry believe to be necessary in fabricating our sophisticated foods. Instead of more mysticism about fabricated foods, there is need for a great deal more exposure and information about them. Obviously it is not in the interest of consumers to exempt from label declaration the presence of antioxidants used as chemical preservatives of fatty emulsifiers that are components of food.[48]

REPORTS ON ADVERSE EFFECTS FROM BHT/BHA

Both BHT and BHA have been demonstrated as harmful to sensitive individuals. Consider the case of Mrs. X[49] who had enjoyed excellent health and been free of allergic reactions. Her food intake was mostly from sources known to her, and her meals were made largely from basic commodities that she prepared in her own kitchen.

After eating commercially processed instant mashed potatoes for the first time, she suffered severe reactions, with skin blisters and hemorrhaging in one eye. This processed food was the only newly introduced item in her environment. When she ate it again and the symptoms recurred, both her physician and ophthalmologist suspected BHA and BHT present in the instant mashed potatoes. They advised her to avoid foods containing these antioxidants. She did so, and the symptoms subsided.

At a later date, her symptoms flared up again. This time they were traced to a breakfast cereal, never before used in her household, which contained BHT and BHA. Mrs. X became a concerned label reader and studiously tried to avoid foods containing these two additives. Again the symptoms returned. This time the problem was traced to a shortening that Mrs. X had previously tolerated. Upon examining the label closely, Mrs. X was astonished to find that the shortening was labeled "new and improved" with BHT and BHA added.

Mrs. X and her physicians tried to learn from government officials what foods were free of the two additives, and what foods would be safe for her to eat. Letters and telephone calls were either ignored, or at best, answered unsatisfactorily. She was told that all she had to do was to READ THE LABEL.

There was a similar lack of response or unsatisfactory answers from food companies. It was repeatedly stated that: "BHT and BHA are completely safe for foods used in amounts currently sanctioned." Mrs. X was assured by all that no substances may be added to food until their safety has been established and approved for use by the FDA.

In the case of these antioxidants, reading the label gives no assurance that one can avoid these materials. Since BHT and BHA may be incorporated in food-packaging materials, and in animal feeds, as well as in ingredients used for foodstuffs, they can enter the end product *indirectly*. Since these antioxidants are also used in a wide range of other consumer goods as well as in foods, it becomes virtually impossible to avoid them.

Mrs. Z[50] is another victim of severe reactions to BHT. After eating reconstituted dehydrated potatoes she developed symptoms of tingling sensations on her face and hands, extreme weakness, fatigue, edema, chest tightness, and difficulty in breathing. She received medical treatment. At a later date, after eating a packaged breakfast cereal, she experienced the symptoms again. Again she received medical treatment. She responded negatively to allergen tests subsequently administered. The only common factor in both foodstuffs was BHT. She was advised to avoid this additive.

Other individual cases have been brought to my attention in which BHT and/or BHA have caused adverse effects. The lack of many other reports of severe allergic reactions to BHT and BHA— or to the thousands of additives permitted—does not signify that other individuals do not suffer adversely. It may merely mean that others have not recognized the source of their problems, or that physicians have been unable to discover them. In view of the absence of allergenic tests for chemical food additives prior to the FDA approval, our ignorance is profound. Because of an ever-increasing complexity of chemical and physical exposures in our modern environment, it becomes increasingly difficult to relate cause and effect. Physicians are beginning to suspect chemical additives, as well as pesticide residues in foodstuffs, as possible sources of an increasing number of allergic reactions. Dr. Edward Mellanby, in speaking of the chemical manipulation of foods, noted that "even when such chemical substances have passed through a battery of tests from the view of toxicology, unexpected harmful results have often ultimately been demonstrated."[51]

HOW INFORMATIVE IS THE LABEL
FOR THE ANTIOXIDANTS?

The advice given by the federal government in the USDA yearbook *Consumers All* is grossly misleading:

> When you read a list of ingredients on a food package and see something like butylated hydroxyanisole added to prevent rancidity, you need not worry about whether it is safe. If its safety were in question, the FDA could and would stop its use. If you prefer nevertheless to buy a product without the preservative, this is your prerogative, too. That is why the label must tell you the additive is there.[52]

Even if BHA and/or BHT are added to a food, the consumer may not necessarily find them listed specifically. The FDA and the USDA allow the general terms "freshness preserver," "antioxidant added," or similar phrases to appear on the label, which give no clue to the exact material used. Is it BHA? BHT? Propyl gallate? Octyl gallate? NDGA? Or some other antioxidant officially sanctioned?

In other quarters, officials have taken measures to restrict the use of these antioxidants. The Joint Food and Agriculture Organization of the World Health Organization (FAO/WHO) Expert Committee on Food Additives has repeatedly recommended a "conditional" intake limit for BHT, with expert supervision and advice.[53] BHT was deleted from the list of permitted food additives in Sweden and banned in Romania for use in foods. In Australia, where much of the BHT research has been conducted by the Commonwealth Antioxidant Research Project, the substance has not been included in the government's list of permitted antioxidants.

In Great Britain, the use of BHT is restricted, with limited use permitted in butter, lard, margarine, and essential oils. Moreover, the British Food Standards Committee has denied several appeals from industry to extend its use to other foodstuffs. In 1958 the Committee re-examined and re-evaluated data and recommended that BHT be withdrawn from the list of permitted antioxidants. The recommendation was followed by the customary "full consideration to any representations made by the interests concerned" just as American industry is given an opportunity to protest a proposed regulation. British industry protested, and the Committee's recommendation was not acted upon.

In 1963, the Food Standards Committee reviewed the subject, and again recommended that BHT should no longer be permitted because "the margin of safety for BHT is less than for the other permitted antioxidants."[54] Two years elapsed. In 1965, the Committee examined new evidence. Experimental rats, fed on diets containing BHT, suffered adverse effects in growth and in their ability to bear their young. In view of these findings, the committee studied a recommendation *to ban BHT entirely from food.* However, because of the inconclusiveness of the evidence, the Committee withheld final judgment until experiments now in progress are completed.[55] Although it was not banned outright in all foods, *BHT was banned from baby foods, and its amount in other foodstuffs reduced by half.* The British Industrial Biological Research Association had gone on record requesting the banning of BHT in baby foods.

Many baby foods sold in Europe are imported from the United States. They are sold in pharmacies rather than in grocery stores. According to *Food Chemical News*,[56] European nutritionists are insisting that the U.S. manufacturers of baby foods eliminate the antioxidants.

Although our own federal officials have shown no similar inter-

est to that of British officials in re-evaluating the safety of these
antioxidants, you, the consumer, can take individual action through
writing letters to food processors. Some protest letters to the
processor of a popular breakfast cereal, and other letters to a
processor of wheat germ, succeeded in having BHT and BHA
dropped from these two products.

NOT SAFE—BUT NOT BANNED

The FDA may be forced to re-evaluate BHT and BHA as well as
other antioxidants, in view of events with nordihydroguaiaretic
acid (NDGA). This antioxidant, on the GRAS list (Generally
Recognized As Safe), was used in meat products, shortening, cake
mixes, and soft drinks, including synthetic orange drinks.

After reviewing available scientific data from the Joint FAO/
WHO Expert Food Additives Committee reports of 1962 and 1965
on NDGA, the Canadian Food and Drug Directorate decided the
information was "inadequate for evaluation" and launched its own
research. Its experiments showed that "NDGA fed to rats at
levels as low as 0.5 per cent produced certain undesirable effects."[57]
Among these were lesions in lymph nodes, enlarged kidneys
with cysts, hemorrhaging, and depressed growth. R. A. Chapman,
Director-General, notified all Canadian food manufacturers on
Sept. 20, 1967, that NDGA "may result in hazards to health" and
he recommended that it be banned for use in foods.[58]

This decision proved awkward for the FDA. Although NDGA
was on its GRAS list, it could no longer be considered generally
recognized as safe because of the Canadian ban. The decision was
equally awkward for the USDA, which had recently *extended* the
clearance of NDGA, along with other antioxidants, for use in dry
sausage.

Two months after the Canadian ban the FDA announced that it
had conducted recent studies that "complemented the Canadian
studies."[59] Later, the FDA was forced to admit that it had *not*
engaged in any studies. It would take action only because of "a
lack of sufficient toxicological data."[60]

In November 1967 the FDA proposed removal of NDGA from
GRAS. Comments were received from three main manufacturers.

The FDA deemed that they provided "no substantive evidence to alter the proposed course of action."[61] In April 1968 NDGA was removed from GRAS and reclassified as a food additive "for which a food additive regulation is necessary to permit its use."[62] *Note that this action does not ban the use of this antioxidant in the United States but merely removes it from the GRAS list.* Compare this with the Canadian action which banned outright the use of NDGA in food.

In personal correspondence with the FDA regarding NDGA, the following was supplied: "Now that the Canadian Food and Drug Directorate proposes to ban its food use, we cannot consider that its safety is generally recognized; *but this would not prevent its future approval, providing scientific data are submitted which prove its safety for general use in foods.*" (Emphasis mine.)[63]

The FDA's action was followed by the USDA's barring the use of NDGA in most meat food products.[34] However, NDGA can still be used for rendered animal fat or in combinations of animal and vegetable fats. The USDA's Consumer and Marketing Service announced that NDGA is considered safe for use in these products, such as lard or shortening. You, the consumer, may well ask: If there is a "lack of sufficient toxicological data," on what scientific basis can NDGA be considered safe in lard and shortening?

HOW THE GOVERNMENT SANCTIONS CANCER-INCITING SUBSTANCES

Prior to the Delaney hearings on chemicals in foods, manufacturers could incorporate harmful materials into foods (as well as drugs and cosmetics) without prior testing. The FDA could not compel any industry to remove the substance until evidence concerning its danger was actually proved. This resulted in lengthy court actions, during which time the consumer was still exposed to the risk.

As a result of the hearings, some features in the proposed legislation were designed to strengthen consumer protection. The burden of proof for safety was shifted to the manufacturer, with provisions for prior testing and approval before a new substance could be sanctioned for use in food (as well as drugs and cosmetics). But a number of loopholes still existed. Many substances already in use were exempt from testing merely because of long-term usage, a practice already demonstrated as one fraught with pitfalls. Intrastate sales were not covered. Chemicals advantageous to food processors, but not necessarily useful to the consumer, could be sanctioned. Such an arrangement, in effect, could exploit pretesting as a device to introduce many new chemicals into foods, and legalize adulteration on an unprecedented scale.

The worst loophole, however, was the lack of control for carcinogens. Tests for cancer-inciting properties in additives were not made mandatory, nor was there any special prohibition against the use in food of any substance found capable of inducing cancer in man or in test animals. George Larrick, the FDA Commissioner at that time, opposed any mandatory carcinogenic tests, and refused to admit any reason to single out cancer causation for special mention.[65]

The need for specific regulation was apparent in the case of Aramite, a pesticide which had been found carcinogenic. The FDA had issued an order preventing continued contamination of food with residue of this substance, but the order was reversed after proceedings initiated by its manufacturer. This case established a precedent for introducing so-called "safe amounts" of cancer-inciting additives into foods, and seriously impaired any protection that might have been afforded by pretesting. Repeatedly, cancer specialists have stated that at present no safe amount of cancer-inciting substances can be established.

To close this loophole, Representative Delaney proposed an amendment—later known as the Delaney clause—which provided that "no additive shall be deemed safe if it is found to induce cancer when ingested by man or animal, or if it is found, after tests which are appropriate for the evaluation of the safety of food additives, to induce cancer in man or animal."[66] Mark well the word "appropriate" in the phrase just quoted, since it was to play a decisive role in what followed, which affected the health and welfare of every American.

The proposed Delaney clause was opposed vigorously by industry and the FDA. The clause would place the onus of costly testings on the food, drug, and cosmetic industries, and might result in the need to withdraw many consumer goods from use. In addition to the economic losses, anxieties would be aroused in the public. Only when Delaney threatened to block the FDA's own bill from coming to a vote did the agency reluctantly agree to include the clause in the proposed amendment to the Food, Drug, and Cosmetic Act.

Over strong industry protests, the Delaney clause was written into the amended law in 1958, as well as into the amended Color Additive Act in 1960. The clause made it mandatory for the FDA to withdraw aminotriazole-tainted cranberries, as well as stilbestrol-contaminated chickens, since both substances showed cancer-inciting properties in test animals. Because of this clause additional chemicals have been undergoing scrutiny.

Industry spokesmen conducted vigorous campaigns to prove that the Delaney clause was "rigid," "unscientific," "working against the broad public interest," "imposes limitations upon agricultural progress through research," and "allows no scientific judgment of the results of research."[67] The "confusers" were at work.

Because of the great emotional impact of the subject of cancer, realistic industry spokesmen recognized the obstacles to outright repeal of the clause. As an alternative, they cast about for some means of circumventing it, and found what they sought in the word "appropriate."

The Food Protection Committee of the Food and Nutrition Board, with Dr. Darby as chairman, issued a report, "Problems in the Evaluation of Carcinogenic Hazards from Use of Food Additives." In discussing the various ways to administer carcinogenic tests with experimental animals, the report was critical of subcutaneous injection (intramuscular) as a technique. "It does not withstand a critical appraisal," according to the report, and several characteristics "throw doubt on its usefulness." When used repeatedly for large doses of material, subcutaneous tests were declared "of limited value and of dubious interpretation."[68]

This downgrading was done by a "scientific" body which included industry-associated individuals. The report served a useful purpose. Industry could challenge subcutaneous tests as not being "appropriate" for determining the cancer-inciting properties of a chemical.

Traditionally, and universally, cancer specialists have accepted it as proof that a chemical is carcinogenic if it produces cancers in test animals by any route (injection, application, inhalation, or ingestion).* As a rule, subcutaneous injection has been found to be *the most sensitive* method. It is also the one by which cancers have been induced with the majority of carcinogens, and in the majority of species of test animals. Obviously, a sensitive testing technique is likely to produce the most damaging evidence.

Dr. Hueper, then chief of the Environmental Cancer Section of the National Cancer Institute, disputed the arguments set forth in the Food and Nutrition Board's report. He stated that the widely accepted subcutaneous tests were downgraded only after environmental chemical carcinogens had become a serious, practical, and economically important issue. Up to that time, no objections had been raised against the scientific and practical validity of this procedure. Its appropriateness was brought into question only when subcutaneous testing became unsuitable for industries' needs. Hueper charged that the policy "has opened, intentionally or unintentionally . . . the door to a legalized inclusion of carcinogenic chemicals in consumer goods, especially foodstuffs, and thereby has become the pernicious instrument in perpetuating the avoidable and needless exposure of the general public to certain environmental chemical cancer hazards."[69]

Hueper's prediction proved correct. The downgrading of subcutaneous tests has resulted in *official justification by the FDA of materials in foods and other consumer goods that are recognized as actual or potential cancer-inciting substances.* The Delaney clause remains "on the books," but its effectiveness has been circumvented. The Delaney clause does not justify a distinction

---

* Justification for this viewpoint will be found, among many others, in the following: E. Boyland, "The Determination of Carcinogenic Activity." *International Union Against Cancer,* Vol. 13, 1957, p. 271; *Evaluation of the Carcinogenic Hazards of Food Additives.* 5th Report of the Joint FAO/WHO Expert Committee on Food Additives. Geneva: WHO Technical Report 220, 1961, pp. 16–17; Dr. H. F. Kraybill, "Carcinogenesis Associated with Foods, Food Additives, Food Degradation Products, and Related Dietary Factors." Symposium on Chemical Carcinogenesis. *Clinical Pharmacology and Therapeutics,* Vol. 4, No. 1, Jan.–Feb. 1963, p. 78; Franklin Bicknell, M.D., *Chemicals in Food and in Farm Produce: Their Harmful Effects.* London: Faber & Faber, 1960, p. 47; and Dr. Harold L. Stewart, *testimony.* 86th Congress, 2nd session, Hearings before the Committee on Interstate and Foreign Commerce, House of Representatives, on Color Additives, 1960, p. 413.

between oral and subcutaneous carcinogenicity. This interpretation, made by the FDA, has been branded "arbitrary and unscientifically unsound."[70] On the basis of the Food Protection Committee's report, the FDA has sanctioned the continued use of food dyes which are known cancer-inciters. Triphenylmethane dyes (light green SF, brilliant blue, fast green, Guinea green, and wool violet), investigated here and abroad, with repeated subcutaneous injections, have produced malignant tumors in rats. This evidence has been judged sufficient to prohibit their use in foodstuffs in several European countries, but the FDA considers it "inadequate" and permits their continued use.

How does this affect the consumer? It is difficult to avoid artificial dyes, not only in food but in innumerable other consumer goods. Dyes are used in gelatine desserts, margarine, fats, oils, butter, cheese, bakery products, sausage casing, spaghetti, puddings, frozen desserts, ice cream, maraschino cherries, soft drinks, candies, confections, canned vegetables, pie fillings, oranges, sweet potatoes, drugs (watery and oily solutions), cosmetics (toothpaste, soap, suntan oils, skin creams, lotions, hair oil, pomades, shampoos, bath salts, lipsticks, rouge, face powders, nail lacquer, mouth washes, and hair-waving fluids and hair rinses.

Many artificial flavors, sanctioned officially for use, are also suspect as carcinogens. Dr. Hueper suggests the advisability of investigating approximately 300 flavoring agents presently used in the preparation and processing of foods, on the basis of evidence that they have induced liver cancers in experimental rats.[71]

The FDA continues to sanction the use of carcinogenic chemicals as drugs (iron-dextran complex, polyvinylpyrrolidone, and others). Food additives known or suspected as cancer-inciting, such as emulsifiers, stabilizers, and thickeners, are also given official blessing. Some of these deserve examination in some detail.

EMULSIFIERS—"NOT SAFE FOR MAN"

In the 1940's, at the urging of the chemical manufacturers, bakers began to substitute certain synthetic chemicals or emulsifiers for natural shortenings. They made the bread softer, kept it from becoming stale, and reduced by as much as half the quantity of natural fat usually used.

Nutritional scientists estimate that by using emulsifiers to replace fats and to increase the volume of the bread, the baker
reduced the nutritive value of the loaf by as much as 20 per
cent.[72] In the absence of dated bakery products, emulsifiers can
give stale bread an appearance of freshness.

But far worse than the nutritional shortchanging and deception
were the dangers. No systematic tests had been made to learn
what happens to the human being who consumes small amounts of
these emulsifiers over a period of time. Yet long before their safety
was investigated, the materials had been in widespread use in
bakery products, ice cream, and other foodstuffs.

By 1950, the *Bulletin of the Association of Food and Drug Officials of the United States* reported: ". . . from the data available,
these compounds [i.e. the artificial emulsifiers] seem to be relatively inert. However, a number of relevant facts, some more or
less fragmentary as yet, have developed." There followed a list of
possible ills which "may result" from eating these particular compounds. The ills included absorption of certain poisons, especially
pesticide residue, which "has been established in laboratory experiments." Other ills included gastrointestinal irritation, changes
in the intestinal flora, bladder stones, hives, and a disturbance in
the bile secretions, as "possible risks run by anyone eating these
substances."[73]

This warning was reinforced by another report, from the Connecticut State Agricultural Station, noted for its unwavering interest in food purity and safety: "There is some doubt as to the
innocuousness of these preparations [the artificial emulsifiers]
because, while they are relatively inert physiologically, there is
some evidence from animal experiments that they modify fat
absorption and enhance the absorption of certain poisons."[74]

Investigation of these emulsifiers, especially the polyoxyethylenes, directly spurred initiation of the Delaney hearings. Sensational evidence was given in testimony by Dr. Edward Eagle, of
Swift & Co. The polyoxyethylene compounds, fed in foods to
experimental rats, hamsters, and rabbits, produced extensive diarrhea, inflammation, ulceration, and bleeding from the genitouri-
nary tract. Post-mortem examination showed kidney stones and
damage to that organ, and bladder stones. All hamsters fed on the
diet were dead within two weeks. Other animals showed retarded

growth, reduced adult size, and poor appearance. Even at low dosages, pathology was extensive. Dr. Eagle admitted that from his testing, the "material is certainly not safe for man."[75] Later findings showed that these emulsifiers can cause, in addition to the symptoms described, cirrhosis of the liver or cancer; and they can alter the absorption of nutrients from the intestines.[76]

The adverse reports on certain emulsifiers within this group of polyoxyethylene compounds (polyoxyethylene [8] stearate) barred these emulsifiers from inclusion in federal bread standards. The two chemical companies manufacturing the materials promptly appealed the ban, and obtained a stay until the case could be decided by the U.S. Court of Appeals. Although the court ruled in favor of the FDA's ban, the chemical companies did not give up the battle. They appealed the case to the Supreme Court, and obtained another postponement of the date on which the ban against the emulsifier would become effective.[77]

Even the exclusion of these emulsifiers from the federal bread standards failed to keep them out of foodstuffs. Breads and other baked goods distributed locally within any state were not affected except in those states that adopted the federal standards. The emulsifiers were used widely in many other foodstuffs, including biscuits, cakes, cake mixes, ice cream, frozen desserts, and pickles, which did not come under the ban.

The manufacturers of these emulsifiers persisted in their efforts to have them approved. Data were submitted to the Food Protection Committee. The Committee's report was extraordinary. The use of polyoxyethylene (8) stearate was sanctioned because it was not found to be a *direct* cause of cancer. True, the material was found to be instrumental in producing bladder stones, but since the relationship is not direct, the Committee would not admit that the material itself caused the bladder cancer![78]

Dr. Hueper reacted: "To say that I am shocked by the committee's action in approving the use of polyoxyethylene (8) stearate for food would be expressing it mildly. Their action is based on the weird reasoning that this emulsifier is not a cancer producer, but it was 'merely' responsible for the production of bladder stones. Bladder stones, as is well known, are frequently instrumental in the development of cancer."[79]

Dr. Hueper had found that these emulsifiers produced cancer in test rats, and these findings had been confirmed elsewhere. With no semantic hedgings, these materials had been branded as cancer-inciters at the Rome Conference of the International Union Against Cancer in 1956, as well as by the Food Additive Committee of the World Health Organization. Experiments reported in 1960 revealed that these materials had marked effects on animal tissues, gonads, and livers and kidneys of rats and mice, and were also found to produce tumors.[80]

The FDA's reversal, granting permission for the use of the polyoxyethylene compounds, was inconsistent with its earlier policy. The agency had banned the use of an additive (diethyl glycol) to keep tobacco moist, because—like polyoxylethylene (8) stearate—it caused bladder stones and bladder tumors in experimental rats. It is worth noting that the same substance rejected for tobacco is a constituent or impurity contained in the emulsifier now permitted in foodstuffs.

STABILIZERS: "UNDIGESTIBLE MATERIALS"

An official USPHS report described alginates and sodium carboxymethylcellulose as "undigestible materials" which "are often substituted for normal food ingredients in an effort to improve texture and keeping quality or to lower calorie value and cost." The report warns: "If carried to excess, such modification may have serious nutritional consequences to certain segments of the population." And it notes that these additives have "physiological potentials which are . . . incompletely explored at the present time."[81]

Sodium carboxymethylcellulose, prepared from cotton linters, has been used for drilling mud, in resin emulsion paints, adhesives, printing inks and textile sizes and to protect colloids. The *Merck Index* describes it, in the human alimentary tract, as a material which in "large and frequent doses may cause complete intestinal obstruction, especially in the elderly and in the presence of a partial obstruction."[82]

In experimental animals, sodium carboxymethylcellulose induced arterial lesions similar to those produced by high cholesterol in the blood. One intravenous injection resulted in the loss of appetite and weight, progressive loss of body fat, and enlargement of the liver and spleen. Visible to the naked eye, there were thickenings in the arteries, with numerous and extensive splits and tears along the artery walls. Less apparent, but present, were tears penetrating into the deeper layers of the arteries, blood vessels, and heart muscles. Early signs of thrombosis were detected. The mechanism seemed to interfere with nutrition of the blood-vessel walls and caused secondary destructive changes, especially in the muscles and blood.[83]

Although originally the FDA rejected a proposal for the inclusion of sodium carboxymethylcellulose in foods, later the policy was reversed. This "undigestible material" is now sanctioned for use as a thickening or jelling agent in many foods, including ice cream, popsicles, cake, and whipped topping mixes, synthetic fruit drinks, and even in baby foods. Experimentally, there was some indication that sodium carboxymethylcellulose, used as a vehicle for testing the carcinogenic activity of other materials, contributed to the formation of cystadenoma (glandular tumors marked by cysts).[84]

If repeated subcutaneous injections were accepted evidence of carcinogenesis, this material would not be permissible under the Delaney clause. Two years of tests, with experimental rats given sodium carboxymethylcellulose by this route, previously accepted as "appropriate," resulted in malignant tumors. Cancer specialists denounced the FDA's sanctioning of this cancer-inciter in foodstuffs. Sodium carboxymethylcellulose may be technically advantageous for food processors, but it serves no consumer need.

Dr. Hueper stated: "Since the long range effects and particularly any actual or potential carcinogenic effect of many of the presently used food additives either have not been determined or have become apparent so far in experimental animals only, any introduction of such chemicals [as sodium carboxymethylcellulose] into the human food supply represents in my opinion *an unjustified, if not socially irresponsible gambling with the health* and the life of the consumer." (Emphasis mine.)[85]

PART II

◆ ◆ ◆ ◆

THE BASIC FOODS

5

Meat: The Beefed-Up Animal Machine

"As FAR as quality is concerned, is it not a fact that there are millions of pounds of meat sold in this country every week which can acquire a taste on your palate only if they are doused with strong sauces? Are we not, in effect, sacrificing a great deal of quality for quantity in our meat supply?" asked Representative Leo W. O'Brien of New York at a Congressional hearing. He continued: "What I complain about is the lack of taste more than anything else, and it has been my experience, and I assume of many members of this committee, that the meat you get, including steak, is not as tasty as it used to be. In fact, sometimes I have the feeling that I can get more taste out of a pretzel than I can out of a steak. Perhaps I am not a good buyer. I go into one of these large stores and the meat is very prettily packaged, but by the time it gets on the table, I have just wasted my time. There is no taste at all. I think sometimes our wives are unfairly blamed because they do not cook as well as our mothers. I have an idea that our mothers had a little better meat to work with in the beginning."[1]

Animal husbandry once evoked a pastoral scene of livestock grazing on green pastures, a careful farmer guarding and increasing the fertility of his fields, knowing that both the health of his animals and the quality of his family's food depended on wise management. Livestock were permitted to exercise; their bodies grew strong, lean, and healthy. In the edible meat, fat was yellowish, soft, and largely unsaturated.

Beef cattle, as an example, were animals that matured slowly. It took as long as three or four years to produce an animal valued as good beef by the farmer as well as the butcher. The animal was taken directly from the pasture to slaughter. Even with large-scale commercial production, beef cattle went directly from range to packinghouse. Beef eaters recognized good flavor as a sign of quality.

But modern practices in livestock rearing, especially in the last two decades, are based on radically different ideas. Quality and nutritive value are largely ignored in an intensive search for economy, speed, and bigness. The fertility of the pasture may be undermined by repeated applications of synthetic fertilizers, drugs, and pesticides, all of which affect the livestock the land supports. Various means are used to fatten animals quickly and cheaply, get them to market sooner, and sell them at maximum profit. Many of these practices run counter to the health of the livestock and the safety of the food.

The environment that has been created for the animals is far from natural, and the vitality of the beasts suffers accordingly. Forcing practices can only be maintained with continuous ministrations of antibiotics, vaccines, serums, and a vast array of other medications.

As a result, the basic physiology of the animal has been altered. For example, young beef animals, 12 to 18 months old, may be confined to feedlots and encouraged to overeat fattening feeds. Drugs may also be given that change the metabolism and increase fat artificially. This fat is hard, white, and almost totally saturated. Over the years slaughterhouse workers have noted the differences in the appearance of the fat, flesh, and organs of these animals.

FEED—CHEAP, AUTOMATED, AND SYNTHETIC

Animal feeds are chosen, manipulated, and computed for low-cost feeding. Cheap urea-carbohydrate mixtures are substituted for conventional high-protein foods.[2]

In large operations, the feedlot may be highly automated. One farm, typical of many, is described in the *Los Angeles Times Outlook:*

> One man, standing at a large panel board looking somewhat like the complex controls of an airliner, directs the whole operation of processing and mixing the varied feeds and automatically loading them into trucks. Five other men spend all day driving special trucks down lines of feed troughs. Conveyor belts carry the feed from the truck to the troughs. Eight years ago we gave the average animal here 28 pounds of feed a day to fatten him two and a fourth pounds a day. Today, using a rich diet, we get a three-pound daily gain with only 19½ pounds of feed. Feedlot owners dream of the day when a cheap feed will be found that will fatten the animals in 25 or 30 per cent less time and still produce the same quality beef. *Feedlot cattle already live on the edge of indigestion because of the amount of feed they consume. It is as if you would sit down at the table three times a day for 150 days and eat a Christmas dinner each time.*" (Emphasis mine.)[3]

Steers do part of their feeding at night. By continuous lighting of feedlots, the animals are encouraged to feed throughout a 24-hour day. With combined overfeeding and constant stimulation, the average slaughter age of beef animals is now speeded up to 18 to 24 months.[4]

Many farm by-products are salvaged for use as animal feeds. Since these are spent materials, much of their original nutritional value is lost. The *Farmers' Weekly* (England) reported: "a group of housed pregnant sheep on a special food which has dried poultry manure as its protein base. The ewes were a bit put off by the taste of it, but this has been overcome by adding molasses and chicory."[5]

In an effort to salvage inedible tallow and grease, the USDA is developing methods of adding them to livestock feed.[6] Tasteless food-grade plastic has been made into artificial roughage pellets for cattle on high-concentrate or all-grain rations.[7] Ground-up newspapers, mixed with molasses, have been fed to cattle at Pennsylvania State University. Feathers have also been used.[8] Treated wood has been used as a supplement in animal food at the college of agriculture at Missouri,[9] while the conversion of waste wood and paper into animal feed is being investigated by North Carolina State University under a USPHS grant.[10] Experimentally, poor-quality roughage such as wheat straw or peanut hulls has been made more digestible for cattle by chemical treatment with sodium chlorite. This is being investigated at Beltsville, Md., by the USDA. However, the treatment generates high heat, toxic gases and table salt. The heat and gas pose fire hazards, and the gas is noxious to man and animal.[11]

A Swiss physiologist, Gustav Bunge, and his associates had experimented by feeding one group of animals fresh milk and another group equal amounts of a synthetic mixture of proteins, fats, salts, and sugar, all derived from milk. The animals on fresh milk stayed healthy while those fed the synthetics died off.[12]

More recently, the USDA at Beltsville, Md., conducted a feeding experiment in which a cow, identified as No. 248, was given a "chemically pure ration" of food for more than two years, consisting of urea as the sole source of dietary nitrogen. The remainder of the synthetic diet included cornstarch, corn sugar, wood pulp, corn oil, vitamins, and minerals. An identical twin sister, cow No. 247, was on a diet of natural feeds: ground corn, alfalfa hay, orchard grass hay, linseed and cottonseed meals, vitamins, and minerals. Both animals received equal amounts of energy and nitrogen feeds daily. Cow No. 247 had a normal delivery. When cow No. 248 gave birth to a heifer calf, the animal was considered normal at birth but died when only 16 days old. According to the officials:

> Extensive post mortem examination of the calf born to the cow on synthetic feed failed to pinpoint cause of death. Although the Beltsville scientists examined body organs and fluids, they were unable to determine any abnormality or nutritional deficiency that could have caused death. The calf appeared healthy and vigorous less than half an hour before the herdsman found it lying dead in its pen.[13]

In addition to feedstuff ingredients that are nutritionally inferior to those formerly used, many additives are incorporated. Synthetic vitamin A is put into feeds for weight gains in beef cattle and to help dairy cows wean heavier calves. Present agricultural practices also make this practice imperative. Livestock can manufacture their own vitamins, except for vitamin A. This vitamin, made from carotenoids in the green grass and legumes, is depleted in winter, when cured hay is used. For many years green alfalfa hay or pellets were used to correct this wintertime deficiency in livestock. However, the increased use of nitrogen fertilizers in present-day chemical agriculture destroys the carotene in corn and sorghum silages, and prevents the animals from utilizing this precursor of vitamin A. Even though synthetic vitamin A is now added to livestock feed, the large quantity of nitrates in the ensilage may produce such severe deficiencies that some animals may continue to show signs of vitamin deficiency even during spring and summer pasturing.

STILBESTROL—"BIOLOGICAL DYNAMITE"

Medications in feed are used to increase weight rapidly. The most sensational gains are achieved by adding hormones and hormone-like substances to the feed. One university averages at least $100,000 yearly in royalties from these materials under its control. It is estimated that their development has added some $90 million yearly profits for cattle growers. Stilbestrol is used extensively; one of its largest suppliers has hailed this hormone as probably the most important happening in cattle feeding in the last hundred years. In 1945 stilbestrol was officially sanctioned in the feed of beef cattle. Currently, it is estimated that 80 to 85 per cent of all beef cattle[14] are being fed on feed containing stilbestrol. It is also used in the feed for sheep and lambs. In 1955 the FDA permitted the use of stilbestrol pellets as implants in the ears of beef cattle and, later on, in the ears of sheep. But farmers were advised in *Farm Journal:*

> If you feed stilbestrol to your cattle, better not say anything about it when you send them to market. You might end up getting less money. One packer has this to say: "Stilbestrol cattle just don't cut out a carcass that's as good as they look on the hoof." But it's not only stilbestrol that's responsible—it's the short-cut, cheaper fattening methods promoted by every agricultural college around. The beef we're seeing today doesn't measure up to the old corn fed beef. It looks plump and good on the outside, but when you cut it open the quality isn't there.
>
> Can buyers tell by looking at cattle whether they've been fed stilbestrol? Generally not.

So while it's hard to nail down anything concrete at these markets, one fact stands out: if you feed stilbestrol, better keep mum about it.[15]

Stilbestrol yields poorer meat because it produces weight that is watery fat, but not protein. It creates more marbling of fat throughout the edible portions of the meat.[16] From the consumer's viewpoint this is not only undesirable, but an economic fraud.

However, the problem is far graver than merely one of adulteration and low quality. Stilbestrol has been acknowledged by scientists as a potent carcinogen, and has been labeled "biological dynamite." Warnings against its use in foods were made repeatedly at the Delaney hearings before Congress in the 1950's, by the International Union Against Cancer in 1956 and by scientists.

Quantities of stilbestrol as small as 2 ppb are toxic in diets of experimental mice. Cancers in these test animals have been induced by daily doses as low as 7/100,000,000 of a gram (one fourth of a hundred-millionth of an ounce).[17] It can also cause leukemia and cysts in animal organs. In human beings, it has produced breast cancer, fibroid tumors, and excessive menstrual bleeding in women, sterility and impotence in men, and arrested growth in children.[18] *The Medical Officer,* an English journal for government health officers, reported that hormone traces in the meat of chemically fattened livestock are causing British schoolgirls to mature at least three years earlier than in the past.[19]

More important than an occasional large dose of stilbestrol is the hazard of *repeated small amounts.*[20] Since consumers may be ingesting small amounts repeatedly in food consumed over a period of years, this is a factor of prime importance.

The use of stilbestrol for livestock is permitted by the FDA as long as no "detectable" residue of it is found in the edible portions. However, when fully examined, this position is seen to be untenable. The method used to analyze possible residues is of utmost importance. It is not enough merely to test for stilbestrol. Testing must also be done for related chemicals that may be break-down products of the original materials.

Stilbestrol fed to experimental rats broke down into four or five products, and they were found in areas of the animals' bodies not previously known to contain such residues. Using radioactive tracing technique, the break-down products were found in the muscles, livers, kidneys, lungs, and skeletons.[21] Such materials also may be present in treated livestock.

The usual method of testing for stilbestrol residue is a bio-assay technique in which the amount of hormone present is *inferred* from certain of its biological effects but *not* from direct chemical identification. The residues are not necessarily detected, unless they happen to have the same chemical reactions in the test. Stilbestrol residue may be present in consumable meat in the form of other residues that would not be revealed by the testing method used. These residues are not destroyed by cooking or in digestion.

Despite the hazards of this hormone, in late 1970 the FDA doubled the amount of stilbestrol permitted in the feed of beef cattle.

ANTIBIOTIC WEIGHT GAINS

Antibiotics, added to animal feed, make young calves grow at a faster rate. This shortens the growing period and makes them ready for market sooner. Many antibiotics, used for this purpose, now supplement animal feed. Because many bacteria have become resistant to the older antibiotics, newer and stronger ones are added to an ever-growing list.

Cooking does not eliminate antibiotic residues. They may pass into the body, and cause reactions such as nausea, vomiting and diarrhea in humans. Prolonged ingestion may stimulate hardening of the arteries and lead to heart diseases.[22] Adverse effects of certain antibiotics are more likely to occur when they are ingested in small amounts over a period of time than with a single large dose.

HEALTH HAZARDS

The wisdom of using antibiotics routinely in animal feed has been seriously questioned.[23] These drugs change micro-organisms in the animal's body. Resistance is lowered, and the animal may be unable to withstand disease-causing bacteria. Food-poisoning outbreaks, which are increasing in numbers, are frequently caused by pathogens like salmonella and *escherichia coli*, organisms found in livestock. One type of salmonella is a common and often fatal infection for calves. Proof now exists that this infection has been transmitted from calves to man, resulting in serious outbreaks.[24]

Antibiotics in meat came under sharp criticism at the 10th Annual Food and Drug Law Institute meeting in 1966, held jointly with federal officials and industry representatives. Dr. Herbert S. Goldberg, professor of microbiology, University of Missouri school of medicine, pointed out that there was a sevenfold increase in nonmedical antibiotic sales. More than one half of the $114.6 million worth of antibiotics sold in the United States yearly—some 1,800,000 pounds—is used in animal feed added to food and on crops. Almost 98 per cent of all animal feeds contain some additive. Dr. Goldberg discussed how this created problems for physicians who use these antibiotics against infections. Their use in food "complicates the role of regulatory agencies . . . with the problem of potential health hazards, such as toxicity, hypersensitivity, and emergence of microbial resistance."[25]

Earlier reports from England, Japan, and elsewhere had warned that the indiscriminate use of antibiotics in livestock and poultry feed might result in an epidemic of resistance to a broad array of drugs on which physicians depend to treat human infections. This danger of multiple drug resistance was confirmed by Drs. Sherwin A. Kabins and Sidney Cohen. Various researchers joined these two physicians in recommending drastic curtailment of antibiotics in agriculture.[26]

In 1967 the FDA held two conferences on the problem of antibiotics in animal feeds. The following year, the agency proposed a total ban on certain antibiotics currently given to farm animals. "New information about bacteria that develop resistance to antibiotics given animals and transfer this resistance to humans who consume the animals, meat and milk" was one of many concerns expressed in the policy statement.[27]

On Nov 20, 1969, the British government announced a restriction on two antibiotics in livestock feed as a result of a study committee report. Great Britain became the first country in the world to take such action. The report said: "We do not accept the statement that twenty years of experience goes to show that there are no serious ill-effects from giving antibiotics to animals." The committee added, "In the long term we believe it will be more rewarding to study and improve the methods of animal husbandry than to feed diets containing antibiotics."[28] Immediately following the British curb, in Washington, D.C., a spokesman for the FDA announced that no antibiotics had been banned from animal feeds by the federal government.[29]

Cortisone, another potent drug, had been suggested for beef cattle. Studies at Colorado State University showed that cortisone, injected into an animal, increased the fat marbling and decreased the waste fat.[30] Approval was never granted. In view of the recent reappraisal of drugs in animal rearing, consumers may be spared this hazard.

TRANQUILIZERS—"THESE MISCHIEVOUS DRUGS"

In the late 1950's tranquilizers were tested by large pharmaceutical companies for use in animal feed. In one experiment, the weight of steers on such diets was boosted an average of 12 per cent, and lambs gained a startling 25 per cent.[31] The company enthusiastically predicted profitable sales. Several other large drug companies explored new outlets for their products. Tranquilizers were found to make animals eat more food in a given period of time, and convert it into body tissue faster. These drugs also prevented losses of appetite and weight in cattle during shipment.

When tranquilizers were used along with antibiotics and stilbestrol, the combination "increased the rate of gain and feed efficiency over and above improvements resulting from use of any of these materials alone."[32] Thus, rather than competing against other materials, the newly applied drugs boost sales of all three.

The FDA approved the use of tranquilizers in livestock feed, and by injection before slaughter. The use of these drugs is now common for both purposes.

A newer use of the tranquilizing drugs, publicized recently, is to stimulate a part of the brain—the hypothalamus—which in turn increases milk production. This research, conducted in Israel with the USDA's financial support, demonstrated that these drugs offer the possibility of increasing milk production in dairy herds. Other potentialities include increasing milk flow in animals nursing their young, and using hypothalamus-inhibiting drugs when it is desirable to stop milk production.[33]

At an agricultural symposium held by the USDA in 1960 it was admitted that almost nothing has been published on residues and the metabolic fate of tranquilizers in animals.[34] Dr. Franklin Bicknell had questioned "whether feeding young cattle on tranquilizers to increase their rate of growth leaves enough of these mischievous drugs in their meat to affect man."[35] The question remains unanswered.

When the metabolic rate of the animal's body is slowed down, more fat can be produced and deposited. A thyroid-blocking drug is being tested, which, when fed to a steer in the feedlot, gives the animal a "push" for the market by putting on more weight with less food.[36]

MANIPULATING THE BREEDING

Sometimes unnatural practices have been with us so long that they draw little attention. An example is the castration of livestock. In the public mind the steer, an emasculated bull, produces meat of superior quality. Yet the process alters some basic physiology of the animal, resulting in overweight and a deficiency of hormones. For the consumer, the nutritional implications are as yet unexplored. The risks involved in adding stilbestrol to animal feed may be compounded by the possibility that the same hormone may be used to castrate bull calves by implanting pellets at the time of their birth.[37]

By 1967, nearly 650,000 beef animals were bred by artificial insemination.[38] In order to achieve high breeding efficiency, at reduced costs, artificial insemination has replaced the farm bull. In a pasture, one bull may service some 20 to 35 cows yearly. By dividing the semen of a donor bull, some 20,000 cows may be serviced. Close to eight million dairy cows are now bred artificially in the United States annually, representing nearly half the cows and heifers in the country.

Although artificial insemination may be efficient, the technique has created problems in the new agriculture. A two-year study, made jointly by the Arkansas Agricultural Experiment Station and the Arkansas Artificial Breeders' Association, was concerned with abnormal sterility and economic losses to dairymen caused by artificial breeding. Attempts were made to inseminate artificially more than 30,000 cows, but only 66 per cent conceived. This percentage is far below the normal conception rate. Many cows failed to conceive even after three or more attempts.[39]

Breeding is manipulated in other ways. The cow may be injected with hormones to make her shed several eggs at each heat period. This is done with the hope that she may give birth to twins instead of the usual single calf. Attempts are now being made to transfer the fetus from the uterus of one cow to another, and thus make a beef cow incubate a dairy calf, or vice versa. Or, a prize cow may be inseminated artificially and the fertilized egg removed and planted in a scrub cow that merely acts as a live incubator. The calf can be born as a "quality" animal with none of its mother's poor blood line. Scientists look ahead to selling farmers packets of fertilized ova to manipulate stock. To obtain enough eggs for this, it is suggested that donor cows could be fed hormones to superovulate.[40]

Experiments are in progress to have virgin heifers produce milk, by incubating artificially inseminated eggs of superior cows by virgin or sterile heifers. Attempts are made, with the use of hormones, to obtain fertilized eggs from newborn calves. No inefficiency is tolerated; sterile female cattle have been made to produce milk through the use of heavy stilbestrol implantations.[41]

Sex hormones may revolutionize the future of animal breeding, according to one of the developers of birth-control pills for human beings. Sex hormones might be used to induce multiple births in food animals, and also to make the flow of milk from cows more regular as well as of a longer duration.[42]

Combinations of female hormones (progesterone and estrogen), as well as ovulating hormones, have been administered to experimental breeding flocks of lambs to produce two crops yearly. Lambs, normally born only in the spring, have been produced both spring and fall by means of this hormonal stimulation. A lamb crop every eight months was pronounced close to a commercial reality.[43]

Another approach to hormonal manipulation of breeding involves the insertion of a polyurethane sponge, treated with a hormone compound, into the vagina of the animal. Absorption from the sponge prevents the animal from ovulating. The sponge remains in the cow from 16 to 20 days and then is removed by means of an attached drawstring. Timed-breeding is being developed, among other reasons, to reduce insemination costs.[44]

One farm writer predicted: "The battle for the heat-control market will be fierce, for the market is a big one. One drug company official estimates that the U.S. market for the synchronizing drugs for cattle could, with the expected growth in beef-cow numbers, reach $75 million a year by the early 1970's."[45]

A university scientist summed up the outlook: "It's the biggest profit-making tool ever handed to the commercial cowman."[46]

"EFFICIENCY" MANAGEMENT

Suckling temporarily reduces the amount of salable milk, and the usual procedure is to separate the newly born calf from its mother and place it on substitute dry rations. The farmer is encouraged to do this by the ads for "calf starters" that ask him: "How much money could you make if you sold ALL of your milk? Just 25 pounds of calf food replaces 225 pounds of milk." These calf-starter rations generally consist of milk powder, synthetic vitamins, minerals, and antibiotics In order to have "less bawling and fence walking" at weaning time, and to reduce the natural desire of the calf for activity—which would in turn require more feeding to produce the energy—the calf, too, may receive tranquilizers.

Reducing costs, an important phase of "efficient" management, is not left to chance. Synthetically produced urea, added to the feed of cows, partially substitutes for protein, such as soybean, which is twice as costly. Although it is admitted that the urea produces less energy, the dairyman is assured that "high grain" or "challenge" feeding offsets this deficiency.[47]

Formerly the cow was given fresh legumes and sprouted grains by the good animal husbandman during winter feeding to make up for seasonal deficiences. At present, the cow is given dry fodder, hay, and ensilage, with little or no fresh greens during the winter. Mash may be given for fattening and conditioning. Bone-meal supplements replace the natural calcium acquired in pasture browsing.

All food rations are closely calculated. The cow may be confined by being stanchioned in a small stall, since any movement increases food requirements without increasing the profitable milk yield. Physiological alterations develop from confinement, as noted in *American Agriculturist:* "We recently had a professional foot trimmer in to work on some of our cows' feet. They tend to grow too long now that the cows aren't walking up a long dry lane to pasture. This man shortened up the toes and sloped the foot back to front so as to improve posture. This will help them to stand better on their feet with less injuries."[48]

INSTANT AGED BEEF

Formerly, to produce tender beef, the animal was hung in a refrigerated room from 14 to 21 days. During that time there was shrinkage, discoloration, and a need for trimming. Since all these factors were costly, methods were explored to make the process speedier and cheaper. A technique developed by one of the major meat packers called "tender aged" beef speeded up the hanging to two days, and eliminated shrinkage and trimming. The meat was chilled, then the temperature was raised to room heat with controlled humidity, and then rechilled. This activated natural enzymes present in the meat, which tenderized it and helped to retain its natural juices.

However, from the meat packers' viewpoint, this process was still costly. It required time, warehouse space, and handling. Therefore, another process was developed that tenderized beef on the hoof by the injection of enzymes into the circulatory system of the animal just prior to slaughter, or into the carcass after slaughter.[49] The enzyme-tenderizing action begins when the meat is cooked. Other packers treat cut meats, such as steaks, by dipping them into an enzyme solution immediately before freezing and packing.[50] Under this method, the enzyme does not become active until the meat is defrosted. If a meat cut is treated with an enzyme in a federally inspected plant, the treatment must be stated on the label.

Neither the enzymes (usually bromelin, from pineapple, or papain, from papaya) nor the process is hazardous to the consumer. But they *can* disguise the true nature of meat from stringy, worn-out old bulls and milk cows. Such practices attempt to alter food and to sell mediocre commodities as high-quality products.

PESTICIDES IN MEAT

Pesticides are used directly as well as indirectly on livestock. In addition to the sprays used on pasturage and in barns, animals may be sprayed, dusted, or driven through dips.[51] A systemic insecticide may be incorporated into the minerals, salt, or supplements in feeds. As the animal eats, the insecticide passes through its digestive system and is eliminated in the manure, where the chemical prevents certain flies from breeding. The livestock serves as a vehicle for the insecticide. Charcoal may be incorporated in dairy feeds, to absorb pesticide that might otherwise be excreted in the milk.[52] Grub-killer compounds may be administered internally to kill parasites before they reach the animal's intestines through its hide.

In the early 1950's, the Texas Research Foundation, an organization financed by private industry, analyzed samples of meat products purchased at various stores. DDT contamination—only one of many which might have been present—ran as high as 69 ppm.[53] Only five ppm had been established by the FDA at that time as maximum permissible residue in meat, an amount that experimentally will produce slight but definite liver injuries in rats. The high residues revealed a shocking situation for the consumer. Subsequent studies, of DDT and many other pesticides used in livestock operations, reveal that pesticides continue to contaminate meat and run especially high in the fat. Frequent warnings to livestock farmers are issued in trade magazines, reflecting the fact that pesticide residue is a common problem.

ANIMAL HUSBANDRY'S "NEW LOOK"

A new look is developing in animal husbandry, and like a miasma, is spreading throughout the land. The sight of browsing herds silhouetted against a ridge, or animals grazing in the field, has pleasant associations enjoyed by man since animals first became domesticated. This scene is slowly vanishing, and in its place are modern factorylike structures, which combine housing, manure disposal, and feeding operations for animals in a single functioning system.[54] "Controlled environment housing" consists of window-less structures where temperature and humidity are manipulated. Slatted floors eliminate bedding costs and reduce labor. Animals require less space than in conventional open lots with shelters.[55] Operating under such a system, the farmer expects higher daily gains, increased feed efficiency, less labor, less disease, and no bedding.[56]

Normally, sheep breed only once a year, when the autumn days begin to shorten. In early experimentation with "controlled environmental housing," the amount of indoor light to which sheep were exposed was regulated. By manipulating it, researchers were able to get two or more lamb crops yearly, and to schedule lambing around the calendar.

Claims that controlled environmental housing offers improved health conditions for livestock are not always justified. A veterinarian noted that respiratory troubles have become more damaging under increasingly intensive methods. Calf pneumonia, for example, can be far worse in a large spotless calf house than in a dilapidated, but isolated building.[57]

So far, the effect of modern practices on animals has been described in relation to all livestock, with many examples cited from beef. Now let's examine specific types of livestock.

MILK-FED VEAL—THE SHOCKING FACTS

The consumer has been conditioned to accept the white flesh of "milk-fed" veal as a sign of superiority. In reality, it represents a shocking practice. The "milk-fed" veal is an animal fed on an imbalanced, malnourishing diet of milk or milk substitute, and purposely kept in a state of induced anemia to keep the flesh white. Veal production in England has been described by Ruth Harrison in *Animal Machines*.[58] Perhaps not all of the conditions that she describes prevail in America. But Mrs. Harrison points out that many of the deplorable practices being used in England and other parts of Europe originated in the United States. Mrs. Harrison describes how English milk-fed veal calves are housed. In very small covered pens, surrounded by straw, with a few holes for breathing, calves are immobilized to increase the growth rate, and kept in darkness to favor white flesh. They are confined by short tethers so that the only possible movement is to stand up or lie down. The animals must constantly strain to balance themselves on slats in the pens. Confinement prevents development of muscle pigment in the flesh. Tethering at the head and a bar behind the legs prevent vices like suckling and urine licking. Neither vice is normal. Suckling results when the calf is separated from its mother too early, and urine licking results from dietary deficiency, especially from insufficient iron. Calves normally have a marked sense of cleanliness and avoid their own urine. The bar behind the legs results in further filth, since the calf becomes matted with dung. The animal is unable to use its tail to free itself from tormenting flies.

PITY THE POOR PIG!

Present procedures in hog rearing also deserve closer examination. The notorious practice of feeding garbage to these animals is well known. Although all states now bar feeding raw garbage to hogs, the Wisconsin legislature proposed to eliminate all processed-garbage feeding.[59] Components of this material are suspected of spreading trichinosis, cholera, and brucellosis.

Not only does the practice of garbage feeding offer public-health hazards, but it fails to serve the health requirements of the pigs. Stomach ulcers, now contracted by nearly 53 per cent of all American pigs, have been traced partly to a diet of cooked foods in which heat treatment has destroyed a number of essential vitamins and amino acids.[60] Other contributory causes of the ulcers may stem from overcrowding, competition for food, and the use of commercially prepared "complete feeds" instead of natural foodstuffs.[61]

Anemia in pigs has also been related to cooked food. Two farmers who insisted on feeding their pigs raw garbage were taken to court by a state sanitary board. The farmers testified that they were unable to prevent anemia in their pigs if they were fed cooked garbage.[62]

Present practices of pig feeding include other hazardous features. Copper sulfate, a cumulative poison, may be added to hog feed to stimulate growth. Antibiotics are widely used with these animals, although the drugs hasten senility and shorten their life span. The use of antibiotics in hog rearing is an admission of deficiencies in existing methods rather than proof of any true progress. The antibiotic feed supplements make poor management possible and profitable; they have become substitutes for good management.[63]

PSE—which stands for pale, soft, exudative (watery)—is the label given by animal scientists and meat packers to characterize the present poor pork quality. They admit that one out of every five cuts of pork the housewife buys has lower quality than it should. What causes pale, soft, watery pork? It is most likely to occur in the fastest-growing hogs—the type farmers are being given encouragement to develop.[64]

Boar semen has not been stored successfully for more than a few days. For this reason, artificial insemination has not been successful with hogs. In 1967 only 8,000 sows were inseminated artificially.[65] However, a new drug is being developed, hailed as the "greatest advance in hog production since the development of antibiotics."[66] If approved for use, this drug will be added to the feed of the gilt (a young female sow) to induce or delay her heat period. If heat synchronization is achieved, breeding by means of artificial insemination will become more feasible.

Because of low standards of management, hogs are susceptible to a number of diseases and infections that reflect their general lack of resistance. As a result, piglets may be taken away from the sow at birth and reared on a "scientific" diet with the aid of artificial warmth to eliminate accidental deaths and enable weaklings to survive. This practice also makes it possible for a sow to be mated again at once, and bear three litters yearly instead of the customary two.[67]

An even greater refinement of this artificial environment is the surgical hysterectomy which removes the embryo piglets and the entire uterus of the sow. The piglets are maintained in sterile incubators until they are sent to a farm. In this way they are infection-free as long as they remain isolated from other pigs, and may form the basis of a new disease-free herd.[68]

The unnatural conditions under which hogs are now raised have reached a new extreme in England, as described by Mrs. Harrison. In the name of space economy, the trough as well as the feeding and dunging passage have all been eliminated. No bedding or cleaning is provided, and the animals are placed in a "sweat box." Disease and deaths are rampant from high-density stocks.[69] Although these extremes may not yet be found in America, will the ever-pressing demand lead in this direction? There are already straws in the wind that it will. For example, a recommendation was made in *American Agriculturalist*[70] to suspend a chain from the rafters to get the attention of bored, confined hogs. This device is an attempt to reduce tail biting, a vice usually encountered when animals are crowded. At an animal research conference it was reported that "excessive energy reduces the litter size and also reduces the productive life of the sow."[71]

Poor feed, overfattening, drugs, vaccines, and an artificial environment are all part of the pattern of current hog management. The last insult comes before slaughter. The hog may meet its fate in one of several ways. It may be immobilized by carbon dioxide.[72] Or it may be put into a hot room (about 100° F.) for a half hour and then given a cold-water bath (about 35° F.).[73] Or it may be exercised or given limited feed or a tranquilizing drug. A common medical anesthetic (sodium pentobarbital) may be injected into its blood stream a half hour before slaughter. The anesthetic slows the post-mortem muscle changes and keeps the flesh of the pork red rather than pale and watery.[74]

The current rearing of hogs provoked Jonathan Forman, M.D., to remark: "We know . . . that the typical pig ready for market is a sick animal—the victim of obesity—who would die long before his time, if we did not rush him to market for the city people to eat."[75]

POOR LITTLE LAMBS, WHO HAVE LOST THEIR WAY

In addition to sheep dips and many other chemical exposures on the farm, sheep may soon be defleeced with chemicals. The materials being tested are potent chemicals, also used in anticancer studies to stop cell growth. These drugs interrupt the cell growth in the bulb of each wool fiber as it grows. In current tests, a typical compound was given to sheep by mouth or injection, with high levels being fatal, and low levels causing "no apparent harm," and no "undesirable side effects detected." Further studies are necessary to determine whether chemical defleecing is economically practical and "whether it causes chemical residues in the meat."[76]

There has been a sharp decline in the health and reproductive capacities of sheep in the last two decades, since radical changes in their feeding and management have come into practice. Lamb meat is sometimes featured in butcher shops as "hothouse" lamb. In 1942, one of the early synthetic drugs (phenothiazine) was introduced as a killer of worms and parasites often found in sheep. This material is not readily broken down by digestion or by microbes in the soil. Dr. William Albrecht posed the question: "Shall we not connect our troubles in growing sheep possibly with our own inclination to use drugs to fight worms, microbes and disease, when we ought to be looking to better feed and normal nutrition for good health of our animals via more fertile soils?"[77] This question might be posed not only for sheep but for all our livestock.

THE DETERIORATION OF ANIMAL HEALTH

These radical changes in livestock rearing have resulted in a dramatic deterioration of animal health—of concern to producers and agricultural officials,[78] and a concern which should be apparent to the consumer as well. Animal vitality is low, and the control of infectious diseases has only been possible by continuously resorting to a vast aggregate of drugs. In the period from 1950 through 1959 cattle with cancers of lymph- and blood-forming organs condemned at federally inspected meat-packing plants increased nearly 100 per cent; cancerous hogs, 97 per cent.[79] The U.N.'s Food and Agricultural Organization, after examination of farm livestock in 136 countries, concluded in 1960 that diseases are a more serious problem than ever. Dr. S. Perry Abraham, a government meat inspector in New Zealand, considered 50 per cent of all lambs and 90 per cent of all ewes to be diseased at killing time. Although overt signs of some diseases were masked by the use of inoculations, abscessed livers reflected the general illness of the animals.[80] Another report, from the United States, stated that an average of 10 to 30 per cent of beef livers at slaughterhouses are condemned because of abscesses.[81] USDA records showed that during the 1968–69 period, Americans ate millions of pounds of beef from cattle that had "cancer eye" or similar tumorous disorders. The diseased parts were merely cut out and the remainder of the carcass was permitted to be marketed. Agriculture officials claim that such localized tumors pose no threat to human beings eating meat from other portions of such animals. The 1968–69 report showed that more than 10 per cent of the 30.1 million cattle carcasses approved by federal inspection underwent some post-mortem cutting for removal of diseased parts.[82]

Livestock magazines are filled with articles on illnesses and diseases in livestock, including kidney stones, blood parasites, stiff lamb, anemia, hog cholera, ulcers, virus, diarrhea, and gastroenteritis. Numerous advertisements for vaccines, sera, antibiotics and other drugs interlace these articles. So many drugs are being administered to livestock that, in England, broken hypodermic needles as meat contaminants have become a problem.[83]

Yet this worsening dilemma can be reversed. Even while the average meat producer continues to use drugs, pesticides and other materials to cut costs and increase profits, there are some livestock raisers who produce meat of purity and superior food value. Raising their animals in a natural environment, they encounter few health problems, no chemical residues, lower fat content in the meat, better flavor, and satisfied customers.[84]

IS MEAT INSPECTION A REAL SAFEGUARD?

When the livestock industry was young, the consumer had a close association with meat production. Many families butchered their own animals, cured their hams and bacon, and prepared their own sausages. The producer-consumer was his own inspector and carefully selected animals that appeared sound and healthy.

As meat processing shifted away from the farm to centralized plants for slaughtering, curing and processing, unsanitary conditions were prevalent. These were described luridly in Upton Sinclair's *The Jungle,* and led to the passage of the Federal Meat Inspection Act in 1906—a milestone year in which the Pure Food and Drug Act was also passed. Both pieces of legislation attempted to assure consumers of clean, wholesome foods.

Today all meat and meat products sold interstate must be federally inspected at the packing plant.[85] The carcass is stamped; processed meat products (canned, packaged, and frozen) also receive inspection marks and must comply with labeling regulations.[86]

How adequately is the consumer protected with federally inspected meat? Officials examining live animals can remove the obviously sick or suspect animals. Although many are removed, not all are spotted. Inspection of slaughtered livestock includes a check of internal organs and carcasses. If disease or abnormality is found, the parts are tagged and examined further. Spot samples may be sent to federal laboratories for microscopic examination. If the disease is rampant, the whole animal may be marked "unfit for human consumption." However, if the condition is not deemed widespread, the affected part may be cut out and the remainder of the carcass approved.

The mortality statistics of diseased livestock and poultry in America are shocking. Figures given by the USDA in its *Animal Diseases*[87] (data for 1954) showed extremely high losses:

Cattle	1,500,000
Calves	2,500,000
Sheep and lambs	4,000,000
Swine	10,500,000
Chickens	235,000,000
Turkeys	7,200,000

In addition, 2,400,000 cattle whose cancerous or tubercular livers were discarded had the rest of their carcasses sent on to be processed for food.[88]

There are many transmittable animal diseases that have only vague clinical symptoms, or none at all even in advanced stages, so this procedure may protect packing-house profits, but not the consumer.

In attempting to obtain more recent mortality statistics of dis-

eased livestock and poultry,[89] I noticed what appeared to be a drop
in the figures:

	Mortality reported in 1963	Mortality reported in 1964
Cattle	Nearly 400,000	Over 400,000
Sheep & goats	Nearly 78,000	Over 51,000
Swine	Nearly 300,000	Over 300,000
Poultry	Over 7,000,000	Over 12,000,000

Inquiry at the USDA's Animal Health Division produced the
following comment on the far lower figures in 1963 and 1964: "The
low figure is the result of adding the sum of the several reports
from each state. The effectiveness of reporting in each state varies,
but seldom reaches even a 25 per cent effectiveness. This is
because veterinarians may not be called to the farm, and never
diagnose the loss, or after a diagnosis, the loss may not be reported. Further, the mortality statistics for 1963 and 1964 are
concerned with only a few of the many causes of livestock losses.
In the main, those diseases reported upon are communicable, or
represent diseases which can be diagnosed clinically."[90] (Emphasis mine.)

Although pork may be stamped "U.S. Inspected" and passed, it
has *not* been inspected for trichinosis, which can be serious and
even lethal for man. There is no way to determine, by visual
observation, whether hogs are infested with trichinae.[91] The
USDA's policy has been that microscopic examination for trichinosis was too costly, and that no practical system of inspection
existed by which it could be done. However, in some European
countries, microscopic inspection of pork for trichinae is done
routinely in meat inspection. The USDA has relied on the fact that
the trichinae are killed by thorough cooking of all pork products
before consumption. Such wishful thinking is no substitute for
adequate protection. Cases of trichinosis have been traced to
butcher shops where pork residues in the meat grinder have
contaminated beef or lamb ground subsequently, in machinery
inadequately cleaned.[92] Other cases involved restaurant hamburgers, grilled on the rare side, in which pork was mixed with the
beef. The inadequacy of pork inspection in the United States has
been revealed in our shockingly high incidence of trichinosis. *We*

have had at least three times as much trichinosis in America as in the rest of the world.[93] The figure may be even higher, since clinical symptoms of the disease resemble viral infections. Many acute cases of trichinosis are suspected of being wrongly diagnosed as flu or virus.

In April 1969, the USDA reported a new trichinosis-detection test, and claimed it to be efficient and effective. The method, called the "pooled-sample digestion technique," can be used on hogs slaughtered under high-speed commercial meat-packing conditions.[94]

WHAT THE FEDERAL LABEL MEANS—
AND DOES NOT MEAN

How protective is the labeling on federally inspected meat? The purple circle stamped on the carcass is seldom seen today by the consumer, who purchases meats in markets that sell prepackaged serving-size cuts. This inspection mark is usually trimmed off when the cuts are prepared for retail sale.

Labels for federally inspected canned, packaged, or frozen meat must list all the ingredients, common name of the product, name and address of the processor or distributor, mark of approval and accurate weight. However, meat can be processed legally with sodium nitrate, sodium nitrite, sodium ascorbate, and many other chemicals sanctioned by the FDA. These chemicals retain meat color and appearance of "freshness." Their harmfulness was amply demonstrated by Dr. Harvey W. Wiley more than a half century ago.[95] Because of the depressing effect of saltpeter on gonads, as well as other deleterious effects on the human system, Wiley refused to approve its use in cured meats. In his famous *Bulletin No. 84* on food adulteration, Part VII dealt with saltpeter, particularly in meats. As a result of political machinations and pressures from the food processors at the time (1906), the USDA refused to publish the findings.

Wiley demonstrated that such chemicals are not needed to preserve meat products, but are "used solely to give the reddish color of fresh meat" and, although their use "has never been forbidden by official ruling, and only small amounts are found . . .

the purpose for which [they] are used is clearly misleading . . .
it seems to me obvious that [their] use in a food product is undesirable, no matter how small the quantities may be."[96]

Despite the incriminating findings and Wiley's warnings, these
materials are sanctioned for use in meat products and other foodstuffs. The fact that their presence must be stated on the label is,
in a sense, a tacit admission that the consumer needs to be
warned.

Presently in the United States, up to 500 ppm of sodium nitrate, and up to 200 ppm of sodium nitrite are permitted in certain
meats and meat products (and in certain fish and fish products,
poultry, and wild game). Far lower limits are set in Europe.

Nitrites should be immediately reduced or eliminated as food
preservatives, especially on meat and fish. This recommendation
was made jointly in February 1970 by Dr. Samuel S. Epstein of the
Children's Cancer Research Foundation of Boston and Dr. William
Lijinsky of the college of medicine at the University of Nebraska.
Noting that nitrosamines—which include nitrites—can produce
mutagenic changes, the researchers suspect that by similar pathogenic processes, these agents are carcinogenic and teratogenic
as well.

STATE MEAT INSPECTION—HOW PROTECTIVE?

Despite the inadequacies of federal meat inspection, at the state
level, it has been chaotic. No generalization can be made of all, or
even of most of the states. Inspection in a few states has been
exceptionally good, probably better than federal inspection. But
for the majority, inspection has been poor, frequently below federal standards; some have voluntary inspection only, and 22 states
have had *no meat inspection of any kind.*

Thousands of local meat packers have escaped federal control
by doing business within states. Some of the big national meat-
packing corporations also have circumvented federal inspection by
setting up one-state operations. About 20 per cent of the meat sold
has not been federally inspected.

Attempts to extend federal meat inspection were made in 1961,
1963, and 1965. All bills died.

Year after year, conditions worsened. The USDA dispatched a fact-finding committee on intrastate meat slaughtering and processing operations. The report, prepared by Dr. M. R. Clarkson, was presented to a House appropriations subcommittee in 1963. Included were criticisms of packers and processors for:

> allowing edible portions of carcasses to come in contact with manure, pus and other sources of contamination during the dressing operations; . . . allowing meat food products during preparation to become contaminated with filth from improperly cleaned equipment and facilities; . . . use of chemical additives and preservatives that would not have been permitted under federal meat inspection; . . . failing to use procedures to detect or control parasites transmitted to man that could lead to diseases such as trichinosis and cysticercosis; . . . inadequate controls to prevent possible adulteration of meat food products, during their preparation, with substitutes such as water, gum, cereals or sodium caseinate; . . . use of false or deceptive labels on packaging; . . . failure to supervise destruction of obviously diseased tissues and spoiled, putrid and filthy materials.[97]

These charges were made in the public portions of the report. The nonpublic portion was said to be filled with sickening pictures, affidavits, and other documentation which remained inaccessible in the USDA's files.[98]

The authenticity and accuracy of the documentation contained in the Clarkson report was challenged. Investigations conducted by a reporter of *The National Observer* unearthed an official USDA memorandum sent to its compliance officers. They were told to "look for 'horrible examples'" and "try to find evidence of contaminants on the meat if possible." The reporter charged that a propaganda campaign for the legislation developed from "tainted evidence," and examples were "concocted in whole or in part" by "zealous officials eager to get a new law at all costs." An editorial, in the same newspaper, suggested that a question just as serious as protection from tainted meat is "how to protect the citizen from an overwhelmingly strong, maybe even well-intentioned bureaucracy that is so convinced it knows what is best for everybody that it will use all means to impose its program."[99]

Repeatedly, the USDA had been accused of sniping at state inspection laws.[100] The Clarkson report precipitated action. Aroused individuals and Congressmen who were shocked by its horror stories clamored for more federal meat inspection. There was little dispute among informed people that unsanitary conditions did exist, but *the question that remained unanswered was whether meat inspection could be done better under federal jurisdiction rather than with tightened controls under state and local authorities.*

New federal legislation was proposed, and stormy battles raged. The USDA faced criticisms from the meat industry, state officials, and individual critics. The USDA also faced interdepartmental difficulties with the FDA, since both agencies share responsibilities for meat inspection. The USDA is responsible for inspecting meat from its source through the time it gets to the exit door of the slaughterhouse. The FDA supervises it from there until it reaches the consumer. The FDA is also responsible for the legality and safety of any additives in meat.

THE WHOLESOME MEAT ACT OF 1967—HOW GOOD?

The new legislation, passed in 1967, must have state compliance by 1970. The act makes it mandatory for all states to legislate inspection and quality standards according to federal specification. Some critics have charged that the new law requires a federal inspector to be stationed at every private meat plant in the country—a great expense that adds nothing to the consumers' protection.

How does the new law fail to protect? By extending federal inspection, the USDA tries to convince the consumer that the "U.S. Inspected" tag on meats (and poultry) means they are free of disease-producing organisms. This is not true. Dr. Oscar Sussman, chief, veterinary public-health program for New Jersey, charged:

> No present method of U.S. meat or poultry inspection can assure disease-free, noncontaminated raw meat or poultry products. Reliance by the housewife on the U.S. inspected legend alone has, can and will cause countless cases of food infection such as salmonellosis and trichinosis. In none of the testimony on this meat Act, or in the resultant consumer education efforts, were housewives told that there can be hazards to their families in U.S. inspected meats. Such failure

to inform rests squarely on those public health authorities who were silent then and who maintain silence now.

Dr. Sussman added that under the present system, U.S. inspected meat and poultry can contain pathogenic organisms. Trichinosis is not eliminated in U.S. inspected raw pork, and salmonella organisms are found presently in great numbers in both red meat and poultry that are U.S. inspected. Dr. Sussman suggested: "Elimination of such hazards lies in proper food processing, food handling, and cooking techniques. The housewife must guard her family against these disease-carrying bacteria. Proper cooking, of course, kills them. But the danger is that they may be transferred, in the kitchen, to food that's served uncooked. For that reason, the housewife must always wash her hands, after handling raw meats or poultry—before touching other foods. And she must always scrub a cutting board or drainboard, which raw meat or poultry has touched, before placing on it salads or other uncooked foods. Preferably she should not use the same surface."[101]

Dr. Sussman explained that the major share of bacterial contamination occurs on the surface of the meat. Searing the outside normally eliminates the hazard. However, this is not true with hamburger, which may be contaminated throughout.

PRESENT INSPECTION—"OUTMODED, INEFFECTUAL"

Dr. Sussman charged that the new law perpetuates an outmoded ineffectual method of carcass-by-carcass inspection which needs overhauling. At present, U.S. inspectors must determine—in as little as two seconds—the wholesomeness and freedom from infection of the meat of the animal. This is, of course, impossible. "This type of inspection is unnecessary, and perhaps dangerous, because it breeds complacency against disease that may actually be present," said Dr. Sussman.[102]

The government inspection seal may be worth having, but it falls far short of being a guarantee of safety and wholesomeness. Although the federal legislation has been responsible for inspection in states where heretofore there was none, or where standards were notoriously low, the shortcomings of federal inspection are apparent. In cases where the state and local authorities have maintained high standards of inspection and have enforced them vigorously, controls have been highly effective.

DOES GRADING HELP?

Many consumers confuse grading with inspection, yet these operations differ distinctly. During the early period of large-scale commercial meat packing, haphazard quality manipulation dominated the market place. During World War II meat grading was compulsory. After the end of the war the meat-packing industry pressed for a rule to make grading voluntary, and the USDA acquiesced.[103] Now packers and processors who wish to have their meat and meat products graded pay for official grading services from the Livestock Division of the USDA. The shield-shape grading mark is stamped on the outer fat on the meat carcass.

Grading of meat *should* be beneficial to the consumer by providing a constant, unprejudiced quality measure, and a means of price comparison. Grading can also assist the small independent processor who takes pride in producing a quality product, by enabling him to compete with the large national advertisers. Such competition also stimulates price competition, which in turn benefits the consumer.

There has been a long struggle for grading. Consumers, institutional meat buyers, and independent and chain-store supermarket operators favor grading. Many large meat packers oppose it. They prefer to have the consumer rely on the brand image, backed by large promotional expenditures. Only about half of all beef is graded, and even lesser amounts of lamb and mutton. The packing industry has successfully resisted hog grading.

A PIG IN A TIN-PLATED POKE

Pork products have never been graded, making quality uncertain. This omission is disadvantageous to the consumer. Canned ham, for example, has been fittingly described as buying a "pig in a tin-plated poke,"[104] and "no bargain when fat and gelatine are sold at ham prices."[105]

Bacon, another ungraded pork product, produced a complaint from one consumer who was "tired of paying 50¢ to 80¢ a pound for bacon fat."[106] Representative Charles A. Vanik reported that 75 per cent of the bacon he tested was "unusable fat and water."[107] In the absence of standards and grades, there is no specification of the lean-to-fat ratio. Although meat packers themselves buy from farmers on a grade basis, they prefer to have consumers gamble on trade names.

Despite the lean meat that peeks through the window of the bacon package, the consumer experiences the all-too-common disappointment of discovering that the product, when unwrapped, is largely fat. Tests showed as much as 60 to 80 per cent waste in cooking bacon, and "too often the strips all but disappear in puddles of their own drippings."[108]

Sausage is another pork product that is frequently disappointing. Results of a 1968 survey revealed that "whether the sausage came from a federally inspected packing plant or from the unchaperoned meat grinder of a local butcher, it was often sour or rancid and frequently contained an overabundance of bacteria. Some of it was contaminated with filth. Not one sample, out of the 177 packages tested for quality and flavor, could be judged really outstanding."[109]

THE GREAT HAM ROBBERY

The story of smoked ham represents the quintessence of what has happened in the absence of standards and grading. Formerly, ham was cured by salts, spices, sugars, and other preservatives applied to the surface of the meat, which, together with the natural juices of the product, formed a brine or pickle. Or the ham was soaked in a liquid brine for about two months. After curing, it was smoked for flavoring and drying, as well as for some spoilage protection. The method took time and care.[110]

In the 1930's, a new method for curing ham was introduced. A curing liquid was pumped into the meat through a series of needles inserted into the tissues, and the technique became known as "pumping." Saturation of the meat with the pickling fluid could be done quickly. Then an even faster method was devised. One needle, inserted into the chief artery of the ham, pressure-pumped the pickling water through the arterial cavities of the tissue. This new technique provided an opportunity for cheating. By 1937 overpumping of hams became a real problem. For many years the packers argued with the USDA about how to control the "dishonest ham." In July 1950, the USDA issued a regulation requiring that pumped hams be reduced to their original or "green weight," as it was known in the trade.[111]

After the 1950 regulation, another innovation was developed. Phosphates were added to the ham pickle. These chemicals served to help absorb the fluid shot into the tissues. But they also helped to increase the amount of water that could be absorbed into the meat. In addition, a pumped ham with a pickle containing phosphates was able to hold the additional moisture *without appearing wet*. Hence, with phosphates, an adulterated overpumped ham could not be detected easily, especially by the average consumer. The phosphate additives provided an even greater opportunity for cheating. Nonetheless, in 1952 the USDA officially sanctioned the use of phosphates in pumping hams.

In plants operating under federal inspection, or in those few states where enforcement procedures were high, cheating was prohibited by the 1950 order that required pumped hams to be brought back to their green weight. But these regulations did not cover intrastate inspection; as already noted, many states have notoriously low standards, or none at all. To evade the 1950 order, some large packers began to use local branch plants for ham curing. Others sold their green hams to smaller plants for processing. Intrastate overpumped hams, containing as much as 30 per cent water, began to flood the market. The practice became so prevalent that poor-quality ham began to drive the good products from the market. Many farmers opposed overpumping for fear that the public image of pork products would force consumers to other protein foods. An editorial in *National Hog Farmer* deplored the situation in which: "every dollar that the housewife spends for water at the ham counter is a dollar she won't buy pork with."[112]

The packing industry attempted to circumvent the 1950 ruling. One large company requested and received permission to over-pump under federal inspection, with the proviso that its products be tagged with the legend "imitation ham."

The practice drew this comment from the editor of *The National Provisioner,* the leading packer journal:

> There is more than smoke in the smoked meat business these days—a hotter and hotter fire seems to be building up among consumers and retailers in regard to the qualities of these products, and especially with respect to ham. . . . If the trend continues, ham—which once enjoyed a prestige position in the pork field—may lose much of its popularity and value as well. One thing is certain: *this particular fire cannot be extinguished by applying more water.* There already may be too much in the business. [Emphasis supplied.][113]

Meat packers wanted no regulatory control. Recognizing that some rules must be forthcoming, they pressured for a legal tolerance for added water.[114] Ultimately the USDA weakened. The 1950 order was rescinded, and the agency officially redefined federally inspected ham as a food that may be diluted with water. The order was issued at the behest of the meat packers, but *without public hearing or public record.* It was merely published in the *Federal Register*[115] and automatically became law.

No one claimed to want water in hams or official sanctioning of overpumping—rather, federal minimum standards of identity, adequate labeling of smoked products, and stricter state laws were needed.

The USDA justified its actions because "consumer demand for juicier smoked meats is increasing."[116] This tactic of hiding behind the name of the consuming public was questioned in *Consumer Reports,* and termed "an old public-relations gimmick."[117] During years of lobbying, both Congress and various state legislatures have witnessed a variety of commercial interests seeking vested legislation, all requested in the name of the consumer. Upon investigation, it was obvious that no "consumer demand" was voiced for overpumping hams. The new ruling was solely an accommodation for the meat packers.

After the announcement of the ruling there was sufficient public outcry to cause the then new Secretary of Agriculture, Orville L. Freeman, to reopen the case by calling for public hearings "to allow further opportunity for consumer groups to be heard."[118]

This was an unprecedented move. Not a single consumer spokesman testified in favor of the new order. The ruling was characterized by a representative of a women's organization as constituting "governmental approval of cheating," and by another witness as "government approval of short weight." Senator Maurine Neuberger noted that in Portland 12,000 pounds of water could be purchased for 35¢, yet 35¢ is the price of water in a five-pound ham at 79¢ a pound. She also said that ham sales probably totaled $875 million (in 1960) and that 10 per cent of that "would be $87,500,000 worth of federally inspected water."[119]

On Oct. 31, 1961, Secretary Freeman rescinded the order, effective Nov. 17. This order was contested by Armour & Co., which took the case to court. The government lost,[120] and packers were able to put water in hams up to 10 per cent without labeling them "imitation." Freeman announced that the label for federally inspected hams would be "ham—water added."

The court decision not only weakened consumer protection, but placed in jeopardy other regulations under the Meat Inspection Act, as well as under the Federal Food, Drug, and Cosmetic Act. The word "imitation" on labels traditionally has denoted substandard products. Even with the label "ham—water added," the USDA has no control over actions taken at the retail counter, where the label can be removed, especially when the meat is sold sliced.

The aftermath of the watered-ham affair has been that the bulk of smoked hams continue to be cured in intrastate plants, outside of federal jurisdiction. Frequently hams processed in these places contain as much as 30 per cent water.

THE POPULAR HAMBURGER—WHAT'S IN IT?

In the healthy, live animal, meat is fairly sterile. The number of bacteria found in the meat in the market place can be considered as the post-mortem history of the carcass: how hygienically it has been handled, how long it has been stored, and at what temperature. When meat is ground, tissues are broken and cell fluids mix with bacteria to provide an even more favorable environment for the growth and multiplication of micro-organisms. Meat with a high bacterial count implies poor sanitation. Yet most communities have no limit on the number of bacteria that may be present in meat. Meat is a perishable food, yet there are no standards of bacteriological quality to function as an effective legal weapon enforcing meat cleanliness.[121]

The inadequacies are prevalent in ground beef. The All-American Hamburger offers many opportunities for economic frauds, such as additives and illegal extenders. It may be adulterated with coal-tar colors, cochineal, and sodium nitrite or benzoate of soda. Dr. Freese at the National Institutes of Health has strongly recommended that sodium nitrite be banned from use in foods. In the human stomach, sodium nitrite is converted to nitrous acid, which is mutagenic in a variety of lower organisms.[122] Sodium sulfite, another additive, can mask the smell of deteriorating meat, and give it a fresh-meat redness. Such meat is injurious, especially if eaten rare. Sodium sulfite is a poison that destroys vitamin B, and is capable of causing considerable damage to the digestive system and other organs. Yet tested samples of ground beef purchased as ready-chopped hamburger, or sold at hot-dog stands, cafeterias, and restaurants, frequently show adulteration with this chemical.[123] Hamburger meat served in restaurants often contains sodium nicotinate to preserve its bright red color. Although this chemical is illegal in some municipalities, 37 states permit its use.[124] Several outbreaks of poisoning have been traced to this additive.[125]

Much-handled trimmings and scraps may be incorporated into hamburger meat, which can raise the total bacteria count. Limitations of fat content vary from state to state, reflecting the chaotic situation regarding meat. Although federal standards limit fat content to 30 per cent, most states lack such a regulation, while others, although limiting it, allow as much as 50 per cent fat. Michigan's standards are higher than federal ones, allowing 30 per cent fat in hamburger, but only 20 per cent in ground beef—a low and eminently desirable limit.[126]

In a 1962 New York City scandal, the Department of Markets accused some butchers of selling hamburger meat containing as much as 90 per cent fat. Illegal addition of beef blood stained the product, and disguised the fat in the meat. Industry representatives, conferring with the commissioner of markets, sought permis-

sion to use beef blood in hamburgers, claiming that they were
"performing a service to poorer people by making the meat more
nutritious and better looking."[127] The request was rejected, and
the practice denounced as fraudulent.

Watering of ground hamburger has been another deceptive
practice. Sometimes water has been mixed directly with the
ground meat, but at times a more subtle method has been used.
The meat is soaked in water—often ice water—on the pretext of
refrigeration.[128] Tongues and corned beef have also been found
to contain excessive water.

Although we tend to think of filth and contamination of foodstuffs as evils of the past which have been corrected by present-
day sanitation, now and then cases crop up. Samples of ground
hamburger meat were found at various times grossly contaminated, with substances such as unfit meat,[129] mold growth, rodent
hair, [130] insects,[131] and "manure-type soil."[132]

Butchers are known to have incorporated horse meat, kangaroo
meat, lungs, pancreas, testicular tissue of a bull, muscles of lips
and snout, and other exotic substances in ground hamburger.[133]
Ideally, the consumer should purchase whole cuts of meat and
grind them at home, to be certain of wholesomeness.

In the absence of a home grinder, or if grinding at home seems
like too much effort, it is still possible for the consumer to have
hamburger ground to order. If possible, this should be done in the
consumer's presence, where the machine is in view. The cleanliness
of the machine can be checked, and the selected cuts will not be
adulterated by *sub rosa* addition of fat chunks. If this is impossible, the consumer should select only preground hamburger that
is bright red in color. If excessive fat is present, the meat will be
pinkish; if not fresh, it will be dull, darker red, or brown. The
package should be dated and it should not be displayed in a
counter where red spotlights can give the product the illusion of
brightness.[134] Such lighting, illegal in some localities, is used in
others.

Meat discolors in one or two days after it has been cut. However, its "fresh" appearance can be extended by wrapping it in a
packaging film in which the antibiotic chlortetracycline has been
incorporated.[135] The possibility of using a combination of antibiotics, radiation, and sorbic acid for better preservation of freshly
cut red meats has been considered.[136] Such practices should make

the discriminating consumer demand meat cut to order, and refuse precut and prepackaged cuts that, in many instances, are "updated." Another objection to prepackaged meats is that the excessive fat or bone is often concealed at the bottom of the container. In some areas containers are used that are transparent on all sides. This practice, while allowing better examination, reduces food value by exposing surfaces to light. Nor do the transparent containers absorb dripping blood as do the porous pulp trays.

10 BILLION HOT DOGS

Frankfurters, first introduced into the United States in 1893 at the Chicago World's Fair, became popular overnight. Americans consume about 10 billion annually. The hot dog has become a highly fabricated, questionable item. Spicing, smoking, and processing may conceal the identity of the raw materials used. Frankfurters vary widely in composition, depending on market conditions and trade practices. As with animal feeds, computers may be used by frankfurter producers to calculate precisely the cheapest mixture as raw-material prices fluctuate.[137]

About one third of all frankfurters consumed are not federally inspected, resulting in many unsavory, unsupervised practices. Without U.S. grading, the protein content, less than in most cooked meats, varies widely. Although the USDA sets a 10 per cent limit for water added to frankfurters processed in federally inspected plants, the water content in uninspected places, in one survey, was as high as 63 per cent. The USDA had set no ceiling for fat. In the same survey, in uninspected places, fat content in some instances was found to be more than 35 per cent.

In 1969, after hearings, the USDA established the fat limit in frankfurters at 30 per cent.[138] But the ruling, which was supposed to be implemented on Oct. 23, 1969, was quietly "subverted," charged Senator Abraham Ribicoff. Early in 1970 the Senator produced a USDA memo, sent to its regional directors, advising that no deadline was set for enforcing the regulation, in order "to give co-operating management time to adjust their formulas."

Another objectionable feature in frankfurters is the misuse of extenders. These materials, including nonfat dry milk, cereal or starch, are not offensive in themselves, but the consumer may be paying costly meat prices for inexpensive ingredients. Extenders *must* be declared on the label. When they exceed the maximum legal limits, they are considered adulterants. The presence of extenders in frankfurters labeled "all meat" or "all beef" is considered misrepresentation.[139]

The USDA permits up to 15 per cent poultry meat in products such as hot dogs without declaring its presence on the label. This has allowed the poultry industry a profitable market for "spent pullets." Such birds, having gone through their laying period and being considered "worn out" to the point where they no longer lay eggs, formerly had been used in soup stock. Now these birds bring a higher price as an ingredient in hot dogs.

Preservatives similar to those in ground beef may also be used in frankfurters. Other additives may also be present, such as antioxidants to retard rancidity, or tenderizers. A coal-tar color (Red No. 1) was commonly used in the casings of frankfurters until banned by the FDA[140] after this material produced liver damage in experimental animals. Casings are still dyed with artificial colors, and proof of their safety is not conclusive. Although regulations prohibit the use of coloring if it penetrates the product, on occasion dyes on frankfurters have been found to penetrate as much as one fourth of an inch into the meat. Frankfurters made of beef, pork, and cereal are likely to be a bland shade of tan rather than the red of the all-beef variety. Court action was taken in New York City against meat companies using cochineal, a dye from insect scales, to color pale frankfurters. The commissioner of markets disclosed that the practice was extensive.[141] Lately, some cochineal has been found as a carrier of salmonella organisms.

Poor sanitation at the packing plant, improper refrigeration, or overlong shelf life at the retail level all may be responsible for high bacterial counts in frankfurters. Although the product may be coded for the storekeeper, it is not dated for the consumer.

MEAT, ANYONE?

Try to find suppliers who raise their animals in a healthy, natural environment. Meat from healthy, well-raised animals is not only wholesome, but of superior flavor. This fact is confirmed by persons who eat such meat.

Other measures are less satisfactory. However, you can limit your selection to fresh meat which is inspected and graded. Ask to see the inspection and grading mark on the carcass. Have the meat cut or ground in your presence. Have all visible fat removed. Avoid processed meats, which include factory-made sausages and luncheon meats.

6

Poultry: The Remade Bird

OLD-FASHIONED poultry husbandry has been converted into the modern poultry industry. Formerly poultry were range birds allowed freedom to scratch and root in the soil. They found earthworms, grubs, larvae, natural sources of antibiotics, and many other materials in the earth; the nature of some of these still eludes us, but they contributed to the bird's health and vigor. Flocks were exposed to sun, air, and the elements, with modest shelter against extremes, but plenty of space for movement.

Today the poultry industry is geared to mass production; quality is sacrificed for uniformity. It may be possible to apply such methods to automobiles, plastics, or thousands of products that can be produced efficiently by automation. But living organisms are vastly more complicated than inanimate objects, and to date, the techniques of assembly-line production have ignored the basic facts of animal nature.

INTENSIVISM

Crowded indoors in unnaturally large flocks, fed processed foods containing drugs and hormones, without access to earth and sun, birds have succumbed to disease.

In a radio interview billed as "Gambling with Public Health," Dr. Gordon Douglas Cambell asked his interviewer:

Have you consumed chicken livers recently? Have you tasted anything worse? They used to be delicious things. The facts are that the grain fed to chickens in our chicken factories, because that is all they are, is heavily exposed to pesticides, more in one farm or factory than another, and the livers show it in their taste. I have developed a very simple test for the acceptability of chicken for eating at my own table. I offer a piece to my cats; cats love chicken, of course, and I was amazed to discover, quite accidentally, that they would refuse to eat chicken, when I knew that the cats were quite hungry. So I now use it as a test. If they won't eat the chicken, I won't either.[1]

What has happened to poultry to make it unpalatable and lower in quality? It begins on the huge breeding farms, which may number birds in the millions, at which only hens are raised; and others, at which only roosters are reared. By tabulating all pedigree information and measurement records on card indexes, and feeding this into machines, choice genetic information is gathered and used. Artificial insemination as well as natural mating may be practiced. Chicks are bred in separate hatcheries for broiler production, or egg laying, and then sold either to the broiler men or egg farmers who raise them for their respective markets. Since the flocks cannot perpetuate themselves under these conditions, it is necessary to have regular replacements.

Today, linear programming with electronic computers selects feed for poultry. Operations are completely automated from bulk storage bins to the feeders in the poultry house. Bulk feed may be blended and ground in a commercially built, automatic electric hammer mill, conveyed to the poultry houses by a low-volume, medium-pressure pneumatic conveyor system, and distributed in feed troughs by auger-type conveyors.[2]

As with livestock, the composition of the feed is determined by the cost of the materials: the least expensive for fattening the birds and getting them to market as quickly as possible. In 1935 it required 16 to 17 weeks, with five pounds of feed, to produce a pound of poultry meat. Twenty-five years later, a broiler could be produced in only nine weeks, with half as much feed to produce a pound of meat. Still dissatisfied, the hatchery-feed and broiler-processing industries set a 1967 goal of under two pounds of feed, with less time for maturation.[3]

THE ARSENIC SPEEDUP

Since 1950 small amounts of arsenic as arsanilic acid have been incorporated into poultry feed to stimulate early maturation, increase efficiency of feed utilization, produce more eggs, "improve" skin coloring and feathering, and yield more profits. Arsenic-fed chickens have more sales appeal by looking yellower than other chickens.[4]

Currently 90 per cent of all commercial chickens are raised with arsenic in their feed. The phrases arsanilic acid or arsonic acid appear on the feed labels. These materials are advertised to farmers with the slogan: "Make your hens work harder."[5]

The arsenic-containing feed must be discontinued long enough before slaughter for the birds to eliminate most—but not all—of it from their meat. Even though arsenic is listed by the USPHS as a carcinogen for man, the FDA allows tolerance residues of 0.5 ppm for it in chicken and turkey tissues, and twice that amount in the by-products of these birds.[6] Former Secretary of Health, Education and Welfare Arthur S. Flemming testified in 1960 that an FDA survey revealed that some poultry raisers were not withholding arsenic-containing feed from their flock for the required time before slaughter.[7] The liver is the detoxifying organ of animal and man. Dr. Manuel Schreiber, FDA toxicologist, stated that dangerous accumulations of arsenic have been found in chicken livers.[8]

THE ANTIBIOTIC SPEEDUP

"Continual medication of poultry feed is like a cowboy riding the range, firing his six-guns to frighten away Indians. When he runs out of ammunition, the Indians appear," wrote a critic in *Farmers Weekly*.[9] Antibiotics destroy bacteria found normally in the guts of the birds. These bacteria do not cause any overt illness, but they impair growth. Such bacteria can be transmitted from one bird to another, or be harbored in the environment. On free range, these organisms do not present any great problem. When poultry is crowded together indoors, with an allowance of half to three quarters of a square foot of space per bird, infection can become rampant.[10]

Routine use of antibiotics with poultry for quick growth has come under severe criticism. These drugs hasten senility and shorten the life span of the birds. Their use enhances the growth of fungus and mold infections in the intestinal tract of chickens. There is grave danger that antibiotic feed supplements are being used to make bad poultry husbandry possible and profitable, rather than good husbandry more efficient.[11]

Antibiotics in feed are most effective in hastening weight gains in birds kept under unsanitary conditions. Criticism has been aimed at pharmaceutical companies that fail to make it clear to farmers that not all poultry needs medicated feeds. The popularity of these feeds has resulted from advertising pressures by some manufacturers who claim them to be essential. To meet competition, feed companies are forced to include them.[12]

Intensivism has produced conditions that increase the need for dependence on antibiotics for disease control. This was admitted at a symposium on chemicals in agriculture: "Under conditions of stress, that is, presence of unfavorable organisms, extremes in ambient [surrounding] temperature, disease and crowding, antibiotics have proven most effective. In commercial broiler production, one or more of these conditions is almost invariably present."[13]

"FRESH" KILLED POULTRY?

Until 1955, the federal government considered any residue of antibiotics in poultry sold interstate to be in violation of the law. Commercial pressures prevailed, however, and, since that time, 7 ppm of antibiotics in the uncooked poultry carcass is permitted. An antibiotic treatment was introduced in which the chicken or turkey was dipped in one of the tetracyclines to prolong the normal shelf life of the bird from seven days up to 21 days. Presumably the antibiotic disappears when the bird is cooked. Although this treatment is not nearly so popular as when first introduced, it is still permitted.[14]

A recent innovation to "preserve" fowl is the application of

sorbic acid to all exposed surfaces.[15] This is being practiced in
some states but has not yet been approved federally. The treatment extends the shelf life of the bird for about 18 days. Although
sorbic acid may be less hazardous than the antibiotic dip, both
treatments should be viewed in their true light. *Consumers' Research Bulletin* commented: "It is well to remember that if a food
is treated so that it can keep longer, it often has been [kept
longer]. . . . Those who regard fresh-killed poultry as a sign of
quality will not regard this longer shelf life as an advantage."[16]

The antibiotic hazards in poultry are compounded *thrice*. These
drugs may be present in the feed, administered to control disease,
and used in a carcass dip.

Drug resistance is a new problem that has arisen from the long-
term use of antibiotics in animal feeds. Certain strains of bacteria
evolve which are resistant to control. Such resistance can be
passed from one strain of bacteria to another. Strains of salmonella, now resistant to antibiotics, may multiply within the fowl.
The prevalence of antibiotics in the feed lowers the resistance of
the birds. When the drug *is* needed for disease control, it is
ineffective. The FDA's former Commissioner Goddard had initiated steps to halt the use of chlortetracycline in poultry (and fish),
as well as oxytetracycline in poultry. Pointing out that their use
can induce the emergence of resistant strains, resulting in food
spoilage from mold and yeast, it was concluded that their use "on
poultry and seafood may be a substitute for a good manufacturing
practice with consequent poor sanitation."[17]

STILL MORE DRUGS!

Another group of anti-infective agents, the bacteriostats, are incorporated routinely in poultry feed to control the growth of
undesirable bacteria. These include drugs which can cause dermatitis in man when applied to the skin, and others which are toxic.
Little is known about the general effects of these materials when
eaten frequently in small amounts.[18]

A tranquilizing additive is permitted in broiler feed to ease
tensions and stresses during hot weather, handling for vaccination,
debeaking, or moving.[19]

Currently, aspirin is added experimentally to poultry feed. This has increased the fat on chickens suffering discomfort from crowding or other conditions that usually lessen weight gains.[20]

To some extent, artificial insemination is being practiced with chickens and turkeys, but semen production is significantly poor in unhealthy or diseased birds. The possiblity of using drugs similar to those now used in human birth control is being investigated to manipulate timing in turkey breeding.[21]

THE CHEMICAL CAPONETTE

Hormones in poultry production have been used even longer than with livestock. The estrogenic female sex hormones, especially stilbestrol, were first used to caponize birds chemically. It was easier and faster than the older castration process. Poultrymen without special training necessary for caponizing could castrate with the hormone. A castrated male bird loses many characteristics. Comb, wattle, and reproductive organs shrivel. The natural instincts of crowing and fighting disappear. It may assume female characteristics, develop greater deposits of fat, grow faster, and become more tender. Such a chemically caponized bird becomes a "caponette."[22]

The use of stilbestrol was extended to include the treatment of all types of table poultry of both sexes, being highly profitable to the poultrymen. It put weight on birds quickly, and could even give old birds the appearance of youth, with plumper, more attractive flesh.

The use of stilbestrol in poultry is not in the consumer's interest. There are greater cooking losses in hormonized birds, in some cases 20 per cent more than in untreated ones.[23] Dr. Robert K. Enders, professor of zoology at Swarthmore College, testifying at the Delaney hearings, said that the use of stilbestrol to induce weight gains in poultry is "an economic fraud. Chicken feed is not saved; it is merely turned into fat instead of protein. Fat is abundant in the American diet, so more is undesirable. Protein is what one wants from poultry."[24]

In 1947 the FDA approved the use of stilbestrol pellets for "tenderizing" the meat of poultry, provided they were implanted one or two months before the birds were marketed. This assumed that in the interim the pellets were completely absorbed. After pellet implantation was practiced for 12 years, during which time the consumers were eating hormonized poultry, evidence was found that the pellets were not always absorbed. Residues of hormonized chickens sold to mink farms caused sterility in the minks.[25] Since the cancer-inciting nature of stilbestrol was established, the FDA was forced to take action. The agency chose a course least upsetting to the economics of poultrymen, by persuading the industry to "voluntarily" discontinue the use of stilbestrol implants.[26]

Despite this agreement, hormonized birds continued to be shipped by individual poultrymen.[27] In New York City, 25,000 pounds were seized by the Department of Markets. The shippers complained that New York City is "the only city in the country where the FDA ban is being rigidly enforced."[28]

The consuming public, learning of the FDA's ban, assumed that government officials had corrected a dangerous situation. This was erroneous, however, for two reasons. First, in a move to avert economic losses, the USDA asked for bids to convert its nearly three million pounds of caponette surplus into canned boned-meat products. This agency took 12 million pounds of caponettes withdrawn from the market, and made them available for state distribution.[29] Second, although the stilbestrol *pellet implants* were banned, *the use of stilbestrol was, and still is permitted in poultry and livestock feed.* In addition, a U.S. patent was granted to allow stilbestrol as an additive to the drinking water of poultry, to increase "meat-producing efficiency."[30]

POULTRY FEED

It is assumed that poultry raisers read label instructions on the medicated feeds they use. The tags bear warnings that medicated feed must be discontinued at a specified point before birds are slaughtered for use as human food. However, these warnings are not always read or heeded. At times, even with inspection, birds contaminated with illegal excessive residues reach the markets.

The effect of potent chemicals may be noticed more readily in small poultry than in larger livestock, and quickly traced to their sources. At times, poultrymen have experienced considerable losses from feeding their flocks on heavily fumigated grains or on meals containing excessive amounts of arsenic compounds. From October 1957 to February 1958, in less than six months, an ingredient in poultry feed caused the death of several million broilers. It was traced to a black tarry residue found in the bottom of vats used to make soap. Transformed into a white substance, this fatty material had been added to poultry feed without adequate testing. It was so toxic to poultry that healthy chickens, injected with fluid from the bodies of the broilers that had died from it, quickly succumbed.[31]

PESTICIDES IN POULTRY

The FDA has set official tolerance levels for pesticide residues in the flesh, fat, and by-products of poultry.[32] *Florida Poultryman* warned farmers not to use lindane and BHC, pesticides used in poultry production, in the hen house. Odors produced by these chemicals "come through" in cooking chicken, and resemble the strong smell of musty grains in stale sweet corn.[33]

In 1965 the USDA tested 2,600 poultry samples in every federally inspected plant throughout the nation, and found *all* birds contaminated with pesticide residues. No one section of the country was better than another. Primary sources of infection were traced to sprayed grain and animal tallows in the feed and to poor husbandry practices. No seizures were made, nor did the USDA divulge specific results, such as the most common contaminant or levels of pesticides found.[34]

STRESS IN POULTRY

Problems with poultry are often directly related to present rearing methods. An article in *Farm Journal* asks: "Having trouble with hysteria in broilers?" The writer suggests that a radio be placed in the poultry house to calm the birds.[35] Conditions in the intensively controlled poultry house may produce stress. Birds are crowded in darkness for the first two weeks, fed medicated food mechanically, and sprayed regularly with insecticide. The birds may be condemned to virtual darkness to prevent fighting. The hen house may be lit dimly with red light, or dull amber lights may go off and on at regular intervals round the clock.[36]

When birds are crowded, feather pecking and cannibalism are prevalent, resulting in lower productivity and lower profits.[37] Producers try to reduce these vices by debeaking the birds.[38] At times, even more extreme measures are used, such as bespectacling the birds with tinted glasses to neutralize the color of the red combs.[39] Vices are far lower among flocks of free-ranging birds or among those well housed, properly fed, and under good supervision.

DISEASE AND DEATH RAMPANT IN THE HEN HOUSE

During the short life span that poultry now have, disease is rampant and mortality rates are high. One of the leading poultry diseases is parasitic: coccidiosis. Even with increased knowledge of the disease, its incidence has soared. The USDA admits:

Farm-raised flocks generally suffer less from coccidiosis than flocks raised under crowded conditions. Because of the space over which farm birds can range, their chances of picking up heavy or fatal doses of *coccidia* are less great—the droppings are scattered over a wide area and the sun and wind dry them quickly so that the oöcytes are destroyed.

Outbreaks . . . have occurred in farm flocks, it is true, but they occur less often and are less severe than outbreaks in large commercial flocks that are crowded together. Instead of being exposed to large numbers of oöcytes in a short time, the farm-raised bird may pick up a few oöcytes each day and eventually develop a resistance. This may explain the relatively few deaths from coccidiosis in farm-raised poultry.

Poultry production has increased tremendously in a few years. Flocks numbering thousands of turkeys are common. The increase in numbers of birds and higher costs of production have brought about a tendency to grow two birds where one grew before. This tendency to crowd birds sometimes has been carried to the point where control measures for parasites and other disorders, particularly respiratory diseases, are inadequate.

Crowding should be avoided, because it favors disease by contributing to a build-up of the number of disease organisms. It also deprives the birds of the exercise they need. A comfortable, sunny, well-ventilated poultry house, free from drafts or dampness, favors good health."[40]

Even with intensivism, there are other controls of this disease that could be palliative, but frequently they are rejected by poultrymen.[41] Isolation of infected birds is recommended, but this is considered "impractical" under present-day management. Continued medication throughout the bird's life is recommended, but this suggestion is considered too expensive. Building up flock immunity is also suggested, but poultrymen are not interested in this approach. Instead, there is greater dependence on drugs for coccidiosis, without any attempt made to minimize the infection at its source. At the same time, it is admitted that no drugs exist that are effective against all nine species of this parasite, and four or five of them are frequently present in most infections.

There are many indications that point to the prevalence of other poultry diseases and to the dilemma the industry faces. At a national poultrymen's meeting a resolution was passed requesting manufacturers of veterinary antibiotics to change their advertising. They were urged to stop emphasizing diseased poultry, and show instead healthy birds benefiting from antibiotics.[42] In *New England Homestead*, poultry raisers were urged to dispose of dead birds promptly. This was presented not only as part of a sanitation program to keep profits high, but also "to present to the consuming public the image of a poultry industry that is vigilant in protecting the quality of its product."[43]

A special incinerator pictured in *Poultry Tribune* is equipped to dispose of 30 dead birds every four hours.[44] Poultry raisers were also advised that dead birds make good pig feed, provided they are cooked.[45]

FLAT AND TASTELESS POULTRY

Flavor in food is closely associated with quality. No wonder poultry reared under present conditions is flat and tasteless. The industry has been aware of this, but instead of changing rearing methods food technologists have attempted to disguise unfavorable qualities.

Additives may be put into poultry feed, masking the unattractive whiteness of broiler flesh and giving it instead a yellowish appearance. An additive advertisement mentions that the coloring helps satisfy consumer demands for "rich golden skin."[46]

All manner of barbecue sauces, seasonings, and even honey are recommended to improve palatability of poultry.[47] The latest technique is to inject poultry, just prior to slaughter, with an enzyme (hyaluronidase), containing a solution of seasoning ingredients such as sage, garlic, nutmeg, or sesame. The solution is injected under the neck and skin of the bird, and spreads quickly and uniformly throughout the flesh. This process acts as a deodorant to disguise unsavory cooking odors, and gives the bird "palatability."[48]

Another recent technique to create "tasty" and "tenderized" chickens is to use chemical injections (epinephrine and sodium iodoacetate) prior to packing and freezing. These chemicals eliminate the need for the more expensive aging process used on commercially packed frozen chickens.[49]

EUROPE TURNS THUMBS DOWN

American poultry is being subjected to severe restrictions in many European countries. It is considered substandard under certain European food health laws. For example, in 1965, the French Ministry of Health banned the use of all antibiotics, hormones, and other drugs in the feed of animals intended for human consumption. The importation of poultry raised on additives of doubtful safety, such as arsenicals, and others, is prohibited.[50] German and Swiss officials[51] have taken similar stands, although in 1968 Switzerland lifted its ban on the importing of uncooked frozen poultry parts. In 1963 West Germany's health minister reported to his government that imported samples of frozen U.S. chickens were contaminated with salmonella organisms capable of carrying typhus.[52]

Since the economic stakes are high, such complaints jeopardize our poultry export trade. The USDA sent a representative to Europe to create a more favorable image for American fowl. The

United Nations World Health Organization plans an international conference on food standards, aiming to achieve a code acceptable to all countries represented. If such a World Codex Alimentarius is formulated, it may force many changes in American poultry husbandry, as well as in other areas of our food production.[53]

"U.S. INSPECTED FOR WHOLESOMENESS"— WHAT DOES IT MEAN?

When the Meat Inspection Act was passed in 1906, and for many years following, there was very little interstate shipment of poultry. For a long period the poultry business remained a side line of grain farming; fowl was sold and dressed locally. In many cases the consumer was his own inspector and could judge sanitation and wholesomeness. No appreciable amount of poultry was brought under federal control. After the industry became a large-scale operation, conditions changed radically, and the need for inspection became urgent.

For many years inspection was voluntary, and a strange loophole existed. Poultry could be graded, and *yet not inspected for wholesomeness.* "Grading" is confused with "inspection." Misinformed consumers believed that they were protected in purchasing graded poultry, when in reality they were not.

In 1959 the USDA made inspection mandatory for all poultry processed in plants that ship interstate.[54] Both viscera and carcass are examined; parts may be condemned. According to the USDA statistics, in one year alone, nearly a million pounds of inspected live poultry and more than 10 million pounds of slaughtered birds were condemned.[55]

However, inspection still had certain weaknesses.[56] If antemortem inspection is not done carefully, sick poultry may get through to the consumer. This is risky, since at least 26 diseases that infect poultry may be transmitted to man. In addition, there are other diseases that the birds do not contract, but with which they may become contaminated during processing. At least two other problems are created by faulty ante-mortem inspection. If the diseased poultry is not discovered, the farmer who supplied the birds cannot be given an early warning that sickness may be invading the remainder of his flock. Also, poultry workers are exposed to sick birds. In 1964, the death of more than 12 million diseased poultry was reported to the USDA by co-operators.[57] Unreported cases would have made the total figure far higher. Undoubtedly, additional diseased birds reached the slaughter-houses.

Another weakness in the law was that poultry could be "New York dressed." This meant that only feathers and blood were removed from the bird. Viscera were left in the carcass and held for a time while shipped. Delayed evisceration may result in mass contamination of carcasses. Public-health and consumer groups had hoped that the 1959 law would specifically ban "New York dressed" poultry, but no direct reference was made to it. Since the regulations for post-mortem inspection of each bird require exami-nation of the viscera, "New York dressed" poultry could not be sold to consumers from federally inspected plants. However, such birds could be shipped between two plants, and this type of poultry has been supplied to processors for soups, chicken pies, and other food products containing poultry.

THE NEW POULTRY ACT—HOW PROTECTIVE?

In 1967, when public attention was focused on the problem of wholesomeness of meat, similar problems with poultry also came under closer scrutiny. Many states made no provision for inspec-tion. The USDA conducted a national survey of poultry packing plants, and uncovered, among other things, the fact that one out of every five birds not federally inspected was unfit to eat. The survey also revealed "gross lesions of disease" in uninspected poultry products, and "failure to remove infectious processes and contamination of the body cavity with stomach contents of fecal materials" as well as a high incidence of bacterial contamination.[58]

As with the USDA's meat survey, the poultry-inspection survey was criticized as a bid by this agency for more control. Consumer reliance on the "U.S. Inspected" tag was demonstrated to be no assurance of safety. In one study, poultry bearing the U.S. inspec-tion emblem was examined. Despite the official inspection, 50.8 per cent was found to be contaminated with salmonella. The examiners then chose an equal number of carcasses of *uninspected* poultry, and made the surprising discovery that its contamination with salmonella was slightly lower, being 48.7 per cent.[59]

Since the passage of the Wholesome Poultry Inspection Act of 1968 an incident raises further doubts about the effectiveness of federal inspection. In 1969, shortly before Thanksgiving, a processor of canned turkey products in Minnesota contacted USDA officials. Frozen turkeys, shipped to the processor from Arkansas, were tested in the company's own laboratory, and some of the birds were found to be contaminated with heptachlor epoxide residue in their fatty tissue in amounts ranging between 2 and 9 ppm.[60] Under federal regulations, residue from this pesticide is barred from food products. Note that although the turkeys, shipped interstate, had been subjected to federal inspection, the contamination was not discovered by federal inspectors. Official investigation showed that some 8 million pounds of turkey was involved, both in live birds and frozen carcasses. The source of contamination was traced to land that had been treated with heptachlor for the control of chiggers and other insect pests.[61]

Despite the USDA's pose of *raising* standards under the new Poultry Inspection Act, in one area of concern, chicken virus, the agency was agreeable to the idea of *lowering* standards. Chicken virus, or leukosis, the largest single cause for condemnation of young chickens, is estimated to cost the nation's poultry industry $200 million yearly. The disease is so prevalent that, according to a recent report from the Surgeon General, "Over 90 per cent of chickens from most flocks in this country and abroad are infected with leukosis viruses, even though a much smaller percentage develop overt neoplasms" (tumors).[62]

Until 1970, the USDA's policy had been to condemn the entire carcass of the chicken if any organs or sections of the bird showed signs of leukosis. The poultry industry considered this to be an economic hardship and it pressured for lowering the standards for condemning birds. The USDA appointed a panel of veterinarians and animal-disease specialists to review the problem. Although the panel recommended continuing the policy of condemning birds whose internal organs show active signs of leukosis, it suggested that chickens bearing cancer virus be allowed on the market if they "do not look too repugnant." The USDA endorsed the proposals. Officials from the agency said that if tumors were detected on the wing of a bird, the wing could be cut off and used in products such as hot dogs, while the rest of the bird could be cut up as chicken—all without posing a threat to human health.[63]

To justify the suggested lowering of standards, the panel cited recent experiments that failed to show poultry cancer viruses as presenting any dangers to man. Dr. J. Spencer Munroe, who had injected a leukosis virus into monkeys in 1963 and found that the monkeys developed tumors, expressed reservations about the panel's recommendations. Rodney E. Leonard, former administrator of the Consumer and Marketing Services of the USDA, admitted that while he had been in office, the poultry industry had buffeted him with complaints and pressures on the issue. Mr. Leonard added, "The industry expects the program to adjust to the economic needs of the industry rather than the health needs of consumers."[64]

U.S. Secretary of Agriculture Clifford N. Hardin awaited an opinion from the Surgeon General before taking action on the proposed change in standards. In what insiders called "a highly unusual move," Hardin rejected the advisory panel report, saying that the decision to continue present inspection standards was reaffirmed after having received a separate report from the Surgeon General. The latter report had advised that the ban on diseased poultry should continue "predominantly on esthetic" grounds and because scientists do not have all the answers.[65]

THE "BLOOMING" TURKEY

Although much of this discussion of poultry is applicable to all marketed fowl, a few special points about turkeys should be made. Mass-scale turkey production developed later than with chickens. It burgeoned during World War II, when meat rationing forced consumers to turn to other sources of protein. However, at the end of the war, with the elimination of meat rationing, the turkey industry went into a slump. The feed mills supplying the turkey raisers were reluctant to allow their newly found profits to slip. Extending liberal credit to turkey raisers, the feed industry promoted the idea of raising larger and larger flocks. As the numbers of turkeys began to rise rapidly, the feed companies became increasingly involved in turkey raising. Many small independent producers were forced out. The critical decisions of management and marketing of turkeys shifted from grower to feed mill. As turkey growing became an adjunct to the supplier, turkey processing began to attract the big packers. Turkey retailing, as did that of other foods, shifted toward the big supermarkets, where success is based on volume operation. Self-service retailing of a packaged bird went along with the big packers' interest in freezing turkeys. This permitted the packers to level out production schedules by processing birds throughout the year, holding them in storage, and releasing them as needed, especially at Thanksgiving and Christmas. However, consumers prefer fresh turkeys over frozen ones. What consumers consider "fresh turkeys" often turn out to be thawed-out frozen birds, since not enough fresh ones reach the market to take care of holiday demands.[66]

Meanwhile, a process was developed to make frozen turkeys indistinguishable from fresh ones. Technologists achieved the pink-white appearance of fresh turkeys, and eliminated the unattractive reddish-brown look characteristic of frozen ones.[67]

Fresh versus frozen turkeys created problems, both of misrepresentation and safety. What is the actual weight of a defrosted turkey? Or the still-frozen turkey? How can the consumer know if the labeled weight is correct? A bird prepared for freezing has first been soaked in a chill bath to "put a bloom" on it, to make it appear plump and waxy. As it soaks, the turkey absorbs moisture, the greater part of which is lost in thawing before roasting. Charges were made that at times the amount of absorbed moisture was excessive. A weights-and-measures department in one state found, upon investigation, weight losses as high as one and a half pounds on a 12-pound bird. In buying a frozen bird, the consumer pays for the water at turkey prices. There is also some evidence that when he buys the thawed bird under the illusion that it is "fresh," he also pays for the water in the bird when it was frozen. In this instance, he pays for the water at an even higher rate, for turkeys claimed to be fresh command a higher price.

Because of these problems, the USDA in the summer of 1960, without hearings, issued a regulation to control the added moisture in frozen birds. However, the requirements are not stringent, and are more an accommodation for industry than a protection for consumers. Independent experiments showed it possible to freeze turkeys efficiently with less water absorption than allowed by the new regulation. Furthermore, the tolerance does *not* include moisture from the giblet bag inside the turkey. As any experienced buyer knows, this item may be an almost solid block of ice.[68]

STUFFED FROZEN TURKEY—HOW MUCH TURKEY?

A long legal tangle over label requirements for stuffed frozen turkeys pointed up the fact that the much touted federal requirements do *not* necessarily serve the consumer's interests better than state regulations. The USDA and the State of New York were at odds for some years over the question of the labeling of frozen stuffed turkeys. The federal agency claimed that it was neither reasonable nor feasible to require processors to label separately the weight of the turkey and stuffing, as well as the combined weight. The State of New York championed the consumer's interests by insisting on separate weights on the label; any bird with a stuffing exceeding 25 per cent of the total product weight could not be sold in New York State.[69]

It was demonstrated that the amount of stuffing in stuffed frozen turkeys of identical weights, prepared by the same company with the same stuffing, can vary over a range of 14 per cent.[70] Therefore the simple, honest separate statements of weight of bird and weight of stuffing would be indispensable for the consumer who reads labels carefully and tries to make wise selections on the basis of information supplied.

The USDA and the State of New York clashed in courtroom battles concerning two of the large poultry-processing companies. They claimed the right to continue their sales in the State of New York, using weight labels approved by the USDA but not by the State of New York. The counsel for the State of New York Commissioner of Agriculture and Markets contended that the consumer was entitled to a more informative label.[71]

The USDA argued that more informative labeling would increase production and inspection costs, which would be passed along to consumers in higher poultry prices. As Consumers' Research pointed out, this unconvincing argument ignores the fact that all weight and volume marking adds to production costs in weighing, checking, and inspection operations. Nonetheless, information on net usable weights is conceded *universally* as a necessary and important right of the consumer.[72]

Consumers' Research noted another irrational policy. At the same time that the USDA argued against more informative labeling on frozen stuffed turkey, the producers of frozen stuffed Cornish game hens were permitted to state the two separate weights on labels, without the USDA expressing concern about extra production costs.

By 1967, both the State of New York and the USDA had modified their views. New York now requires only that the processor state on the label the minimum weight of the turkey, but no longer requires a statement of the weight of the stuffing. The stuffing still may not exceed 25 per cent of the total weight.[73] The USDA proposed modification of its regulations. It would require processors to append to their statement of the total weight of the product "a statement specifying either the maximum weight of stuffing or the minimum weight of turkey in the product."

Consumers' Research concluded that the USDA's proposed revision of labeling *still fails* to offer as much information as the consumer deserves. Whereas formerly the consumer had to make an "educated guess" regarding the weight of the turkey and the weight of the stuffing, now the USDA proposes to substitute formal government guesswork by using averages calculated by means of statistical techniques. This is contrary to a position taken repeatedly by some weights-and-measures officials who contend that the manufacturer or packer has a duty to go further than merely supply the *claimed* weight on the *average* purchase.[74]

Furthermore, the USDA's new proposal establishes a bad precedent. There are many other food combinations being concocted, to which, in the future, this new plan may be extended. Such a policy is clearly against the consumer's interest.

HOW FRESH IS FRESH?

Many thawed birds are sold as "fresh." This involves a potential loss of quality, and safety too, if the uninformed consumer tries to refreeze the bird. There is virtually no way of knowing whether the turkey is truly fresh or merely defrosted. In any case, fresh birds are scarce. *Consumer Reports* suggested that it be made mandatory for the inspection seal and/or grade label to carry the word FROZEN along with other official descriptions now required.[75]

There are poultry producers who raise healthy birds in wholesome environments. *Farm Quarterly* described the operation of one such turkey ranch. The owner, formerly employed as a feed salesman, objected to the growing trend of medicated feeds and the poor flavor of the birds reared on them. He decided to raise his own turkeys, using natural foods and methods. By culling out the occasional sick bird from his flock, he reduced his mortality rate to less than 5 per cent—an average far below current levels. The turkeys take longer to be raised and brought to maturity. Sanitary methods are used for rearing, slaughtering, and cleaning processes. The birds develop a fine flavor, which has resulted in enthusiastic customers year after year. This producer has reaped profits, even at times when other turkey raisers have sustained losses. When more consumers learn to demand healthy, flavorsome birds, more individual poultrymen will be encouraged to supply them.[76]

POULTRY, ANYONE?

Whenever possible, try to find poultry raisers who have range flocks, or at least sunny, well-ventilated poultry houses. Ask them about their feeding practices. (Feed mills will supply unmedicated feeds upon request.) Observe sanitation and slaughtering practices.

If such raisers are inaccessible, buy inspected and graded fowl. Try to find out whether the bird is truly fresh or merely thawed out.

THE AUTOMATED EGG

The quest for profit at the expense of animal health and quality food is reflected more clearly in current egg-production practices than in any other area of modern factory farming. Gone are the days of laying hens, along with chickens, a small barnyard flock spending their days scratching in the yard, flirting with the rooster, and letting other fowl learn their place in the caste system. Summertime offered herbage, abundance of insect life, some grains and seeds, and long days of light, air, sunshine, and movement. The presence of the rooster was not only a symbol of rural life but assured perpetuation of the flock. Egg production, poultry as food, and, possibly, livestock and produce were segments of a varied farm operation. Eggs frequently provided extra cash for the farmer's wife, who referred to it as "egg money." Grateful customers who purchased farm fresh eggs were assured of wholesome food with fine flavor from healthy hens.

Today, laying hens have become victims of automation, and many a farmer who raises them is put into an equally unenviable position. The would-be egg farmer is enticed by these typical statements: "Would you like to produce eggs for four cents less per dozen? Mortality 1 per cent or less per month? Cracks less than 3 per cent? Average production per hen 230 eggs on four and three tenths pounds of feed per dozen? Labor costs less than a cent and a half per dozen?"[77]

To achieve this highly improbable goal, the farmer is encouraged to expand, raising larger and larger flocks. The 10,000-bird flock is considered a bare minimum for a livelihood.[78] A 50,000-to-100,000-bird flock is no longer uncommon,[79] with indications pointing toward 200,000 in the future.[80] Depending on the degree of automation, one man can handle up to 25,000 layers.[81] To make this possible, techniques euphemistically described as "confined rearing," "high density housing," "battery units," or "caged layers" are common.

Laying hens are reared in factorylike structures, with ventilating systems and controlled lighting, that may cost, equipped and with birds, as much as $60,000 per unit. Several groups pressure the farmer to convert to this costly equipment. Huge cartels, which control the egg industry, arrange financing. By signing a contract for the entire egg production, the farmer, formerly independent, has lost his identity. He serves as virtually nothing more than a hired hand, in return for some elusive "security" with a guaranteed income. The large hatchery also encourages the farmer to raise large flocks, and arranges to place starter pullets with him. At a later date the hatchery gets a return on its investment by receiving a percentage from the sale of the eggs. This becomes a leasing operation, based on the performance of the pullets. Both the feed company and the dealer encourage the egg farmer to expand his operation. They may even furnish the feed in exchange for a percentage of profit earned later in egg production. Manufacturers of building supplies, ventilating systems, electrical generators, feed cards, cages, and other costly equipment necessary to stock and maintain these laying houses encourage the farmer to increase the flock.[82]

The new laying houses are huge structures or sometimes a complex of buildings. The structures are usually windowless. High-density housing fills the air with bacteria, dust, ammonia, and excess moisture. This foul air must continuously be carried off through an exhaust ventilating system.[83]

The birds may be crowded on the floor. Eggs are laid in roll-away nests instead of roosts, and gathered via a belt collection system. Or, the birds may be placed in cages, singly or a few to each cage, depending upon the cage size. The actual space allotted each bird is incredibly small, measuring at times as little as .5 to .7 square foot per bird.[84] The cages are stacked in three or four tiers.

Hens thrust their necks through the cages for feed, which is placed, sometimes automatically, in troughs. The birds may have restricted access to water, since it has been found that feed conversion is somewhat improved by withholding water for periods of time. Hence, a valve may automatically turn the supply of water off and on at regular intervals.

For greater economy in feeding, laying hens have been denied food rations for an entire day. This has been tried at Wye College, an agricultural school attached to the University of London. A saving of 3/6d (under 50 cents) on each hen could be made through its laying life by witholding food one day a week.[85]

Hens usually take slightly more than 24 hours to produce an egg. Current research, using electronic recorders that make hourly checks on egg laying of individual hens, is aimed at cutting production time.[86]

The hens drop their eggs on an inclined wire floor, and the eggs roll outside. They may be collected by hand or go from an automatic counter onto a conveyor belt. Another conveyor belt may remove the droppings. Outside the cages are laying records. When production drops for an individual hen, it may be set aside for the stew pot.

MANIPULATING THE LAYING HEN

It has long been known that light speeds up the hen's sexual maturity and egg production. Under natural conditions, the increasing amounts of daylight in springtime, when food and temperature are suitable for rearing the young, triggers egg production through a complex chain reaction of eye, brain, pituitary, ovary, and oviduct, with hormones acting as messengers. Now, all these biological processes may be manipulated artificially.[87] The windowless structures of the modern hen house black out the seasons. In present research experimental flocks are exposed to artificial light up to 18 hours a day. "Stimulighting" increases the hours of light during the pullets' development, forcing them into early production. Light control is also manipulated to delay sexual maturity. These artificial operations with light can overstimulate birds, lead to nervousness, and create vices.

Since a caged laying bird does not live in a healthy state, its life has been shortened from the normal span, formerly measured in years, to one now measured in months. For this reason, commercial layers must be replaced frequently. Thus, hatcheries that specialize in breeder hens, and others raising starter pullets, are assured of profitable business by repeatedly replacing stock.[88]

Semen may be collected and inseminated artificially in breeder hens to produce fertile eggs, which when hatched will form the stock for laying pullets.[89] At the hatcheries these fertilized eggs may be removed from the breeder hens and placed in special incubators. Mechanical devices turn the eggs and maintain constant humidity.

At present, fertile eggs can be stored only seven to ten days before incubation; attempts are being made to prolong this short shelf life.[90] Experimentally, fresh hatching eggs have been packaged and vacuum-sealed in airtight plastic bags, chilled at 40° F., and kept for periods of more than a month before incubation.[91]

Normally, after a certain period of egg laying, hens go through a natural molt before they continue egg laying in their second year. But "force molting"[92] may be induced, allowing the farmer to profit from egg production at times of the year when market prices are high. This is done by turning off the lights, and either withholding water or supplying the birds with a medicated "molting feed." Hens manipulated in this way may later lay eggs of inferior quality, with "checks" (cracks), poor shells, and other defects. Some dealers require force-molted eggs to be identified by the supplier, so that they may be handled separately. Hence, the egg farmer must decide if a force molt is to his financial advantage. In a farm magazine, the question was raised regarding the hen: "Should we retread the old girl and get her ready for another run around the racetrack?"[93]

Breeders have experimented with a featherless laying bird. Protein content is lowered in the hen that is forced to produce many eggs. Since part of the protein intake goes into the production of feathers, it was reasoned that, in a featherless bird, this protein could be diverted to achieve higher protein content in the eggs. Devoid of their natural insulation, such birds had to be kept warm under lamps or dressed in vests.

THE FATE OF THE FLAGGING HEN

When laying hens flag in egg production they are culled from the flock. As *Poultry Tribune* reports, the sale of these birds is becoming difficult:

> There was a time when an egg producer got a good price for his layers when they had completed the laying period. This price was almost equal to the cost of producing a pullet. But those days are long gone and there are indications that disposal of fowl is becoming an increasing problem. More recently Leghorn-type fowl from cage operations has been looked upon with disfavor by processors and buyers because of *brittle and shattered bones*.
>
> One egg producer had to give his hens to a mink ranch in order to get rid of them.
>
> The time may come when producers may have a hard time giving away old fowl. It is quite possible that the producer may even have to pay to have worn-out layers hauled away. [Emphasis mine.][94]

INTENSIVISM BREEDS DISEASE AND MORTALITY

Laying hens are subjected to many of the same practices as broiler birds. High density causes high mortality rates in young chicks.[95] Occasionally, as an infection rages through the laying house, it may wipe out nearly the whole flock. The editor of *Poultry Tribune* commented:

> Our service mail indicates that the biggest problem that producers have with their flocks is disease. Laying flock mortality in the U.S. runs 20 to 25 per cent a year. This is too high. The annual loss from poultry diseases exceeds $240 million. Losses are not only reflected in mortality, but lowered egg production and fertility, and inefficient use of feed.[96]

Infectious diseases are far greater among caged birds than among those which range free. Fowl are particularly susceptible to upper respiratory diseases, especially when they are overcrowded and overheated. Some diseases result from uncontrollable stresses that reduce egg production. Diseases may also appear in eggs from sick hens. A brightly colored full-page advertisement of a large chemical company in a farm magazine stated that the use of its medicated feed would keep a sick bird producing eggs with no time lost during illness.[97]

WHAT'S IN THE EGG?

Eggs are vehicles for residues of a wide range of chemicals present in the diet and environment of laying hens. Antibiotics in feed may more than double the egg laying in low-producing hens. There is also pressure to include antibiotics in the drinking water of layers as well. Feed medicated with antibiotics must be withheld from birds when they are laying. But even when this recommendation has been followed, antibiotics have been detected.[98]

Although the FDA has set "zero" or "negligible residue" tolerance levels for pesticides in eggs, there is no assurance that this food is uncontaminated. Poultry management and poultry feed may both contribute to pesticide residues in eggs.[99]

Experimentally, white Leghorn hens, fed pesticide-contaminated feed, excreted substantial amounts of residue in their eggs:[100]

Hens fed DDT at dosages in feed of:	Laid eggs that contained DDT at:
0 ppm	1.2 ppm
50	23.7
100	44.7
200	56.3

Raisers of laying hens are warned to "air out" fumigated grain before feeding it to birds.[101] Grain with residue may permanently injure the livers of the birds and reduce egg size. Pesticidal contamination is such a widespread problem that the USDA awarded contracts to food scientists and poultry experts at the University of Georgia to find ways of eliminating DDT residues in eggs as well as in the fatty tissue of chickens, where a pesticide is likely to concentrate.[102]

Drugs may be used with laying hens. A tranquilizer, used in conjunction with antibiotics in layer feed, was advertised as boosting egg production since it "calms birds, reduces blood pressure and heart rate, increases respiratory rate."[103] Experimentally, hens fed aspirin laid more eggs.[104] Another drug has been found to be effective in reducing "laying slump"; at the same time it cuts feeding costs.[105]

DYED EGGS (NOT EASTER)

What happens to the eggs of laying hens raised under such conditions? The green grass in spring feeding of farm flocks produces fine flavored eggs with deeply colored yolks high in vitamins A and D.[106] But the eggs of confined birds show little seasonal change in yolk color or vitamin content. Since they tend to be pale and watery, as well as flat-flavored, additives are supplied to the feed to darken the yolk color; synthetic vitamins may also be supplied. An antioxidant may also be used to "improve yolk pigmentation";[107] residues of this may turn up in tested eggs. A new process uses a compound that ties up certain pigment-destroying factors in the layer's digestive tract. It is billed as making the yolks "as colorful as Van Gogh's sunflowers."[108] Some current egg contracts base payments on color of yolks, which further encourages the egg farmer to manipulate his feed to obtain the desired hue.[109] Dr. Franklin Bicknell condemned the practice sharply:

> The pallid yolks of commercial battery eggs can legally be colored with any yellow dye, however dangerous, if, being fed to the hen, it is excreted into the yolk. This deluding the public by providing battery eggs with yolks dyed to the golden yellow of the yolks of "farm" eggs is a dangerous swindle and should be banned.[110]

Enlarged, blotchy egg yolks have been traced to a feed ingredient used to control disease in growing birds, but carelessly fed to laying hens.[111] Severely mottled egg yolks have been increasing. Some may result from estrogenic hormones, and others from chemicals in feeds. High temperatures and prolonged storage are also implicated in the increased incidence and intensity of mottling.[112] Although egg producers claim that mottled eggs are edible and not harmful, consumers object, and rightly so, believing that such yolks indicate poor management, low quality, or spoilage.

Blood spots in egg yolks are also objectionable to the consumer. Although careful breeding is considered a factor in reducing them, it is admitted that there is "an unknown factor in nutrition concerned with blood spots. For example, layers on range will produce fewer eggs with blood spots than the same birds in confinement. It is entirely possible that there is something in green grass or legumes that helps to prevent blood spots."[113]

The shell is another indication of egg quality. The well-nourished hen produces a durable shell which resists cracking. But poorly fed battery hens, low in calcium, may produce shells that crack readily. Under present management, egg producers attempt to correct this condition by adding terephthalic acid and antibiotics to the feed, sodium bicarbonate to the drinking water, or a toxic material, "three-niter mash," to harden eggshells.[114] Another technique is to pump carbon dioxide into the hen house. Birds inhaling this gas lay eggs with thicker shells.[115]

THE OBSOLESCENT ROOSTER

The presence of the rooster in the barnyard makes it likely that the free-range egg is fertile, whereas the egg produced by a confined bird is not. By analysis, there are critical differences between the two.[116] A fertile egg has a well-defined estrogenic value, and the ability to hatch out the embryonic chick.[117] It is likely to be produced by a better-nourished hen with a properly functioning endocrine system. The fertile egg shows a superior albumen quality. It is apt to be fresher, and far more flavorsome. There is clinical evidence that persons allergic to ordinary nonfertile eggs can tolerate and thrive on fertile ones.[118]

For several reasons the rooster is eliminated in modern factory egg production. Since it is not essential for egg-laying purposes, its absence does not hinder production. On the contrary, its presence would only lower production because of the excitement that it provokes. It would be physically impossible to introduce a rooster into the present caged-layer system. It is also more costly to produce fertile eggs, with at least 10 per cent more feed required, for an efficient cock must be well fed. Fertile eggs are more perishable than nonfertile ones.

But wait. Science may change all this. Dr. Edward F. Godfrey, associate professor of poultry science at the University of Maryland, predicts that the days of a rooster's idleness are numbered. A technique is being perfected to change the sex of a fowl. If successful, the rooster may be called upon to lay eggs and earn its keep. At present, every batch of 100 eggs produces about 40 males and 60 females, but only eight of these males are necessary for breeding. By injecting eggs with synthetic female hormones when the embryo is in a sexually undistinguished stage, and repeating injections until the chick is hatched, a rooster with an egg-forming organ can be produced. To date, about 50 per cent of such treated roosters have developed ovaries, but these organs are not yet functional. But, given time, the scientists are optimistic, predicting roosters with egg-laying organs that will function properly.[119]

HOW FRESH IS FRESH?

Eggs are perishable. Farm eggs have always been valued because of their superior fresh flavor and nutritional value. Each passing day lowers the quality; for this reason many consumers have insisted on day-fresh eggs.

Battery eggs can scarcely be considered fresh. Although they are cooled immediately after collection, it may be a long time before they actually reach the consumer. They may be washed with water, detergent, and sanitizer to cleanse them and remove stains.[120] Although this process may give more uniformity and sales appeal, it is of doubtful benefit to the consumer. The shell of an egg, having some 6,000 to 8,000 pores, can absorb foreign substances and odors. For this reason eggs should be washed just prior to being used.

To extend shelf life, commercial eggs are dipped or sprayed with a commercial oil or oil solvent.[121] This treatment makes it impossible, even in the absence of refrigeration, for the consumer to distinguish between the day-old fresh and several-weeks-old oiled eggs.

In large-scale operations, where space permits, eggs may be held in the storage cooler for two weeks before actual delivery to stores. Many eggs are held much longer in cold storage.[122] This is advantageous for producers, who can profit from market-price fluctuations. Experimentally, it has been learned that during a full year of cold storage, under ideal conditions of temperature and humidity, shell eggs lose protein, B complex, and other vitamins.[123]

The consumer has no way of distinguishing fresh from cold-storage eggs. In some states, cold-storage eggs are still permitted to be marketed as "fresh." When an egg is broken, if the yolk tends to look flat or contains blood spots or mottling, or the white runs rather than holds firmly, it is probably not fresh.

Many attempts are made to prolong the shelf life of eggs. Aluminum covers have been devised to place over individual eggs, and whole boxes of eggs, to seal out air and permit them to remain unrefrigerated.[124] A technique was developed to envelop each egg in a transparent plastic shell, vacuum-seal it, and then sterilize it with ultraviolet radiation. Such eggs had a shelf life of at least two years, and withstood rough handling.[125] Both features would be attractive to egg sellers. Similar experimentation involves encasing the eggs in plastic or exposing eggs to steam heat to destroy bacteria. Unpackaged, such eggs become hard-boiled within five seconds.[126]

EGG GRADING—HOW RELIABLE?

At present, less than 30 per cent of all eggs sold in food stores are graded, and repeatedly surveys indicate that graded eggs do not live up to the grade, either for state or federal standards.[127] Although enforcement inspectors may check, relatively few stop-sale orders are issued, compared with the number of violations.

Compulsory egg standards of some states may be stricter than the voluntary ones of the USDA.

Even with grading, one survey showed that half of the eggs were below the minimum standards.[128] There was little difference in the eggs sold in national chain or local stores or in independent supermarkets. Quality varied slightly between large packers and small. Supermarket eggs produced under the so-called "rigid quality program with supervision from the producer to consumer" showed some 30 per cent substandard. Only 55 per cent of eggs labeled "Grade A" in a regional chain actually met that grade. In one large city, the lowest-priced eggs graded higher than the highest among different supermarkets. One chain posted three different prices for "Grade A" large eggs in three different stores in the same city on the same day. A county agent who graded eggs from five different supermarkets found that nearly half were not up to the grade stamped on the carton.

Other surveys seem to indicate that consumers concerned with getting the egg grade paid for are best served by a new USDA egg grade begun in 1959, called "Fresh Fancy Quality."[129] Cartons of these eggs carry the words "Produced and marketed under federal-state quality control program" and are usually "Grade AA." Cartons are dated for easy reading by the concerned consumer, and not mysteriously coded. They may not be sold after the tenth day following inspection, thus insuring freshness.

Federal standards of egg quality judge shape, texture, and condition of the shell, shape and condition of the yolk, and firmness and clarity of the white.

The standards of quality offer very little useful information to the consumer. It would be far better to know things such as the degree of freshness; fertile or nonfertile; free range or confined; if feed additives are used and what they are; biological content for protein, vitamins, and so forth. It would be far better if grading were based on flavor and nutrition rather than on superficial characteristics of external uniformity.

PROBLEM EGGS

Even with some grading of eggs, there appear to be flagrant inspection inadequacies. When battery eggs are collected, they are candled to cull out imperfect eggs. The large egg producers salvage almost all eggs, even cracked or dirty ones, and pool them together for freezing or drying.[130] These are used by bakeries or to produce "convenience foods." Some of these eggs should be considered unsafe and unfit for human consumption.

In confined rearing, when birds are crowded on the floor rather than in cages, there are many "floor eggs" that are broken and dirty.[131] Also, because of the prevalence of diseases among battery birds, many imperfect eggs become contaminated with harmful bacteria from the hens. It is suspected that egg washing and processing equipment may contaminate sound eggs.

In addition, there are practices by unscrupulous individuals.[132] At the hatcheries, after 18 to 21 days at high heat and humidity, some fertile eggs fail to hatch out. By this time these eggs are partially decomposed, and often contain dead chick embryos. Such incubator-rejected eggs have been partly sterilized and deodorized with chemicals. In other cases, these rejected eggs have been added to good eggs, frozen, and sold for use in processed foods. Such practices receive little publicity.

Current practices with "floor eggs," diseased birds, and contaminated eggs have created a major problem of salmonella infection. There is a high incidence of reported cases of food-borne illnesses, and many more are suspected but unreported.[133] It is believed that many attacks are not diagnosed properly, and perhaps misjudged as "virus." One public-health official estimated the yearly total as 2,000,000 cases.[134] Many of these have been traced back to contaminated, cracked eggs.

Since each egg pore is about a hundred times larger than salmonella, this organism can enter the egg easily. There are frequent seizures of decomposed eggs contaminated with salmonella. This organism is found especially in dried and frozen eggs and in processed foods made with them. About 10 per cent of all egg powder exported from the United States to Great Britain in one year was found contaminated with salmonella, including strains not previously found there.[135] In Newfoundland, the eggs in packaged cake mixes were contaminated.[136] Frozen egg whites are used for meringue, cream pies, éclairs, and tapioca pudding (to which egg whites may be added after the pudding is cooked). Cracked eggs are also used extensively in mayonnaise, salad dressings, noodles, and other factory-processed foods.

Salmonella outbreaks from processed eggs could have been controlled to a large extent if the USDA had chosen to act vigorously, by requiring pasteurization of all frozen or dried eggs. Eggs heated sufficiently to kill salmonella unfortunately lose desirable baking properties, especially for angel-food cake. Since substantial amounts of public funds are used for research on this particular item, a disinterested observer might conclude that angel food is a basic foodstuff necessary for the nation's survival.

With salmonella contamination widespread, the USDA urged voluntary pasteurization of dried and frozen eggs. The industry conducted a series of soul-searching meetings, at which its members were advised to "face up to the salmonella problem,"[137] to avert economic chaos.

After much research, late in 1965 the USDA scientists working on this problem announced "a perfect method" for pasteurization of commercial egg whites "without significantly lowering the whipping quality or cake volume."[138] A picture in a monthly USDA publication proudly pictured two angel-food cakes, identical in appearance, one made from egg white pasteurized by the new technique and the other with unpasteurized egg white. This scientific breakthrough permitted the USDA to amend its regulation. Effective Jan. 1, 1966, all egg products under federal inspection had to be pasteurized or at least analyzed for salmonella in the absence of pasteurization equipment. Effective June 1, 1966, egg-white products also had to be pasteurized. This ruling did not cover intrastate eggs and egg products.

THE ARROGANT MANIPULATORS

Our present methods of factory animal farming, reaching their lowest point in the caged layer, reflect our arrogant and futile attempts to subjugate by force the biological world of which we are a part. We must stop ignoring the nature of these creatures and learn to work with their biological patterns. In addition to the low quality of animal food that is being produced, with consequent hazards to human health, there is another question that needs to be answered. Have we the right to manipulate living creatures in this manner, and at what point do we acknowledge cruelty?

EGGS, ANYONE?

Try to find a farm where laying hens are free-range. This may require some effort, but the result will be rewarding. If there are roosters on the farm, so much the better. About 98 per cent of all animal feed contains some kind of additives, but most feed mills will make up formulas to order without chemicals or drugs. The following formulas, high in nutrients, can be suggested to the farmer.

For Growing	Pounds	For Laying	Pounds
corn	240	corn	300
wheat	240	wheat	300
oats	100	oats	100
alfalfa meal	100	alfalfa meal	100
soybeans	120	soybeans	100
gluten meal	100	meat scrap	50
meat or fish meal, or 50		dried-milk powder	20
per cent of each	60	bone meal	20
cod-liver oil	8	limestone	10
limestone	12	salt	10
dried-milk powder	20	sunflower seed	50
salt	5		1,060
	1,005		

In large cities, there are stores which feature fresh, fertile eggs. The consumer will discover that the few extra cents charged for such quality products are worthwhile in terms of flavor, quality, and wholesomeness.

7

Fish: Its Poisoned World

FISH, HARVESTED as nature's crop, has been the least tampered with of all our basic foods. The flavor of trout, caught in the clear mountain stream, cooked and eaten at the campside, epitomized a gustatory treat. A bounty of shellfish, gathered from coastal shores while the pot of water was being prepared, symbolized high-quality protein with excellent flavor.

But in recent years, water pollution now almost universally contaminates fish as well as other aquatic life. Industrial and radioactive wastes as well as sewage are spewed into fresh-water streams. Coastal areas, which nurture shellfish, are contaminated with bacteria and poison-laden excrements. Even the vast oceans are fast becoming reservoirs of effluvia.

Fish are extremely sensitive to pesticides. They sicken or die at very low concentrations, much lower than for most living organisms. Concentrations as low as two parts per trillion of DDT were found to cause problems in the Great Lakes.[1] The consumer can be harmed by eating fish that has been poisoned but not killed outright, since fish have been known to concentrate these poisons 2000-fold over the amounts in the water where they were found.[2]

THE RIVERS OF DEATH

Repeatedly, incidents of masses of fish dying from pesticides have been publicized. Dramatic ones occurred in 1954 in the Miramichi

180

River near New Brunswick, Canada, where DDT killed vast numbers of Atlantic salmon returned to spawn.[3]

Stream contamination shows up repeatedly in all areas of the country. This was demonstrated in U.S. Fish and Wildlife studies.[4] Ground water can carry poisons great distances: fish can be affected far from the actual site of pesticide application.

Incidents in the Miramichi River, in Maine, and elsewhere were preludes to those in the Mississippi River from 1960 to 1964. The death of more than nine million fish in the lower part of this river was traced to a pesticide (endrin) and two compounds associated with it.[5] U.S. Fish and Wildlife reported that the maximum residue of this highly toxic compound that can be tolerated in rivers containing fish is only 1/600 part per billion (ppb). Levels tested in that area had reached as high as one ppb.[6]

The USDA's past position had been that no food containing endrin should be sold; the FDA permitted no tolerance for its residue in foods. However, after the massive fish kills, samples of processed seafoods from the New Orleans area were examined; 89 out of 93 cans of oysters and shrimp examined contained traces of endrin.[7] The FDA failed to make seizures. Instead, the agency announced that humans beings will not be harmed by eating such products.

THE DYING LAKES

The Great Lakes have served as bountiful sources of fish for human consumption, but they have become focal points of pollution in recent years. More than 2600 square miles of water in Lake Erie are so depleted of oxygen that only the most primitive forms of life survive.[8]

Until the spring of 1969 no permissible limit of DDT in fish had been established. In April 1969 the FDA seized more than 34,000 pounds of pesticide-contaminated coho salmon that had been caught in Lake Michigan, processed in the state of Michigan, and shipped interstate to Wisconsin and Minnesota. Residues of DDT and another pesticide, dieldrin—considered even more toxic than DDT—were found in the seized fish. DDT contamination ranged up to 19 ppm,[9] which was several times higher than levels permitted as "safe" in other foods. Contamination of the lake was probably caused by the runoff of DDT and dieldrin applied to crops and trees, as well as home gardens and forests around Lake Michigan. Fears were voiced that the entire year's commercial harvest of over two million pounds of fish might be found to have excessively high levels of pesticide residue. Senator Gaylord Nelson of Wisconsin, a crusader for the banning of DDT and other persistent pesticides, expressed concern about the future of commercial fishing on Lake Michigan.[10]

The seizure of the coho salmon precipitated several official actions. The FDA set an interim limit of 5 ppm for DDT in fish shipped as food in interstate commerce until a "full scientific review" could be completed.[11] After this limit was established, the Michigan State Department of Agriculture tested samples of processed chubs already on grocery shelves within the state, as well as fresh chubs fished in Lake Michigan. In both instances DDT contamination of the fish was higher than 5 ppm.[12] In the wake of the coho salmon seizures, Secretary of Health, Education, and Welfare Finch announced the formation of an expert advisory committee to review the extent of human health hazards created by all types of chemical pesticides. Meanwhile, the FDA advised that much of the DDT could be eliminated by filleting fish, since this disposes of concentrations of fat found under the spine and near the head and tail of the salmon.

Following the coho salmon seizures, the Michigan State Agriculture Commission announced that DDT would be banned from sale within the state, although no provision was made to prohibit anyone from bringing in the pesticide from elsewhere. In rapid succession other states took action, through legislation or directives, ranging from temporary suspension, limited curb, and gradual phase-out program to total ban. Some limited the action to DDT, while others included all persistent pesticides. Abroad, England had already begun to take action as early as 1962, to prohibit the use of chlorinated hydrocarbon pesticides for grain treatment of seeds used during spring sowing. In 1969 Sweden announced a two-year ban on DDT, while Denmark banned it permanently. Hungary prohibited the use of all persistent pesticides. Australia announced plans to phase-out DDT. The U.S. government took steps in this direction, proposing a two-year period.[13] But the federal directive was weakened. Exceptions were granted for "emergency uses" of DDT. Also, the Pesticide Regulations Division of the USDA permits pesticide manufacturers to appeal cancellations, and allows them to continue selling their products while the case is pending. Promptly, leading pesticide manufacturers filed appeals.

This procedure was protested by a group of leading conservation organizations, which also used the court for appeals. The group contended that all permission for use of DDT should be suspended, pending legal action. The group petitioned to end the legal use of DDT as a pesticide, and to have DDT residues in food declared no longer permissible.[14] At the same time, the group requested a review of an earlier petition concerning DDT residues in foods that had been rejected by the Department of Health, Education, and Welfare. The agency had stated that it was impossible to declare DDT residues in foods as being no longer permissible, since the pesticide was so widely distributed in nature. Former Secretary of Health, Education, and Welfare Finch stated that even if DDT were outlawed immediately, it would take ten years or longer to cleanse the environment from the effects already caused by this pesticide.

The conservation group proposed the immediate initiation of a legal ban on DDT residues in food products, accompanied by waivers that would allow for gradually diminishing pesticide residues within the next few years. This proposal would insure the withdrawal of this pesticide from use.

The conservationists' petitions to the Department of Health, Education, and Welfare cited evidence that DDT has been found capable of causing cancers in mice that are fed large doses of this pesticide. The group requested that the Delaney clause be invoked. *To apply this clause, presumably a legal ruling would be necessary, to classify a pesticide residue in food as a "food additive."* Such reclassification is unlikely. The report of the Commission on Pesticides and Their Relation to Environmental Health, made public by Secretary Finch in December 1969, called for modification of the Delaney clause, to give the Health, Education, and Welfare secretary greater discretion to determine when evidence justifies action. "If this clause were invoked for pesticide residues, it would outlaw most food of animal origin, including all meat, all dairy products, eggs, fowl and fish,"[15] the Commission had said.

DEFILED COASTAL WATERS

Today the consumer who eats shellfish of unknown origin is taking unnecessary risks. Oysters,[16] clams,[17] shrimp, and lobsters[18]— regardless of source—may harbor infectious organisms, some of which are undetectable, but deadly to the consumer. The Connecticut State Department of Health warned that raw clams are suspected as agents of infectious hepatitis.[19] The salt marsh area of Chesapeake Bay, sprayed repeatedly for mosquito control, has experienced massive kills of fish and crabs, with DDT residues as high as 46 ppm. Fishing areas were closed in the west in 1969, owing to DDT contamination of jack mackerel, while in the east, the FDA closed the Sandy Hook area to fishing, because of sludge contamination.

Fishing areas have been closed because of oil spills, and the marketing of oil-contaminated fish and shellfish has been judged to be a public health hazard. After an oil spill off the coast of West Falmouth, Mass., in 1969, the area was studied by scientists from the Woods Hole Oceanographic Institution. Certain carcinogenic hydrocarbons in the oil were found to be ingested and retained by marine organisms, and then passed along the food chain.

By 1970, widespread and alarmingly high levels of mercury contamination of fish in the Great Lakes and other water bodies in the United States, Canada, and elsewhere led to numerous fishing bans.

In recent years, state and federal agencies that control oyster beds and their care have been pouring materials into the sandbanks to protect oysters from their enemies, such as starfish and other sea creatures. These materials are made of insecticide, and a chemical (orthodichlorobenzene) combined with sand. Scientists believe that the chemicals, being insoluble, or only slightly so, "probably" do not pollute the water or damage other plants and animals not in direct contact with them. Sea animals, venturing into the treated sandbank, perish from the poisons in different ways. A starfish, for example, goes into a spasm and disintegrates.

An oyster drill, a member of the snail family, swells up to such an extent that it is forced out of its shell and either dies or is devoured by fish. A crab loses its sense of balance and goes into convulsions.[20] The consumer may well wonder whether the chemicals ultimately make the oyster unfit to eat.

The U.S. Public Health Service certifies the purity of food made from shellfish, but does not guarantee that the shellfish itself is pure. Some states fail to appropriate adequate sums for vigorous surveillance. At a shellfish sanitation workshop held in Washington, D.C., in November 1964, federal officials warned the industry that unsafe shellfish may threaten the market.[21]

THE CONTAMINATED OCEANS

Nor are the oceans spared. Pesticide residues are now found in fish caught far out at sea and in remote areas such as the Antarctic.[22] This is not surprising, for pesticides are air- as well as water- and soil-borne. This was shown dramatically in 1964, when dust settling over a city in Ohio was identified as particles of pesticide and soil carried from Texas. Deep-sea fish, when caught, have been found with concentrations of pesticides in their livers and other organs.

Low-level radioactive wastes are discharged into the oceans, from slowly disintegrating concrete-lined drums. Although officials claim that these materials are largely absorbed by algae and plankton rather than by fish, there have been cases where concentrations are higher in fish than in plants. Ultimately these contaminants may find their way up through food chains[23] to consumers.

AN UNHEEDED WARNING

Fresh-water sport fishing is another area for concern:

> Radical changes have occurred in fish nutrition and culture over the past 10 years. Since the inception of artificial propagation in 1853, trout have been reared almost entirely on meat diets. The increasing competition for slaughterhouse products has gradually priced these meat sources out of the economic range of the trout

producer. Consequently, since about 1930 an increasingly large amount of dry meals (primarily scrap marine fish and liver meals) and cereal grain products have been added to trout diets. The use of fresh meat supplements requires refrigeration, and to overcome this difficulty the first all-dry feed diets began to appear on the fish market approximately 10 years ago. The majority of these are prepared in the conventional pellet form and are liberally supplemented with a variety of vitamins, antioxidants, growth stimulants and other additives.[24]

The feeds developed for trout were similar to those previously used for poultry. When the pellets were fed to baby chicks, the birds developed cancer. Later rainbow trout, raised in hatcheries, were given this feed in hopes of achieving maximum weight gains in the shortest period of time before being released into streams.

In the early 1960's, hatchery-raised rainbow trout that were fed this pelleted feed developed liver cancer in what leading cancer specialists considered *epidemic proportions.*[25] In some hatcheries, 100 per cent of the trout were affected.[26] The outbreak seemed related to a cancer-inciting ingredient, still not completely identified, but present in the fat fraction of the feed. Upon investigation, moldy cottonseed meal in the dry feed was suspected as the most likely cause of the cancer. Dr. Hueper, one of the investigators, reported that the outbreak had "serious financial implications, because the sale of diseased animals for human consumption and their transport through state lines is forbidden by federal law. It has been maintained by some groups that the consumption of fish would not represent any health hazard to the consumer, but this assumption is not justified because of the distinct lack of practical and scientific experience in such matters, and especially because the causal agent of this neoplastic [producing abnormal growth] disease is unknown. The fact that at times carcinomatous involvement affects not only the liver and other internal organs not ordinarily used for human food, but at times also the muscle tissue, provides an additional reason for caution against any laxity in the application and enforcement of existing laws."[27] He concluded:

The occurrence of this epidemic among edible fish subjected to an artificial nutritive regimen provides *a serious warning of the possible future production of a similar cancer epidemic in the human population through an increasing contamination of the human environment*

with some of the many industry-related carcinogenic chemicals.
[Emphasis mine.][28]

HOW FRESH IS "FRESH" FISH?

Benjamin Franklin remarked that a guest is similar to fish: fine the
first day, but stinking by the third. The importance of freshness in
fish has always been recognized by the discriminating consumer,
who examined the brightness of the fish eyes, color of the gills, and
odor of the flesh. Deterioration in caught fish is rapid. Few persons
have ever actually experienced the flavor of truly fresh deep-sea
fish, which has a pleasant and delicate odor and flavor, quite
unlike the "fishiness" which many associate with it, and which is,
in reality, mild rancidity.

For many years chilling of fish was practiced to delay its
deterioration. This was helpful, but not entirely satisfactory. Deep-
sea fishing was conducted in relatively shallow ocean-bank areas,
several hundred miles from port. Since it took a trawler or dragger
several weeks to fill its hold, and more time to sail back to port, the
catch was barely fresh when unloaded. Although the fish was
eviscerated, washed, and packed in ice soon after being caught,
the ones at the bottom of the trawler's ice bins were broken down
by the weight of ice and fish on top of them. On long trips, much
of the ice melted. In unloading, the fish was frequently forked or
otherwise mishandled. Even the fish caught by small boats that
plied waters close to shore and returned daily to port were not
particularly notable in quality, since such fish were often neither
eviscerated nor packed in ice until after landing.

The obvious answer to the problem of insuring freshness of fish
from deep sea to the table seemed to be quick-freezing, which
became technologically possible. Yet in all the years that this has
been in practice, all too often both the fresh-caught flavor and
quality have been absent. The fish may be mishandled before
reaching the packing plant, with early quality deterioration already present.

Or, it may suffer in several ways between packing plant and
delivery to the consumer.[29] It may defrost in transit from the coast
to the distributor's inland cold-storage plant, only to be refrozen

slowly under adverse conditions. It may be held too long in storage by the distributor, defrosting in transit to the retail store, and then be refrozen upon arrival. The retailer may allow the frozen fish to thaw, and refreeze it, or it may be held unduly long in the store, at temperatures below freezing but above the desirable level of 0° F. Freezing, unlike canning, does not completely inactivate the enzymes of fish; slow deterioration goes on, despite low temperatures. The results of such mishandling may be that when fish is thawed for use, there is excessive drip, and the flesh is tough, dry, darkened, or yellowed, with rancid odors and flavors due to decomposition.

For several years the Association of Food and Drug Officials of the United States (AFDOUS) worked, against industry pressure, to develop a frozen-food code, which was especially important for fish. At the annual meeting of the AFDOUS in June 1960 the code was adopted. It established detailed requirements in the handling of frozen products, calling for maintenance of zero degrees Fahrenheit or lower at each stage of operation.[30]

THE DISMAL FROZEN FISH

In the absence of standards through the years, the *quality* of frozen fish has been notoriously low. In several different tests, conducted at various times, *Consumer Reports* regarded the general quality level of all frozen fish products as "dismal" and "highly disappointing."[31] A food editor of *The New York Times* declared that much frozen fish had no more flavor than household paraffin.[32]

Four different frozen-food items bear closer examination: fillets, breaded shrimp, breaded fish sticks, and breaded fish portions. Frozen fish fillets have been marketed for a long time. They should be attractive to the consumer, for they have no waste. With no standards to meet, however, there is wide variation in quality, which apparently has little relationship to price.[33]

Frozen raw breaded shrimp has also been on the market for some years. When first introduced, it contained appreciably more shrimp than breading. In the absence of standards, the percentage of shrimp decreased to the point where some products contained as much breading as shrimp or more breading than shrimp. This particular seafood is more sensitive to mishandling than most frozen items. Even if the original quality of the shrimp is good, if stored too long, or at freezing temperatures insufficiently low, it becomes tough, fibrous, and rubbery, and may develop a flavor like dried salt cod. The breading may become rancid, too, producing sharp or acrid odors and flavors, and the shrimp, after cooking, will be discolored.[34]

In March 1958, voluntary federal grading standards for frozen raw breaded shrimp were adopted by the U.S. Department of the Interior (USDI), with a lenient allowance of 50 per cent breading. This was followed by the FDA hearings to establish standards of identity. Consumer testimony urged less breading, with 60 per cent as a minimum for shrimp content. Others protested that the proposal failed to require any label listing the size of the raw shrimp or their geographic origin, and put no time limit for holding them in storage prior to breading. The standard finally established[35] permitted industry breading a maximum of 50 per cent. However, the federal government has more stringent specifications for its own purchases, allowing only up to 30 per cent in the lightest breading category. The standard permits ascorbic acid and antioxidants to be added, without their presence being stated on the label.

The leniency of the standard elicited this candid comment from *Quick Frozen Foods:*

> Raw frozen breaded shrimp standards have again been revised, this time downward. It may soon be possible to procure a "Grade A" label on a package of breaded shrimp which is only 50 per cent shrimp. This may be a wonderful initial selling gimmick for the packer, but it is not so good for the consumer. Come to think of it, it is not too good for the future of USDA standards in the public regard. Nor is it too good for the shrimp packer who uses only 25 per cent breading and must compete in price with the man who uses 50 per cent breading. Both will wear the USDA's "grade A" label. Eventually, it has to kick back on the entire field, because people will sour on all frozen raw breaded shrimp.[36]

The prediction came true. *Consumer Reports* found the record of this industry's performance one of "poor-quality production, the promotion of mediocre official standards, the advocation of price-boosting tariffs, poor packaging, short weights, and carelessness about uniformity of the product."[37]

In June 1963, the USDI announced grading of frozen fish. In its press release, this agency stated: "Housewives of America should soon be finding two more fish products bearing a U.S. grade shield in the freezers of their favorite food stores. This shield is their assurance that fish products are of high quality and have been processed under continuous inspection of the Department of Interior."[38]

But performance failed to live up to these high hopes. In tests run by Consumers Union, out of ten brands of raw breaded shrimp that had the USDI "Grade A" shield on their labels, only one was judged top quality. But bacteriological tests showed widespread contamination, with 75 per cent of the samples failing to meet minimum requirements.[39] Since frozen shrimp must undergo cooking, this was not judged a health hazard; but better sanitary levels should be achieved by industry.

Deceptive practices have also been found in the frozen-shrimp industry. Large frozen shrimp are more popular than small ones. To exploit this market, an enterprising processor pressed tiny shrimp into a shrimp-shaped mold, and then froze, sliced, and breaded them, selling them as jumbo shrimp.[40]

A hazardous misrepresentation is that "fresh" shrimp sold beyond shrimp ports and adjoining areas may actually be thawed-out frozen shrimp. The unwary consumer may attempt to freeze these "fresh" shrimp—a dangerous practice.

Frozen breaded fish sticks, a processed food handled mainly by machine, first appeared on the market in 1953, and were a sensation.[41] Within two years, the market declined sharply. A packing-company executive accounted for the slump by suggesting that "too many people have turned out too much poor quality merchandise at a cheap price."[42] Instead of trying to raise the quality of the product to recapture the market, industry launched promotional campaigns.

In a process more like woodworking than food processing, mixtures of different species of fish are cut from large blocks into oblong, stick-shaped pieces. The poor quality of frozen fish sticks has been attributed to faulty processing and/or handling. Some fail to meet grading under U.S. standards because the percentage of breading is excessive. Facetiously, the question was asked: "Breaded fish sticks or fishy bread sticks?"[43] Many products fail to pass bacteriological requirements, although if the fish is *properly* heated before eating this failure is not considered a health hazard. However, the frozen breaded fish sticks are already fried as "convenience food" and merely reheated, so there is no assurance that the product will be heated sufficiently to insure destruction of pathogens.

More recently, "frozen breaded fish portions" have been marketed. These are "uniformly shaped, masses of cohering pieces of fish flesh, of established sizes and weights." As with other frozen fish products, these, too, have been pronounced "dismal" by *Consumer Reports*. The most common fault was rancidity, present in more than 80 per cent of all brands tested. "Bilginess" and other putrid odors were described as the second most frequent fault, resulting from bacteriological decomposition.[44]

STILL "A PRETTY BLEAK PICTURE"

The sorry state of frozen fish was described in May 1965 by Harold B. Allen, chief of the branch of technology, Federal Bureau of Commercial Fisheries. Addressing a food-industry audience, he summarized a three-year study, conducted by the USDI, on the quality of frozen fish products purchased from large supermarkets as presenting "a pretty bleak picture."[45] Because overlong storage was suspected as the chief cause of low-quality frozen fish, the USDI deliberately made its purchases in supermarkets rather than small groceries. By doing so, the agency evidently hoped to avoid even older products in small stores, where stock may not move so quickly. Nonetheless, some samples purchased in food chain supermarkets were found to be up to four years old. Even two-year-old frozen fish was admittedly overage. The official noted no real improvement in the quality of frozen fish during the first three years of the USDI grading. Approximately one sixth of all haddock samples were inedible or contained filth.[46]

With this state of affairs, what can be done? Admittedly, keeping frozen fish in a state of high quality is difficult, but it is not impossible. A systematic approach is needed, from beginning to end of the processing of fish. Quality control starts with *mandatory* inspection, instead of the present voluntary one, of *all* raw fish by the USDI. To prevent deterioration after packing, nationwide application of the Frozen Food Code needs to be made. This follows a recommendation for maintaining 0° F. temperature at all times, from packer to consumer. Despite industry resistance, the major provisions of the code have been adopted in some states. Although the code does not guarantee high overall quality, tests show average bacterial counts lower in regulated than in nonregulated states. Consumers can be protected from rancid frozen fish by the requirement of clear and conspicuous dating on each package. Also, states should follow the example of Massachusetts, where despite strenuous industry opposition, a good bacteriological standard must be met.

THE ANTIBIOTIC "FRESH" FISH

The consumer may assume that switching from frozen to fresh fish assures better quality. Unfortunately, much "fresh" fish sold in supermarkets today is stored frozen, and allowed to thaw prior to sale.

Even when the "fresh" fish is sold by a clerk who assures you that it was delivered in a fresh, unfrozen state, the term may be meaningless. Since April 1959, the FDA has permitted the addition of an antibiotic as a dip, or in the ice that surrounds fish during transportation, to lengthen shelf life. Certain raw sea foods, such as whole, headed, or gutted fish, unpeeled shrimp, and shucked scallops may be treated and contain up to five ppm antibiotic residue. For example, haddock on ice keeps "fresh" up to 16 days; treated, up to 25 days; red snappers, 12, but treated, up to 30 days; and scallops 12, but treated, up to 22 days.[47]

A fishing trade journal noted that "preparation and cooking removes most of the antibiotic and what small residues may remain are of 'no medical significance.' "[48] Translated into consumer terms, this may be rephrased: traces of antibiotic still remain, even after preparation and cooking. Added to antibiotic residues from other foodstuffs, amounts may *not* be negligible. As noted earlier, concerning antibiotics in poultry, Dr. Goddard had taken steps in 1966 to halt the use of two antibiotics used on fish. Originally, it was thought that cooking would destroy the antibiotic residues. But concern is now voiced about certain sea foods, such as oysters and clams, frequently eaten raw.

Fresh fish may be refrigerated in crushed ice containing preservatives such as sodium benzoate, sodium nitrite, hydrogen peroxide, ozone, or chlorine, to inhibit spoilage. From the consumer's viewpoint, none of these chemicals is desirable. In recent years cases of illness and deaths were traced to excessive amounts of sodium nitrite added to fish by sellers who hoped to prolong even further the shelf life of their products.

Ideally, live fish should be placed in pools until the time they are sold. This is done with lobsters in many first-class restaurants and hotels. In some European countries, it has been customary to keep fish alive until sold. Unfortunately, this practice has never become common in the United States.

FISH: CANNED AND SMOKED

Canning has been in long use, especially for tuna, salmon, and sardines. Although there are no federal grades, standards of identity for canned tuna have been established by the FDA. In general, a better level of quality has been maintained for canned than frozen fish, but even this could be improved. A large U.S. institutional food distributor stated: "By far the best tuna fish is packed by the Japanese, who fish off the same waters our packers use, but who pack their tuna in a different way—aboard ship, so that it is far juicier and meatier than our brands."[49] In tests, the findings of *Consumer Reports* concurred with this statement.[50]

OUTBREAK OF BOTULISM

For many years commercial canning in the United States has maintained a high safety record in regard to botulism. The few reported cases were mostly from improper home canning. In 1963, however, two Detroit women died of botulism traced to improperly canned tuna fish from a California packing plant.[51] Apparently, after the tuna fish had been thoroughly processed, botulinus spores entered cans with faulty seams. The case, isolated as it was, still pointed up the need for unflagging vigilance at all levels of food processing.

THE FISH PROTEIN CONCENTRATE WRANGLE

A relatively new product has been developed: fish is ground, the fats, oils, and nonprotein nitrogen are removed, and the rest is dried to an odorless and tasteless powder. This product is known popularly as "fish flour," or more properly, fish protein concentrate (FPC). It is highly concentrated: 80 to 85 per cent protein, and 15 to 20 per cent minerals. It is an extremely economical source of protein, and agencies of the United Nations have been particularly interested in making use of FPC to combat malnutrition in underdeveloped countries.[52] The Bureau of Commercial Fisheries, USDI, has been interested in the product to boost fish consumption in the United States.[53] FPC can provide protein adequate in amount and quality for as little as a penny a day per person. FPC has been described as protein rich as meat, but cheap as bread. Both the NAS-NRC and USDI termed the product safe and equal to, or exceeding, the officially accepted protein quality standards.

With all these attributes, the benefits of FPC became publicized. Unfortunately, it was referred to as "fish flour," although it has no attributes of grain flours for baking purposes. Its use as a supplement, however, could raise substantially the nutritive values of breads, crackers, breakfast cereals, cakes, and other processed foods. For example, only 3 to 5 per cent FPC added to a cereal gives the mixture a protein quality equal to milk and meat.

FDA considered standards of identity for FPC,[54] an action that caused a violent protest from the wheat-producing Midwest and the baking industry. Apparently, these groups viewed the suggestion as an admission that their products were overprocessed and low in nutritive value.

The flour interests waged a campaign to discredit FPC, issuing statements not based on fact. Claims were made, for example, that fish flour would replace wheat. This is untrue, for FPC would be used as a *supplement*, not as a *substitute* in baked products.

The wheat interests conducted a campaign to spur individuals to write protests to the FDA. The majority of letters were from women in the wheat-growing area. The response was hardly "spontaneous," since one town in Kansas accounted for 40 per cent of all the letters.

The alarm of the baking industry was expressed candidly by William B.

Bradley, president of the American Institute of Baking:

> The thought that whole fish flour might be an ingredient of commercial bread would harm the acceptance of commercially produced bread and tend to decrease consumption even below the present low figure.[55]

Then, with an illogical bit of nutritional nonsense, he concluded:

> I am not certain that protein concentrates in the nature of fish flour have real merit in the solving of nutritional deficiencies which occur in many of the developing nations. . . . [There] the deficiency of protein is accompanied by a deficiency of calories. The furnishing of protein concentrates without calories would not solve the nutritional deficiencies because the protein would be used for energy. If calories were furnished in forms such as wheat, the protein would be supplied also and thus eliminate the need for a protein concentrate.[56]

Meanwhile, the Nutrition Foundation, which represents both the wheat and fish interests, as well as other segments of the food industry, has been hesitant to take any stand that might arouse the wrath of some of its members. Upon being questioned about fish flour, the Nutrition Foundation president, Dr. Paul B. Pearson, was noncommittal, saying that the developments were "being followed with interest, and could prove highly significant."[57]

Wheat producers, millers, and bakers have had deeply entrenched and powerful lobbies, which frequently in the past have exerted notable pressures on the FDA's policies. The fish industry, on the other hand, is smaller and less aggressive, and has dealt mainly with the USDI for protection of its interests.

Whatever the reasons, the role played by the FDA in the FPC affair can be described as unscientific, irrational, and certainly not in the best interests of the consumer. The FDA began to raise objections to FPC being made from the *whole* fish, which contains eyes, scales, intestines, and some intestinal contents, although the processing largely removes the products of digestion from the fish.[58] George P. Larrick, the Commissioner at that time, found the product from whole fish "aesthetically objectionable," and "not normally considered acceptable for human food." The FPC advocates pointed out that some persons eat snails, oysters, clams, sardines, oxtail soup, kidneys, and the like, which to others might be comparably objectionable.

Larrick echoed the statement of the baking interests by declaring the product from whole fish "filthy." The FPC advocates noted that more objectionable waste matter may be present in the cleanest fish or meat fillet than in FPC made from whole fish. The director of commercial fisheries pointed out that the raw materials used for gelatine consist of calf bones, as well as pork and calf skins. In view of this, he requested the FDA to re-examine its interpretation.

Larrick pronounced FPC from whole fish "adulterated." FPC proponents argued that, on the contrary, the processing of whole fish removes impurities. In addition, it was noted that the FDA sets tolerances for "safe levels of filth" such as rodent excrement and hairs, as well as insect infestations, in a variety of items, including wheat, other grains, milk, meat, and water; the USDA allows for dirty, cracked, and leaking eggs in its consumer grades.

After lengthy consideration, the FDA approved a standard of identity for FPC in January 1962,[59] with a proviso that the product could *not* contain any heads, tails, fins, viscera, or intestinal content of fish. Thus, FPC made from *whole* fish was barred for sale in the United States.

This stiff limitation discouraged prospects for developing an FPC industry. The processing cost for FPC from gutted fish is far more costly than from whole fish. The product would be outpriced for use in underdeveloped countries. This meant the withholding of valuable inexpensive nutrients from protein-starved persons throughout the world who normally are recipients of our foodstuffs. Government agencies that purchase food for export are enjoined from buying products not approved by the FDA. Even if this were not so, selling or giving products to other countries that we consider unfit for home consumption would be a policy scarcely shaped to build good will.

FINAL CLEARANCE—BUT LIMITED

After Larrick's retirement, his successor, Dr. James L. Goddard, made it clear that he did not find the idea of FPC so repulsive as his predecessor. Clearance continued to be held up because of new obstacles: residues of isopropyl alcohol, the presence of lead caused by processing, and high concentrations of fluorides from the fish bones. Techniques were modified, and the FDA finally cleared FPC in 1967,[60] with certain limitations. FPC will not be allowed at present to be used to enrich foods. This was possibly a sop to the wheat and baking interests. Although bulk sales overseas are permitted, FPC can only be sold to U.S. consumers in containers of one pound or less. Allegedly, this was done to placate dairy interests, which argued that cheap fish protein might undercut milk sales. At present only a few types of fish are cleared for use in FPC, including hake. This move, according to an entrepreneur who wishes to develop FPC, was a crippling amendment, since it is difficult to obtain sufficient quantities of hake.[61]

Even after the FDA clearance, a new controversy threatened. Two dairy organizations, representing many milk producers, opposed clearance, with the old "filth" argument once again rearing its ugly head. The real unvoiced worry of the dairy interests was economic. FPC could well cut into dairy-product sales. Dry-milk exports had slipped drastically from 1965 to 1967. The FDA overruled the dairy organizations' objections, and noted that they were "not supported by grounds legally sufficient to justify the relief sought."[62]

The FDA approval of FPC, even with its limitations, represents a victory. It has been a long struggle to develop and make available this valuable concentrate which has been termed a "life line of the future."

FISH, ANYONE?

Choose ocean fish rather than inland varieties, for the degree of contamination will often be less. Ask about the freshness of the fish. Was it frozen and thawed? The time-honored guides of appearance and odor are no longer trustworthy. According to Dr. Bicknell, the white opacities that develop in the eyes of fish that have been frozen and then thawed "are only recognizable by an expert and are of little help to the housewife trying to tell if fish are fresh."[63]

Eat shellfish only if you are absolutely certain that it comes from unpolluted water, and even then, to be on the safe side, cook it well. Sport fishermen should check the safety of streams or coastline.

8

Nuts: Nature
Versus Technology

NATURE HAS provided nuts with an excellent packaging that
should be admired by modern technologists. The shell, being
durable and quite impervious while intact, provides a long shelf
life for the nut inside.

But the trend toward "convenience foods" has introduced many
objectionable processing methods that degrade nuts. For example,
cashews may be heated in liquid to make the shells brittle, and to
extract oily substances; English walnut shells may be loosened by
exposure to ethylene gas. Once nuts are shelled, they are subjected
to fumigants like methyl bromide to keep them insect-free.

As any cook knows, blanching of nuts to remove the inner skin
can be done simply by soaking the nuts briefly in hot water. But
commercially, pecans and English walnuts are often dipped in hot
lye and then rinsed in acid. Or they may be put into a hot solution
of glycerine and sodium carbonate; the skins are removed with a
jet of water, and the nuts are then dipped in a citric-acid solution.

Walnuts, which may have variations of light and dark nutmeats,
are frequently bleached in a solution of chloride of lime and
sodium carbonate to give them a uniform appearance. Pistachios,
which have good nutritive value in a natural state, are usually
dyed bright red, and encrusted with an objectionable heavy layer
of salt.

MAKING A GOOD FOOD BAD

Frequently shelled nuts are cooked in oil, and heavily salted or sugared. Such processed nuts are objectionable for several reasons. Vitamin E and as much as 70 to 80 per cent of their thiamin (from the vitamin B complex) may be destroyed. Although the process is known as "roasting," it is actually French frying, an undesirable method that does not even approximate roasting.[1] Yet neither state nor federal officials prohibit such misrepresentations. The oils used may be of poor quality, and there is carcinogenic danger when cooking oils are reheated and reused repeatedly. Salting or sugaring of nutmeats is undesirable, too, for there is already a superabundance of both salt and sugar in the average diet.

Sometimes individuals complain that nuts are "indigestible." Are the nuts themselves at fault, or are the processings the real culprits?

After nuts are shelled, rancidity is hastened considerably. To retard this, several antioxidants may be used. Consumers' Research noted that this practice permits: "great latitude in shipping, handling and storage, so that grocers or restaurant keepers do not have to provide favorable storage conditions for items that would normally deteriorate so as to be unappetizing or unsalable in a few days or weeks. These undesirable practices could be corrected to some extent, if state and federal agencies would require the date of manufacture to be put on every packaged food."[2]

Nutmeats may be coated with acetylated monoglyceride and an oxygen interceptor to extend shelf life for a year or longer, as well as to pasteurize and "improve" their appearance.[3] Shredded coconut is coated with propylene glycol, and BHA and BHT are also commonly used with nutmeats. Remember, too, that nuts used in bakery products and confections also contain these materials.

BHT and/or BHA are included in most packaged shelled nutmeats, and may even be put into vacuum-packed tins of nuts—a practice totally unnecessary.

Pesticides tend to concentrate in oils and fats. Nuts, being rich in oil, may concentrate pesticides from the sprayings of the nut trees. The FDA has set official tolerance levels for pesticide residues in nuts.

NUTS, ANYONE?

Purchase nuts in the shell, and crack them as needed. Or buy vacuum-tinned shelled, raw nutmeats uncoated with oil, sugar, salt or preservatives. These superior products are available, although not common. Once the tin is opened, refrigerate the nutmeats and use them within a reasonable time.

PEANUTS CAN BE POISONOUS

Although peanuts are not true nuts, they are associated with them and are frequently packaged with mixed nutmeats.

After eating peanut meal in their feed, some 100,000 turkeys died in England in 1960. Investigation[4] showed that the peanuts were contaminated with *Aspergillis flavus,* an aflatoxin mold commonly found on peanuts, wheat, corn, soybeans, rice, cottonseed, and other grains[5] stored in warm, damp places. It was learned that the toxin could also kill ducklings, pigs, and calves.[6] Cows eating such contaminated food could pass the poison through their milk, and the toxin would still be found after the milk was pasteurized or dried.[7]

In 1965, five bears at the San Diego zoo died from liver cancer.[8] Contaminated peanuts in the feed were suspected as the cause. Experimentally, a large number of different species of animals were fed contaminated peanut meal. *None demonstrated complete resistance to adverse effects.*[9] However, up to that point, there was no certainty that *Aspergillis flavus* caused liver cancer in man, although aflatoxins were termed "the most powerful hepatic [liver] carcinogens known."[10]

Circumstantial evidence was investigated, and a relationship of human toxicity to *Aspergillis flavus* was established. It was found that this aflatoxin could inhibit the growth of human lung cells.[11] Researchers also have reason to believe that it may play an important role in spreading liver disease among human beings and animals in the tropics.[12]

The toxin is common to peanuts grown in many parts of the

world.[13] It is present in raw and in processed peanuts. Roasting does not kill the mold.[14] Hence the poison may be present in roasted peanuts, peanut butter, packaged nuts, candy containing nuts, and peanut meal for animal feed. Peanut oils are free of the poison, because the strong alkalis used in processing neutralize the toxins.[15]

The FDA was alerted to the need for careful surveillance of peanut foodstuffs that might be contaminated. The agency found poisons in some samples tested. Processors of peanuts and peanut butters became jittery that adverse publicity might cause a public scare. When the FDA discovered that some 1,000 cases of contaminated imported peanut butter had been released on the market, the agency conducted a quiet search to recover them. An official admitted: "We are trying to get all of it back without creating panic. We are not trying to recall the product by publicity, because we think it would be a serious mistake to scare the public."[16]

Such a policy may backfire. Unless there is widespread knowledge, even the growers and processors may fail to comprehend the potential seriousness of the problem.

Meanwhile, the USDA has developed a program to minimize *Aspergillis flavus* in domestic peanuts and other crops. The agency offers price supports to growers who will use only high-quality peanuts for food products. The USDA is giving educational assistance to the industry to help improve the quality of peanuts, and conducting research to eliminate mold damage. It has set up a federal-state inspection system for all lots of shelled peanuts intended as food, before they are shipped. However, the screening program is not foolproof. After it was implemented, the FDA recalled thousands of cases of peanut butter contaminated with aflatoxin mold.[17]

PEANUT BUTTER—A SAD TALE

There was a time when flavorsome peanut butter was made solely from freshly ground nuts, perhaps with a little natural oil and a dash of salt, but nothing else. Providing fairly good-quality protein, appreciable amounts of vitamins, and desirable unsaturated fatty acids, this product, enjoyed especially by children, was considered an inexpensive, wholesome food. In limited quantities, it was approved for inclusion in a nutritionally well-balanced diet.

Old-fashioned peanut butter, without preservatives, has a relatively short shelf life. The oil, rising to the top, is exposed to light and air, both elements hastening rancidity. Refrigeration will retard the process. The oil can be stirred back into the peanut butter, or the jar can be turned upside down briefly. Because of its consistency, peanut butter sticks to the roof of the mouth. When taken directly from the refrigerator, it is difficult to spread on soft bread. But none of these features caused undue concern to the peanut-butter lover. Until a decade ago, it was possible to find this type of peanut butter in almost any food store throughout the country.

As food technologists, additive manufacturers, motivational researchers, marketing experts, and advertising agencies began to pool their talents, peanut butter gradually underwent such modifications that the typical present-day product bears little resemblance to the original. Although peanut butter may not be a basic foodstuff, what has happened to it deserves close scrutiny. The changes wrought symbolize how the food interests can convert a simple, wholesome food into a complex adulterated substance.

To prolong shelf life and prevent oil separation in peanut butter, processors began to add a hydrogenated vegetable oil. (This process, described in Chapter 9, on fats and oils, will be shown as objectionable.) In addition, dextrose or sugar was added, acting as an absorbent for some of the oil, to prevent separation. Emulsifiers (monoglycerides and diglycerides) were also added for this purpose. The addition of sweeteners changed the basic quality of peanut butter, converting it into a confection and possibly masking inferior, rancid, or moldy peanuts. The sweeteners are especially objectionable, since the product is so widely consumed by children.

Purist peanut-butter devotees prefer a product made with the entire peanut, including the heart (germ). Since this is perishable, most processors degerm the peanuts. They claim that the heart tends to give a bitter flavor to the product. This statement is challenged by the purists, who claim it is a lame excuse for lowering the nutritional value in order to gain long shelf life.

The means used to achieve long shelf life and to delay rancidity and oil separation may be highly desirable for economy in marketing and distribution, but they are not in the consumer's interest. Nutritionally, peanut butter with limited shelf life is preferable. Fresh stock, refrigerated and dated, delivered frequently to retailers, can minimize the rancidity problem.

FROM BAD TO WORSE

In time, other additives were introduced, to provide "taste acceptability." Texturizers made the product more "spreadable" and counteracted its tendency to stick to the roof of the mouth. In the absence of standards of identity, peanut butter became so adulterated that in many cases about one fourth of the product consisted of additives.

The FDA had no quarrel with the addition of hydrogenated oil, sweeteners, and other materials objectionable to knowledgeable consumers. The FDA merely required that the additives be declared prominently and conspicuously on the label. For years, even this regulation was neither fulfilled by many manufacturers nor enforced by the FDA.

Deterioration of peanut-butter quality continued. In 1958, the FDA inspection of the product revealed only 78 per cent peanuts in the finished peanut butter processed by the largest manufacturer.[18] The following year, the FDA proposed a long-overdue standard, consisting of a minimum of 95 per cent peanuts, and up to 5 per cent optional ingredients. The American Home Economics Association, consumer groups, and individuals endorsed a return to 100 per cent peanuts, but the situation had been allowed to deteriorate so long that this was considered unrealistic. Industry continued to balk at the 95 per cent proposal. Time passed, and the standard was not established.

After numerous negotiations with industry, in November 1961 the FDA proposed a new standard,[19] making further concessions by lowering the proposed minimum to 90 per cent, and raising optional additives to 10 per cent. These ingredients were to be listed on the label after the words "peanut butter." Even this leniency failed to satisfy most of the industry. Peanut-butter makers claimed that a leading product of the largest processor would not have met the new minimum requirements.

The new standard allowed that products containing as little as

75 per cent peanuts be labeled "imitation peanut butter." Rather than adopt this label, one large company chose to use the term "peanut spread," with a disclosure of ingredients on the label. A ludicrous situation resulted from the proposed standard. A small manufacturer,[20] producing 100 per cent peanut butter of high quality, noted that the proposed standards required peanut butter to be made from *blanched* peanuts. Because he had been using the entire nut, including skin and heart, he asked the FDA how his product would be affected. The FDA had made no provision for such a product, which obviously was superior to the maximum requirements in the proposed standards. The agency advised the processor to label his product "imitation peanut butter," if the standard went through! Officially, "imitation" on food labels has been required for products that do not comply with specified requirements, but these items have been *below* standard,[21] such as sausage containing excessive cereal or water in place of meat, jam or jelly with less fruit, and cheese with more water or less fat.

The new standard was challenged bitterly by industry. Preposterous claims were made that the proposal discouraged research and restricted improvements. Translated into consumer language, this meant further adulteration and lowering of quality would be hampered. The new standard was not adopted, but suspended until future hearings.

Meanwhile, old-fashioned peanut butter has virtually disappeared from the shelves of food stores throughout the land. True, there are exceptions here and there, sold as specialty items, or from small producers who take pride in quality products. But by and large, the highly contrived and modified products are the only ones commonly available, with no real choice except among brand names.

THE PEANUT-BUTTER BATTLE DRAGS ON

Again in November 1964, the FDA attempted to issue a modified standard for peanut butter.[22] Again, a ceiling of 10 per cent optional ingredients was permitted, but this time further concessions were made to industry. Hydrogenated cottonseed oil was optional, and various types of corn products were lumped together with sugar and honey under the term "sweeteners." The new standard pleased neither consumers nor processors, and many objections were raised during the hearings that followed.

Dr. Theron Randolph, allergist, objected to the nonspecific term "sweeteners."[23] Many individuals, he pointed out, are highly allergic to corn and corn products; others to sugar cane or beets. Although cottonseed allergy may be less common, the reaction may be acute. Even honey allergy is not rare. A similar problem is created by the inclusion of lecithin as an emulsifier and dispersant. This may be a product of either corn or soybean; the label declaration should be specific.

Objections were also raised to the addition of *any* oil other than that naturally present in the peanuts.[24] The new proposal allowed the addition of oils to nuts naturally low in oil, yet the added oil would be considered as part of the 90 per cent peanut content. Some nutritionists expressed anxiety that animal fats might be added to peanut butter, unless additives were listed specifically. Cottonseed oil was objectionable to some nutritionists; others expressed fear that residues of weed killers used in cotton might be present in the oil. One individual noted that additives cut protein content, but raise calories.

Industry was also dissatisfied, wanting the 90 per cent minimum peanut content reduced to 87 per cent. The makers of corn sugar and the raisers of soybeans opposed limitations on the inclusion of their products. The large peanut-butter manufacturers wanted permission to use additional chemicals to compensate for the shortcomings of off-flavors in peanuts, which sometimes develop from poor crop-drying conditions.

Industry was especially annoyed by the assertion, in the proposed standards, that "artificial flavoring, artificial sweeteners, chemical preservatives, added vitamins, and color additives are not suitable ingredients of peanut butter." The manufacturers and their trade association insisted that present-day peanut butter has been developed to meet consumer acceptance. This distorted claim was discredited when irate homemakers began to flood the FDA with letters demanding a return to pure peanut butter without adulteration. More than 1,500 letters were received—a record-breaking number for any proposed standard.

In July 1965, once again a revised standard was proposed,[25] repeating the 90 per cent minimum. Again it was held in abeyance because of protests. In December 1965, new hearings were begun. This time the FDA attempted to justify its newly proposed regulations by demonstrating that, under them, peanut butter could be made economically and efficiently. The FDA planned to use as witnesses a few peanut-butter manufacturers who had opposed the point of view expressed by the big companies and their trade organization. An FDA lawyer charged that attempts to "gag" them had been made before the hearing and a hearing examiner informed industry attorneys that he would report to the U.S. Attorney General their alleged efforts to change witnesses' opinions or prevent them from testifying.[26]

Despite harassment, one peanut-butter manufacturer, testifying for the government, said that his own peanut butter contained 94 per cent peanuts and voiced hope that the standard would drive from the market borderline products used to wage price wars. He charged that some inferior products contained 20 to 25 per cent corn-syrup solids.

During the December 1965 hearings, Dr. Fredrick J. Stare, appearing as a witness, expressed the opinion that, in terms of practical nutrition, it doesn't make a "damn bit of difference"[27] if it is 90 or 80 per cent peanuts in peanut butter. The FDA's hearing examiner voiced concern about the increased use of chemicals in peanut butter, and he asked Dr. Stare if he objected to them. "Not at all," was the reply. Then the examiner asked Dr. Stare if he considered the FDA's proposed standard reasonable. The reply was: "It is unreasonable to say you must have 90 per cent peanuts in peanut butter, even if you can spread the damn stuff. It is too high." Then he added that the high requirement leaves "no room to manipulate"[28] more chemical additives that might be needed.

Two more years went by, with no peanut-butter standards. In December 1967, the FDA again issued a proposal for peanut butter[29] to contain at least 90 per cent peanuts. The proposal permitted hydrogenated vegetable oils as stabilizers and emulsifiers, provided that these ingredients be declared on the label. The proposal forbade the inclusion of preservatives, artificial flavorings, sweeteners, color additives, and vitamins. Once again, the Peanut Butter Manufacturers Association, representing some 60 companies that constitute most of the industry, challenged the FDA's proposal. The trade organization termed the proposed standard "unreasonable."[30]

By July 1968, the FDA issued what appeared to be its final thoughts on this protracted argument.[31] The agency reaffirmed its position requiring 90 per cent peanuts, but permitting, with a label declaration, hydrogenated vegetable oils as optional "stabilizing ingredients" with fat content up to 55 per cent. Two peanut-butter manufacturers, challenging the proposals, requested a court review. Thus, once again, attempts to establish a definition and standard of identity for peanut butter have been thwarted.

THE LARGER ISSUE IN THE PEANUT-BUTTER BATTLE

Basically, what has been argued was not the acceptable ratio of peanuts to optional ingredients, but the larger issue, business morality. Does the food industry have the right to manipulate public taste and debase a food by removing its nutritive values and adding nonnutritive ones? The food industry and its advertising agencies deny playing this role. They argue that "product evolution" develops to satisfy consumer demands. Using peanut butter as an example, it is apparent that "product evolution" is forced upon the consumer, not created by him. *If given a choice,* he may prefer quality to convenience. The much-touted claims of easy spreading and improved texture are thin pretexts to cheapen a product and lengthen its shelf life. If consumer demands were the sole arbiter of peanut butter, the current market place would not be restricted largely to brand differentiation. The buyer would have a choice between old-fashioned peanut butter without preservatives and the peanut butter that has undergone "product evolution."

During the recent Congressional hearings, Mrs. Ruth Desmond, representing the Federation of Homemakers, a group supporting old-fashioned peanut butter, concluded her testimony by saying:

> Let us hope this matter of an honest standard for peanut butter will be resolved with deliberate speed. We urge that the FDA invite the advice of real homemakers who have no profits to consider except the bonus of good health from wholesome, nutritious foods.[32]

PEANUT BUTTER, ANYONE?

Try to find peanut butter that is freshly ground, from 100 per
cent peanuts, with no additives other than salt. Such products are
available in rare cases in regular food stores, but more frequently
through certain specialty shops and mail-order suppliers. For help,
see the *Consumer Bulletin Annual,* 1969, pages 173–74. Or make
your own peanut butter at home, a small quantity at a time, using
an electric blender or a seed or meat grinder.

9

Fats and Oils:
Some Unhappy Truths

ALTHOUGH FATS and oils are not classified as "basic foods" like meats and other proteins, they are closely associated.

Some fat in the diet is vital, but recent findings show that both *quality* as well as *quantity* are important. Farming and factory practices have drastically altered the original nature of fats and oils, producing foods not only less nutritive, but also actually hazardous. A few basic facts are necessary as background to an understanding of the radical transformation that has taken place.

A fat is distinguished from an oil by its physical consistency. At room temperature, if solid, it is considered a fat; if liquid, an oil. In the natural state, however, either fat or oil can gradually revert to liquid or solid by having the temperature raised or lowered. The characteristic solidity or liquidity depends, generally, on the degree of saturation of the fatty acids. The more solid they are, the higher the saturation; the fluid oils are nearly all unsaturated to some degree.

In general, vegetable and fish oils are highly unsaturated; animal fats are highly saturated. There are exceptions. For example, coconut oil, a vegetable fat, is highly saturated. The unsaturates contain highly desirable "essential fatty acids" (EFA) vital for bodily functions and good health. (These fatty acids are linoleic, linolenic and arachidonic.)

THE ALARMING AMERICAN DIET

Formerly, Americans consumed not only *less* fat but fat that was *less saturated*. Alterations in the composition of fats have come about through changes in farm management. Concentrated feeds and confinement of animals have converted the natural soft, yellow, partially unsaturated animal fat into a hard, white, far more saturated one. The hard fat produced in these foodstuffs is now being consumed in greater quantities than formerly. Demonstrable changes are found in the quality of human fat in persons consuming such foods. Medical authorities warn that most Americans are eating far too much fat in their total diets, and fats of the less desirable type—the saturated ones.

The alarming intake of saturated fats, even by young children, caused a concerned physician, Dr. David Spain, to remark at a White House Conference on Children and Youth:

> If 35 per cent of his calories comes from fats, is junior being prepared, starting in the nursery school, for a coronary occlusion? Frappés, fat-meat hamburgers, bacon and mayonnaise, sandwiches, followed by ice cream, may be good for the farmer, good for the undertaker, but bad for the populace.[1]

Although the scope of this book is limited to food processing and modifications, at this point it is necessary to mention a closely related problem. The shocking rise in coronary disease in the United States has developed along with significant dietary changes. Although controversy rages, many medical researchers have found significant correlations between coronary disease and the consumption of excessive amounts of fats and fats of the wrong kind. The American Heart Association made two recommendations concerning fats: reduction of the total fat intake, and change of the type of fats eaten, from saturated animal fats that predominate in the American diet to the unsaturated vegetable and marine types.[2] These suggestions were made because of certain findings. Although some blood cholesterol is normal, high amounts may be linked to coronary-artery disease. In some instances, cholesterol seems to be related to fat intake. Saturated fat tends to raise cholesterol, while unsaturated fat may lower it.

Groups including the American Diabetes Association have requested the FDA to have specific vegetable or animal fat identification, with percentages, on all food products. The phrase "vegetable oil" is inadequate. There are some vegetable oils, including coconut oil, which are high in saturated fats.

HYDROGENATION: WHAT PRICE CONVENIENCE?

In addition to the abnormal saturated fats produced through farm practices—a situation already fraught with dangers—the problem has been intensified by the factory process of hydrogenation. By saturation, liquid oils are converted into plastic solid fats.

Originally, the process was developed to make low-cost soap, so that waste products of inedible fish and vegetable oils could be substituted for more expensive lard. American chemists adapted the process for food fats. This was described in *Consumer Bulletin* as "an untested novelty in the long history of the human race and its dietary practices."[3]

The process has been in existence for half a century. There is a growing awareness of its harmfulness, with expressions of concern from the medical community. A decade ago the alarm was sounded in a leading article in *The Lancet:* "The hydrogenation plants of our modern food industry may turn out to have contributed to the causation of a major disease."[4]

How is the liquid oil or soft fat hardened? It is exposed to a high temperature and placed under pressure. Hydrogen is then bubbled through the oil in the presence of nickel, platinum, or some other catalyst. The hydrogen atoms combine with the carbon atoms, and the product becomes saturated or hardened. The new compound bears no relationship to the original oil. It is a dark, malodorous grease that would be unacceptable to the consumer. But technologists' skills are used to bleach, filter and deodorize it into a pure white, odorless, tasteless, highly artificial fat. It may be processed further for making shortening, lard, or margarine.

The hydrogenated fats offer many conveniences. They have a high degree of durability, resisting change and deterioration even under poor storage conditions and unfavorable temperatures. "Hydrogenated shortenings can be accompanied by a tenfold increase in resistance to rancidity,"[5] asserts the food technologist. These fats do not absorb odors readily. The baking industry finds them "superior to oils in shortening effect and creaming quality."[6] They are well suited for ease and economy of food preparation in the factory, restaurant, and home.

At what price is this convenience achieved? The process tends to be selective. The greater the degree of unsaturation in the natural oil, the greater its tendency to respond to hydrogenation. The heating of the oil ruins its original character, with destruction of all vitamins and mineral factors as well as an alteration of proteins. The essential fatty acids (EFA) are destroyed, or changed into abnormal toxic fatty acids antagonistic to EFA. The synthetic fat forms new molecular structures unacceptable to the human physiology. This is how Dr. Bicknell described it:

> The abnormal fatty acids produced by "hardening" [hydrogenation] are the real worry. The atoms of the molecule of an essential fatty acid are arranged in space in a particular manner . . . but hardening may produce a different spatial arrangement, so that a completely abnormal . . . unsaturated fatty acid is produced. An analogy is ordinary handwriting and mirror handwriting: both are identical but spatially different, so that at best reading the latter is difficult and at worst serious mistakes are made. The same mistakes are made by the body when presented . . . [with the abnormal] EFA. Not only does it fail to benefit by them, but it is deluded by their similarity to normal EFA and so attempts to use them. It starts incorporating them in biochemical reactions and then finds they are the wrong shape: but the reaction has gone too far to jettison them and begin again with normal EFA, so they are not only useless but actually prevent the use of normal EFA. They are in fact *anti-EFA*. They accentuate in man and animals a deficiency of EFA. An analogy is jamming the wrong key in a lock: not only is the lock not turned but the right key also is rendered valueless.[7]

Dr. Hugh Sinclair at the Laboratory of Human Nutrition, Oxford University, has found that lack of EFA "is a contributory cause in neurological diseases, heart disease, arteriosclerosis, skin disease, various degenerative conditions such as cataract and arthritis, and cancer."[8]

Dr. Ancel Keys has warned that the unnatural forms of poly-unsaturated fatty acids, produced during the hydrogenation processes, have altered biological qualities. "Where there are double bonds, different configurations of the molecule are found. In natural fats, almost all of the unsaturated fatty acids have the *cis* configuration. The molecule bends backwards on itself at this point. When the lipid chemists hydrogenate these fatty acids, some of the double bond remains but the molecule is straightened out. . . . There is much reason to suspect that the *trans* acids are biologically less desirable."[9]

There is no assurance that nickel, if used as the catalyst, leaves no residue in the product. This element, even in minute quantities in the diet, is suspected of being a carcinogen. In addition, the role of "abnormal" metals such as nickel has been studied in relation to atherosclerosis. One metal can replace another and inactivate it in a biologic system, so that there is a possibility that the nickel competes with an essential metal in the enzyme system of the body, and produces a vitamin B_6 (pyridoxine) deficiency.[10] This vitamin plays an important role in converting saturates to unsaturates in the body.

Despite the shocking implications of hydrogenation, the process is used almost universally by food processors. Far worse, it is accepted and fully sanctioned by government agencies responsible for the consumer's welfare. It is difficult, if not virtually impossible, to avoid hydrogenated fats, commonly used in restaurants, bakeries, and hundreds of consumer food products.

In the light of present knowledge, official acceptance of hydrogenation is unpardonable. Labels of many prepared foods merely list the ingredient "vegetable oil" or "shortening" without naming the specific one or stating whether it is hydrogenated. The concerned consumer, wishing to avoid hydrogenated fats, is not afforded even this modicum of protection. At the very least, as pointed out in *Consumer Bulletin*,[11] merely by a simple change of administrative regulations requiring no special legislation, federal and state government agencies could require a label declaration of hydrogenated fats and their amounts.

FROM SOAP DISH TO DINNER TABLE

In a strange way, the increased use of hydrogenated fats through the years has been influenced by a totally unrelated industry. At one time, many fat scraps went into soap production. With the meteoric rise of the detergents, made from synthetics in the laboratory, the demand for soap-making waste fats has declined. Possibilities were explored for other uses. Hydrogenation provided the favorable means of channeling them into the food industry. The process made it possible to salvage waste that otherwise would not gain "consumer acceptance" because of poor color or rancidity.

Old-fashioned lard, fairly saturated but still a natural fat, was acceptable in moderation. Today, lard, too, has been altered considerably. It goes through processes of settling, bleaching, filtration, and hydrogenation. The resulting product does not melt at room temperatures and will keep unrefrigerated. Added antioxidants increase its life tenfold.

As evidence has mounted revealing the menace of hydrogenation, some shortening processors have attempted to change their methods to avoid economic losses. They joined the popular bandwagon of proclaiming their products "high in unsaturates" but adding that they "stay freshly sweet at room temperature." A close reading of label information reveals how this is achieved. These products may contain antioxidants, in addition to emulsifiers, defoamers, and artificial colors and flavors. As noted in Chapter 4, artificial antioxidants in fats are considered possible carcinogens. Hence, one undesirable process has been substituted for another.

Another development has been the attempt by segments of the food industry to modify products, ranging from hot dogs to pastries, by substituting unsaturates for saturates. If carried to a logical conclusion, the practice would have to begin back at the farm, with a complete reversal of present practices. This seems highly unlikely in view of the USDA's role. At the very time that the medical community has been urging people to cut down on fats, the USDA has been encouraging the addition of surplus fats to livestock and poultry feed for rapid weight gains, and feed economy.

MARGARINE—THE GRAND DECEPTION

Margarine, in addition to its hydrogenation, has other objectionable features that make it an artificial product. It is a water and oil emulsion, with chemicals added to maintain its stability and give it other properties. The fat portion of the emulsion must be at least

80 per cent of the finished product, and it may contain animal or vegetable products. A variety of fats and oils are used, with the selection of the essential ones largely governed by price. In 1961, for example, a record amount of lard was used in margarines because it was cheaper than vegetable oils. The remaining nonfat portion may consist of water, milk products, or ground soybeans. The federal standard permits a variety of chemicals,[12] all in a futile attempt to make a synthetic product like the "high-price spread." An artificial butterlike flavor and odor are achieved with diacetyl. To insure enjoyment of these qualities, isopropyl or stearyl citrates are added. These additives are euphemistically labeled "flavor protectors." Additional attempts to achieve butterlike qualities are made with artificial color, lecithin to imitate the frying behavior of butter, and synthetic vitamins to "enrich" the product. Sodium benzoate, benzoic acid, or citric acid may be added as preservatives. The benzoates are known poisons, with severe reactions in sensitive individuals, resulting occasionally in death. In addition to these items, which must appear on the label, emulsifiers (monoglycerides, diglycerides, and others) may be present but undeclared.

Despite the skills of the food technologists, the resulting product seems poor from the viewpoint of palatability as well as nutrition. In sample testing, none was considered the equivalent of top-quality "AA 93-score" butter. Even the highest-ranking brands were judged to have a somewhat "artificial" flavor and "greasier" texture than butter. Most were described as melting poorly in the mouth, "with a feeling reminiscent of salve or vaseline."[13]

Historically, margarine has evolved from lowly beginnings, to a product that at present has taken more than two thirds of the "spread" market from butter. For many years the powerful dairy interests succeeded in preventing margarine from being colored at the factory. The effect of this was to keep sales low, and thus avoid any economic threat to its competitor, butter. Three additional unfavorable factors adversely affected margarine. There was an unhappy emotional association for people who linked it to the food shortages of World War I. The unappealing appearance of the uncolored product resembled cold cream or lard. Furthermore, homemakers disliked the inconvenience of having to color the margarine.

The bitter struggle between the butter and margarine interests began shortly after World War I and continued for three decades. At the beginning, margarine manufacture was in the hands of small processors, and it was simple for the butter industry, being affiliated with the powerful dairy industry, to dominate them and dictate policy. As margarine manufacture gradually became incorporated with other giants of the food industry, the picture changed. By 1952, the sale of colored margarine was legalized in all states except Minnesota and Wisconsin, both predominantly dairy states. At later dates, these diehards also yielded.

Legalizing the sale of colored margarine was probably the greatest single factor in its phenomenal sales increase. The product was offered at a much lower price than that "high-cost spread," and the deft skills of packaging experts made it more attractively wrapped than butter. Motivational researchers removed the onus of low social status by projecting margarine as a modern, efficient product, with its users "forward looking, progressive people."[14] Its "spreadability" was emphasized. By 1958, margarine outsold butter by more than 100 million pounds yearly.[15] But the real bonanza came when the industry began to exploit the public interest in polyunsaturates.[16] The campaign was labeled as "one of the most unprincipled food promotions . . . in the past quarter of a century," with TV commercials "noisy, ubiquitous and shameless. They have promoted a staple food as though it were a drug."[17]

The margarine manufacturers have advertised their wares as containing unsaturates. Significant quantities are unlikely, regardless of the raw materials used, because of the hydrogenation of the product. Many claims fail to tell the whole story, and typify what advertising agencies call "avoidance of negative appeal." Slogans have been devised so that "a little inaccuracy saves a world of explanation." For example, the advertising for one corn-oil margarine states that it has never been hardened by hydrogenation. While this may be true about the corn oil in the product, it fails to state that the cottonseed and soybean oils, *also present, have been hydrogenated.* Another corn-oil margarine is advertised as being made from 100 per cent corn oil. This may be true of the raw material used, but it fails to note that in order to make the product solid, at least part—and probably a large part—of the oil *is* hydrogenated. What percentage is liquid? The consumer is not informed. Most likely the amount is insignificant. As long as margarine is a solid, boxed product, not flowing from a bottle, the consumer can assume that the fat has been hydrogenated.

Another artful device is to label margarine and other factory foods as "partially hydrogenated" or "partially hardened"—with the words "hydrogenated" and "hardened" used interchangeably. These misleading phrases may be misinterpreted as a protection for the consumer. Actually, the degree of hydrogenation to which a food is subjected depends on factors of convenience for the manufacturer, packager, and retailer. The consumer should remember that a product is either hydrogenated or not hydrogenated; any degree of hydrogenation is not in his best health interests.

Some manufacturers of margarines continue to perpetuate their quackery in advertising. Although the FDA has issued mild warnings, it has made no seizures for misrepresentation or deceptive health claims.

Advertising copywriters for margarines have shifted from direct to indirect health claims. References to heart disease or doctors' prescriptions are made less frequently. Instead, these have been superseded by phrases like "high in unsaturates" or "low in saturated fats" to carry the message to a public that has already become somewhat knowledgeable.

It is well to remember the observation of Dr. Bicknell in World War II. In Norway, where margarine factories had been destroyed, arterial diseases decreased. In England, during the same period, with margarine factories intact, arterial diseases increased. He commented: "It is difficult to resist the conclusion that our increasing arterial degeneration is not the inevitable concomitant of old age, which it may antecede by many years or never join at all, *but a preventable pandemic disease of modern foods and especially of modern bread, milk and margarine.*" (Emphasis mine.)[18]

THE UNHAPPY TRUTH ABOUT OILS

Most oils are high in unsaturates. The informed consumer, aware of the role of saturates and factory processings, logically would turn to oils as a source of fats in the diet. Natural oils are desirable foods. For centuries, using crude apparatus, small amounts of oil-producing materials (such as olives, sunflower seeds, sesame seeds) were pressed, and the fresh oil used immediately. This crude oil usually is dark, strong-flavored, and high in nutrients. But such oil, if not used promptly, and especially if exposed to air and warmth, oxidizes. Rancid oil not only has a disagreeable odor and taste, but has lost vitamins, retards digestion, and produces toxic substances.

There are techniques to produce good oil and to retard its spoilage. Oil that is extracted in hydraulic or screw presses, using moderate heat, and refrigerated immediately in dark containers excluding air, will keep fresh for a reasonable time. Fortunately, crude oil contains natural antioxidants, such as carotenoids, vitamin E, and phosphatides, which help keep the oil fresh.

Unfortunately, current methods of processing oil, practiced by most of the industry, differ radically from these techniques. The oil may go through a number of operations. Food technologists admit that "processing may . . . have effect on the nutritional quality of oil, but no serious studies have been devoted to this phase of the problem."[19] It is known that amino acids (especially lysine, methionine, and arginine) are destroyed by the heat used in the processing. The degree of nutritive destruction depends on the severity of the heat.

A LITTLE SOLVENT IN YOUR OIL?

In extraction, the oil-bearing materials are crushed, cooked, and exposed to a light petroleum fraction solvent—commonly found in gasoline—that dissolves the oil. Any residue of the solvent still present in the oil is considered "negligible." But warnings have been given:

> Since various petroleum constituents . . . have produced cancer in man and experimental animals, the presence of such chemicals in foods appears to be objectionable, particularly when such materials are subject to high temperatures.[20]

Food technologists had attempted to use another solvent (ethylene dichloride) as a substitute for flammable petroleum ethers in soybean extraction. This solvent produced a reaction in the proteins, and caused fatal aplastic anemia in calves.[21]

REFINING AND BLEACHING

For consumer acceptance and prolonged shelf life, oil is refined. Regrettably, many Americans associate this word with polite manners or purity in their gasoline. Ignorance of the term, when applied to foodstuffs, is reflected in successful food advertising which boasts of the "purity" of products through refinement.

Refined oil is treated with caustic soda, lye, or other strong alkalis. The oil may be steamed or mixed with water to remove other impurities. Then it is filtered. "Alkali refining . . . removes phosphatides, if not already removed by degumming operation, as well as proteins and protein fragments. A number of minor components of vegetable oils, including sterols, chlorophyll, vitamin E and carotenoids, are affected only to a limited extent by refining."[22]

Then the oil is treated with bleaching earth, fuller's earth, or clay. Again it may be filtered. "Chlorophyll content is effectively reduced by bleaching; carotenoid pigments are effectively absorbed."[23]

After refining and bleaching, vegetable oils have quite an unpleasant flavor and odor. Hence, the oil is deodorized at high temperature. It is stripped with steam distillation, a process that may last for 12 hours, and then cooled. Again it may be filtered. "The contents of sterols, chlorophyll, and vitamin E are lowered only slightly . . . carotenoid pigments are largely destroyed. Deodorization markedly increases the resistance of fats and oils to oxidation. *Even the keeping quality of an oil previously damaged by oxidation can be improved.* If metal scavengers, such as phosphoric, citric, or tartaric acids are added to oils to enhance keeping qualities, they are ordinarily added during deodorization. Lecithin may also be added to improve keeping qualities. True antioxidants are seldom added to vegetable oils, because such additions frequently decrease the resistance to oxidation instead of increasing it. Cottonseed and soybean oils . . . can be made more resistant to oxidation only by adding a powerful antioxidant like propyl gallate." (Emphasis mine.)[24] Remember that the natural antioxidants of the oil have been destroyed!

Some oils undergo further modification. As a convenience for commercial producers of salad oils and mayonnaise, oil may be "winterized." The oil is cooked slowly for a long period, solids are removed, and it is filtered further. This treatment prevents the oil from solidifying when refrigerated.

WHAT IS "LIGHTNESS" OF FLAVOR AND TASTE?

At this point the oil may be bottled and sold as refined vegetable oil, with several antioxidants added. With its long shelf life, such oil is satisfactory to the grocer, but unacceptable to the consumer seeking nutritional value. The oil is a clear, colorless, odorless, bland product. The overprocessing has depleted the oil of whatever individual character it originally had. Advertising writers, stumped by the essential sameness of oils, have had to concentrate on "lightness" of flavor and taste.

Because of this sameness, contamination of one oil by another cannot be detected by flavor. In purchasing a specific oil, the consumer may not be getting 100 per cent of a given kind. Even when oils are processed separately, it is difficult to keep them from contaminating one another. The oil may be extracted in a plant where the crop is grown, but refined at some distant place where several different oils are processed. Usually pressed oils are not refined separately from solvent-extracted ones. At various times the bulk tanks transporting oils contain different kinds. For the person very sensitive to certain foods, this poses a critical problem. For example, an individual highly allergic to corn and corn products may avoid purchasing corn oil. Yet in purchasing another vegetable oil he still runs the risk of exposure to corn, if the oil happens to be contaminated in the handling just described.

WHAT ABOUT OLIVE OIL?

People in other countries still prize and use good oil. In Spain, for example, where huge amounts of olive oil are processed and refined for export, the natives prefer freshly pressed crude oil. Olive oil shipped from Greece is not heated, but our federal laws make it mandatory to pasteurize such oil when it reaches our shores. Dr. E. W. Eckey, an authority in this field, said: "If people would get used to the flavor, many oils would be perfectly edible in the unrefined state, with perhaps a simple filtration."[25]

Olive oil, being one of the most popular vegetable oils, can vary considerably in quality. At one time, the term "virgin oil" meant that the product was from the first pressing of the crop. But modern techniques make this phrase relatively meaningless. "Pure olive oil," which may be a blending of various olive oils, is refined. Italian experts suggested that rigid standards be enforced, since the refining process destroys, removes, or alters vitamins, lecithin, and unsaturates of the more valuable virgin olive oil.

Generally, *genuine* imported virgin olive oil undergoes less modification than most domestic refined oils. Olive oil has the advantage of oxidizing less readily than other oils, although it is more saturated than some. When tinned abroad, the product still comes in honest measures of pints, and other multiples commonly known, thus making it easy for the consumer to compare costs of different brands.

WHAT ABOUT "COLD-PRESSED" OILS?

Cold pressing of oil can be done with the hydraulic and screw-type presses mentioned earlier, but unfortunately the term is misleading when applied to modern methods. At present, the so-called "cold-pressed" oil has been heated. The source material is heated or partially cooked to soften the cell walls so that the expeller, which exerts enormous pressure, can extract the oil efficiently from the seed. The oil is subjected to additional heat, created by this enormous pressure. This generated heat is so great that the meal cake, the material remaining after the oil is extracted, is often quite scorched.

MORE UNHAPPY TRUTHS

There are other aspects of commercial vegetable oils that deserve consumer wariness. Many oil-bearing crops receive extensive pesticidal treatment. Residues, especially concentrated in fatty substances, may contaminate vegetable oils.

Prolonged heating and reheating at high temperatures produce harmful substances suspected as cancer-inciting in oils.[26] Deep-fat frying is favored in many short-order diners and also in good restaurants for economy, speed, and convenience. It is a method also used extensively in processed foods like potato chips, doughnuts, baked goods, and serve-and-heat dishes, as well as in many homes. Consumers' Research recommends that deep-fat frying should be avoided.[27] Also to be shunned are all burned fatty foods and charcoal-broiled meats. All charred, blackened, or burned portions of meats or other fatty foods should be cut off or discarded.

FATS AND OILS, ANYONE?

Choose foods low in saturated fats. These include noncreamed cottage cheese, lean meats, and sea foods (especially cod, flounder, haddock, sole, trout, and sea bass) not breaded, buttered, or fried.

Use cooking methods such as broiling, boiling, baking, roasting, steaming, or poaching. *Consumer Bulletin* suggests broiling with radiated heat, but not with smoke or flame.[28]

Obtain freshly pressed crude vegetable oils, in dark bottles or tins. These products are available for those who seek them. There is a variety of choice, commonly from corn, peanut, olive, safflower, soy, and sesame. Avoid cottonseed oil, for cotton is likely to be sprayed heavily with pesticides. Purchase oil in small quantities, refrigerate, cap tightly after using to exclude air, and use within a reasonable time.

In cooking, learn to substitute oil for saturated fats. Oils can be used successfully for most recipes that list butter, margarine or vegetable shortening as ingredients.*

Seeds (sunflower and pumpkin) and nuts are also good sources of unsaturates. Learn to use them.

Keep intake of *all* fats and oils down to limits now recom-

* For help in adapting recipes, see *The Natural Foods Cookbook* by Beatrice Trum Hunter (Simon and Schuster, 1961).

mended by the medical authorities: about one fourth of the total diet.

Make wise selections from restaurant menus by choosing baked, broiled, or boiled items. Shun fried foods.

Avoid hydrogenated fats by avoiding factory processed foods. Avoid coconut oil, the one liquid oil that is highly saturated. It is used extensively in commercial candies, crackers, and some baked goods because of its superior keeping qualities and other special properties useful to manufacturers. It is also found in "filled milk" and "imitation milk" (see Chapter 10).

Milk:
The Not-So-Perfect Food

WHAT HAS happened to the old-fashioned cow, browsing outdoors in a pasture? Well, it isn't the same creature since scientific dairy farming took over. Its natural ability to produce a yearly supply of milk measuring some hundreds of gallons has been upped into the thousands. Its udder has grown so enormous that it doesn't even look like the Old Bossie many of us knew as children. It gets tranquilizers to keep it from being nervous and to increase its milk flow. It is force-fed on a high-protein diet. These, plus many more innovations, have made it possible for the dairy industry to announce triumphantly that the average yearly milk yield of the New Cow has been increased by more than 2,000 pounds.

Through the years a favorable public image of milk has been developed by aggressive, promotion-minded forces in the dairy industry, and aided by governmental agencies. "Milk is the nearly perfect food" supersedes the older superlative: "Milk is the perfect food." Other slogans include: "Milk, the Magnificent," "Milk, the food for every member of the family," "Drink three glasses of milk every day," and "You never outgrow your need for milk." How good is this much publicized food produced by the New Cow?

CONTAMINANTS IN MILK

Antibiotics, hormones, detergents, viruses, toxins, impurities in the containers, pesticides, and radioactive isotopes are some of the extraneous materials that may find their way into marketed milk, converting it from a food into a potential health hazard.

Penicillin has been described as the least toxic of the antibiotics, but some persons are so sensitive to it that even the sucking of a penicillin-medicated lozenge has caused collapse. Penicillin can cause asthma, gastrointestinal disorders, dermatitis, enlarged glands, swellings, and fever, as well as severe and even fatal shock.[1] For the highly sensitive person, penicillin is hazardous even in exceedingly small proportions of one millionth of the normal medical dose.

Despite potential dangers, penicillin has been used by dairymen since 1945 to treat mastitis, a common inflammation in cows. Residues may contaminate milk and milk products consumed by man.

Strange contradictions exist in the control (or its lack) of antibiotics in the dairy industry. Although physicians urge caution in using antibiotics as medicine for man, dairy farmers depend on them increasingly. Frequently, penicillin is used on cows without the advice of a veterinarian. In 1957, the dairy industry in America was spending $15 to $20 million annually for antibiotics, of which at least 80 per cent was in over-the-counter sales.[2] By 1960, the industry was using 75 tons of antibiotics yearly just for mastitis control. As many as 28,000 international units of penicillin per pint have been found in milk from cows treated for mastitis, or from cows fed penicillin routinely to keep a low bacterial count in the milk.[3]

Pasteurization, high heat, and pressure do not destroy antibiotics in milk; nor is there a legal tolerance for the residue. Nonetheless, various milk surveys by the FDA in 1956[4] and subsequently revealed that small concentrations of penicillin were almost universal. Although some seizures have been made, federal inspectors have no jurisdiction over milk shipped within a state. State standards and quality control vary. Hence, contaminated milk continues to reach markets. The problem became so critical that a ban on the use of antibiotics for mastitis was suggested several years ago by the Joint Conference on Chemical Additives in Foods,[5] although it was not acted upon.

Penicillin preparations used by dairymen bear warnings that milk from treated animals should be discarded, but some farmers have risked possible seizures by selling milk known to be contaminated, rather than suffer economic losses. Some unethical dairymen, faced with the threat of having tainted milk tested, have resorted to subterfuge.[6] When an enzyme (penicillinase) is added to the milk, it fails to show a positive test for penicillin. The enzyme, an illegal additive, can intensify the health hazard. Both contaminants are potential allergens.

Penicillin in milk may not be suspected as the cause of an illness, since human reaction to it may occur as long as 15 days after it is ingested. Even when milk, suspected of contamination, is tested, it may reveal penicillin residue on some days, and not on others. Dairy technologists admit great difficulty in obtaining penicillin-free milk for special testing purposes.[7]

One controversial antibiotic, chloromycetin (or chloramphenicol), is used to treat mastitis in cows, although the Committee on the Use of Antibiotics in Food branded it as a "potentially highly dangerous" residue in milk. This antibiotic was placed in a special category because "it alone among the major antibiotics is capable of exerting a fatal toxic effect when given in normal therapeutic doses."[8] Possible additional hazards have been reported in laboratory experiments. The antibiotic was capable of causing chromosome breakage in human bone-marrow cells in test tube studies, as well as in cultures of human white blood cells (lymphocytes).[9]

Hormones, administered to cows to increase their milk yield, may contaminate the milk. Female hormones, absorbed under the skin of the animal, can pass into its milk in abundant quantities. Milk from cows treated with a female hormone (oestrin) has caused a noticeable "feminization" in males who consumed milk of such origin exclusively.[10]

Detergents have also been known to contaminate milk. In one case, the bacterial count in milk inspected in England was so low that inspectors suspected that a disinfectant had been added. Dairymen denied this suggestion, but upon investigation it was discovered that the milking equipment had been washed with a detergent, and 12 per cent of the milk cans were contaminated with residue.[11] Detergents in milking equipment constitute a problem in the United States as well. Warnings to dairymen are issued about "sanitizer residues" in milk that can "seriously hinder the growth of desirable bacteria used in the preparation of cheese and cultured milks."[12]

On behalf of the petroleum industry, from 1956 to 1959, researchers investigated wax samples taken from milk containers used in different parts of the country. They reported small quantities of a potent acknowledged cancer-producing hydrocarbon (1, 2, 5, 6 dibenzanthracene) present as an impurity in the wax of some samples. Other studies demonstrated that wax, in some degree, went from the container into the milk and cream.[13]

Dr. Hueper, at the time, chief of the Environmental Cancer Section, NCI, stated that in view of this incriminating evidence, it was unwise to use wax-coated containers for food.[14] As a result, many American dairies switched to polyethylene plastic milk cartons. Animal tests, based on repeated subcutaneous injection, were used. As a result, the FDA took no action to prohibit wax in milk cartons. Instead, the agency attempted to establish new "safety" standards for wax, including criteria for its cancer-inciting properties.

Because milk plays a large role in infants' diets, health officials have traditionally maintained that it should contain no pesticidal residue, no matter how minute the quantity. The tolerance was established at zero. But this zero tolerance was an illusion. It was not an absolute zero, but merely a legal one, and authorities took no action if residues were found below what is termed an actionable definition of zero. In the butterfat of milk, as much as .25 ppm, or one fourth of one part insecticide to a million parts of butterfat, was tolerated; .01 ppm in whole milk was tolerated. When amounts were found below these thresholds, no action was taken.

In reality, most milk tested in recent years has contained illegal residues. In 1959 a survey in different areas showed 25 to 62 per cent of all samples contained measurable amounts of residues of those pesticides commonly used in dairy operations.[15] In 1961, almost three quarters of all milk tested in California showed traces of pesticides, but under the legal tests only 28 dairies were actually suspended.[16] In 1963, the FDA admitted that 67 per cent of all milk shipped interstate showed pesticidal residue.[17]

Pressures mounted as the pesticide menace became better known. In 1961 the FDA requested an advisory committee of the National Research Council to evaluate the proposal for tolerances of pesticide residues in milk. The conclusions of the committee, as reported by John L. Harvey of the FDA, "were to firmly and flatly urge that no tolerance for pesticide residues in milk should be established."[18] This sounded like no compromise.

But the FDA failed to support the recommendation. M. R. Stephens, the FDA's director of the Bureau of Enforcement, in addressing a dairy-industry conference the previous year, had said: "If additional research should show that it is possible to set a tolerance for pesticide residues in milk without endangering the public health, the FDA will reconsider its present policy."[19]

A spokesman for the dairy industry admitted that "current and future agricultural practices make it virtually impossible to produce milk and milk products completely free of measurable amounts of DDT and other insecticides."[20] He urged the FDA to set a tolerance of at least 0.1 ppm for residues in milk.

Meanwhile, more sensitive testing techniques had been developed, using gas chromatography, which could detect residues in *parts per billion.* Not only was the testing more sensitive, but it was more rapid, so that many more samples could be tested quickly. This resulted in an awkward situation. With these newer techniques many more cases of pesticide residues were being revealed.

The law had a basic contradiction. The legal determination of "zero" was based on an outmoded test no longer used. With the newer methods, virtually *all* commercial milk could be seized and dumped. In 1966, it was admitted officially that "no milk available on the market today, in any part of the U.S., is free of pesticide residues."[21]

THE MILK SCANDAL

In the spring of 1964, with the consent of the FDA, the District of Columbia Health Department seized pesticide-contaminated milk from dairy farms in the Washington, D.C.–Baltimore milkshed area.[22] Although at first the incident seemed minor, later it was discovered that the FDA had not inspected the milk nor taken direct action. Since many Washington legislators and their families lived in the area involved, the story suddenly took on national significance. A Congressman may view pesticide residue in milk tolerantly when it happens in a state other than his own, but is as outraged as any other citizen when his own family is threatened.

Suspension of the dairymen's permits by the local health department led to newspaper and magazine articles throughout the country. Everywhere the incident shocked dairymen, who recognized the grave implications for themselves and their industry.

The seized milk was contaminated with heptachlor, a widely used, persistent insecticide. It accumulates in the fat of cattle eating contaminated hay or grass, and is excreted in the milk. The insecticide may be stored in the body of a pregnant cow until the following year, and may appear in the milk only after she has calved.

The penalized dairymen claimed that they had used this pesticide according to directions recommended by the USDA. They demanded financial relief from the government. They were angry at being singled out, when the situation was obviously widespread.

PRIVATE PROFIT BEFORE PUBLIC PROTECTION

At this point, the Baltimore testing ended abruptly, with the excuse that the department lacked available time for further tests. There were various attempts to mend fences. Congress authorized subsidies to the dairymen through January 1965,[23] and appropriated $8.8 million to reimburse them. The dairymen would receive payments up to 100 per cent of the value of the contaminated milk. A two-year extension was requested and granted, because the pesticide residue persisted. Then the Pennsylvania Department of Agriculture allowed a dairy to purchase milk showing pesticide residues and to process it into dried milk and cheese.[24] The product would be shipped only within the state, and hence would not come under supervision of the FDA. A few of the farmers supplying this milk for processing were among those whose contaminated milk had been seized in the Washington, D.C.–Baltimore milkshed area. The milk with pesticide residue was blended with "clean" milk until a point was reached where the pesticide residue was considered "insignificant." The milk was no longer considered adulterated! The labeling of the cheese and milk bore no special information for the innocent consumer. In addition, the contaminated milk barred from the whole-milk sales in Washington was reclaimed and used in buttermilk and cottage cheese wherever the producer could satisfy health authorities in his own area.

After the initial seizures, a report was issued in June 1965 by the Pesticide Residues Committee (NAS-NRC), which had been requested once again by the FDA to review a proposal to establish tolerances for pesticide residue in milk. Remember that the recommendation of this Committee in 1961 was "to firmly and flatly urge that no tolerance for pesticide residues in milk should be established." In 1965, the Committee suggested that "no residue" and "zero tolerances" were "scientifically and administratively untenable and should be abandoned."[25] Instead, the Committee recommended that pesticides should be registered either as "negligible residue" or "permissible residue."[26] It should be noted that members of the Committee in 1965 included executives of Merck, Sharp & Dohme, Shell, Atlas Chemical Industries, and others, whose interests would be affected if the FDA were to implement such recommendations.

On the basis of the Pesticide Residues Committee report, the FDA proposed a tolerance of 0.05 ppm for DDT, and its breakdown products DDD and DDE, in milk; 1.25 ppm in butter, cheese, and ice cream; and 2.50 ppm for all three in any one product.[27] Legalizing pesticide residues may be realistic in view of the widespread contamination, but it hardly upholds the traditional image of milk as a pure food.

THE FALLOUT MENACE

Nuclear explosions began in the 1950's, and with them a new, unseen contaminant entered milk. A high percentage of all human exposure to radioactive isotopes of strontium 90, strontium 89, iodine 191, and cesium 137 is associated with dietary sources, especially milk and dairy products.

At first, the problem of fallout in the diet was mainly under the surveillance of the Atomic Energy Commission, with other government agencies participating to a lesser extent. This caused Consumers Union to comment: "It is hard to see why judgment of matters of public health should have to depend primarily on the reports of the very agency charged with the responsibility of manufacturing nuclear weapons, rather than on those of an agency whose specific job is to safeguard the public health."[28]

Consumers Union urged thorough and independent investigations, and ended by launching its own pioneering efforts as a private organization interested in consumer welfare. Starting in 1959, it began to monitor milk, and later made total diet studies,* which have been conducted with the co-operation of home-economics departments at various universities. Milk samples, and later food samples, were taken from 50 different locations throughout the country, and tested for radioactive contamination. This project was the largest study of its kind ever undertaken by any agency, government or private, which seems a sad commentary on the initiative of government agencies responsible for the protection of the public.

Consumers Union reported that the strontium 90 content of milk had been increasing steadily. It soon became apparent that the government policy of monitoring only milk provided a grossly inadequate measure of the total human intake of strontium 90. Milk contributed an average of more than half of the total exposure,[29] leaving the balance unaccounted for. At one point, the government considered the possibilities of decontaminating milk. Experimentally at one pilot plant, up to 98 per cent of the strontium 90 was removed. It was discovered that cesium 137 could also be removed.[30] But neither the government nor the dairy industry attempted to develop the process for widespread commercial production. Costs for industry were estimated at 10 cents per quart, a sum, it was argued, formidable enough to threaten national milk consumption. Later estimates were revised downward to only 9 cents per quart, but the dairy industry still showed no interest in developing decontamination equipment.

Strontium 90 continues to contaminate foodstuffs, and milk remains the dominant source of contamination. Unlike other foods,

---

* Findings were reported in numerous issues of *Consumer Reports*, especially during the period from 1959 through 1962.

milk tends to retain strontium 90. But consumers are urged not to eliminate milk from their diet, since the calcium in milk dilutes the incorporation of strontium 90 into bones. The menace is still here. The presence of any radioactive source becomes perilous in the immediate vicinity of red and white cell formations in the body. While a dilute source, such as that provided by the calcium in milk, may be better than one more concentrated, all sources should be regarded as being extremely hazardous to human health.

THE SKIM-MILK FAD

For years skim milk was fed to hogs and other livestock because it was a by-product of the more profitable fractions of the milk: cream and the butter made from it. When the dairy industry noted that the American public became calorie-conscious and cholesterol-anxious, it responded to changing consumer tastes, and diverted skim milk to this market. The sale of fat-free skim milk began to boom. Soon other skim-milk dairy products were promoted, including cottage and other cheeses, ice milk, and sherbet. The food industry adopted skim milk for bread, cake mixes, frozen foods, meat, and even soup mixes. More recently, the dairy market has capitalized on the 900-calorie craze and the milk-fortified liquid breakfast.

Skim milk must be run through a clarifier and cream separator before pasteurization to remove most of the fat. This lowers its energy value by reducing fat-soluble vitamins A, D, E, and K. Thus, skim milk has all the denaturings of processed fluid milk, with additional losses from fat removal.

The dairy industry welcomes the skim-milk fad, for the separated fat can be processed as whipping cream, coffee cream, and butter or can be used in ice cream, cheese, and other products. Separation increases total milk profits.

NONFAT DRY MILK

Our farm economy, geared to ever higher yields, creates milk surpluses that must be handled. Nonfat dry milk has provided an outlet, and the product seems blessed with that important goal, long shelf life—although this is not actually true.

Two major processes exist for drying milk. Spray drying is *relatively* harmless in destroying food values. The butterfat is removed, and the nonfat portion of the milk is pasteurized and partly evaporated. What remains is blown through nozzles into a vacuum at lower temperatures. These solids may be processed further. Spray drying, when analyzed, shows no destruction of an important amino acid, lysine.

The second process, drum drying (or roller drying), requires excessively high heat. The milk flows over superheated metal surfaces, and the protein pattern of the milk is destroyed. Vitamin C and all other vitamins are reduced. Lysine is impaired drastically or destroyed completely. Experimentally, animals fed drum-dried milk deteriorated rapidly.[31]

Processors of commercial nonfat dry milk do not identify their products as spray-dried or drum-dried. The consumer should demand that this pertinent information be printed on the label.

Other features of nonfat dry milk should be recognized, especially by concerned mothers. Dry milk is an unbalanced food. Although it is used commonly for infant feeding formulas, some professionals consider this inadvisable. The sucrose content in dry milk is many times higher than it is in proportion to other elements in fluid milk. This may adversely affect the calcifying of teeth before they erupt. Another poor feature of dry milk for infant feeding formulas was pointed out by the eminent nutritionist, Dr. Hugh Sinclair of Oxford University. Dry milk is relatively low in essential fatty acids, but high in synthetic vitamin D from "fortification." Dr. Sinclair warned that this combination may lead to the wrong use of calcium in the infant's body.[32]

In 1966, the ubiquitous problem of the disease organism salmonella turned up in dry-milk powder. Contaminated samples were taken off the market.[33] Since salmonella organisms can be fatal to the very young as well as to the old—two groups likely to be large milk consumers—the contamination of dry milk is a serious problem.

The problem is compounded by the fact that dry milk is also used by commercial bakeries and other food processors in large quantities. It is possible for the salmonella infection to spread, indirectly, over wide areas before its source can be detected.

Once a package of dry-milk powder is opened, even a small percentage of moisture can double or triple the bacteria count. Milk powder must be stored in airtight containers, kept cool, and not allowed to become stale.

Using chemical and microbiological tests, a researcher noted nutritional losses and deterioration in dry-milk powder. He warned that "even the seemingly harmless processing methods of the food industry, when drying or dehydrating at higher temperatures and condensing or evaporating at higher temperatures, must be seriously investigated."[34]

Despite such findings, high-heat methods are widely used in experimentation, as the search for long shelf life continues. When experimenters *reheated* pasteurized milk to 195° F. for a fraction of a second, the product had even longer shelf life than usual. Similar experimentation produced milk that kept without refrigeration for six months or longer and was hailed as "the biggest revolution since pasteurization."[35] Eighteen months of milk preservation have been achieved by exposing milk to supersonic sound waves, and then freezing it. This treatment prevents the milk from separating when thawed, and supposedly the milk returns to its original flavor and appearance. At this point, recall what Dr. Harvey Wiley wrote: "Milk which is sterilized at a high temperature, viz., that of boiling water or above, is no longer milk in the true sense of that term."[36]

ABOUT CANNED MILK

The University of Wisconsin has patented a process for making a canned concentrated sterile milk. By removing water, the whole milk is reduced to one third of its original volume. The product is reported to hold its initial physical stability for six months or longer, and its original flavor for four to six weeks without refrigeration. Keeping ability is increased four times as long, with refrigeration. But because the water removed from the milk is taken from the protein molecule, *the protein is denatured.*

Evaporated milk loses half of its vitamin B_6 (pyridoxine) during the heat processing in canning. Babies fed on an evaporated milk formula have developed convulsive seizures until vitamin B_6 was supplied. This was confirmed in experiments with rats.[37] Even its shelf life is more limited than most consumers realize. It must be stored cool, like fresh milk. After two years of storage, analysis showed extensive losses of vitamins A, riboflavin, and E. When it was stored at 100° F. for this period of time, four amino acids were destroyed.[38]

Several additives are permitted in evaporated milk. It may contain one or more of the following: disodium phosphate, sodium citrate, calcium chloride, carrageenan, and/or synthetic vitamin D.[39] Sweetened condensed milk represents the worst debasement of all. It may be sweetened with either refined sugar or refined corn syrup, or a combination of both.[40]

DR. POTTENGER'S 900 CATS—
AND PROCESSED MILK

The full significance of the changes produced in milk as a food were demonstrated dramatically by Dr. Francis M. Pottenger, in his studies of 900 cats. In one phase of the experiment, cats were fed milk as their principal item of diet. Those fed on raw milk reproduced a homogeneous strain and died of old age or injuries from fighting. Some cats fed on raw milk with vitamin D (from cattle fed on irradiated yeast) showed bone changes, including rickets in some young animals. Young male cats did not live beyond the second month, and adult males died within 10 months.

When pasteurized milk was the principal item of diet, supplemented with raw meat, the efficiency of reproduction declined in females. Skeletal changes occurred, and kittens showed deficiencies in their development. Cats fed evaporated milk showed even more damage. However, the most marked deficiencies occurred in the sweetened-condensed-milk-fed cats. Much of the damage was blamed on the excessive carbohydrate.

Later Dr. Pottenger made a similar study of white rats, using different types of milk. The general results duplicated those with the cats. Dr. Pottenger's concluding remarks are important, in the light of what has been presented thus far in this chapter on the effect of heat on milk:

What vital elements were destroyed in the heat processing of the foods fed the cat? The precise factors are not known. Ordinary cooking precipitates proteins, rendering them less easily digested. Probably certain albuminoids and globulins are physiologically destroyed. All tissue enzymes are heat labile and would be materially reduced or destroyed. Vitamin C and some members of the B complex are injured by the process of cooking. Wulzen and Van Wagtendonk have described a thermolabile substance in milk (the Wulzen factor) that may be one of the factors. Minerals are rendered less soluble by altering their physiochemical state. It is possible that the alteration of the physiochemical state of the foods may be all that is necessary to render them imperfect foods for the maintenance of health. *It is our impression that the denaturing of proteins by heat is one factor responsible.*

The principles of growth and development are easily altered by heat and oxidation, which kill living cells at every stage of the life process, from the soil through the plant, and through the animal. Change is not only shown in the immediate generation, *but as a germ plasm injury which manifests itself in subsequent generations of plants and animals.*[41] [Emphasis mine.]

IMITATION MILK

Have you had your imitation milk today, consisting of water, corn syrup, vegetable oil (commonly hydrogenated coconut oil), sodium caseinate (derived from soybean or milk), potassium phosphate, salt, stabilizer, emulsifier, artificial coloring and flavoring, and synthetic vitamins and minerals? This type of drink, now marketed in many states, has enjoyed booming sales and has threatened the market for milk from live cows. "Filled" milk is similar, but it contains some nonfat milk solids.

If processors are successful in having the federal Filled Milk Act and laws in a majority of states either repealed or modified, the market will be flooded with imitation milk and other "dairy" products made with it.

The ersatz-milk producers claim that their product has certain advantages over cow's milk. Flavor stability is easier to control. It has a longer shelf life and is less vulnerable to the action of microorganisms. It meets Jewish dietary laws. But above all, it is cheap to produce.

Price comparisons of dairy versus nondairy substitutes were made in 1968 by Robert F. Holland, head of the food-science department at Cornell University:[42]

dairy product	average price range	nondairy product	average price range
milk	26–27¢ per qt.	imitation milk	19½¢ per qt.
coffee cream	45–49¢ per pt.	nondairy whitener	24–29¢ per pt.
whipping cream	60–65¢ per pt.	synthetic whip	35–39¢ per pt.
butter	79–85¢ per lb.	margarine	22–47¢ per lb.

Imitation milk has been touted as being without the highly saturated butterfat of milk. And so it is. But in filled milk the butterfat may be replaced with *coconut oil, which is also highly saturated.* Coconut oil or hydrogenated fats may be used in nondairy cream substitutes. When analyzed, these products contained a higher percentage of saturated fatty acids than that found in milk fat.[43]

When filled and imitation milks were compared for nutritional values the conclusion drawn was that "they are in no sense a nutritional replacement for milk in proteins, minerals and vitamins."[44] The protein content of filled milk was found to vary from below to above that of natural milk, but the protein of imitation milks, put together from various substances, is lower in efficiency than milk protein.[45] Six nutritional investigators unanimously agreed that "the imitation milks and certain filled milks as formulated today are unsuitable for infants and children . . . from the standpoint of low content of protein, essential amino acids and minerals." These products were also judged to be "potentially harmful for other vulnerable age groups such as pregnant and lactating women, and persons on marginal diets such as those in low-income groups and the aged."[46]

"FACTORY" CREAM AND BUTTER

Although butter is not grouped with the dairy products of "the basic four," it is so closely allied to cream and milk that it will be considered here. Formerly, butter was made on the farm from country-fresh cream. The farmer may have added some salt for preservation, but little else was done when cream was churned into butter. Farm families considered spring and summer butter best, because of its rich yellow color resulting from cows on pasture grazing. If the farm family was dissatisfied with the pale and less flavorsome winter butter, the animal feed could be supplemented with carrots, rutabagas, corn, or clover hay. The word "vitamin" was unknown in those days, but farmers were aware, by eye and tongue, that differences existed in butter quality.

We have learned that the transfer of cows from stable feeding to green fodder can increase the vitamin A in butter as much as 20 times. Green pasturage, added to the cow's rations, contains an unidentified but valuable vitaminlike activator termed "X," which can be increased up to 50 times. This "X" factor plays a vital role in animal and human health.[47]

Today, as butter production has moved from farm to factory, many changes have resulted. Some butter is still made from sweet cream, and is so labeled. Consumers should look for this on the wrapper. However, much butter is produced from stale cream that has soured and has been returned to the creamery to be salvaged. The acidity is neutralized by adding calcium carbonate or sodium bicarbonate or a form of hydroxide, such as calcium, sodium, or magnesium. Hydrogen peroxide may be used as a bleach, and nordihydroguaiaretic acid as an antioxidant. The cream is pasteurized to prolong its shelf life. Off-flavors and aromas which may have developed are often masked by the addition of a "starter." This starter culture not only disguises what would be unacceptable to the consumer's nose and palate, but also retards bacterial defects described as "cheesy, putrid, and surface taint."

After the culture is added, the cream is allowed to "ripen." Then it is churned and may be colored. Dyes from coal tar, as well as vegetables, are permitted in butter. After the public had been exposed for years to certain artificial dyes in butter, long overdue animal tests demonstrated that at least four were cancer-inciting. Belatedly, in 1957, the FDA prohibited their use. At present, however, some coal-tar dyes still permitted (yellow O.B. and yellow A.B.) are suspected of being carcinogens.[48] Until positive proof is presented at some future date, the consuming public is being exposed to unnecessary risks. Although natural dyes such as carotene or annatto, from vegetable sources, can be used, usually the coal tars and the synthetic form of carotene are chosen, because they are cheaper and more uniform.

WHY SALTED BUTTER?

An objectionable amount of salt may be added to retard the growth of yeasts and molds. The salt, in turn, is neutralized by an alkaline salt (sodium carbonate, magnesium oxide, or calcium carbonate). Unsalted butter, which has fewer additives, is a better buy. Its shelf life is shorter than that of salted butter, and therefore it must be handled carefully and sold promptly. Those who still wish to salt their butter can always do so at the table.

BUTTER—HOW FRESH?

The powerful dairy industry has been the *only* food industry legally exempt by Congress from the regulation that makes it mandatory to note on the food label the presence of added color. Thus, the consumer has no means of knowing whether butter (or natural cheeses or ice cream) contain dyes; if they are present, he does not know whether they are natural or artificial. Because of the probable presence of dyes, the consumer is unable to distinguish between summer and winter butter. The time of year the butter is purchased gives no clue, for the "fresh" butter may not have been churned recently. Any coloring of butter, even with harmless dyes, should be considered a deception masking a deficiency.

Rancidity in butter and oils, which destroys fat-soluble vitamins in the digestive tract, is a potential health danger. Special care needs to be taken to insure butter freshness. Much butter reaching the market today is out of cold storage. Since the product is undated, the consumer has no assurance that rancidity has not begun. Now that odors and off-flavors can be disguised artfully, the time-honored tests by nose and palate are no longer reliable guides. Butter that turns rancid during long or improper storage may be salvaged. It is washed, and then impregnated with diacetyl to disguise its aroma.

Proper storage is important in preserving butter's nutrients. Exclusion of air and light and proper refrigeration retard oxidation.

For these reasons, it is wise to purchase well-wrapped butter in preference to tub butter.

Butter quality could be improved without greatly increased production costs. It is estimated that the vitamin A value in butter could be doubled if cows were to be fed legume forage in winter months.

Contaminants in butter and cream are similar to those described in milk. Since pesticides are fat-soluble, a high percentage of their residues may be stored in fat foods. For example, cow's milk containing 2 ppm of DDT may yield butter containing as much as 25 ppm.

SIMULATED BUTTERMILK

Traditionally, buttermilk was a by-product of homemade farm butter. During the churning, when butter began to form, the buttermilk was drawn off through a hole in the bottom of the churn. Unless it was strained, some of the flecks of butterfat remained in the buttermilk. When drunk fresh, it was a nourishing and delicious beverage. Today's commercial buttermilk, however, is completely divorced from the making of butter.

Much commercial buttermilk is made by reclaiming returned stale pasteurized milk. Or it may be made by fermenting skim milk. Whichever milk is used, it is pasteurized. Then a commercial culture is added. The batch is stirred and maintained at a certain temperature so that the milk ferments and develops lactic acid. If the product has been so denatured that it cannot form its own lactic acid, a commercial one may be added. The fermented milk is poured into a churn, *and some extraneous butter is added.* The mass is churned until the butter is broken up into particles to *simulate* real buttermilk. This bottled factory food may be given a "quality approved" rating by the USDA, and legally permitted to be sold as real churned buttermilk.

CHEESES—BLEACHED AND DYED

Cheese, a natural product, results from lactic-acid fermentation. The end product depends on the quality of the original milk, the method of preparing it, types of molds and ferments used to ripen it, and the time and temperature in its aging and storing. Traditionally, enzymes and bacterial cultures were added to milk to develop a particular flavor and character in the cheese. Rennet was used to coagulate the casein into a solid mass, which was processed into a hard cheese. It was never subjected to chemical preservatives that would interfere with the fermentation process.

Today, skim milk, milk enriched with cream or sour milk may be used. Instead of rennet, an acid coagulator, far poorer in calcium, may be introduced. During the processing, salt may be added, as well as calcium chloride to set the milk in a semisolid mass. While none of these features is highly objectionable, there are certain current practices that are not in the best interests of the consumer. Consider bleaching.

Traditionally, Cheddar and Swiss types of cheese have been made from fresh raw milk, carefully handled to keep the bacterial count low. A method was developed and patented by Kraft to make these cheeses from pasteurized milk, exposed to high heat in order to destroy the bacteria. Borden, Swift, and Armour were eager to use the process, but were denied the right. They took legal action, but lost. Cheese production, like any business, is highly competitive. These companies therefore cast about for an alternative. They found it in bleaching.

In June 1959, the National Cheese Institute filed a petition with the FDA to add hydrogen peroxide and catalase (an enzyme) to milk for cheese manufacture—Cheddar, Swiss, and related types. The hydrogen peroxide would destroy bacteria and bleach the cheese. (At the same time it would destroy vitamin A.) The catalase, added later, would remove the hydrogen peroxide.

During hearings Kraft, as well as the State of Wisconsin and the Wisconsin Swiss and Limburger Cheese Producers Association, filed objections. These groups objected to the process, which, they claimed, would lower quality, mask inferior quality, encourage unsanitary handling of milk, and impair the nutritive quality of the product.

Despite these objections, the FDA ruled in favor of bleaches,[49] which are now permitted in many hard natural cheeses. The decision makes a mockery of the pontifical statement contained in the FDA's definitions and standards for cheeses, and other foods, which reads that standards are set so that they "will promote honest and fair dealings in the interest of consumers."

As a result of the ruling, some natural hard cheeses are bleached with benzoyl peroxide, or with benzoyl peroxide mixed with potassium alum, calcium sulfate, and magnesium carbonate.[50] Presumably the consumer is adequately protected by the label, which must contain the information that the milk has been bleached with benzoyl peroxide. When such terms are encountered, is the average consumer well enough informed to interpret the safety or hazards? Also, consumers usually buy small wedges of cheese that have been precut from a large wheel. In such cases, label information becomes inaccessible.

Nor is the consumer adequately informed about dyes permitted in natural cheeses. As stated earlier regarding butter, the dairy interests are the *only* food processors legally exempted from the ruling that added color must be stated on the label. The only admonition from the FDA is that the coloring (or flavoring) added must not conceal damage or inferiority, or make the food appear better or of greater value than it is. How can the consumer determine this? If he does, what recourse does he have?

Blue or green coloring may be added to certain white cheeses to offset the natural yellow color of the milk.

Cheeses *not* colored are cream, Neufchâtel, Gruyère, Roquefort, Limburger, cook cheese (Koch Kaese), and sapsago.

Mold-inhibiting ingredients of sorbic acid, or its salts (potassium or sodium sorbate) or any combination of two or more of these, are permitted in cheese, and are widely used. The presence of these preservatives must be stated on the label. Sorbic acid appears to be less toxic than either salt.

Synthetic vitamin A may be added to certain cheeses (blue, Gorgonzola, Provolone, Parmesan, Romano, and sapsago), since the bleaching process destroys this vitamin.

CONTAMINANTS IN CHEESE

Penicillin residues in milk have caused trouble in cheesemaking, since the antibiotic inhibits the starter cultures. Because of this, some factories have been forced to discontinue cheese and yogurt production. The Microbiological Section of the Canadian Food and Drug Directorate reported: "Where penicillin or other antibiotics are used with dairy cattle the survival of resistant organisms may lead to widespread distribution of resistant strains into the homes of the general populace, since *staphylococci* and *streptococci,* often in large numbers, are of common occurrence in cheese."[51] Another antibiotic is widely used in cheese production to suppress the growth of certain bacteria. Not considered a preservative, it can be used legally.

Cheese rinds may be coated with wax or vegetable oil, which may penetrate into the cheese. Many samples of Edam and Gouda, with their bright red wax, offer visible proof of the migration of dye into the cheese.

As with milk and butter, cheese may be contaminated with pesticide residues. *Legally,* the residue of pesticide in cheese is zero. But as a *practical* matter, residues are permitted. In 1965 the FDA requested a permissible tolerance of 1.25 ppm in cheese. Scientists decided it was "absolutely safe" to allow 0.3 ppm, but even this amount has been exceeded. Contamination is an ever-increasing problem.

This was demonstrated in 1963. The FDA seized cheese, produced in Utah and shipped to California, which contained a pesticide exceeding the permissible tolerance for residue.[52] The cheese company refused to withhold its contaminated product and announced that it intended to continue sales. Further seizures were made by the FDA as well as by state authorities. Subsequent samplings continued to show contamination. Both the cheese company and the Utah Department of Agriculture requested newspapers in the Salt Lake City area not to publicize the seizures because "a newspaper story would cause considerable panic among the consuming public in the state." Despite consent to this agreement, one newspaper leaked the story and stated that the FDA had "headed off a disastrous blow to the Utah cheese industry."[53] Unable to locate sources of uncontaminated milk for its products, the cheese company closed. The dairymen who had supplied the milk were advised that their milk was unacceptable. The Utah Department of Agriculture and the affected farmers requested a moratorium that would allow the contaminated milk and cheese to be acceptable until new forage could be obtained to replace the contaminated forage, which was the source of the trouble. The FDA denied the request, but the USDA appropriated monthly payments to affected dairymen in Utah and elsewhere to cushion a serious setback both to the economy and the well-being of the people.[54]

Large amounts of imported cheeses have also been seized because of excessive amounts of pesticide residue. In 1969 nearly two million pounds of imported cheeses were impounded because of contamination. According to the inspectors, it was a "whopping" increase over previous years.[55]

COTTAGE CHEESE—WHOLESOME AND PALATABLE?

Cottage cheese, a food frequently used by the dieter, invalid, convalescent, and low-budgeter, as well as by the general public, should be of especially high quality. It is an unaged cheese made by coagulating whey. Cream or a creaming mixture may also be added.

Cottage cheese is almost as highly perishable as milk or cream, yet it is seldom subjected to the extensive inspections or controls more commonly applied to them. Since it is usually a local product, it may not be subjected to the federal standard of identity. Although the USDA grades it with a "Quality Approved Shield," such grading is voluntary, and graded cottage cheese is not readily found by the label-conscious consumer. Nor is the product likely to be dated.

A survey released in 1960 by Kansas State University revealed overhigh bacterial counts with slime and mold on the surface of the cheese. Off-flavors such as "bitter," "fruity," and "yeasty" tastes were found in many samples. The researchers concluded that there was "serious need for manufacturers of cottage cheese to pay more attention to details in the manufacturing process to insure the consumer that the composition of the cheese conforms to legal standards and that the cheese is wholesome and palatable."[56]

The reasons for this poor quality in cottage cheese can be ascribed to the lowering of standards by the industry. Sodium hypochlorite may be used in washing the curds, which finishes the process far more quickly than the traditional bacterial one. Diacetyl may be added as a butter flavor. Objectionable amounts of salt may also be added. Annatto or cochineal may be used as dyes, and hydrogen peroxide as a preservative.

In 1960 at a meeting of the American Cottage Cheese Institute, members supported a recommendation for amending the federal standards to permit the inclusion of stabilizers and mold inhibitors: stabilizers for smooth texture, uniform color, flavor, and thickness (heretofore achieved by using good-quality raw materials and careful production), and mold inhibitors for longer shelf life.[57] Both additives are economic short cuts for industry, but not necessarily in the consumer's interest, for they can mask poor quality and staleness.

Processors of starch and adhesive products petitioned, and the FDA later proposed calcium sulfate as a stabilizing ingredient in cottage cheese.[58]

Opposition was voiced by consumer groups, who pointed out that calcium sulfate, related to plaster of Paris, has no nutritive value, and is a material of questionable safety in food. It was described as a material that "hardens quickly after absorbing moisture, and its ingestion may result in obstruction, particularly at the pylorus," and "surgical relief may be necessary."[59]

The FDA answered the objection by explaining that calcium sulfate is not plaster of Paris, and that the dehydrated form does not take up water and harden. Both materials have the same chemical name. Despite this explanation, the FDA failed to comment on the more important point raised, namely the possibility of hazards in the use of the material. Because an objection was filed, consideration of the proposal was extended, but ultimately approved. Calcium sulfate is permitted in cottage cheese. Mold retarders of sorbic acid, or its salts, are also permitted.

SURVEY—DISMAL DISCOVERIES

The deterioration of quality in cottage cheese has continued. Alarming facts, going far beyond the Kansas State University study of 1960, were revealed in 1964. Consumers Union made an in-depth study of cottage cheese in a large single market area, Philadelphia. This indicated the general trend elsewhere. They found overacidity, probably due to poor processing, and flavor defects of bitterness, yeastiness, fermented taste, and rancidity, caused, it was believed, by heavy microbiological growth. There were dangerously high counts of coliform bacteria, yeasts, molds, and other micro-organisms that grow well during long storage at refrigerator temperatures. These contaminations indicated laxity in production and distribution, with a breakdown of sanitary controls of ingredients or manufacturing equipment, improper refrigeration, and overlong storage or careless handling.

Brand names proved no guide to sanitary quality. At least one sample of every brand had objectionably high microbial counts. Investigators felt that the entire industry was badly in need of reform. Many samples failed to meet the composition require-ments of the federal standards of identity, and some were judged mislabeled. Findings revealed not only poor quality, but potential health hazards.[60]

PROCESSED CHEESES: "PLASTIC MASS"

"One of the major atrocities of this age is the disappearance of natural cheese and the substitution for it of what is called process cheese, made by grinding cheese of very low quality or any quantity that happens to be available and mixing in chemicals as emulsifiers," wrote F. J. Schlink, of Consumers' Research, as early as 1935.[61]

Three decades later, the situation has not been improved: "Process cheeses are the TV dinners of the cheese world," wrote Vivienne Marquis and Patricia Haskell in *The Cheese Book*. "Kept in the arrested state in which they reach the consumer, they can easily survive him, and sometimes do. They belong to the present, and equally to the past and future, because time has stopped for them."[62]

Processed cheese is described in the federal definitions and standards as "prepared by comminuting [grinding up] and mixing with the aid of heat, one or more cheeses of the same or two or more varieties . . . with an emulsifying agent . . . into a homog-enous plastic mass. One or more of the optional ingredients . . . may be used."[63] What this description fails to note is that different grades of cheese, both green and cured, may be used. Whereas enzymes make natural cheeses mature slowly, the processed ones are made quickly by heat, and then aerated to increase their volume. The end products have undergone such modifications that they scarcely deserve classification as food.

REMEMBER WHEN ICE CREAM WAS ICE CREAM?

Once, ice cream was a special treat, often made on the back porch in a home freezer, with quantities of fresh fruit and thick country cream. Remember how it tasted?

Sadly, the ice cream you take home from the supermarket freezer will probably be a synthetic ghost of the old-fashioned one. It has become a victim of large-scale factory techniques. The story is a depressing one, of deterioration, adulteration, misrepresentation, inadequate safeguards, and a lack of federal standards, grading, or controls.

WHAT'S IN THAT ICE-CREAM CARTON?

Under the 1938 amendment to the Food, Drug, and Cosmetic Act, ice-cream makers (and 10 other food groups) were granted official freedom from labeling restrictions. This exemption was granted "for a reasonable time" of two years to allow the FDA to establish definitions and standards. When this time proved insufficient, the FDA announced that no "formal extension" was granted but enforcement on label rules would be withheld. During a long interim, more than 20 years, the ice-cream manufacturers could ignore label rules with impunity. Finally, in June 1960 standards were issued, and amended in 1964. As they stand now, the standards virtually *exempt* ice cream from informative labeling that would be of value to the consumer. The only items that must appear on the package include the name of the food (ice cream), with flavor identification; if artificial flavoring has been used, this must be stated.[64] *This is all that needs to be printed.* Such inadequacies do not bear out the late President Kennedy's recommendation to Congress: "Consumers have a right to expect that packages will carry reliable and readily usable information about their contents."

It is not necessary for the ice-cream manufacturer to list all ingredients, yet there is a wide choice of about 60 now permitted in this product. As someone expressed it, "The consumer has no basis for choice; *he* takes his chances."[65]

In reading the list of permissible dairy products in ice cream the consumer may wonder if ice cream has become a convenient dumping ground for practically every product devised by the dairy industry. Instead of the traditional sweet cream and sweet milk which went into ice cream, the optional dairy ingredients, as amended in 1964, now include[66] cream, dried cream, plastic cream (sometimes known as concentrated milk fat), butter, butter oil, milk, concentrated milk, evaporated milk, sweetened condensed milk, superheated condensed milk, dried milk, skim milk, concentrated skim milk, evaporated skim milk, condensed skim milk, sweetened condensed skim milk, sweetened condensed part-skim milk, nonfat dry milk, sweet cream buttermilk, condensed sweet cream buttermilk, dried sweet cream buttermilk, skim milk that has been concentrated and from which part of the lactose has been removed by crystallization, skim milk in concentrated dried form that has been modified by treating the concentrated skim milk with calcium hydroxide and disodium phosphate, concentrated cheese whey, and dried cheese whey. The bulk of the low-priced ice cream may contain as much air as it does ice cream. This is achieved by the use of cheap thickeners, beaten into the ice-cream mixture to increase its volume, and allow it to remain in an unmelted state after serving.[67] Gelatine or gum, used for this purpose, may favor germ growth in a mixture that is already a dangerous culture medium for bacteria.

ICE CREAM—A DUMPING GROUND?

The dairy interests proposed additional by-products for inclusion in the standards. Their proposals were rejected. They had wanted to include a partially "delactosed" milk product, as well as soured skim milk treated with a neutralizer. Caseinates of milk were also proposed, which would have involved considerable manipulation of skim milk, treating it with alkalizing reagents and then working out excessive alkali.

Although some dairy products were rejected, the strange case of whey remains to make the consumer question whose interests the FDA has at heart. During the 1960 hearings, cheese whey was proposed as a component in ice cream but rejected as "inferior in some respects" to other dairy products used in ice cream. The FDA stated: "There is no evidence . . . that would indicate that the consumer would expect ice cream . . . to contain even limited amounts of this byproduct from cheese-making in substitution for the customary ingredients."[68] Its use was prohibited. By December 1964, with revised standards, however, the FDA reversed its former position. Concentrated cheese whey and dried cheese whey were added to the list of optional dairy ingredients. Where is the logic? Since no declaration of whey is necessary on the ice-cream label, the same unsuspecting consumer described by the FDA in 1960 still has no indication now that whey is being substituted "for customary ingredients." Although whey is an acceptable nutritious food component, it scarcely substitutes for cream in ice cream.

SOME SHODDY PRACTICES REVEALED

During the 1960 hearings, considerable testimony became indirect admissions of many long-standing uncontrolled, shoddy commercial practices.

"The usual household practice of preparing ice cream is to prepare it from sweet cream or a mixture of sweet milk and sweet cream. However, a large proportion of commercially prepared ice cream is prepared from various dairy products, *with or without water, so combined that in composition the mixture closely resembles cream or a mixture of cream and milk.*"[69] (Emphasis mine.)

A whole range of additives had gradually entered the scene, including antioxidants, neutralizers, buffers, bactericides, stabilizers, and emulsifiers. Formerly eggs, milk protein, fat lecithin, and other natural substances like gelatin, agar-agar, or seaweeds were used as emulsifiers and stabilizers, but these have been replaced gradually with cheaper ingredients by many manufacturers. Testimony at the hearings continued: "It is possible to increase the property referred to as smoothness by the judicious use of nonfat milk solids and some stabilizing and emulsifying agents and by heat treatment of the milk before freezing."[70]

Stabilizers also help to hold the air incorporated into the ice-cream mix, and "produce a smoothness suggestive of richness."[71] (The hazards of certain stabilizers have been discussed in Chapter 4.)

In 1942, when hearings were held on frozen dessert standards, three chemicals (two emulsifiers and one stabilizer) were considered for inclusion but rejected because the FDA judged that their safety had not been established. By 1960, the FDA authorized their use *in separate food-additive regulations,* but they were not named in the official definition and standard of identity. The emulsifiers were the notorious polyoxyethylenes (described in Chapter 4), which have been labeled as potentially cancer-inciting materials. The third was propylene glycol alginate, not named in the standards, but allowed in "standardized" ice cream. In 1942, reports had been submitted on this material, which had been used in germicides and antifreeze substances and as a paint remover. In experimental tests with this stabilizer, some rats developed diarrhea and others fed on the lowest levels soon died. No attempts were made to find the causes of the diarrhea or deaths, but the chemical was rejected as a stabilizer for ice cream.

However, by the time of the 1960 hearings, the FDA reversed its former position, claiming that reliable conclusions could not be made from earlier experiments. Possibly additional information had been filed by the manufacturers *in confidential petitions* that convinced the FDA that the material was safe. The consumer, however, had no way of obtaining this information. Conceivably, new information might justify change in a ruling. The lack of access was deplored in *Consumer Bulletin:*

> It is beyond our comprehension that materials considered so doubtful a few years ago as not to be permitted in ice cream at all should now be thought so unexceptionable that they may be used without even mentioning their presence on the label and without revealing in official publications all the facts upon which the FDA decided on their safety.[72]

Sodium carboxymethylcellulose, still another substance which has been labeled as potentially cancer-inciting (described in Chapter 4), was also allowed in the new standards.

OTHER QUESTIONABLE INGREDIENTS— OFFICIALLY SANCTIONED

At this point, the reader may feel that ice cream, under present federal standards, is a pig in a poke. The fact that it contains still other officially sanctioned but questionable ingredients will not be very reassuring. These are the sweeteners, flavorings, and colorings.

Formerly, sugar was the common sweetening agent in ice cream. Today, although some permissible sweeteners may be considered acceptable, others can only be viewed as cheap substitutes that lower quality. Refiner's syrup is one. It has been described as "the last liquid product of the refinery [which] has such a salty taste and such a peculiar flavor, acquired during the process of manufacture, as to be practically inedible."[73] This product was proposed for ice cream. The FDA approved, reporting: "There was no evidence that any designation of a kind of ice cream has ever contained a reference to refiner's syrup, but there is no reason to conclude that refiner's syrup cannot be used in a special type of ice cream without jeopardizing the consumer's interests."[74] Other permissible sweeteners included glucose, related products, and cheap adulterants that are health menaces. (They are discussed in Chapter 14.)

Artificial flavors are largely replacing the natural ones in ice cream. The FDA expressed its viewpoint on this:

> When so used that they do not create a misleading impression as to the presence of a natural ingredient or the amount of a natural ingredient present, artificial food flavorings are suitable ingredients of ice cream. Consumers quite generally prefer natural over artificial flavorings and desire to know when artificial flavorings are present in ice cream. *To the extent that accurate information can be conveyed to consumers by labeling on ice cream, label statements of the use of artificial flavorings are in the consumer's interest.*[75] [Emphasis mine.]

If you, the consumer, were provided with accurate information regarding the artificial flavors likely to be present in ice cream, would you buy the ice cream?

The true vanilla bean, or an extract of it, are both expensive. Yet, as any cook knows, the amount of vanilla required for flavor is so small that it is difficult to understand why such an item needs to be cheapened. The answer is found in the *Merck Index*. One part of vanillin, the synthetic substitute, equals 400 parts vanilla pods; two and a half to three parts of vanillin replace 500 parts of vanilla extract. Other synthetics also replace real vanilla, notably vanildene ketone and piperonal, a well-known louse killer.

Chocolate is another popular flavoring. Chocolate ice cream, when artificially flavored, may contain very little cocoa flavoring extract, but it will have amylphenyl acetate, vanillin, aldehyde C_{18}, veratraldehyde, n-butylphenyl ethylacetal, and propylene glycol.[76]

Strawberry ice cream is also a favorite. If it happens to be artificially flavored rather than made with real strawberries, it may have Corps Praline, alcohol, propylene glycol, glacial acetic acid, aldehyde C_{16}, benzyl acetate, vanillin, methyl cinnamate, methyl anthranilate, methyl heptine carbonate, methyl salicylate, ionine beta, aldehyde C_{14}, diacetyl, and anethol.[77]

Similarly, highly complex formulations are made for imitation flavors of banana, cherry, pineapple, black walnut, and a host of others that go into ice cream and other foodstuffs.

THE INADEQUATE LABEL THAT MISINFORMS

Label information on ice cream is not only inadequate but misleading. You, the label-conscious shopper, in reading the words "artificial flavor" may assume that artificial color has not been used. This is a wrong assumption. Although the ice-cream producer *must* declare the presence of an artificial flavor on the label of his product, he has no obligation to declare the presence of an artificial color.

Furthermore, you may assume that artificial flavor is the *only* additive used in the ice cream, since it is the only one listed on the label. In reality, many other additives may be present, but not declared on the label.

The artificial colors used in ice cream are the dyes, already discussed in Chapter 4, about which there is no universal agreement concerning safety. To achieve a yellow color in ice cream, a producer may use tartrazine or sunset yellow FCF; for orange,

orange I; for red, amaranth, ponceau 2R, Carmoisine, or Lissamine Red 6B; and for blue, Indogotine.[78] Technical materials sent to manufacturers usually bear warning words: *"CAUTION:* consult latest government regulations before using this dye in foods, drugs and cosmetics"—underscoring the need for considering these materials as being far from innocuous.

DAIRY PRODUCTS, ANYONE?

If you wish to use dry nonfat skim milk, write to the producer of the brand of your choice and ask if the milk has been spray- or roller-dried. At the same time, suggest that this information be printed on the label as a consumer service.

Choose well-wrapped unsalted butter.

Try to find natural cheeses produced by cheese makers who still take pride in quality production. These products are properly aged, without artificial colors or other objectionable additives. Some are made without salt.

If you cannot locate a source for fresh cottage cheese of good quality you may wish to try making your own. Directions will be found in Home & Garden Bulletin No. 129, USDA, "Making Cottage Cheese at Home." (Supt. of Documents, U.S. Government Printing Office, Washington, D.C. 20402, 5 cents.)

Demand informative ingredient labeling on ice cream. Until this is achieved in your area, plan to make your own, using simple, natural ingredients. Occasionally there is a heartening sign, such as this full-page advertisement that appeared in the *Milwaukee Journal:*

"At last! *OLD FASHIONED WISCONSIN ICE CREAM.* Remember how good old-fashioned ice cream used to taste? Rich! Creamy! Smooth! Heavy! . . . With real fruits and the very best ingredients? Now you can enjoy it again!"

This was followed by a listing of ingredients:

"The finest fresh fruits; pure vanilla beans; extra high-grade chocolate; fancy premium nuts—freshly roasted; and the richest, freshest cream in the land."

Those who subscribe to the belief that milk and dairy products—even those of good quality—should not be consumed, especially by adults, may find some reassurance in the fact that the Eskimos, the Maori, the Australian aboriginals, and other groups of people whose traditional diets did not include dairy products nevertheless maintained themselves in good health.

11

Produce: The Chemical Tomato—and Others

AT A Congressional hearing, Representative Morgan R. Moulder commented: "The tomatoes you buy in the grocery store, or chain stores, or other stores . . . they may look pretty, but they are the most tasteless, mushy, worthless product I have ever seen in a grocery store. I wonder if the Department [of Agriculture] has any jurisdiction over that? And are these worthless tomatoes the result of chemicals being used in their production on the farms that the chain grocery stores themselves operate, produce, and sell to the consumer?"[1]

M. R. Clarkson, associate administrator at the USDA's Agricultural Research Service, answered: "No sir, it is the result, first of the selection of certain varieties in the hands of the grower and the person to whom he supplies his material. Secondly, in the producing of fruits and vegetables of a perishable nature for the intricate channels of commerce today, they are oftentimes picked at an early stage of their development and do not carry the same flavor as though they had been freshly picked off the vine just before they are eaten."[2]

Representative Moulder added: "I have searched for them in the summertime and wintertime, and they are always wrapped in the same fancy cellophane packaging, and you go to all the stores and they are all just alike in any season regardless of when they

255

are picked, synthetic and tasteless . . . There are many other vegetables and products sold to stores that have the same so-called quality . . . there are many . . . that I have looked for, and I have searched very carefully, and they certainly are not what they used to be."[3]

Just as animal husbandmen have devised means of increasing yields of milk, livestock, poultry, and eggs at the expense of quality, so too have fruit and vegetable growers been following a similar pattern. Not only are tomatoes "synthetic and tasteless" as Moulder charged, but as the late columnist Robert Ruark put it: "Our fruit has attained that delicious arsenic flavor . . . the leathery lettuce has probably come to stay," and, "they make strawberries out of some kind of colored plastic. They're big as apples but they taste like cardboard."[4] A panel about to award prizes to fruit and vegetable entries at a Royal Horticultural Society exhibit in England was instructed to judge the produce for its *edible* qualities. The jurors were cautioned that in the past prizes had been given to a "cucumber which tasted like turpentine, carrots . . . like soap, and peas with beautiful plump pods but which tasted of nothing at all."[5]

Many factors combine to produce fruits and vegetables that may be beautiful to behold but insipid to taste. These include the choice of variety, farm management, preparation for market, handling in transit, and extension of shelf life. The sophisticated consumer has been conditioned to expect certain produce year round, rather than in the season when it reaches its normal peak of goodness. Markets that offer exotic produce grown at distant places emphasize the uniformity of size and color instead of taste, and perfection in appearance instead of tolerance for nature's occasional blemish. This great variety of produce has been achieved at the expense of flavor, nutrition, and safety.

WHY WORRY ABOUT FARM MANAGEMENT?

Health and well-being—or disease and illness? The difference may lie in the gardens and fields where your fruits and vegetables are grown. So it is important for you, the consumer, to know something about the methods of farm management responsible for the garden and orchard produce that pours into the food market year round.

Crop farming, like all other areas of agriculture, has been invaded by factorylike automation. The selection of the crop variety may be determined by such factors as what will ship well or store longest. Of the hundreds of varieties of succulent apples developed through the years, few reach the market today. Where are the Belle Flower, Harrison, Sheep Nose, Fall Pippin, Red Astrachan, Canfield, Gravenstein, and Russet, just to name a few from yesteryear? Despite many varieties of crisp, savory garden lettuce developed by seed companies, the shopper is usually resigned to the wilted iceberg lettuce found in supermarkets throughout the land. Similar limitations exist with many other fruits and vegetables.

Automation on the farm may determine the selection of crop varieties. Machine harvesting, directly in the fields, requires crops with toughness and durability. Thus, the fine flavors associated with tender varieties are often ignored; those chosen are ones that can withstand the rigors of being shaken, pulled, and hauled without bruising. A pear-shaped tomato, for example, was especially developed because it was adapted to the needs of the harvesting machine. A square tomato is being bred to reduce shipping damage.[6] Scarcity and high cost of labor for hand-picking may force more and more crops to be machine-harvested. The USDA admits that "unless machinery is designed to harvest the crops economically many fruits could disappear from the marketplace."[7] At the same time, machine harvesting has created other problems. Since it is not selective, it picks green along with ripe tomatoes. A considerable percentage of the unripe tomatoes are salvaged by gassing them with ethylene to hasten their "ripening." This treatment is permitted officially by the USDA.[8]

FERTILE SOIL—FLAVORSOME CROPS

Traditionally, any farmer knew the importance of suitable soil for growing flavorsome crops. This, in turn, is partly dependent on soil fertility, either maintained or restored with well-composted organic matter. The chemical industry has perpetrated a myth that organic matter is in short supply. The facts do not confirm this. It is true that in former years the mainstay of organic matter was barnyard manure. Although the tractor has largely replaced the horse and ox, our supply of organic matter has not decreased. On the contrary, it has increased. The diversity of modern industry provides us, more than ever before, with materials for soil enrichment. We fail to utilize many of them. Instead, many valuable materials are wasted in the town dump, which, in turn despoils the landscape; or burned, polluting the air; or spewed into waterways, contaminating streams.

These materials could be salvaged and converted into valuable soil amendments providing nutrients and flavor to crops. Conversion of these materials is not highly lucrative, compared with the sale of chemical fertilizers.

THE NPK MENTALITY

The application of chemical fertilizers, notably NPK (nitrogen, phosphorus, and potash), has given produce quick, lush growth— but poor flavor. But there are far more serious problems, not yet adequately appreciated, created by the long-range use of these materials.

NPK can increase crop output at relatively low cost and with little effort. In emergency situations, such as an impending famine, these materials can produce immediate results. But when used for a lengthy period, they unbalance the soil, lower the nutritive quality of foods, and produce hazards.

Over the years, for instance, Kansas corn, fertilized with NPK, increased substantially in yield but deteriorated in quality. Its valuable protein declined (by as much as 22 per cent) while its carbohydrate content rose. Kansas wheat suffered a similar loss. Whereas in 1940 the protein in wheat had ranged from 10 to nearly 19 per cent, by 1949 it had dropped to a range of from 9 to less than 15 per cent.[9] Such protein losses shortchange the consumer. Increases in carbohydrate, at the expense of protein, are nutritionally undesirable and constitute a health hazard.

A distinguished agronomist, Dr. William Albrecht, who has studied this problem, has this to say about soil:

Man has become aware of increased need for health preservation, interpreted as a technical need for more hospitals, drugs, and doctors, when it may simply be a matter of failing to recognize the basic truth in the old adage which reminded us that to be well fed is to be healthy. Unfortunately, we have not seen the changes man has wrought in his soil community in terms of food quality for health, as economics and technologies have emphasized its quantity. Man is exploiting the earth that feeds him much as a parasite multiplies until it kills its host. Slowly the reserves of the soil for the support of man's nutrition are being exhausted. All too few of us have yet seen the soil community as the foundation in terms of nutrition of the entire biotic pyramid of which man, at the top, occupies the most hazardous place.[10]

Along with the decline of protein, the subtle balance of amino acids is disturbed within the protein molecule. This succeeds in lowering the *quality* as well as the quantity of the protein.

Quality protein can only result when all the essential and probably semiessential amino acids are present in optimal ratios to each other. Then the body can use the materials efficiently to repair old tissue and form new. Nonessential amino acids must be present in sufficient quantity to prevent any of the essential ones— of which there are ten—from being diverted from their tissue-building function. Protein balance is upset even if one essential amino acid is absent. Present-day foods generally have unbalanced patterns of amino acids.[11] To compensate for this partial deficiency and imbalance, an excess of protein is consumed. This is not a satisfactory substitute for an adequately balanced amino-acid pattern. It wastes protein—often the most costly item in the diet. In addition, there is evidence that increasing the total protein of the diet steps up the need for each essential amino acid.

Ironically, protein is declining in quality at the very time when world food problems force us to be aware of the need for quality. Many of the world's malnourished exist mainly on proteins of plant origin, which are lacking in one or more essential amino acids. We can no longer think of rescuing a famished world merely in terms of a quantitative increase in food production on a caloric basis. *Even with a high daily intake of calories, if quality protein is lacking, starvation can still triumph.*

The problem of the protein-carbohydrate ratio in our foods is only one of many imbalances created by the long-time use of chemical fertilizers. Another, to date largely ignored, concerns the mutagenic effect of imbalanced elements. Shortages or excesses of fertilizers were shown to produce extensive chromosome injury in plants. High concentrations of nitrogen were particularly damaging, causing erosion and breakage of chromosomes.[12]

Plant nutrition requires far more than the mere blending of three major elements. At least 13 major elements are considered essential for normal plant growth and development; many additional trace elements also play vital roles. Nutrients in the soil antagonize or stimulate each other. Heavy application of one element can upset the balance. The level of one cannot be changed without influencing the others. Such imbalances are felt directly by the consumer. For example, it was shown that excessive nitrogen used in growing celeriac produced overlarge, hollow tubers; in wet years especially, the vegetable was susceptible to rust and rot during winter storage.[13] Similarly, the keeping qualities of the potato, cabbage, winter radish, apple, and strawberry were poor when excessive nitrogen was used.[14] The strawberry became soft and lost its typical aroma, and the tomato lost flavor.[15]

DEFICIENCIES CAN AFFECT YOUR HEALTH

When crops are overfertilized with phosphorus, a zinc deficiency may result; potash fertilizers may lead to boron deficiency. Excessive potash treatment decreases valuable nutrients in foods, such as ascorbic acid, carotene, chlorophyll, and total acids. Overliming, by making the soil too alkaline, may reduce the availability of many vital trace elements to plants. This, in turn, affects nutritional quality and flavor.

Proper balance of the soil results in health-giving foods; soils deficient in certain minerals modify or disturb the cell metabolism, resulting in disease. This has been especially true of deficiencies in trace elements such as copper, zinc, calcium, or magnesium.[16] Some investigators suggest that the control and prevention of many degenerative diseases rightly begins with a better understanding of nutrition, starting with the study of the soil and its treatment and cultivation.*

* A few leading exponents of this belief are Professor William A. Albrecht, *Soil Fertility in Its Broader Implications*. Extension Bulletin 66. Durham:

Continuous applications of NPK have other drawbacks. These materials do not enrich the soil with organic materials that decompose to form humus. On the contrary, the accelerated plant growth induced by chemical fertilizers has the effect of speeding up the rate at which humus is exhausted. Our soils have continued to be depleted of humus at a faster rate than organic matter has been replaced. As this depletion proceeds, plant pests—both noxious insects and diseases—attack the crops.

NITRATE POISONING

"Modern chemical agriculture can honestly claim only two notable crops—disease and pests," noted a soil scientist.[17] We can now add a third: poison. Nitrate poisoning is a long-range problem. We have only begun to appreciate its enormity and complexity. Truly, we have opened a Pandora's box.

Ever since chemical fertilizers have been in use, the nitrates have been especially popular because they boost crop yields. After World War II the sale of nitrate fertilizers soared, far exceeding that of potash or phosphate fertilizers. By 1961 there was a sevenfold increase over the 1940 to 1944 sale of nitrates.

When nitrate fertilizers are used on cultivated fields, the surface runoff water may seep into farm wells and ponds. Many of these have had to be abandoned for both human and animal use owing to their high levels of nitrate.

Under some conditions, nitrate is transformed into highly toxic nitrite. A large amount has been responsible for sudden death in livestock. In lesser quantity, it interferes with the animals' utilization of feed; livestock may suffer from subclinical poisoning, resulting, for example, in a lower milk yield from cows.

All plants need nitrogen for growth. But when oversupplied, they may develop watery tissue and be susceptible to disease. The range is narrow between too little nitrogen and too much. Natural

General Extension Service, University of New Hampshire, June 1944; Sir Albert Howard, *An Agricultural Testament*. New York: Oxford University Press, 1943; Weston A. Price, D.D.S., *Nutrition & Physical Degeneration*. Los Angeles: American Academy of Applied Nutrition, 1950 (5th printing); and André Voisin, *Soil, Grass and Cancer*. New York: Philosophical Library, 1960.

nitrogen compounds found in the soil, in the air, in rich compost, in ripened manure, and in leguminous crop residues do not create this problem. The nitrogen supplied by these sources is released slowly, and is long-lasting and beneficial. The effects are entirely different from those of the readily soluble, quick-acting chemical nitrate fertilizer.

NITRATE POISONING MAY AFFECT YOU

Canners are faced with a problem of internal can corrosion caused by certain foods, especially tomatoes and sweet potatoes. Excessive amounts of nitrate in these vegetables are suspected as the prime culprit.[18]

Excessive nitrate accumulates in the leaves and stems of plants. Commercially grown vegetables frequently contain excessive amounts of nitrate.[19] For example, unbalanced nitrogen fertilizing increases the oxalic acid in spinach. Even a slight increase in the nitrate content in the sap of plants may lead to iron chlorosis, a metabolic disorder of plants caused by a nutritional deficiency.

Although healthy people excrete excesses of nitrates, these materials place an undue burden on the body, especially in the ill. Under certain conditions the bacteria that live in the intestinal tract can convert nitrate to nitrite, resulting in harmful effects on the body. Nitrite, reaching the blood, can tie up hemoglobin in a form that destroys its ability to carry oxygen from the lungs to the tissues. In large amounts, nitrite can result in respiratory failure and death.

Increasing numbers of cases of fatal infant cyanosis have been traced to excessive nitrate in water. The intestinal flora of the infant, as compared with the adult, is far more apt to include types of bacteria which convert nitrate to nitrite.

There is growing concern over the effect of the increased nitrate content of foods, especially for infants. A recent study at the Missouri Agricultural Experiment Station showed that commercial baby food contained as much as 0.8 per cent nitrate nitrogen (as dry weight). At this rate, an infant fed a two-ounce jar of baby food could receive as much as 40 milligrams of nitrogen as nitrate. Public-health officials recommend no more than 12 milligrams of nitrate nitrogen daily for infants. *Presently, some infants' diets exceed these upper recommended nitrate limits.*[20]

Is there a solution? There are reasonable alternatives that can still produce safe crops with good yields. One university reported:

Natural nitrates have something that the artificial lacks, and there is no completely adequate substitute for them in the field of agricultural fertilizers. Chilean [natural] nitrates contain small amounts of vital impurities, such as magnesium, iodine, boron, calcium, potassium, lithium and strontium, which are to plants what the vitamins in fresh foods are to human beings. It has been found that natural nitrate does something that makes apples stay on trees; that it does something to corn that results in better livestock fattened on it; that chickens raised on nitrated feed lay better eggs of greater fertility. It is . . . impossible to make artificial nitrates that duplicate natural nitrates.[21]

FEAR OF PUBLIC PESTICIDE PANIC

Fruit and vegetable crops are subjected to many insecticides and weedicides. The FDA has set official tolerance levels for specific produce. Public concern about pesticide residues in foods prompted the FDA to launch "market basket studies" to determine the extent of the problem. The method used by the FDA has been criticized as unscientific, and the selected menus as unrealistic. Devised tests understating the problem prompted the *Wall Street Journal* to comment that "there's more pesticide in our foods than Uncle Sam's random sampling methods might disclose."[22]

The high tolerances of pesticide residues permitted on American produce exclude many of them as imports into some European countries.[23] Action was taken to minimize these economic losses and to quell public concern at home. In 1968, at the suggestion of the President's Science Advisory Committee for Control of Persistent Pesticides in the Environment, the FDA and the USDA jointly proposed a reduction of maximum residues allowed on fruits and vegetables. In some instances, as in the case of DDT, the proposed cutback was up to 50 per cent.[24]

Despite official assurances regarding "safety," the consumer remains inadequately protected. Frequently seizures are made of foodstuffs with pesticide residue exceeding the tolerances. By its own admission, the FDA can give only token surveillance to all foodstuffs transported interstate. Within any state, the situation may be worse.

For the concerned consumer who wonders if these chemicals can be removed by washing, rinsing, or peeling, unfortunately the answer is "no." The nature of the problem is described by Dr. O. W. Grussendorf, Research Station, Canada Department of Agriculture:

> The housewife cannot play around with hexane to wash lettuce, cabbage, spinach, cauliflower, etc. Hexane is our chief stripping solvent, followed by acetonitrile; these solvents are too dangerous even to consider them as "food cleansers." Moreover, the residues are mainly in the entire system of the plant, hence of the food product. We must distinguish somewhat between "deposits" on the surface and "residues" in the sense of contamination; both are "residues" in the sense of contamination, and are objectionable per se. The chemicals are intimately interwoven in the structure of the plant. The insecticide can be entirely intra-cellular, and nothing of it can be found on the surface of the plant.[25]

PLANT-GROWTH REGULATORS—
"BIOLOGICAL DYNAMITE"

Some 42 growth-regulating chemicals are now approved by the USDA for more than 100 different uses in crop production, and it is predicted that more are on the way. Root crops such as potatoes and onions may be treated to prevent sprouting. A chemical sprayed on the leaves of these crops several weeks before harvesting is absorbed by the foliage, travels down the stem to the edible portion, and prevents further cell division within the tuber or bulb. Such treated produce can be kept from sprouting for as long as a year, leading the consumer to believe that a treated old crop is new. Aside from the deception, the decline in food value should be of concern. The ascorbic-acid content of potatoes freshly dug may range from 50 milligrams to 100 grams; after storage for a period of many months, this may drop to less than 10 milligrams.[26]

In addition to these unfavorable factors, there is a far graver problem. These antisprouting materials stop cell division and are capable of producing mutations in the genes.[27] *This hazard is biological dynamite.* Sprout inhibitors have been condemned as potential cancer-inciters.[28] Early tests with maleic hydrazide, one of the inhibitors commonly used on potatoes, onions, and tobacco, showed that this chemical produced an unusually high incidence of local malignant growths in three out of 52 rats, with none in control rats.[29] In 1967 tests, cancer researchers found that 55 milligrams of this chemical injected into mice produced numerous live tumors. In extrapolating these findings for man, the annual total exposures, on potatoes, onions, and tobacco, was estimated at about 630 milligrams, which would be over 11 times as great as the dose found to be carcinogenic in the mice. There may be certain protective factors in man, such as quick elimination of this chemical, that might conceivably buffer the effects on the body. But "the risks are the results of the ubiquity" of the chemical, and the "progressive exposure of entire populations," noted the researchers. "It would thus seem appropriate to reduce tolerance levels of maleic hydrazide or ban its use, except when human exposure can be minimized."[30]

Further evidence against maleic hydrazide as an adjunct to agriculture was presented in 1969. Dr. Samuel S. Epstein, a researcher at the Children's Cancer Research Foundation in Boston, reported a method of detecting potential chemical hazards. Test materials were injected into newborn mice during their first three weeks of life and checked a year later to see if tumors had developed. It was found that maleic hydrazide caused liver tumors. Dr. Epstein stated that over a period of twenty years human beings ingest enough of this material from potatoes alone to approximate the dose given to the newborn mice.[31]

Other warning signals about sprout inhibitors have been raised, but ignored. Pigs fed on potatoes treated with a sprout inhibitor failed to reproduce. Another unanticipated and freakish result was experienced by two Connecticut potato farmers. Having used an approved sprout-inhibiting chemical on their crop, they discovered much to their horror that the material caused the sprouts to grow inside the potatoes. This resulted in crop losses of nearly $150,-000.[32]

You can examine purchased onions to determine whether or not they have been treated with a sprout inhibitor. Cut an onion crosswise at either end. Long before the sprout actually emerges, the color of the sprout in an untreated onion will become yellow or green at the top of the bulb. It will also develop dark spots around the future root growth at the bottom of the bulb. Treated onions remain light in color.[33]

Other types of growth regulators increase the size of the produce. For the last century the size of the produce, as a criterion of quality, has dominated the technical journals. At horticultural shows and agricultural fairs, the prize-winning squash, cabbage, apple, and so forth usually have been mammoth. Today there is still admiration for the size of produce, even though it may have an inverse relationship to flavor. For example, large peas are usually less tender and sweet than small ones. Within the same planting, smaller heads of cabbage may have higher contents of valuable elements. Nevertheless, size continues to be stressed. Hormonal material such as gibberellin is used to produce larger grapes; beta-naphthoxyacetic acid to yield bigger strawberries. These growth regulators may adversely affect quality. Grape consumption in California was reported falling sharply because of the flatness in flavor. This was attributed to too many unripe grapes and too many that were artificially enlarged by treatment with gibberellic acid, which plumps up grapes 20 to 60 per cent above their normal size.[34]

Herbicides, which also affect plant hormones, are widely used to control weeds among food crops. Additional hormones are used as sprays to retard the ripening of fruit or to keep it on the vine or tree longer, facilitating economical harvesting. Such tampering with basic processes may create hazards far beyond our present comprehension. The case of one weed-killer serves as an example.

After World War II many herbicides that had been tested and developed for biological-warfare use were marketed for civilian purposes and used by farmers and homeowners for killing weeds and controlling brush. One of them, 2,4,5-T, had been sanctioned for civilian use by three federal agencies: the USDA, the FDA, and the U.S. Fish and Wildlife Service. It has been widely used by the federal government as a defoliant in Vietnam. A State Department report, made public in March 1966, gave firm assurance that "the herbicides used are non-toxic and not dangerous to man or animal life. The land is not affected for future use."[35]

Concerned biologists began to raise questions regarding the long-range ecological effects of herbicides, as well as their possible direct hazards to life. In sections of southeast Asia where massive amounts of defoliants have been used by the Department of Defense, there has been grave disruption of life. Rubber plantations have been damaged, as well as farm and garden crops. Such crop destruction is especially deplorable in an area where people already suffer extensively from endemic malnutrition.

By the late 1960's various reports were disturbing to concerned scientists. In 1968 a group of investigators reported that 2,4,5-T had been found to cause widespread chromosomal defects in plants.[36] In December 1969, the World Health Organization released a report dated Nov. 21, 1969, that defoliants, used in huge quantities in Vietnam, are possible causes of birth defects in children.[37]

In the late 1960's the National Cancer Institute had begun a series of investigative studies of some two hundred compounds, mainly pesticides, to determine whether these materials induce cancer-causing changes, fetus-deforming changes, or mutation-causing changes in experimental animals. As part of this study, a contract was given to the Bionetic Research Laboratory in Bethesda, Md., to study the possible carcinogenic properties of a number of compounds. Among them was 2,4,5-T. Laboratory studies there showed that mice and rats given relatively high oral doses of 2,4,5-T in early stages of pregnancy "showed a higher than expected number of deformities" in their offspring. The report noted that after administration of 2,4,5-T, with the exception of very small subcutaneous dosages, "all dosages, routes, and strains resulted in increased incidence of abnormal fetuses." These abnormalities included lack of eyes, faulty eyes, cystic kidneys, cleft palates, and enlarged livers. On the basis of these results, in October 1969, the USDA curbed civilian use of 2,4,5-T effective January 1, 1970, although use of this defoliant was permitted to be continued by the U.S. military.[38]

It has been suggested that the fetus-deforming effects of this herbicide may not be from the defoliant itself, but from dioxin, a common contaminant in 2,4,5-T. If this is so, further grave questions are raised. Under high heat, dioxin can be produced in a group of chemical substances that include certain fatty acids used in detergents and animal feed. Studies had been made of the deaths of millions of young chicks after they had eaten certain kinds of chicken feed. Government scientists now speculate about the possibility that those deaths may have been the end of a chain that began with the spraying of corn crops with 2,4,5-T. The theory is that possible residues of dioxin, present in the 2,4,5-T, remained in the harvested corn, and were concentrated in certain by-products that were then sold to the manufacturers of chicken feed. In turn, the dioxin was absorbed into the systems of the young chicks.[39]

2,4-D, a commonly used herbicide, is a close chemical relative of 2,4,5-T. Dr. Samuel S. Epstein told the Senate Subcommittee on Energy, Resources and the Environment in April 1970 that potent dioxin contaminants have been associated with 2,4-D as well as with its chemical relative. To date, federal restraint applies only to 2,4,5-T, although 2,4-D is used far more extensively on food crops.

"TO MARKET, TO MARKET"—QUICKLY

Because of long shipping distances, much produce is picked unripe. As a result, neither maximum flavor nor full nutritional content develops. The folly of this procedure is typified by the picking of unripe oranges.

According to L. P. De Wolf, a veteran citrus grower:

> Citrus fruit cannot be artificially ripened. If it is picked green and immature, it will remain immature until it rots, regardless of the kind of treatment to which it may be subjected. It does not have to be picked green in order to be shipped to market in good condition. Neither does it have to be picked as soon as it ripens. It will remain on the tree in good condition for several weeks, and even months, and then it can be picked and sent to market in good condition. *In fact, it deteriorates more quickly when it is picked green than when it is allowed to remain on the tree until it gets ripe.*[40] [Emphasis mine.]

The consumer may wonder, then, why citrus fruit is picked so early. It is a repetition of the old story: the shipper wants to get to the market for a quick profit. Although not all produce may hold, ship, and store as well as oranges, there are many other foodstuffs which could be allowed to mature on the tree, bush, or vine.

ARTIFICIAL RIPENING

The vine-ripened tomato is vastly different from the insipid product that comes packaged, four or five in a cellophane-wrapped box. The former may have a high vitamin C content as well as fine flavor. The latter may appear red but taste green. Its appearance of ripeness may be an illusion. One technique is to soak the tomatoes in a brine through which sulphur dioxide has been bubbled for five days. They can be kept undamaged for an additional month in fresh water. Tomatoes have been kept "fresh" with this method for as long as four years. Appearance of ripeness in the tomato can also be achieved by means of artificial hormones.

The papaya, if forced, never develops the full flavor or sweetness of the naturally ripened fruit. Honeydew melon can either be ambrosial or flat-tasting. A gas, which develops naturally within the melon, triggers a ripening process while on the vine; this occurs only a few weeks after the melon has reached its full size. Picked prematurely, the ripening process never takes place. Green unripe fruit, such as banana, orange, lemon, cantaloupe, persimmon, and pear, may be exposed to ethylene gas to produce "fresh ripe fruit," a fraudulent phrase. This practice allows growers to extend their marketing season.

PHENOLS—"POISONOUS AND CAUSTIC!"

Produce shipped long distances may be treated with chemical preservatives applied either directly on the raw commodity or indirectly by treating the shipping container or impregnating the wrapper. Toxic materials may be incorporated in the paper or packing boxes to prevent rotting. Toxic phenols (such as biphenyl and 2-4-dichlorophenoxyacetate) are also used.

Phenols are capable of causing destruction of the chromosomes, and can lead to genetic mutations.[41] Sodium-o-phenylphenate can cause death, if as little as one and a half grams are ingested. Among other effects, it can cause nausea, vomiting, circulatory collapse, paralysis, convulsions, coma, and necrosis of the mouth and the gastrointestinal tract, as well as death from respiratory failure.

Dr. Werner Schuphan, a scientist, said that it is unknown whether phenolic treatment of produce damages the biological value of the fruit, directly or indirectly. Investigations pointing to its harmlessness on produce have not been convincing. Testing has been limited to the action of *isolated* biphenyl, *not in combination with the produce*.[42]

In the late 1950's, the FDA made it mandatory to declare the presence of these preservatives. George P. Larrick, Commissioner of the FDA at that time, said that "the consumer has a right to know whether a preservative is added to food and what it is."[43]

As a result, a 4¾ × 2¾-inch card was required to be displayed near the treated produce at the time of the retail sale. The innocuous-sounding phrase TO MAINTAIN FRESHNESS at the top in bold letters seemed to give cheer rather than warning to the consumer. The chemicals, however, were listed in much smaller type. Was the average homemaker aware of the hazardous nature of these chemicals? Certainly there was no official educational program to enlighten her. Not only was the sign inconspicuous, but frequently, in violation of the ruling, it was not displayed.

Growers and chain-store and supermarket operators, all fearing adverse effects on sales from this requirement, began to pressure the FDA.[44] The agency eased the regulation.[45] The card displayed alongside the treated citrus fruit was no longer required to name the specific chemical or chemicals used. Even this accommodation did not fully satisfy industry.

Various trade groups pressured Congress to exempt *all* fresh fruit from the requirement. By 1960, the short-lived attempt to warn the consumer, weak as it was, ended. The original act was amended by Congress, at the request of industry organizations, so that "no declaration shall be required while such commodity (produce) having been removed from the shipping container, is being held or displayed for sale at retail out of such container in accordance with the custom of the trade."[46]

WITH DIPHENYL, PEEL UNSUITABLE FOR CONSUMP-TION must be stamped on U.S. citrus fruit shipped to some

European countries, such as Germany and Italy.[47] Thus, the consumer abroad is given more warning than those at home about phenolic treatment. The residual odor of these phenols is sufficiently strong to be smelled on the treated produce, as well as in the containers.

A fungicide, DPA (diphenylamine) is widely used to treat wrapping paper used on apples and pears. Although it was cleared by the FDA on the basis of some animal experiments, the British Ministry of Health remains unconvinced of its safety.

MINERAL OIL—ALSO QUESTIONABLE

Mineral oil is another "protective" coating used for certain produce. It has been used to impregnate wrappers on fruits, such as pears and apples. Since 1964, it has been permitted directly on raw fruits and vegetables.[48] The wisdom of this regulation should be challenged, in view of the FDA's repeated warnings of the dangers of ingesting mineral oil. Since 1938 it has been forbidden as a coating on produce in Germany. Dr. W. C. Hueper has identified mineral oil as a possible cancer-inciter.[49]

Physicians at Johns Hopkins Hospital estimated the yearly consumption of mineral oil in food at nearly 50 grams per person, in addition to what is taken as medicine. Mineral oil droplets showed up in the lymph nodes and other tissues of about 78 per cent of the persons examined in the hospital study. The physicians engaged in this study suggested that this high percentage may account for a high rate of mysterious tissue injuries.[50]

WAX—MORE PROBLEMS

Waxing, a technique that can disguise the lack of freshness in old produce, is more likely to be found on fruits and vegetables shipped long distances than on produce locally grown. The wax heightens the luster, prevents shriveling, and gives easily bruised produce some surface lubrication that prevents chafing.

The thick coating of wax can be felt and seen readily on a cucumber or rutabaga, but it may not be apparent on many other treated items. Wax may coat, among other produce, carrot, orange, lemon, lime, apple, pear, plum, peach, melon, parsnip, eggplant, summer squash, potato, tomato, green pepper, or strawberry. Though the wax can be removed along with the thick skin of some items, particles of wax stick to cut surfaces of produce. Even after peeling, residue may still be present.[51] Also, how can wax be removed satisfactorily from a tomato, green pepper, or strawberry? Nutritionists have stressed the importance of using the great concentration of nutrients in some produce just below the skin surface. Why should the consumer be forced to discard valuable elements? Washing does not remove wax. Applied just before shipment of produce, it may cover and entrap whatever residues of pesticide, dye, or gas remain on the food. Although wax has been cited as a potential carcinogen,[52] the widespread practice of waxing fruit and vegetables continues to have official sanction.

MORE TECHNIQUES OF KEEPING PRODUCE "FRESH"

Prior to shipment, lemons may be washed in chemicals to retard decay. Carrots with tops cut off may be subjected to enzyme-inhibiting chemicals, to prevent further leaf growth. Frequently, fruit is washed in detergent baths for cleaning. Any of these materials may be present on the produce as residue. How adequate are the safeguards?

Official approval has permitted the use of antibiotics on seeds, vine, and plant beds before the edible fruits and vegetables appear.[53] Official approval has not yet been granted for direct antibiotic treatment on produce, but food technologists, looking toward future possibilities, have been engaged in experimentation.[54]

"PAINTED HUMBUG!"

The story of "color-added" oranges epitomizes the manipulation of foods for profits. They are colored to boost sales through "improved appearance," the resulting nutritional losses and hazards being quietly ignored.

An official of the USDA once stated that the treatment given the unripe oranges simply unmasks the ripe color that nature, if given some weeks more in which to do its work for consumers, would have put upon the oranges. To which Senator Royal S. Copeland snapped back: "Painted humbug!"[55]

For years, the Florida and Texas citrus industry was allowed to use a coal-tar dye (Red No. 32) to mask the greenness of the fruit. Industry spokesmen insisted that the practice was necessary for consumer acceptance. Ultimately, long overdue tests revealed the danger of the dye.[56] The material was delisted,[57] with a lenient provision that the citrus industry could temporarily continue its use until a substitute could be found. In 1959, Red No. 2 was substituted. This material, still in use, was *not* given a clean bill of health, but described as "less toxic" than Red No. 32.

Industry was given another period of grace, during which it was advised to seek a harmless alternative. Instead, the industry lobbied. As a result, the citrus industry has repeatedly been granted liberal extensions of time. Artificially colored oranges continue to be sold to the American consumer, but are banned as imports in Canada, Great Britain, and elsewhere. In March 1964, the British Food Standards Committee recommended that all coloring of citrus fruit be prohibited.

To date, toxicity studies on Red No. 2 are few, and not reassuring. Rats fed this dye metabolized it in their bodies and excreted a substance (1-amino-2-naphthol) suspected as a carcinogen. When implanted in the bladders of mice, the metabolite produced cancer.[58]

The consumer may feel that there is no particular danger in using color-added oranges, since the thick skin of the fruit can be removed and discarded. But there are factors to consider. In addition to the deception of making the fruit appear other than what it really is, what about the shortchanging of nutritional values? Orange peel has been found valuable in controlling diarrhea in babies.[59] Some consumers use orange skins for marmalade, candied rind, or flavoring. Many children like to eat oranges cut in half or quartered. What assurance do we have that they are not ingesting dye? A boy in Florida died after peeling an orange with his teeth; his death was attributed to the dye. How many more cases have there been, which have not been traced to the offending dyed rind?

Furthermore, the coloring of oranges is not just a simple procedure of exposing them to the dye. Objectionable preliminary
processings destroy much of the original value and flavor of the
fruit. This is well described by L. P. De Wolf, the experienced
citrus grower previously cited:

> No color can be added to a green-skinned orange. First it has to be
> "degreened." This is done in what is known as the "coloring room,"
> where it is shut up air-tight and then doused with a gas. The gas now
> universally used is ethylene gas [which can cause asphyxiation]. This
> gas destroys or removes the chlorophyll from the rind and leaves it,
> according to the degree of greenness, all the way from a sickly or
> lemon color to almost white. I have seen them come out of the
> coloring room looking almost like peeled potatoes.
> While it is being gassed, the fruit is subjected to artificial heat and
> is sometimes held in this room for three or four days. It impairs its
> flavor and has a tendency to hasten its deterioration and decay. After
> coming out of the coloring room the fruit is washed and then run
> through the "color-added" machine—that is, if they want it to have
> any extra color. The color is added by passing the fruit through a vat
> of hot dye or else spraying it on hot while the fruit is subjected to
> steam heat.
> Practically all of the Florida citrus that goes to market through
> regular commercial channels before the first of the year is artificially
> colored. It should be borne in mind that maturity laws are laws of
> nature and are not affected by court decisions or acts of the legisla-
> ture. Florida's so-called Maturity laws are not really Maturity laws at
> all, but just plain Green Fruit laws designed for the specific purpose
> of providing a legitimate means of shipping green immature fruit to
> the market under false pretenses.[60]

The consumer should learn how to choose. The appearance of
an orange has little or no relationship to flavor. Greenish- or
brownish-skinned oranges, even with external blemishes, may be
ripe, more palatable and sweeter than the brightly colored ones.
This has been the experience of persons who order directly from
Florida groves, and receive tree-ripened citrus fruit, grown without poisonous sprays, and not subjected to gassing, waxing, dyeing, or even washing.

The Economic Research Service of the USDA made a survey in
a large city of the orange-buying habits of consumers. The artifi-

cially colored oranges sold twice as fast as their naturally colored counterparts in a nearby display. It would not require great expenditures, either on the part of the USDA or the citrus industry, to re-educate the public, rather than perpetuate fraud and hazard.

MORE DECEPTION

Last year's white potatoes may be dyed red to make them appear like "new" potatoes. The FDA's Bureau of Education and Voluntary Compliance admitted:

> We have considered the possibility that such colored potatoes might be deceptive and therefore illegal, but we have not encountered an instance where we felt we had evidence to establish in court that the colored potatoes were, in fact, deceptive. To prove this we would need clear-cut proof that potatoes of a lower quality were dyed and sold as of a higher quality, or a lower priced white potato, after being dyed was sold at a high price as a red variety of potato.
>
> Although we sympathize with those who object to the penetration of the color into the flesh of the potato, the law contains no provisions which would permit us to outlaw the dyeing of potatoes solely for that reason.
>
> Certainly, however, the consumer has the right to know when the potatoes are colored. Under the law, not only must the bags of potatoes be labeled to show that they are colored, but when sold in bulk in the retail store, a sign calling attention to the presence of added color should be displayed.[61]

How many consumers see potatoes displayed in the original shipping container? How many see a placard in the potato bin stating that the potatoes are dyed? This regulation appears to be honored in the breach, and contains loopholes that permit deception.

For years the skins of sweet potatoes have been dyed artificially. The heightened color makes them appear like more expensive yams. This deceptive practice had been banned in Canada. The FDA finally ruled in June 1968 that "artificially red-dyed yellow varieties of sweet potatoes would be deemed adulterated," and their interstate shipment would be banned.[62]

SULPHUR DIOXIDE IN YOUR FOOD—
NO UPPER LIMIT SET!

It is commonplace to find dried fruits with the warning label
PREPARED WITH SULPHUR DIOXIDE, and they are rarely
found unsulphured, except through special sources. Nor is there any
educational campaign to inform consumers. Sulphured fruits, being brighter, plumper, moister, and "fresher" looking, are foisted
upon consumers, as are the deceptively bright oranges and
potatoes.

The practice of exposing fruits to the poisonous fumes of
sulphur was investigated by Dr. Wiley during the early days of the
Pure Food and Drug Act. He demonstrated that sulphur dioxide
harmed the body, destroyed the fine flavor of dried fruit, and
furthermore, was unnecessary. His assistant, Dr. W. D. Bigelow,
developed a practical method of dipping fruit into a harmless,
weak saline solution whereby the color and flavor were retained.[63]

Wiley proposed a regulation which would have banned the use
of sulphur dioxide. A storm of protests from fruit packers followed. They took advantage of Wiley's temporary absence in
Europe to exert pressure. As a result, the regulation was killed.[64]

Bigelow's work, "Experiments Looking to Substitutes for Sulphur Dioxides in Drying Fruits," was submitted in 1907, but
denied publication by the U.S. Department of Agriculture.[65] Since
that crucial reversal, sulphur dioxide has been permitted on dried
fruits, as well as many other processed foodstuffs, including
molasses and candied citrus peel and in fruit marmalade. It is
used to keep commercially prepared fresh foods from browning.
For example, slices of potatoes, intended for French frying in
restaurants, may be dipped in a solution of sulphur dioxide; or
slices of fresh apple, apricot, or peach may receive similar treatment. It prevents browning of fruits just before commercial freezing. Fresh asparagus may be blanched in it. Commercially stored
dehydrated fruits and vegetables may be treated with sulphur
dioxide. Fresh peaches, apricots, and nectarines may be dusted
with sulphur as a fungicide, and sulphur dioxide is used as a
fumigant for many grains. Certain dry wines and fruit juices are

processed with it. The whole kernels of corn may be soaked in a sulphur-dioxide solution for processing; in turn, this imparts sulphur to many manufactured corn products, including cornstarch, corn flour, corn sugar (dextrose and glucose), corn oil and corn dried dextrins. It is also used in the processing of cane and beet sugar. In addition, sulphur dioxide has become a major air pollutant. Thus, it can be readily seen that exposure to this poisonous material is compounded.

In 1911, the USDA instructed a group of "scientific experts" to investigate sulphur dioxide. The report, never published, found that a portion of from three tenths of a gram (the equivalent to be found in from six to eight ounces of dried fruit) up to one gram daily gave rise in some individuals, over a period of months, to signs of injury. The symptoms included an increase in uric acid, a destruction of corpuscles in the blood, belching of sulphur-dioxide gas, teeth on edge, inflammation of the mucous membrane of the mouth, symptoms of malaise, headache, backache, sick appearance, nausea, albumin in the urine, sensation of cold, anemia, dull eyes, and a listless manner.[66]

Despite these findings, the use of sulphur dioxide continued to be sanctioned. No limit was set on the amount of sulphur dioxide that could be used in drying fruits. The amount was left to the discretion of the fruit processors. Amounts found were several times that which originally had been considered a "safe" maximum, already set generously high to accommodate industry.

In 1929, an official of the USDA testified before Congress:

> Technology had developed, and it has gone, we believe, entirely too far. It has gone so far that the American dried fruit is now in very considerable disfavor abroad. In fact, England, France, Germany and Switzerland have placed partial embargoes on American dried fruits because of the excessive sulphur content. Japan has intimated that a complete embargo will be placed on American dried fruit. [We believe that] this enzyme [the cause of the darkening] can be controlled in other ways than by the use of sulphur dioxide. If we can do that, it means the salvation of the whole dried fruit industry and particularly . . . where sulphur is so largely used.[67]

At the time of this plea, by a USDA official, the Bigelow report remained interred within the same government agency.

WHAT DOES SULPHUR DIOXIDE DO TO FOOD?

Although little, if any, of the free sulphur dioxide may remain in foodstuffs, their biological patterns have been altered, with a destruction of at least part of the valuable B complex: thiamin. In addition, sulphur dioxide has been used to conceal inferiority of fruit. During the Congressional hearings on chemicals in foods, Vincent A. Kleinfeld, chief counsel for the government, produced information indicating that the dark pigmentation of rot spots in fruits such as maraschino cherries can be bleached out with sulphur dioxide. After this treatment, the color of the rotten portion cannot be distinguished from the sound.[68]

Frequently "scientific research" is cited to vindicate the use of sulphur dioxide on dried fruits. A study was made in California, a state which leads in the sulphuring practice. The research showed that sulphured fruit contained a higher vitamin C content than dried fruit without bleach or preservative. What the report failed to note was that vitamin C, present in the raw dried fruit fed to laboratory animals, was lost in the cooked dried fruit consumed by man. Yet the cooking is necessary to eliminate a portion of the sulphur dioxide. One of the findings in the report is not usually quoted. *A slight chalkiness and brittleness of the cutting teeth was observed as an abnormality in the animals fed the sulphured fruit.*[69]

Only certain portions of this report have been quoted. For example, an article appeared in a leading medical journal assuring physicians that sulphured fruits are not harmful.[70] Such a misstatement is important, for dried fruits are a favorite food for invalids and those on hospital diets. The limit of residue tolerance was wrongly cited in the article as only a tenth of the actual amount used in commercial practice. The excessive amount was admitted officially to be neither legal nor regulated.

Although at present sulphur dioxide as a preservative in dried fruits comes under the jurisdiction of the Federal Food, Drug, and Cosmetic Act, *the FDA has never established upper limits for its use.* Despite its toxic nature, sulphur dioxide is regarded by this agency as an additive "generally recognized as safe." When questioned, the FDA supplied the following information: "In order to contain enough sulphur dioxide to be unsafe, a food would first become so distasteful as to be inedible, so its use is self-limiting. However, the regulations specify that sulphur dioxide shall not be used in a food recognized as a source of vitamin B_1."[71]

This position is arbitrary as well as unscientific. "Self-limiting" is a fatuous criterion for the use of sulphur dioxide or any other chemicals in food. Additives should not be allowed in quantities up to the limit of consumer tolerance. *The point of harmfulness and toxicity may be reached at a far lower level than that which affronts the tongue or nose.*

RAISINS AND PRUNES GO MODERN

Although "sun-dried" raisins and prunes are still commonly available, even these dried fruits are no longer the simple unsophisticated foods they once were. They may be dried on pesticide-treated drying trays to reduce insect-control costs.[72] Even the added raisin-seed oil is flavored artificially with a preservative, which in turn contains five ingredients. The "golden" raisins are bleached. To achieve their light color, both the fat- and water-soluble vitamins are destroyed.

The consumer pays for water at fruit prices by purchasing "tenderized" prunes, or "hydrated" dates. In addition, sorbic acid may be added as a preservative.

METHYL BROMIDE—
ANOTHER POISONOUS FUMIGANT

Methyl bromide, another hazardous chemical, is used to fumigate dates. Although the FDA claims that methyl bromide goes out of the food, this assurance is based on outmoded tests. Methyl bromide is characterized as "only slightly soluble in water," and dates may retain some fumigant even after being washed. Such chemical treatment usually causes some modification of the food product, as well as contamination.

Dr. Theron G. Randolph, an allergist, has found that highly sensitive patients show allergic reactions to dates fumigated with methyl bromide, but no adverse reaction to unfumigated dates grown in the same grove. This physician suggests that the commonly experienced laxative action of dates is *not* from the fruit, but from the residue of the fumigant.[73]

Continuous exposure to low concentrations of methyl bromide is especially dangerous. The material is injurious to all forms of animal life. Yet this fumigant is used not only on dates, but with many other foods, including dehydrated vegetables, flour, feeds, nutmeats, beans, peas, spices, chestnuts, macaroni products, chocolate, and dairy products.

Adequate industrial safeguards for workers handling methyl bromide were instituted only after several hundred date packers were poisoned, some very seriously. Two, made temporarily insane by the poison, were confined to an asylum.[74]

Methods exist for drying fruits satisfactorily without resorting to hazardous materials. Safe substitutes should be mandatory, to safeguard workers and consumers, and the poisons should be prohibited.

The FDA has begun to express long-overdue concern about the total intake of bromide from foods and other sources. R. E. Duggan, assistant director for science, Bureau of Regulatory Compliance, the FDA, wrote: "Bromide values exceeding 25 ppm in any composite warrant further investigation." But bromide tolerances ranging from 25 to 400 ppm are established for many foods. The FDA arranged composite samples of 82 food products likely to be purchased by the average consumer, and tested mixtures of five or six of them. Duggan admitted: "If any mix has 25 ppm bromide, then one or more of the foods in the mix might have a rather high residue."[75]

HOW GOOD ARE FROZEN FRUITS AND VEGETABLES?

Modern techniques of freezing *can* provide good possibilities for harvesting fruits and vegetables at their peak of goodness, and at the same time conserve most of their flavor and food value. Although truly fresh produce should always be the first choice, quality frozen produce can serve as a satisfactory supplement. The home gardener who freezes surplus fruits and vegetables appreciates these foodstuffs during the winter, when the variety of fresh food is limited.

Commercial freezing, using current knowledge and facilities, *could* produce frozen produce superior to what is now being offered. Freezing avoids the destructive high heat of canning, with the need to reheat. Freezing should also eliminate the need for additives, since the freezing process itself preserves.

However, the quality of the thawed-out produce depends on the agricultural management of the crop, as well as its handling, at each stage from farm to table. The same chemical agriculture that produced fresh produce with excessive nitrates, pesticide residues, or poor flavor also provides the raw materials for frozen fruits and vegetables.

Commercial freezing may cause needless nutritional losses. For example, the microwave method of blanching broccoli commercially was shown to result in far more loss of ascorbic acid than the conventional hot-water blanching method usually used in home freezing.[76]

To prepare produce for commercial freezing, fruits and vegetables may be washed with detergents. At times, these materials have been found as contaminants in frozen produce.

Although the homemaker can freeze fruits and berries with a minimum of sweetening, or none at all, all too often commercially frozen fruits contain a large amount of sweetening.

The consumer has no assurance that adequate safeguards have been taken to keep frozen produce well frozen at all times, with sufficiently low temperatures. (This was discussed in Chapter 7, dealing with frozen fish.) If frozen produce has been allowed to thaw and to refreeze at any point between processing and its use, there is a loss of flavor and nutrients; hazards may be created with microbiological growth. There are many instances—which shoppers can cite—when frozen produce has been stacked above the temperature control line or the temperature in the freezer case in the store was not sufficiently low.

In the absence of package dating, there is no way to know the age of frozen food. Even when stored at zero Fahrenheit, over a period of time serious losses of flavor and nutrition occur. A device indicating freshness or spoilage of frozen food has been patented.[77] A small litmus-paper disc, visible through a precut hole, can be inserted into the frozen-food packaging material. If the food is fresh, the disc remains a certain color; if the food begins to deteriorate, the color changes. The consumer would benefit from the use of such a device if the frozen-food industry could be persuaded to adopt it.

WHAT PRICE THE CAN OPENER?

"The path of civilization," said Elbert Hubbard, "is paved with tin cans." Judging by statistics, Mr. Hubbard was right. We eat most of our pineapple from cans, 90 percent of all beets, 80 per cent of tomatoes and tomato products, 65 per cent of apricots, sweet corn, and green peas, 50 per cent of asparagus, and many fruits.[78] Is the convenience worth the price?

To prepare fruits and vegetables for commercial canning, produce may be soaked in lye or other caustic solutions for easy peeling.[79] Or a vegetable may be dipped in a chemical bath that converts the skin to a jellylike pulp for easy removal.[80]

Additives, not used in home preparation, find their way into commercial canning. Calcium salts (calcium chloride, sulfate, citrate, monocalcium phosphate, or any mixture of these) may be added to canned peppers, lima beans, potatoes, or tomatoes to keep them firm. Green peas may be treated with magnesia or magnesium carbonate to prevent the breakdown of chlorophyll, and retain the color. (These materials are laxative, and are used also in fireproofing woods, in disinfectants, and in the manufacture of cotton fabrics.) Tin salts (stannous chloride) may be used to keep glass-packed asparagus looking green.[81]

Official USDA publications assure the consumer that "good commercial canning methods cause relatively little loss" of nutritional values.[82] Is this true?

CANNED PEAS—"GREEN GUNSHOT"

It does not require a particularly discriminating palate to note the tremendous difference between sweet fresh green peas and canned ones. How can two items differ so radically? Canned produce undergoes alteration of the mineral balances found naturally in the raw commodities. Comparing the sodium and potassium content of fresh and canned peas, processing lowers the potassium 66 per cent. At the same time, sodium rises as much as 1,421 per cent in canned peas![83]

This derangement of mineral balance is accompanied by losses of other nutrients. The green peas, ready for canning, may be soaked in a 2 per cent solution of soda for 30 minutes to an hour to preserve the color and "improve" the taste. Then they are subjected to water or steam blanching. During the latter process, the potassium in peas falls 39 per cent, vitamin C loss is about 30 per cent, and the taste—even if originally present—has been impaired.[84]

Then the peas are exposed to a combined purifying and cooling process in the form of a shower bath of cold water, while they travel on a conveyor belt. During this time additional minerals are dissolved in the water. At this point, the blanching water, freed from suspended particles by filtration, is discarded from the peas. Along with it go the minerals. The peas are put into cans, and charged with tap water and salt. Sugar, corn syrup, or both, in addition to monosodium glutamate, may be added. Calcium oxide may be used to precipitate the bicarbonate, and this is added to the liquid used for filling up the cans. Once the cans are sealed and sterilized, the leaching process of the peas continues. The high heat necessary to kill bacterial contaminants causes a 30 to 40 per cent vitamin C loss. If the canned peas are stored as long as nine months after processing, as much as 90 per cent of the original quantity of vitamin C may be lost. Some destruction is attributed to the catalytic action of the iron dissolved from the can lining. Both vitamin B_1 and B_2 also suffer losses during processing; there are also small losses of protein during the blanching.[85] No wonder canned peas are dubbed "green gunshot"!

OTHER CANNING CHANGES

Other canned produce undergoes similar alterations. *Potassium losses* in typical foods include:[86]

> 47 per cent in spinach
> 51 per cent in tomatoes
> 60 per cent in green beans
> 65 per cent in carrots

At the same time, there are tremendous *increases in sodium,* the following canned foods being typical:[87]

357   per cent in spinach
368   per cent in carrots
450   per cent in tomatoes
5,857   per cent in asparagus
45,554   per cent in green beans

HOW SAFE ARE CANNED FOODS?

Poisoning from the metal of cans is rarely reported, but it does exist. Manifestations are similar to those of chronic lead poisoning. Canned orange juice, when analyzed, was found to pick up tin dissolved from the container. Some samples showed up to 150 ppm of tin contamination.[88] Canned fruits and vegetables may have a long shelf life, but they do show signs of deterioration, Dr. Wiley wrote, as early as 1912: "In my opinion, it would be a great step forward, if the package should carry not only the net weight, but also the date of manufacture, so that goods could not be held too long on the grocer's shelves. This is especially true in the case of . . . such vegetables as asparagus . . . berries, some of which are especially apt to attack the inner surface of the container."[89]

Consumers often ask the question: how safe is food left in a can after it is opened? Both the USDA[90] and the National Canners Association[91] have given assurances that such food is safe, but tests suggest otherwise. After a can has been opened, tin contamination of the food remaining in it may rise by leaps and bounds. For example, when canned grapefruit was first opened and tested, the juice contained 20.3 milligrams per kilogram of tin; after two days, 87; and after four days, 364.[92]

The relationship of canned foods to cancer was explored. Many possibilities of contamination from metals were uncovered, which may present hazards. These include metals present in tin plate, solder sealing, lacquer linings; also traces from soil, the air, sprays, machinery, storage, cooking containers, or cutting tools.[93]

FRUITS AND VEGETABLES, ANYONE?

Try to find sources of vine- or tree-ripened fruits. Some tomatoes and melons bearing special labels "vine-ripened" reach markets.

Certain commercial growers take pride in raising apples, melon, pineapple, papaya, avocado, and citrus fruit of good biological quality without pesticides, dyes, waxes, or fumigants. Such produce is shipped to special outlets as well as to individuals. There are also suppliers of untreated white potatoes and onions, and well grown vegetables that store well, such as carrots, kohlrabi, and cabbage. Fresh fruits can be supplemented with unsulphured and sun-dried ones. Read labels carefully.

For the suburbanite and rural dweller, a vegetable and fruit garden, however small, should be considered. A surprisingly large amount of produce can be grown, even in a backyard plot. Convert lawn area to productivity. Use edible-berry-bush plantings as ornamentals. If space is limited, consider dwarf fruit trees. Interplant for efficient use of areas. Look for neighbors who raise produce of biological quality, and buy or barter surpluses.

12

Our Impoverished Grains

BREAD: "PRESLICED ABSORBENT COTTON"

"OUR BREAD is sliced, wrapped, steamed and whitened to duplicate the consistency of old newspapers . . . [an] unforgettable aroma of nothingness."[1]

". . . pre-sliced absorbent cotton."[2]

". . . cotton fluff wrapped up in a skin."[3]

". . . pappy, tasteless, soft aerated substance that is as appetizing as white foam rubber without the spring and the bounce."[4]

Such reactions to modern commercial bread, and others in the same vein, have led to some soul-searching by the editor of *Bakers Review:*

> We cannot escape the unpleasant fact that dissatisfaction with the contemporary loaf is pretty general. And what troubles me even more . . . is the fact that the trade in general appears to be indifferent to it. . . .
>
> For years, the consumption of white bread has been falling. Added to the growing criticism of bread, there emerges an obvious conclusion: there must be something wrong with the product.[5]

The manipulation of grains for bread and cereal, unlike most other foodstuffs, is not a recent innovation. Adulteration and short weight of grain, meal, and bread down through the centuries had

286

made both the miller and the baker traditional objects of contempt and distrust.

Historically, bread has been a potent status symbol. Dark-colored bread was associated with the poor working people; light-colored bread was a sign of wealth and prestige.

Although whole-wheat flour contains more nutrients than after it is processed, its excessive roughage, especially in the outer bran, does not make flour of 100 per cent extraction a suitable food for everyone. Many people cannot tolerate it. This fact has long been recognized. The sieving and bolting of meal to remove the coarse outer bran has been practiced for at least two thousand years.

During the 18th century the miller began to extract from 60 to 80 per cent of the grain as white flour for the household. In a world of free competition, it was in the miller's interest to satisfy his customers: the baker and the consumer. White flour was especially prized by the baker. As a craftsman, he preferred to turn versatile white flour into tarts, cakes, pastries, and other specialty items more profitable than bread. White flour was not readily infested by insects, nor did it quickly turn rancid or moldy with age.

Competition to meet the public demand for cheap white bread was keen. The baker adopted various tricks to make the flour go a little further or to increase the whiteness of the loaf. Alum, chalk, and ammonium carbonate were commonly used as whiteners or improvers. Wheat flour was adulterated with potato or barley meal; stale dough might be incorporated into the new batch. Many of those early tricks served as precedents for later practices.

Although adulterated bread and cereal inevitably went to the poor in cities, the rural population fared well. Each town had at least one gristmill. The farmer took his sack of wheat, corn, or rye to the miller. The grain was stone-ground, and reduced to flour or meal, with the cellular structure and air sacks containing the nutritious elements kept reasonably intact. The meal was promptly converted by the farmer's wife into savory and sustaining bread or gruel, with optimal flavor and nutritional values conserved.

Scientific advances and chemical manipulations have wrought many changes. A technological development shortly after the Civil War led to the demise of the local gristmill. A current of air was used to separate the bran from the flour. This required more complicated machinery and greater power than the local gristmill could supply. Local milling operations were shifted to mass production in the Midwest, centered in Minneapolis.

With the introduction of the steel rolling mill in 1874, speedy large-scale milling of white flour became feasible. The grain was crushed, rather than ground. The germ and bran were flattened. When the flour was sifted, the starchy part passed through, and left the germ and bran on the screen. The flour, without the fat from the germ, could be stored or shipped long distances without turning rancid.

This processing reduced risks, because the white flour had long shelf life. Other fractions of the wheat could be sold separately, including the bran, germ, "shorts" or "middlings," and gluten. For example, in the city, bran was used as horsefeed or processed into ship biscuits. Bran sent back to the country was eaten by the rural population or used as animal feed. The removal of the brown bran and cream-colored germ gave the flour a whiter appearance. These practices served the ever-growing demands for whiteness.

Because of the favorable keeping qualities of white flour, its price was low. Contrariwise, owing to the perishable nature of whole-wheat flour, with the risks of losses in shipping and storing, its price was held high. For the first time in the history of bread, the symbols were reversed. Whole wheat became a mark of luxury for the rich, and the goal of eating white bread finally was achieved by the common people.[6]

"REAL BREAD HAS BEEN TAKEN OUT OF OUR MOUTHS"

The milling operations impoverished the flour in a manner which, even today, the average consumer scarcely appreciates. By crushing it, the roller mill destroys the cellular structure of the grain and changes its biological pattern. Roller milling reduces both the quantity and quality of the proteins.[7] Good-quality proteins are removed with the germ and bran; only those of poor quality are left in the white flour. For example, the amino acids essential for growth (lysine and tryptophan) are reduced. The balance of minerals is disturbed. For instance, the altered ratio of potassium to magnesium is considered harmful to health.

The grain contains valuable unsaturated fatty acids and vitamin

E. In roller milling, the grain loses about half of its fat content.[8] One of the richest natural sources of vitamin E is found in the germ of the wheat, with lesser amounts in the bran.

A number of important minerals are reduced substantially, with percentages varying for different wheats and different degrees of extraction. The following are taken from a study at the University of California college of agriculture:[9]

manganese	about 98 per cent lost in roller milling
iron	about 80 per cent
magnesium	about 75 per cent
phosphorus	about 70 per cent
copper	about 65 per cent
calcium	about 50 per cent
potassium	about 50 per cent

Other studies indicate about 72 per cent loss of zinc and 15 per cent loss of cobalt.[10] Similarly, vitamin losses are serious. The same California study found:[11]

thiamin	about 80 per cent lost in roller milling
niacin	about 75 per cent
riboflavin	about 65 per cent
pantothenic acid	about 50 per cent
pyridoxine	about 50 per cent

In addition, the study reported that biotin, inositol, folic acid, choline, and para-aminobenzoic acid are all reduced. These vitamins, from the B complex, are found in greatest abundance in the bran and wheat germ. There are at least four other vitamin factors (and possibly more as yet unidentified) also found in the portions discarded in the milling.

The nutritional inadequacies of white flour were questioned in England as well as in America. *The Lancet,* in 1911, stated: "Real bread has been taken out of our mouths by modern methods of impoverishment."[12] The USPHS had issued a warning bulletin that experimental animals fed on highly milled wheat and corn died; those on unmilled grains thrived. The millers objected. Although the USPHS was on sound scientific ground, the agency issued a "corrective" bulletin, explaining that white bread is wholesome if balanced in the diet by an adequate consumption of the protective foods. As already demonstrated, this rationale has been used repeatedly, and still is, by apologists for impoverished foods. The obvious fallacy, noted by nutritionists at the time, was that low-income families simply could not afford the protective foods that would have been necessary in order to build an adequate diet around white bread.

ATTEMPTS TO IMPROVE BREAD BY RAISING THE EXTRACTION RATE

During World War I, attempts were made to improve bread nutritionally. England raised the extraction rate of wheat flour to a compulsory 90 per cent. U.S. millers were opposed to the raising of the extraction rate. They were successful in having it held at 75 per cent, and using other grains along with the wheat.

After the end of World War I, at the millers' insistence, the U.S. government dropped control of the extraction rate. By so doing, the government lost an opportunity to campaign for a nutritionally improved bread.

Scientific investigations continued, and more evidence revealed the inadequacies of white flour and other highly refined foods. Sir Robert McCarrison's *Studies in Deficiency Disease*[13] showed that varied diets of European people did not protect them from deficiency diseases caused by modern food processing. Noting that beri-beri was established as a vitamin B deficiency in the Orient, McCarrison suggested that the absence of the same vitamin complex in white flour, the staple for many westerners, was "peculiarly significant."

The Health Committee of the League of Nations stated: "White flour in the process of milling is deprived of important nutritive elements. Its use should be decreased and partial substitution of lightly milled cereals . . . is recommended."[14]

ATTEMPTS TO IMPROVE BREAD THROUGH ENRICHMENT

Despite these recommendations to decrease the use of highly refined white flour and products made from it, official U.S. records of the 1930's showed that white-flour products constituted about 55 per cent of the total food intake of the average urban person during those depression years.[15] Numerous surveys at the time revealed grave nutritional deficiencies.

Two events in the late 1930's affected bread. Several vitamins were isolated and synthesized. The approach of World War II placed a new emphasis on physical fitness and improved food. Both developments were factors that led to the enrichment program, launched as an attempt to improve white flour.

The idea of enriching white flour by adding synthetic vitamins was first suggested in 1936, before the Council on Food and Nutrition (then known as the Committee on Foods) of the AMA. Because of the interest in the newly synthesized vitamins, two years later, the same Council met jointly with the Council on Pharmacy and Chemistry of the AMA, and the principle of food enrichment was endorsed.

The enrichment formula for bread specified a minimum standard of three synthetic vitamins (thiamin, riboflavin, and niacin) and one mineral (iron). Later, a revision included two optional additions (calcium and vitamin D). Among many factors *not* restored by the enrichment program are ones acknowledged to be vital in human physiology: vitamins (biotin, pyridoxine, and pantothenic acid); minerals (phosphorus, potassium, manganese, and copper); and protein amino acids (lysine and tryptophan). These factors, as well as others present in the wheat berry, have been shown to constitute an interlocking nutritional mechanism that can be destroyed by the removal or impairment of any one essential factor. However, despite its shortcomings, the enrichment program should be regarded as an attempt to improve the nutritional qualities of white flour and products made with it. Perhaps a wiser policy would have been to undermill the grain or to seek other techniques for conserving nutritional values.

WHAT ABOUT 100 PER CENT EXTRACTION?

Despite the seemingly high nutritive value in 100 per cent extraction of wheat, it is necessary to point out several unfavorable factors. As mentioned earlier, not everyone's digestive tract can handle the roughage of bran. The proteins in the bran are digested only with great difficulty and are only partially utilized.[16] Modern methods of bread baking have created new problems of additional indigestibility in the commercially baked 100 per cent whole-wheat loaf. Traditionally, when bread was made, the dough was allowed to rest for a number of hours to allow time for certain enzymes to work. In the same time, the moistened bran had a chance to become softened. With present speeded-up methods in commerical baking, the resting time of bread dough may be cut considerably by the introduction of various chemical agents, and the bran may not be given enough time to become softened.

Wheat—even when of high quality—contains phytin, an organic phosphorus compound that interferes with the body's utilization of important nutrients. For example, when whole-wheat bread is eaten along with foods containing calcium and iron, the phytin combines with them to form calcium and iron phytates. These compounds are insoluble, and succeed in making the calcium and iron in the food unavailable to the body. It has also been found, through human experiments, that minerals in whole-wheat flour, such as calcium, magnesium, phosphorus, and potassium, were less completely absorbed with high extraction flour.[17]

In recent years, additional problems with bran have developed because of various contaminants. Strontium 90 is absorbed readily by wheat. About 25 per cent of this radioactive material has been found in its bran. Current attempts are being made to remove the strontium 90 with strong acids. Also, residues of pesticides and fungicides, permitted officially, concentrate in the bran of the wheat.

BLEACHING: "AN ABOMINATION, A DECEIT, A SERIOUS COMMERCIAL VENTURE"

Despite early legislation forbidding adulteration of flour, millers have been using bleaching agents of various kinds. As flour ages or matures, its bread-making qualities improve. But aging flour involves the cost and inconvenience of storage, as well as the element of time. Bakers discovered that the same bleaching chemicals that whiten flour also "age" or "improve" it. The bleach was also found useful in keeping the flour sterile and preventing it from weeviling or souring.

Bleaching was also useful because inferior flours could be substituted for high-grade ones. Among the millers themselves, some were frank to admit that:

> Overbleaching flour shows upon the face of it that it has been treated with some villainous process which has destroyed its character. It is lacking in bloom, is a deception wherein the miller has attempted to profit. It enables the miller to avoid skill, and the bread-producing quality of the flour is damaged just in proportion as the miller cheats by this artificial means.
>
> We do not consider bleaching to be beneficial in the true sense of the word, and intelligent bakers and consumers do not like to be deceived and are, therefore, opposed to this process. Aging produced in the flour by the quick process does not correspond to that produced by nature. The bleaching destroys the essential oil and . . . also the flavor, and any expert would at once detect a bleached flour by the taste as compared with the unbleached.
>
> Bleaching is a reproach to the milling trade. It is an abomination, a deceit, a serious commercial venture.[18]

Dr. Wiley had opposed the use of bleaches in flour on the grounds that objectionable substances were being introduced for the unethical purpose of concealing inferiority. His views were confirmed by studies he submitted with his recommendation for the banning of bleached flour. Evidence was presented in federal court, and bleached white flour was declared unfit as human food. The government won its case in seizing flour bleached with nitrogen peroxide as "adulterated and misbranded." The millers fought the decision bitterly and appealed. The battle dragged on for a decade, the issues submerged by the legal technicalities. Finally, through the unrelenting pressures of the millers, enforcement of the bleaching ban was made ineffective. In 1920, when Wiley was no longer in government service, the agency he once led issued an announcement that no further action would be taken against bleached flour. This was done on the grounds that poisonous substances, such as flour bleaches, might be added to foods unless "a quantity was added that made injuriousness susceptible to proof in court."[19]

AGENE—CAUSE OF RUNNING FITS IN DOGS

Agene (nitrogen trichloride), a flour bleach introduced in 1920 without adequate testing, was widely used for nearly three decades in the United States and England. This chemical, suspected of being toxic, was investigated in England. Experiments confirmed its harmfulness. In 1927 the British Ministry of Health recommended that agene be prohibited.[20] But no official restraints were actually instituted, and millers continued to use it. At a later date, an English physician from Hull, Dr. J. J. Coglan, produced clinical evidence of the damaging nature of this material in a memorandum to the British Ministry of Food, but there was no official action. Apathy prevailed until strange behavior in animals aroused interest.

Running fits in dogs had first been noticed in the southern United States. Later, the fits grew in intensity and were more widespread. Dogs lost interest in their surroundings, ran or walked more slowly, had dry mouths, sought shade, were frightened and unfriendly. Finally, they frothed at the mouth, collapsed, and had ataxia and epileptiform fits.

A miller, who wished to remain anonymous, suggested to Sir Edward Mellanby in England that agene might be the culprit for the running fits in dogs. Dr. Mellanby experimented, and found that he could produce hysterical outbreaks at will by exposing the dogs to flour containing agene. He wrote: "The abnormal behavior of the animals affected by the agenized flour suggests that the central nervous system is primarily affected by some toxic agent, but other organs may also be involved."[21] Dr. Mellanby's published report was followed by a film in which Mellanby showed the dogs' symptoms after they ate agenized bread.

Tests conducted in the United States corroborated Mellanby's findings. Agene was banned in the United States on Aug. 1, 1949. On Jan. 27, 1950, the British Ministry of Health agreed to discontinue agene at an unspecified date and to replace it with another bleach. The Ministry's scientific committee insisted that the general public would be dissatisfied unless an improver was continued in bread. Although the general public was not represented on this committee, the flour millers were. However, the new alternative bleach could not be introduced readily, and the banned agene continued in use in England, despite its known dangers, for six more years. In 1956 it was replaced by another bleach.

After agene was banned in both countries, proof of its harmfulness to man was firmly established.[22] Later, more adverse data were forthcoming. Agene was suspected as a cause of some myopia and allergies in children.[23]

At the Sloan-Kettering Institute the toxic substance formed in bread by agene (methionine sulphoximine) was used experimentally to retard tumor growths in seven patients with advanced cancer. Although it failed to arrest the tumors, in four patients it caused psychosis: "frank hallucinations, disorientation, and marked agitation which continued for from one to three days after administration of the compound was stopped."[24]

BLEACHES: "SOCIAL CUSTOM AND BIOLOGICAL STUPIDITY"

Although agene was banned, the bleaching of flour has been continued. Other poisons have been substituted, notably chlorine dioxide. Dr. Bicknell wrote: "The chlorine dioxide of today is as miraculous as was agene from the commercial point of view and is as harmful from the point of view of the consumer."[25]

In technical literature intended for millers, chlorine dioxide was described as "more powerful than nitrogen trichloride [agene]; the quantities used are one-third to half those of nitrogen chloride. Chlorine not only oxidizes the flour pigment but also has a valuable bleaching effect on the coloring matter of bran, which makes it particularly valuable for bleaching very low grade flours."[26]

Present evidence is sufficiently damning of bleaches to demand that they be outlawed. Dr. Anton Carlson, professor of physiology at the University of Chicago, termed bleaching a "social custom and biological stupidity."[27]

Investigations have shown that agene converted an amino acid, methionine, into a toxic material that is, according to Dr. Mellanby, "very poisonous indeed."[28] Chlorine dioxide has been found to destroy all of the vitamin E in flour that may have escaped in the milling process;[29] or if not to destroy it, to form a toxic product or a perverted one with the oil's EFA (essential fatty acid).[30] As with agene, chlorine dioxide may also form a toxic material with methionine.[31] An official report from England admitted that *although no trace of the chlorine dioxide may be left in the flour, the product formed may act injuriously or impair the nutritional qualities of the flour.*[32] Recent experiments showed that growth was stunted in mice fed flour treated with chlorine dioxide.[33]

After examining the evidence of the dangers and destructiveness of chlorine dioxide as a substitute for agene, Dr. Bicknell remarked: "Add to this graveyard of nutrients a lingering miasma of chlorine dioxide, and the millers have achieved a flour as nearly non-nutritious as is possible and as covertly, as insidiously corrupting to the body as food well can be."[34] Indeed, there seems to be some foundation for the rhyme:

> *The whiter the bread,*
> *The sooner you're dead.*

THE FINE ART(IFICES) OF BAKING

"The ultimate goal of the present trend [will] probably be reached when a bread substitute made up primarily of starch, air, water, polyoxyethelene stearate and a little saccharin [is] found acceptable to the general consumer."[35] This statement, by Dr. Mellanby, exaggerated as it may seem to be, suggests the trend in the fine art of baking.

Technologists have devised many chemical short cuts that permit bakers to manipulate the ingredients of their products toward these objectives: to create the biggest loaf, with greatest speed, the least work, and the longest shelf life, with the greatest economy.

Yet the label on the bread may list only one chemical additive: a mold retarder (usually calcium or sodium propionate). It would be a severe shock for the public to know that not one, but nearly 60 chemicals may be present in a loaf of bread, without label declaration.[36]

The lack of informative bread labeling was established when this food was standardized by the FDA. From 1941 to 1951, when bread standards were being considered, discussions and controversy dragged on endlessly. As with other federal food standards, any original intention of consumer protection was ultimately perverted. The standards succeeded in concealing rather than revealing facts of interest to the consumer. Meanwhile, industry kept pressing for inclusion in the standards of all the improvers, conditioners, leaveners, extenders, dyes, antioxidants, and other chemical adjuncts of the baking trade.

In the absence of consumer counterpressure, industry representatives were able to have a number of ingredients included in the bread standards, and others added later. Current regulations include more than 80 ingredients,[37] of which about 75 per cent are chemicals not found in a home kitchen. Commercial bread is no longer a simple food made of the familiar flour, salt, milk, yeast, and water. Nor do commercially baked goods necessarily include the traditional eggs, butter, or other ingredients usually associated with homemade cakes, pies, cookies, and pastries. The baker is even unlikely to start his production from scratch. He may employ such short cuts as processed Danish pastry mix, sweet dough preparations, icings, cremes, and frostings processed for him. In order to be preserved, these concoctions already may be interlaced with additives. The baker may add any number of improvers, dough conditioners, leaveners, yeast foods, enzymes, bacterial and mold inhibitors. Many of these additions ultimately give the consumer a low-quality food at a high price. Common synthetic fats (monoglycerides and diglycerides) and hydrogenated fats are used. Silicones may be used as pan glazes, and white mineral oil as pan grease. The low cost of mineral oil is stressed as a selling point by manufacturers selling bakers' supplies.[38] "Cultured butter flavor" is billed as adding "that special touch of richness which tastes exactly the same as butter in finished goods, with many additional advantages . . . it costs much less, yet goes much further than butter . . . it needs no refrigeration . . . guaranteed to stay sweet and fresh . . . a single ounce will flavor 60 pounds of dough."[39] Nitric acid "imparts a yellow tint" as a substitute for egg yolks. Cheap emulsifiers substitute for milk to give a "rich feeling."

Artificial dyes, caramel coloring, flavor enhancers, and cost-cutting imitation flavors are commonplace. For instance, "imitation banana flavor has the aroma and taste of the genuine fruit so closely duplicated that it has everything but the peel [and a] total

absence of the familiar synthetic nail polish odor and taste."[40]
Other artificial flavors are offered that are "so carefully compounded that only an expert can distinguish them from the natural
product . . . their cost is low, as one fourth that of pure spice."
To complete the deception, some of these artificial flavors contain
"color specks to appear in the finished product."[41]

"MORE BREAD FOR LESS DOUGH"

The federal government officially sanctioned additives to be put
into bread dough to increase its water absorbing capacity, and
thus increase the weight or size of the loaf. "More bread for less
dough" is the oft-repeated appeal to the baker in his trade magazines. Shortenings with emulsifiers hold promise of "greater than
ever volume." Oxidizing agents (potassium or calcium bromate,
potassium or calcium iodate, calcium peroxide) keep the air in the
dough while it bakes. Other compounds "trap and hold more air
and moisture in the batter . . . more batter . . . 10 per cent
more cakes . . . more profits."

Some bakers achieved such monstrously blown-up bread that
one-pound loaves were baked to the size and shape of the usual
one-and-one-half-pound loaf. This deceptive practice led to official
action in Oregon, where the legislature decreed that such bread
must be labeled "balloon bread." The ruling, contested by the
bakers, was upheld in court.[42]

So many additives now replace basic ingredients in baked goods
that, at present, flour makes up only 50 per cent of the average
bread loaf, and as little as 25 per cent of a cake.[43] The baking
industry is the largest user of sugar—another impoverished product. The use of sugar by the baking industry has jumped nearly 70
per cent since 1952.[44]

"STAY FRESH LONGER"—
THE MOLD-RETARDING PROPIONATES

Shelf life is important to the baker. Manufacturers of many substances used in commercial breads appeal to the baker with

catchwords such as these: "stay fresh longer," "reduce stale returns," "reduce baking costs." Leavening agents are offered for self-rising flours that "extend the shelf life of from four to six weeks up to several months or more." The mold retarders are well known to the consumer for extending the shelf life of bread.

Both industry[45] and the FDA[46] are quick to affirm that calcium and sodium propionate are salts of propionic acid, which is produced naturally in cheese during its manufacture. It sounds reassuring to learn that the additives are harmless natural substances. The truth is that the propionic acids used in bakery products are made synthetically, by large chemical and pharmaceutical companies, from ethylene, carbon monoxide, and steam. Since fungi and molds are closely related, it is not surprising to find that these materials are also common ingredients in solutions, powders, and ointments used to treat athlete's foot, *tinea cruris*, and other mycoses. Sodium propionate is also used as a fungicide in the production of the garlic crop, and as a preservative in salad greens and vegetables intended for human consumption. In this capacity, it is exempted from an official FDA tolerance. Sodium propionate has also been used as a preservative for tobacco, a practice since the end of World War II.

Although these materials have been considered harmless, from past experience we know that such assurances are not always well founded. They may merely be based on inadequate testing.

Dr. S. C. Werch reported allergic reactions from propionates, which began with upper gastrointestinal disturbances 4 to 18 hours after eating foods containing propionates, and ended with partial or total migraine headache. Since the gastrointestinal symptoms are similar to gall-bladder attack, the symptoms may be severe in cases where an allergy to the propionate is combined with a gall-bladder ailment. Dr. Werch charged that authorities have failed to find harm in the propionates simply because they have not looked for it.[47]

Furthermore, when sodium salt of propionic acid is used, this places an additional burden of sodium on the body. When the calcium salt of propionic acid is used, this destroys the enzyme that normally makes it possible for the body to assimilate any calcium—present naturally or through enrichment—in the bread.

A large manufacturer of propionates had conducted an exten-

sive national promotion campaign, advertising for several years in
women's magazines, to educate "discriminating homemakers"
about the benefits of these products. The copy was aimed at
"thrifty homemakers" who would benefit from using propionate
that "makes food last longer"[48] and "at no additional cost."[49] An
advertisement of a rival manufacturer, aimed at professional
bakers, claimed that the propionates gave two to four days' extra
shelf life.[50]

The consumer should recognize these materials for what they
are. These preservatives help cut bakers' losses by reducing the
return of stale baked products. In the absence of dating on these
goods, the buyer has no way of knowing whether they are fresh.
The mold retarders can give stale goods the appearance of freshness. Homemade breads keep very well without benefit of these
preservatives. If baked goods were prepared daily, as they used to
be, and still are in some small bakeries, there would be no problem
of freshness. During humid, hot weather baked products should
be refrigerated, whether at home or in a store. Under such conditions, there is no need to artificially prolong the shelf life of baked
goods.

One indication that food is alive is its ability to become moldy.
When this living quality is destroyed, the food itself has been
robbed of something important. This was expressed colorfully by
the nutritionist Elmer V. McCollum, professor emeritus, Johns
Hopkins University, who advised: "Eat only those foods that spoil
or rot or decay—but eat them before they do."[51]

BREAD, ANYONE?

Try to find a small bakery that takes pride in the quality of its
products, uses simple ingredients, and bakes daily. Such a place is
not likely to use preservatives.

If you cannot tolerate a high extraction, use bread made from
unbleached flour. So-called French and Vienna breads may *not*
contain shortening. A "home loaf" may be labeled specifically to
show that it contains no lard, fat, or sugar.

If you cannot locate such a bakery or products, consider baking your own bread. Baking bread requires no special skill or equipment, and you can control the ingredients.

BREAKFAST CEREALS

Attention has been focused on wheat, the grain most commonly used by Americans. However, when analyzed in detail, other grains would be found to be similarly impoverished.

Today's degerminated cornmeal differs from old-fashioned bolted cornmeal. Overmilling has resulted in serious losses of protein, fat, thiamin, riboflavin, niacin, phosphorus, iron, and vitamin A.[52]

Equally tragic is the devitalization of rice. The natural brown whole grain has been a sustaining staple for countless numbers of people in many sections of the world. But modern polished white rice, overmilled, is so refined that a diet composed largely of it usually produces severe nutritional deficiencies.

Unfortunately, untreated brown rice has a relatively short shelf life—a few weeks or, at most, months. Then it becomes rancid. Undermilled rice can be stored longer, while overmilled rice has a long shelf life.

The degree of milling varies. Traditionally, hand-milled rice was undermilled and retained many nutrients. The present-day overmilled whiter products, widely produced since the introduction of milling machinery, have suffered losses of nutrients. For example, nutrients in the hull, embryo, and outer layers of the rice are lost. Proteins are decreased, and their quality is lowered. This occurs because the lysine content (an essential amino acid) present in the discarded germ and bran is much higher than in the remaining endosperm (starch). Thus, milling reduces the percentage of lysine in the protein.[53]

Some of the corn fractions are sold profitably, as, for example, corn oil. Both rice bran and "polish" are important ingredients in animal feeds, and the rice oil finds a lucrative market in leather treatment, hair tonics, and fine soaps. However, the real financial bonanza for the grain processors has developed with the rise of a peculiarly American institution: dry cereals.

SNAP, CRACKLE, AND POP

The ready-to-eat cold cereal products, invented at the turn of the century, have virtually revolutionized the American breakfast. Richard Carter noted that Americans "actually glow with a sense of well being" as they eat such food. "Decades of tradition and millions upon millions of dollars in advertising have trained them to regard their ready-to-eat breakfast cereal as the last word in morning nourishment. Any suspicion that the stuff is nutritionally inferior to other breakfast foods is bound to be dispelled by the sales literature printed on the brightly colored boxes."[54]

The flaking of the grains is only one of several ways in which their basic nature is changed. They are also mauled by being shredded, crinkled, popped, and puffed. As early as 1921, a puffed-oat company announced with fanfare that a way was found "to explode the food cells in whole grains. The grains are sealed in guns and long subjected to a fearful heat. The moisture in each food cell is changed to steam. When the guns are shot, more than 100 million steam explosions occur in every kernel. The grains are puffed to bubbles, eight times their normal size. The grains are flimsy, flaky food confections, fascinating in their texture and their taste."[55]

EXPERIMENTAL RATS FARE BADLY ON BREAKFAST CEREALS

The effects of processing on the biological and nutritional quality of the grains have concerned scientific investigators. The growth-promoting quality of the grain's protein is reduced so drastically that experimental rats fed on it were unable to grow.[56] The grains are exposed to excessively high heats (up to 392° F.) for toasting, gun exploding or puffing. Lysine and other valuable amino acids, as well as parts of the vitamin B complex, are lost. In addition, if sugar is added to the cereal, the value of the protein is reduced further. Valuable vitamins like thiamin, already low in many highly refined foods, are less available to the body.[57]

PROMOTIONAL BALLYHOO

Despite these nutritional shortcomings, the promotional ballyhoo of the breakfast cereals has stimulated an ever-expanding market. Long ago, an official of one large cereal producer was quoted as saying: "It's not enough to just make and sell cereal. After that you get it half way down the customer's throat through the use of advertising. Then, they've got to swallow it."[58] In order to do this, cereal manufacturers currently spend more than $72 million annually in America for promotion.[59]

More than 70 different cereal brands compete for the consumer's attention, with an annual sales volume now estimated at $600 million.[60] The dry cereals are lucrative, with a considerable price spread between the basic commodity of grain and the highly processed cereal. The bulk wholesale market prices of grains— approximately two and a tenth cents per pound for corn, two and two tenths cents for oats, and three and four tenths cents for wheat—may soar to 30 cents to $1.20 per pound as processed cereal.[61]

The industry has shown great ingenuity in boosting profits ever higher. One approach has been through the mystical virtues of these depleted foods to provide strength, vigor, and athletic prowess, in promotion described as "the protein bandwagon."

"Protein content and protein quality," noted Dr. D. L. Emmett Holt, Jr., school of medicine, New York University, "have become sales gimmicks in the food industry."[62] The cereal manufacturers have been among the chief offenders, despite the fact that nutritionists agree that cereals, even the best of them, are not dependable sources of proteins.

NOT "HIGH PROTEIN"—HIGH CARBOHYDRATE

All breakfast cereals are predominantly carbohydrate. When sweetened, either at the factory or at the table, their carbohydrate content is further increased. Whereas wheat or rye bread averages about 50 per cent total carbohydrates, the processed cereals have substantially higher percentages:[63]

oat breakfast cereals average about	70 per cent carbohydrates
bran flakes	79 per cent
wheat flakes	80 per cent
puffed wheat	80 per cent
corn flakes	85 per cent
rice flakes	88 per cent
puffed rice	88 per cent

The reason cereal manufacturers are interested in joining "the protein bandwagon" is stated clearly in a USDA publication: "Breakfast cereals promoted as extra high in certain nutrients also are apt to be higher priced."[64]

Another lucrative innovation by the breakfast-cereal manufacturers was the sugar-coated or "presweetened" cereal, begun in 1949. Once again, a USDA publication stated bluntly: "Sugar-coated cereals that are ready to eat cost more, per ounce, than many common unsweetened ones. Buying sugar-coated cereals can be an uneconomical use of food money."[65] However, the USDA makes no attempt to warn the consumer about the nutritional inadequacy of these cereals or the harm of sugar in the diet, especially for children. This government agency not only sees no harm in the increasing consumption of these foods, but has actually promoted them. A USDA release described "cereals shaped like stars, doughnuts, and snowflakes . . . cereals with cutouts and games on the back . . . and sugar-coated cereals" as "good for between-meal snacks. They're all available at your local food store in an almost endless display."[66]

Many of these cereals contain more sugar than grain. Some contain several different types of sugars, and others have a mixture of sugar and artificial sweeteners. Gradually a basic grain has undergone such modification that it has been transformed into a confection.

Nutritional researchers have reported that the high carbohydrate in refined corn flakes, wheat flakes, oatmeal, white rice, and white flour products cause tooth decay in experimental animals. The same cereals, made with natural, unrefined grains, cut tooth decay drastically.[67]

Along with the high carbohydrates, numerous additives are incorporated in the boxed cereals. There are also problems of slack fill, ingredient listings difficult to locate and more difficult to comprehend, the odd fractional weights that make it virtually impossible to figure cost per unit. When added together, what does the consumer have? According to the cartoonist Bob Barnes, breakfast cereal "looks like shavings, tastes like sawdust, chews like cardboard and swallows like sandpaper."[68]

The nutritional content of 40 leading breakfast cereals is so low that they constitute a threat of "empty calories," testified Robert B. Choate, Jr., a former government adviser on hunger, on July 24, 1970, before the Consumers Subcommittee of the Senate Commerce Committee. Speaking as a private citizen, Mr. Choate charged that cereals "fatten but do little to prevent malnutrition" and that "for a budget-conscious family, they are a bad nutrient investment for the dollar." Citing a survey of cereal advertising, he said that children are "being countereducated away from nutrition knowledge," "deliberately being sold the sponsor's less nutritious products," and "being programmed to demand sugar and sweetness in every food."

Cereal processors countercharged Choate with technical errors, including his condemnation of presweetened cereals that may lead to the consumption of too much sugar. "In our opinion," one manufacturer said, "exactly the opposite is true. Presweetened cereals provide a measure of control over sugar intake that is not present when the young consumer sweetens his own."

WHY DO WE EAT CEREAL?

The breakfast-cereal sellers have done well in their hucksterings. They have not only sold dreams of strength and boundless energy, but the pleasures of consuming confections. Now, with the help of professional motivational researchers, they move forward to greater vistas. Dr. Ernest Dichter announced:

> The high percentage of people who want crush-resistant cereals proves that they look upon breakfast as a sort of adversary which has to be conquered. The greater fighting attitude people have toward the struggle of the day, the more they seem to be insisting upon consuming a good breakfast. This is one of the reasons why mushy soft cereals are rejected unless they happen to be hot, since heat substitutes for the feeling of resistance offered by cold cereals.

Cereals, to a large extent, fulfill our tactile curiosity. You can play with cereals in an oral fashion. They have interesting shapes that can be cracked with a snap, crackle, and pop. In a psychological research study of the cereal of the future conducted for a major food company, it was found that, contrary to a purely logical expectancy, the future trend will not be a supermodern pattern of "atom-powered" cereals. The truly modern cereal will combine all the warmth and affection of the substantial old-fashioned cereal with the fun, lightness, and convenience of the modern dry cereal.[69]

CEREAL, ANYONE?

Old-fashioned cooked cereals may not fulfill the "tactile curiosity" but if used in limited amounts, they can provide good nutrition. Even the best are predominantly carbohydrate, and should not be considered as substitutes for quality protein.

In addition to commonly known grains such as wheat, rye, oats, corn, and brown rice, consider buckwheat and millet.

SOME FINAL THOUGHTS ON GRAINS

We can recognize the useful role of cereal foods, especially in times of emergency, such as in famine or war. But we should also remember that people such as the Eskimos and others had enjoyed robust health without grains in their traditional diet.*

Grains rank high on the list of common allergens. Many people suffer great discomfort and ill health because of an unawareness of their sensitivity to certain grains.

From the viewpoint of optimal nutrition, cereal foods—even those of good quality—do not afford the high values of the "protective foods," such as proteins, fruits, and vegetables. Dr. Aaron M. Altschul warned that the lack of proteins in grains is particularly harmful to children in areas of the world where cereal foods

* See H. P. Pickerill, M.D., *The Prevention of Dental Caries and Oral Sepsis.* London: Bailliere, Tindall and Cox, 1912; Weston A. Price, D.D.S., *Nutrition and Physical Degeneration.* Los Angeles: American Academy of Applied Nutrition, 1950 (5th printing); and Vilhjalmur Stefansson, *The Fat of the Land.* New York: Macmillan, 1957.

form a major part of the diet. Lack of protein, he pointed out, often results in permanent physical and mental damage.[70]

In the United States, where protein foods are plentiful, the consumer is not dependent on grains. The carbohydrates of wheat, corn, rice, barley, and other grains cannot be considered as basic foods in the same sense as proteins, fruits, and vegetables. Through the aggressive efforts of the millers and the bakers, abetted by governmental policy, grains and grain products continue to be highly overrated.

PART III

◆　◆　◆　◆

A CLOSE-UP
OF SPECIALTIES

13

Baby Foods:
What's in Them?

WRITING ABOUT commercial infant formulas as early as 1912, Dr. Wiley made an observation that is still timely:

> It is hardly necessary to say that none of these efforts have met with complete success. There is no so-called commercial "infant's food" that can be recommended for general use. A large percentage of the commercial infants' foods are offered, not as complete foods, but as milk modifiers. One of the virtues urged in their behalf is the substitution of sugar and dextrin (derived from starch from cereal products) for the natural milk sugar or lactose. It is difficult to believe that nature has made a mistake in placing lactose instead of sucrose, maltose, or dextrin, in the milk of mammals. That infants often thrive on these substitute sugars is an evidence of the ability even of the babe to tolerate a strange environment rather than a proof of the waywardness of nature. It is more logical to believe that lactose, the natural sugar of little sweetness, is not only the normal, but the best carbohydrate for the baby.[1]

The alimentary tract of the infant and young baby has been subjected to the same pressures from the food revolution as other age groups. Time-honored breast feeding was downgraded, and ridiculed as "old fashioned," when both pharmaceutical companies and dairies discovered the profits in selling infant feeding formulas. Uninformed mothers hailed the new "freedom" and looked upon the "convenience" of prepackaged formulas, billed as offering "ease of digestion" and "optimal nutrition," as the latest advances of medical progress.

Efficiency-minded hospital administrators were quick to accept bottle formula feeding. The charge has been leveled that the reasons babies born in hospital A are started off on formula Y, and those in hospital B are fed formula Z, are "likely to be a combination of convenience and economy from the hospital's viewpoint. Sales promotion finds its way even into the hospital nursery, and the manufacturers have found that it pays long-term dividends to spend some money getting a baby started off on their own particular products."[2]

This is accomplished by supplying a hospital with an unlimited free supply of a commercial formula. As a follow-up, printed formula slips are provided for the hospital to present to the departing new mother and child. At times, she is given a send-off supply of the formula itself, thus establishing brand loyalty. The pediatrician and general practitioner are supplied with formula sheets, supplemented with impressive references from the professional journals.

INFANT FORMULAS—HOW SCIENTIFIC?

Cow's milk is usually the basic ingredient of infant-feeding formulas, and differs considerably in composition from human milk. This is apparent from the comparisons listed in *Composition of Foods,* Agriculture Handbook No. 8:[3]

	human milk, U.S. samples (100 grams)	fluid whole cow's milk (pasteurized & raw, 3.7 per cent fat) (100 grams)
protein	1.1 grams	3.5 grams
carbohydrate	9.5 grams	4.9 grams

Other differences in nutritional components include the types and amounts of fats, vitamins, and minerals.

To adapt cow's milk to the infant's need, the excessive protein content must be lowered. Hence the formula is "modified" with water. To compensate for the lack of lactose in cow's milk, the formula is supplemented with additional carbohydrates. The source may not be lactose, but ordinary table sugar (sucrose), maltose, or dextrin.

In addition to the questionable wisdom of substituting a contrived feeding formula for breast milk, there are other important considerations. The act of breast feeding provides psychological as well as physical benefits both to the infant and mother. Also, a considerable number of children develop allergy to cow's milk. Many physicians believe that breast feeding circumvents this problem. Dextrin in the formula, derived from starch, is another potential allergen. Table sugar, which may be present, is undesirable.

BABY FORMULAS—FACTORY-MIXED

A growing number of commercial enterprises are now established throughout the country which provide ready-to-drink baby formulas to hospitals and homes. The formulas provide whatever the doctor orders. According to the *Wall Street Journal* this may include "Coca-Cola and strawberry Jell-o concoctions that combat diarrhea, a goat's milk formula for babies allergic to cow's milk and a formula that uses natural mother's milk" among some 156 different kinds of formulas. It is not known how many babies are using factory-mixed formulas at present, but the number is sizable. A San Francisco service supplies 70 of the area's largest hospitals, and a Chicago company filled 2,000,000 bottles in the first five months of 1966. At least 11 other cities have similar service, many for hospitals. Mothers using the service claim that it saves time, prevents other children from upsetting the sterilizers, and is "the greatest thing since diaper service."[4]

HAZARDOUS CONTAMINANTS IN
BABY-FEEDING FORMULAS

Nitrate poisoning, (discussed in Chapter 11) presents hazards in formula feeding. Water high in nitrates, if used to dilute the formula, poses a special threat to a tiny infant. The blood hemo-globin of babies up to the age of 16 weeks differs from that of the adult. At this early age, the infant is highly sensitive to nitrate poisoning. If the water is contaminated, powdered milk prepara-tions, evaporated milk, and formulas, all diluted with water, may increase the infant's nitrate intake. He may drink ten times as much water per body weight as an adult, thus ingesting far more nitrate, proportionately, than the adult drinking the same water. The dyspeptic infant may convert the nitrate, already a toxin, into the even more poisonous compound nitrite. Hence, a sickly infant is more endangered than a healthy one. As mentioned earlier (see Chapter 11), cases of fatal infant cyanosis have been traced to nitrate poisoning.[5]

Strontium 90 also poses a threat to the infant fed commercial baby foods. Commercial dried infant foods, reconstituted in water, have been found to contain up to six times as much radioactive material as human milk.[6] The higher percentages of radioactive strontium come from water used to mix the formula, as well as in dried cow's milk used in its manufacture. Mother's milk is lower in fallout residue than cow's milk because the human diet contains less radioactive material than the cow's.

CEREAL SOLIDS—"NUTRITIONAL PROGRESS"?

The food industry has been aggressive in its campaign to switch the growing infant's diet from a liquid formula to cereal solids at an earlier age than formerly. Among 2,000 pediatricians surveyed a few years ago, more than half admitted that they were being strongly pressured for an early switch in the baby's diet by mothers who regarded the addition of solid food as "a form of nutritional progress."[7] Leading baby specialists said that the very early addition of solids offered "no added advantage," and one child psychiatrist charged that the practice was "part of the general cultural trend to speed up everything."

Dr. Allan Brown, a pioneering Canadian pediatrician and former physician in chief of the Toronto Hospital for Sick Chil-dren, remarked that refined white flour in infant cereals has "about as much food value as powdered glass."[8] Other physicians have pointed out that infants lack the enzyme ptyalin in their saliva until they are about six months of age. The pancreatic gland does not develop any starch-digesting enzymes until the molar teeth erupt. Up to that point, the infant can digest milk, meat, and fats, but not starches. Hence, such foods as cereals, mashed potatoes, rice, pablum, and other starch foods cannot be digested. Instead, these foods may ferment, causing gastrointestinal upsets, rashes, respiratory disturbances, and other discomforts or potentially dangerous conditions.

Nonetheless, the processors of baby pap have pressured mother, physician, and grocer with all the resources they command. This multimillion dollar business is among the leading national advertisers.[9] One of the largest processors of baby food claims to reach more than 70 per cent of all new mothers through direct mailings.

The baby-food processors employ "detail" men, similar to the salesmen employed by the pharmaceutical firms, to visit physicians, and extol the benefits of early and broad use of their products. Physicians are further "educated" through the extensive advertising placed in professional journals.[10]

The supermarket also has felt pressures from the sellers of baby food. In one location, field salesmen were charged with buying out competitors' stock secretly in an effort to force customers to switch to their own brand, rearranging the shelves to put competing brands in less accessible places, and intermixing cans and jars of different competitive products, as well as hiding more desirable items behind the slow sellers.

Commercial baby foods lack vitamin E. This conclusion was reached by researchers who examined six popular commercial infant formulas and ten baby cereals. Processing destroys substantial amounts of vitamin E tocopherol. The researchers wrote: "Although the requirements of the infant are not clearly indicated, it would appear that the infant formulas should be supplemented."[11]

JUNIOR BABY FOODS—WHAT'S IN THEM?

After the formulas and the cereal foods, the growing baby is introduced to the meats, chickens, fruits, vegetables, and puddings devised by industry. Meat is a comparative late-comer in the commercial baby-food venture. The industry was started in the late 1920's, but strained meat was introduced only at the end of World War II. The neglect of meat for the baby had a sound nutritional basis. The chief contribution it makes to the diet is protein. Physicians have maintained that adequate amounts of protein are already obtained from milk in the normal baby's diet.

In the early period of commercial baby-food preparation, products were kept bland. Through the years, baby foods have been used increasingly by adults with ulcers, by persons with chewing problems, and by the elderly. In addition, many mothers select baby foods that appeal to their own eyes and taste. These adult consumers and testers of baby foods have changed the very nature of the products. Now baby foods are flavored, salted, and colored to appeal to adult tastes, not child needs.

To gratify adult desires, numerous additives have been incorporated that are unnecessary, undesirable, and even dangerous. Examination of the labels on typical baby foods in a supermarket shows many additives.

Strained ham and ham broth, meat sticks, and frankfurters for juniors contain, among other ingredients, salt, sugar, and sodium nitrite. All three of these additives are objectionable, and especially in baby food. Sodium nitrite is used to keep the color of the meat bright and appealing to the adult who makes the purchase. In the presence of ascorbic acid, the sodium nitrite becomes more potent. Yet both may be present in meat for infants.

Chicken and chicken broth contain, among other ingredients, sodium carboxymethylcellulose (discussed in Chapter 4), a hazardous material. This cheap emulsifier is used for appearance, to keep the broth from separating. Processors claim its "usefulness" is to save the busy mother the time it takes to stir the food before serving! A check of brands without this material reveals that the gelatine found naturally in chicken apparently keeps the product from separating without resort to cheap emulsifiers.

Many fruit-starch puddings contain more sugar than any other ingredient, a highly objectionable feature. Calcium sulfate is added as a stabilizer to some baby dessert fruit gelatines.

Sugar is all too common an ingredient in baby foods. In orange juice especially processed for babies, sugar is "added to maintain a uniform sweetness." Sugar is added, not only to fruits and baby-food dessert, but even to some meat foods.

The consumer may wonder just how much meat is contained in the junior "high meat dinner." There is no requirement for listing the percentage of meat, or any other ingredient, on the label of foods consumed by the baby, or for that matter, for any food consumed by human beings. *Ironically, this essential information is required on the labels of foods for dogs and cats!*

Mono- and diglycerides, the synthetic emulsifiers (discussed in Chapter 4), have been added to some baby foods. MSG (discussed in Chapter 3) had been added to commercial baby foods containing meat or vegetables, until this "flavor enhancer" was found to cause brain damage in experimental animals. The processors voluntarily withdrew MSG from baby-food products.[12]

Salt in baby foods, especially deplorable, is almost universally present in meats, vegetables, puddings, and fruits, appealing to jaded adult taste buds rather than to the young child. The salti-ness is increased by the presence of sodium in some of the additives, such as *sodium* nitrite, *sodium* carboxymethylcellulose, and mono*sodium* glutamate.

In 1963 researchers at the Brookhaven Institute analyzed differ-ent samples of strained meats sold as baby foods. They found the salt content among most samples of vegetables and miscellaneous mixtures in concentrations far higher than those in nonprocessed meats and vegetables:[13]

	sodium range per 100 grams
processed:	293 to 510 milligrams
unprocessed:	144 to 357 milligrams

Five out of seven experimental infant rats fed on a diet of these commercial baby foods quickly developed high blood pressure. The control infant rats, fed a mixture of freshly prepared strained meats and vegetables plus a small daily dose of multivitamin mixture, showed no signs of the disease. The researchers suggested that high intake of salt in infancy may be implicated in the development of high blood pressure in the adult.[14]

Four years after the Brookhaven studies, an analysis made of

318 CONSUMER BEWARE!

many commercial baby foods showed that excessively high levels of salt were still present. "Data on the sodium in infants' feeding diets indicate that those receiving commercially prepared infant foods are ingesting a level that far exceeds the needs for growth and to compensate for obligatory losses through the skin and kidneys. . . . Since the high sodium in infants' foods is the result of the addition of sodium chloride to make the products more palatable to the mother, consideration might also be given to encourage manufacturers of baby foods to reduce the amount of salt added. There is no evidence that the infant rejects bland foods."[15]

The presence of food additives in commercial baby foods is regrettable. In addition to the hazards, it offers a specious justification for the general practice of food processors to use additives. The reasoning is: if additives can be used in baby foods, then certainly they must be harmless for the general public.

The mother responsible for feeding a child should be aware of certain facts, stated in a report issued in 1962 by FAO/WHO:

Foods that are specifically prepared for babies require separate considerations from *all* other foods as regards the use of food additives and toxicological risks. The reason for this is that the detoxicating mechanisms that are effective in the more mature individual may be ineffective in the baby. The committee strongly urges that baby foods should be prepared *without* food additives, if possible. If the use of a food additive is necessary in a baby food, *great caution should be exercised* both in the *choice* of the additive and in the *level* of use."[16] [Emphasis mine.]

In 1966, the same organization recommended once again that "synthetic or even natural products should not be added to baby food unless absolutely necessary, and in only very limited quantities." An additional recommendation made by the Committee was: "In the case of special cereals or enriched foods, the label should state clearly the ingredients, so that allergic babies could be switched to other compounds."[17]

In view of the special toxicological problems posed for infants, the Federation of Homemakers has urged repeatedly that the FDA set up a separate classification of additives permitted in baby foods. To date, this suggestion has not been acted upon.

Pesticidal residues, already discussed as present generally in commercial foodstuffs, pose even greater hazards in foods intended for infant consumption. A scientist in charge of special technical projects for one of the largest processors of baby foods testified before the Delaney hearings on chemicals in foods that his company had developed a considerable research program to minimize pesticidal residues in baby foods. "Primary consideration," he said, "was given to the evidence that young animals are usually more susceptible than older ones and occasionally exhibit marked changes in certain organs, even though the body growth may be normal, when subjected to the chronic toxic effects"[18] of certain pesticides. He admitted that his company was forced to reject crops that showed contamination. However, such produce was not destroyed, but sold to less particular processors or on the open market. His company had spent nearly $700,000 during a five-year period to maintain minimum residues in baby foods. Despite these efforts, the scientist admitted that the company was "unable to develop any washing, peeling, or inactivation procedure which will completely remove" the pesticide residue or off-flavors resulting from its presence.[19] "Processing, in many instances, tends to accentuate the off-flavor, which continues to develop for some time after processing, while the produce is on the shelf." Attempts to keep baby foods relatively free of pesticide contamination, testified the scientist, "involves a hardship on both ourselves and the farmers, and certainly does not make for good farmer-canner relationships." Then he added: "But it has to be done not in our interest, or that of the farmer, but in that of the ultimate consumer, the baby."[20]

BABY FOODS, MOTHERS?

Consider breast feeding the new infant. Help can be obtained through your physician, as well as through La Leche League (Franklin Park, Ill. 60131), a group of women interested in helping to advise others on breast feeding.

Babies are born with the instinct to suck. Many pediatricians believe that feeding problems are created by forcing solid foods on them too early in infancy. Because an infant has little control over his tongue, and throat muscles are underdeveloped, swallowing solid foods is difficult. Apparently, the young child, protected by nature, has an impulse to reject such foods. Infants vary in developing their ability to swallow. When the infant is ready, solid foods can be started without resistance. Dilute the food with milk or fresh fruit juice, and feed it from a bottle that has an enlarged hole in the nipple.

Although the thought of home preparation of solid baby foods may sound tedious, it need not be. A food mill for fine mashing and straining, as well as an electric blender, can simplify the procedure. Many of the fresh fruits and vegetables, as well as protein foods such as eggs, fresh meats, and fish, used by the rest of the family can be blended or mashed and strained for the baby. Omit salt, sugar, and other additives.

While the child is still eating only very small quantities, it may be convenient to blend enough food for several meals and quick-freeze individual portions.

Meat, cooked just enough to sterilize the outside surface, can be scraped with a spoon for easily digested protein, with vital enzymes and other elements conserved. Liver can be simmered briefly and ground, along with the water in which it was cooked.

Better Food for Better Babies is a pamphlet that offers many helpful suggestions for preparing nutritious foods for infants. (Write Mrs. Gena L. Larson, P.O. Box 582, Leeds, Utah 84746, $1.25.)

The advantage in home preparation of baby food is the precise knowledge of what it contains. The food can be of high quality and free of the hazards of additives. Dr. Wiley's words are still valid: "The best place to prolong life is at the beginning of life."[21]

14

Sweet, Cheap, and Detrimental

"In a state of nature man's sweet taste was a blessing, by attracting him to the many fruits that are rich in vitamins. But today the refining of sugar has reached such a state of perfection that all vitamins and minerals that are present in the cane or beet are left behind with the molasses and benefit only the cattle that are fed the molasses or its residue after distilleries convert molasses into alcohol. The glistening white crystals of sugar provide man with his cheapest and purest food, yet the very purity makes it objectionable. It is pure calories which man . . . woman or child . . . does not need, or at best would much better obtain from foods that also give . . . a balance of protein, vitamins and minerals," wrote Dr. Ralph W. Gerard, in Food for Life.[1]

The historical development of white sugar bears some resemblance to that of white flour. When sugar refining was first begun, poor people who could not afford this costly commodity used dark sugar or molasses. In 1880 a centrifugal machine was devised, separating sugar from the cane, making it possible to manufacture a highly refined product with a long shelf life, and cheap enough for all to afford.

What happened to the sugar?[2]

In its natural state, sugar also contains significant amounts of other vitamin B complex fractions, notably pantothenic acid and carries

321

	one tablespoon of light cane molasses	one tablespoon of refined white granulated sugar
calories	252	385
total carbohydrates	65 per cent	99.5 per cent
(milligrams) calcium	165	0
(milligrams) phosphorus	45	0
(milligrams) iron	4.3	0
(milligrams) sodium	80	0.3
(milligrams) potassium	1500	0.5
Vit. B_1 (thiamin)	.07	0
Vit. B_2 (riboflavin)	.06	0
Vit. B_3 (niacin)	0.2	0

the Wulzen factor (an antiarthritic agent), vitamin E, and trace elements such as copper, manganese, zinc, and iron in a form most easily assimilated.

WHAT ABOUT BROWN SUGAR?

Brown sugar offers no advantage over white sugar. If anything, it is even *more* refined, and the refining process itself presents hazards.

Don't let the color fool you. The raw sugar is washed to remove the film of molasses present on the surface of the raw sugar crystals. The mixture is put into a centrifuge machine, where it is separated from the crystals. Then it is heated to a melting point, filtered, and "decolorized" with animal-bone charcoal. By boiling it repeatedly, the decolorized liquid becomes crystallized and concentrated. *The "brown" coloring in this sugar comes from the bone-charcoal treatment rather than from the residue of molasses.*

Regarding this "decolorizing" process, Dr. Hueper has said: "In themselves, sugars may not be carcinogenic—but carcinogenic impurities may be introduced into sugars when concentrated sugar solutions are filtered for decolorizing purposes through improperly prepared charcoal containing polycyclic hydrocarbons. Chemicals of the dibenzanthracene type are eluted [washed out] from charcoal by concentrated sugar solutions. Traces may be introduced in this manner and may remain in apparently chemically pure sugars."[3]

WHAT ABOUT RAW SUGAR?

Some 64 food ingredients have been isolated in the raw juice of sugar cane. These include many essential minerals such as potassium, magnesium, calcium, iron, manganese, phosphate, sulfate, and others; seven vitamins: A, D and five of the B complex; four enzymes needed to assimilate sugar; all of the essential amino acids for forming proteins; and two important unsaturated fatty acids (linoleic and linolenic).[4]

However, in making sugar, when the juice is pressed from the cane, it is treated with heat and lime to precipitate some of the so-called "impurities." These include some of the valuable elements found in the raw juice of the sugar cane.

After the heat and lime treatment, the resulting products are raw sugar and blackstrap molasses. The molasses probably gets the bulk of the vitamin B complex, which is water-soluble. The raw sugar is still a good repository of minerals. However, it should still be viewed as a processed food, modified from the raw juice of the sugar cane. Raw sugar should be used sparingly, if at all.

WHAT ABOUT REFINED WHITE SUGAR?

Although sugar is not a basic food, it accounts for a sizable portion of the average American's total daily food intake. Like salt, it is found in nearly all processed foods. Chefs, homemakers, and consumers all may use sugar with a heavy hand, helping to perpetuate a myth that sugar "brings out the flavor" in food.

Per capita use of sugar and syrups has more than doubled since 1889.[5] Worldwide, the United States ranks among the highest in sugar consumption. A conservative estimate of the average *daily* American sugar consumption is a quarter of a pound. The Sugar Institute crooned: "Sugar must be one of our most needed foods— that's why we like it so much."[6]

As for the individual who assumes that he avoids sugar by not dipping into the sugar bowl, even he rarely escapes. Breakfast may begin with sweetened canned or frozen juice. Cereal may be presweetened, even if not sugared at the table. The bread, biscuit, muffin, waffle, or pancake contains sugar. Additional sweetening may be added with jam, jelly, marmalade, or syrup. Sugar may lace the coffee, tea, or cocoa.

The midmorning snack of Danish pastry or doughnut, possibly accompanied by a beverage, adds more sugar.

The lunchtime soup, crackers, sugar-cured ham in the sandwich, pickle, and apple pie à la mode are all vehicles for sugar.

The midafternoon candy bar "for quick energy" or the stick of chewing gum adds more.

The evening meal carries its fair share. The alcoholic drink, possibly a mixture with ginger ale, has sugar in both its constituents. The salad may be garnished with a sugar-containing dressing, the meat gravy with a dash of sugar, and the canned or frozen vegetable processed with sugar. The dessert, if cake, pie, cookie, custard, gelatine, or canned fruit, adds its quota.

For television snacks, the candy dish and Coke or beer bottle may be handy. The total daily intake of sugar adds up quickly!

"When it comes to human diets," wrote Dr. Michael H. Walsh, instructor in clinical nutrition at the University of California, "there is no object in furnishing sugar unless appropriate amounts of proteins, fats, minerals, and vitamins are also furnished. Refined sugar, because of its highly concentrated form, and being completely devoid of essential proteins, vitamins, and minerals, is now regarded nutritionally *as a diluting agent* of the modern diet. It is a displacer of other factors far more essential than sugar. Thus, the more sugar consumed, the less opportunity for getting essential nutrients into the diet. If sugar is furnished as a replacement of proteins, fats, minerals, and vitamins, then serious physiological consequences follow. This is the essence and the crux of the physiological problem we have to deal with, not only in dentistry, but also in medicine."[7] (Emphasis mine.)

SWEETEN IT UP—FOR "CONSUMER ACCEPTANCE"

Commercial cakes, ready-mixed cakes, and cakes made from recently devised recipes are likely to have *twice* as much sugar as formerly. Bakers have found that cakes made with more sugar hold their moisture better and last longer. Whereas formerly the wedge of pie or cake, scoop of ice cream, or piece of confection was an occasional treat, these have become routine in the daily menu.

The typical American palate is jaded by sugar, which predominates over other flavors. At a 1959 California fair, for example, samples of canned peaches were displayed with varying concentrations of sugar in the syrups, ranging as high as 55 per cent. In tabulating answers to the questionnaire given to persons sampling the peaches, it was found that the samples with the *highest* sugar content were preferred. This response made the sugar interests advise canners to sweeten syrup at least 60 per cent over previous levels to "gain maximum consumer acceptance."[8]

The food industry happily obliges, since sugar, a cheap commodity, can replace more expensive ingredients. At times the sweetness of processed sugary items is so excessive that even jaded palates rebel. At this point, to counteract the cloying sweetness, citric acid may be added to the heavy syrup in canned fruit.

"QUICK ENERGY"

"Eat sugar for 'quick energy' " has been the advice of Sugar Information, Inc. Most nutritionally ignorant people have come to accept the idea of "quick energy" as beneficial. In reality, it can be harmful, especially when dietary habits are poor. Excessive amounts of sugar consumed for "quick energy" are burned at the expense of inadequate amounts of protein and fat, which supply essential elements necessary for proper metabolism.

The quick assimilability of refined sugar is actually responsible for *unfavorable* effects. It plays havoc with the normal function of the blood-sugar level by raising it temporarily, and then lowering it dangerously. This can lead ultimately to chronic partial blood-sugar starvation and diseases.[9]

Sugar Information, Inc., crowed: "Nutritional findings show that your need for nature's own sweetener is as deep-seated as the human body's need for energy. Although sugar has been extracted from plants and used by man as one of his most valued foods for thousands of years, scientists are just beginning to appreciate the important role sugar plays in the life processes."[10] Surely, the last sentence of this quotation was meant to convey the impression that refined sugar benefits mankind, but its overtones are ironic.

Yes, refined sugar *does* play an important role in the life processes—but, when used in excess, a detrimental one. Such use has been denounced by nutritionists, physicians, dentists, anthropologists, and scientific researchers.* Other than industry-associated persons, refined sugar has few defenders. Excessive sugar consumption has been suspected of being implicated in a wide range of conditions that lead to ill health and degenerative diseases.

HOW THE FDA DISCOURAGED
NUTRITIONAL IMPROVEMENT

Officially, federal agencies endorse the principle of "enrichment" and "fortification" of foods. In practice, the FDA has taken action to discourage some food processors from attempting to improve the nutritional qualities of impoverished, overprocessed foods such as sugar. The Dextra case serves as an illustration.

A Florida food processor, recognizing the debasement of refined sugar, developed a special process that added nutrients to it. The label on the product said: "Now, at long last, many of the vitamins and minerals lost in the refinement of cane juice have been restored to Dextra Fortified Cane Sugar. Almost any diet can be nutritionally improved by the use of Dextra Fortified Cane Sugar in place of sweetening agents containing only 'empty calories'— calories unaccompanied by nutrients."[11]

* Among many other authorities who might de cited are E. M. Abrahamson, M.D., and A. W. Pezet, *Body, Mind and Sugar.* New York: Holt, 1951; T. L. Cleave, M.R.C.P., G. D. Campbell, M.D., and N. S. Painter, M.S., *Diabetes, Coronary Thrombosis and the Saccharine Disease.* Bristol: John Wright, 1969 (2nd ed.); Weston A. Price, D.D.S., *Nutrition and Physical Degeneration.* Los Angeles: American Academy of Applied Nutrition, 1950. (5th printing); Vilhjalmur Stefansson, *The Fat of the Land.* New York: Macmillan, 1956, pp. 117–120; Dr. John Yudkin, "Dietary Fat and Dietary Sugar in Relation to Ischemic Heart Disease and Diabetes." *The Lancet,* Vol. 2, No. 7349, July 4, 1964, p. 45; Margaret J. Albrink, M.D., J. Wister, and Evelyn B. Man, Ph.D., "Serum Lipids, Hypertension and Coronary Artery Disease." *American Journal of Medicine,* Vol. 31, July 1961, pp. 4–23; and Albrink and Man, "Serum Trigylcerides in Coronary Artery Disease." *Archives of Internal Medicine, American Medical Association,* Vol. 103, No. 1, Jan. 1959, pp. 4–8.

On the basis of this label, the FDA seized the product as "misbranded." The action was contested by Dextra in a federal court. The judge, ruling in favor of Dextra, stated: "The sole basis of the government's charges is that the added nutrients are of no value because they are already in adequate supply in the American diet. This is clearly an untenable basis for holding the product misbranded. The provisions of the Federal Food, Drug, and Cosmetic Act did not vest in the FDA or any other federal agency the power to determine what foods should be included in the American diet; this is the function of the marketplace."[12] The FDA appealed the decision to a higher court. The original court decision was upheld in favor of the manufacturer.

GLUCOSE—"THE CHAMPION ADULTERANT"

Glucose, the cheapest sugar, has had a long history of use as a filler, or adulterant, of many foods. The consumer may be unaware either of its presence or its dangers. It was termed the "champion adulterant" by Dr. Wiley.[13]

Glucose is made from cornstarch, a natural product with minerals and vitamins. But the original starch is converted, by means of sulphuric or hydrochloric acid, into a soluble carbohydrate that dissolves readily in solids or liquids. The strong acid destroys all the nutritional values (phospholipids, phytates of calcium and magnesium, and fractions of the vitamin B and E complexes) contained in the original starch. Arsensic residue, present in either acid, may contaminate to some degree the resulting product, which at this stage is ill smelling and dark. These objectionable qualities are removed by filtration and deodorization. The end product, glucose (or dextrose, "corn syrup," or "corn sugar"), is clear, odorless, and nearly tasteless.

Glucose products need not be declared on food labels. Unsuspected, they may be present in many processed foods, including canned fruit and fruit juices, fruit butters, syrups, preserves, jams, jellies, soft drinks, candy, canned vegetables, spiced cheeses, ice cream, sweetened condensed milk, catsup, and bakery products. Often dried fruits are saturated with glucose to increase their weight, so that a consumer pays fruit prices for a cheap filler.

Glucose is a dangerous form of sugar because it has very little sweetness. Without realizing it, the unsuspecting customer may eat quantities of it. Glucose can displace vital foods in the diet to an even greater extent than refined cane or beet sugar.

The "quick-energy" factor, already demonstrated as undesirable in cane or beet sugar, is far worse in glucose. Of all sugars, it is the fastest to diffuse through the intestinal wall.[14] When levulose sugar (from fruit) is eaten, it enters the blood stream within four hours; glucose is in the blood stream within 15 minutes. This may be a virtue for intravenous feeding of hospital patients who cannot take food by mouth. But as Dr. Wiley pointed out long ago, "What would be all right" in that situation would be "all wrong" for "the conservation of natural digestion."[15]

The harmful effect of glucose was well described by Wiley, who testified: "The burning of the sugar in the blood is activated by the pancreas. Now if we flood our stomachs with dextrose (glucose), then we will need half a dozen artificial pancreases to take care of it, and there is the real danger, the threatening danger, as every wise physiologist will tell you, from that source."[16]

When glucose was first introduced on the retail market in 1902 the public had the impression that it was made from glue. To overcome this prejudice, the company renamed it "corn syrup," under which misnomer the product became popular.[17]

Dr. Wiley condemned its use. He charged that the term "corn syrup" was misbranding, since glucose was made from neither corn nor syrup. A food was considered misbranded if it bore the name of another substance. In this case there *had* been a true corn syrup earlier, from the expressed and concentrated juice of the corn stalk.[18]

The presence and unsuspected nature of glucose in food today is the direct result of a long but unsuccessful battle waged by Dr. Wiley to keep it out of food. Hearings were conducted, with the powerful glucose-refining interests exerting strong pressure on the Department of Agriculture, on Congress, and on the President. Among other things, Dr. Wiley charged that chemists in colleges and universities were paid honorariums of $50 each to sign testimonials favoring the term "corn syrup."[19] After the hearings were concluded, the government assented to the term "corn syrup" and allowed its use in foods.

Since Dr. Wiley's time, additional evidence has implicated glucose in numerous conditions and diseases. Glucose was found to be the *only* known sugar capable of inducing diabetes in test cats. The experiments demonstrated the destructive effects of glucose on the pancreatic tissues.[20]

SACCHARIN—"A NOXIOUS DRUG"

"Saccharin is a noxious drug, and even in comparatively small doses it is harmful to the human system," wrote Dr. Wiley in 1913.[21] He tried to keep this nonnutritive adulterant out of food and drink.

Saccharin, a coal-tar product synthesized in 1879, is intensely sweet, cheap, and not bulky to handle. Such qualities appealed to the food industry, which began to flood the market with candies, soft drinks and bakery products using saccharin as a sugar substitute. By 1890 the Commission of the Health Association in France decreed saccharin harmful,* and forbade its manufacture or import. Eight years later the German government limited its use, and expressly banned it from all food and drink. Similar actions were taken in Spain, Portugal, and Hungary. But attempts to keep saccharin out of food and drink in America have been unsuccessful.[22]

As early as 1951, three FDA scientists reported that saccharin at certain levels showed a high incidence of unusual combinations of cancers. The FDA chose to ignore the report. In November 1969 Dr. George T. Bryan, a tumor expert and cancer researcher at the

---

* The harmfulness of saccharin has been of concern to the medical community. Among other works which could be cited are Robert D. Barnard, "The Effect of Saccharin Ingestion on the Blood Coagulation and the *in vitro* Anticoagulant Effect of Saccharin and of Ferriheme." *Journal of the American Pharmaceutical Association*, Vol. 36, No. 8, Aug. 1947, pp. 225–228; Albert A. Bianca, M.D., "Sugarless Sweetener Changes Blood Sugar." *Science News Letter*, Vol. 79, No. 17, p. 264; R. G. Hogarth, "Case in Which Acute Pain in the Region of the Stomach and Pancreas was Apparently Produced by the Continuous Use of Saccharin." Memoranda, *British Medical Journal*, Vol. 1, 1897, pp. 715–716; H. C. Ross, M.D., "The Danger of Saccharin." Correspondence, *British Medical Journal*, Oct. 9, 1915, pp. 552–553; and Conrad Stritzler, M.D., and Dominick C. Oddo, M.D., "Acute Urticaria Caused by Sensitivity to Saccharin." *New York State Journal of Medicine*, Vol. 55, No. 23, Dec. 1, 1955, p. 3479.

medical school of the University of Wisconsin, reported to the FDA that using saccharin, he had produced bladder cancer in 47 per cent of the mice in one group, and in 52 per cent of another group. In a press interview, Dr. Bryan admitted that although direct cancer hazard to man from saccharin has not yet been established, he was "very suspicious." He added, "It may take many years before it is known exactly how dangerous the substance is, and until then its use should be restricted to those who need it for medical reasons."

Following the curbing of cyclamates in 1969, the FDA announced in March 1970 that saccharin would be reviewed by the NAS. The panel concluded that "on the basis of available information, the present and projected use of saccharin in the United States does not pose a hazard." But FDA officials noted that there are still unresolved safety questions. By mid-September 1970, the FDA announced that restrictions on the use of saccharin were being considered.

THE ARTIFICIAL-SWEETENING CRAZE

In 1950, a new type of artificial sweetener was developed. Cyclamates, some 30 times sweeter than sugar, offered certain advantages over saccharin to the food industry for use in processed foods. Cyclamates did not lose sweetness in cooking, canning, or baking. When first introduced, cyclamates could be substituted for sugar at half the cost. Later, about 64 cents' worth of cyclamates replaced as much as $6 worth of sugar.

Manufacturers of cyclamates, as well as the food processors, recognized a huge potential market. Special dietary foods would no longer be sold only to diabetics, but to a larger, more profitable group, those who wanted to reduce their weight.

No clear definition existed of what constituted a dietary food. Dietary value of artificially sweetened foods was claimed on the questionable basis of reducing calories by omitting sugar. The dietary tag was used by packers and retailers as a promotional gimmick. Increasingly, artificially sweetened foods and the sweeteners themselves were used by the general public.

For years the FDA had banned the use of artificial sweeteners in certain foodstuffs. Thus the agency had implied an awareness that unrestricted use for the general public, or for certain groups such as children, might be undesirable. The officials were undecided about the safety of the artificial sweeteners. No major research on saccharin had been conducted in recent years; even less was known about the relatively new cyclamates.

The FDA requested the Food Protection Committee, Food and Nutrition Board (NAS-NRC) to review the safety of artificial sweeteners for use in foods. This Committee, with Dr. Darby as chairman, issued a report in 1955 recommending that "the toxicity of these substances must be known, and their potential intake by significant segments of the population must be estimated."[23] Further: "There has not been extensive controlled studies of the use by people in various physiological states."[24] The Committee concluded that "there is no evidence that use of non-nutritive sweeteners, saccharin and cyclamate, for special dietary purposes is hazardous."[25]

The important issue remained unresolved. These foods were *not* being used solely for special dietary purposes, but *indiscriminately* by the general public. By June 1959, under new standards of identity, the FDA allowed food processors to sweeten fruits, jams, and jellies with artificial sweeteners in various combinations.[26] In rapid succession, artificial sweeteners were to be found in some ice creams, ice-cream cones, cookies, candies, canned fruits, juices, sodas, "diet" colas, puddings, toppings, syrups, breads, breakfast cereals, "900 calorie" drinks, salad dressings, and even vegetable soups and canned chicken dinners.

By sly editing, some manufacturers transformed the warning words into sales assets. "Nonnutritive" was explained as "no calories." "Should be used only by" became "recommended for." "For those who must restrict" was translated as "by persons who desire."[27]

In 1962, the FDA asked the Food Protection Committee for a second review. Although the safety of these substances was reaffirmed for use in foods, the report cautioned that "the question of the safety of cyclamate for all classes of people is not settled . . . its safety for expected use levels [cannot] . . . be guaranteed until the level at which it can be tolerated in various age groups and physiologic states is ascertained." Further warning was given that prolonged experience with the use of cyclamate "has not accumulated and little is known of the results of its continued ingestion in large amounts, in a variety of situations in individuals of all ages and states of health. The priority of public welfare over all other considerations precludes, therefore, the uncontrolled distribution of foodstuffs containing cyclamates."[28]

Despite the recommendations in this review, the FDA made no attempt to restrict the use of artificial sweeteners for the general public, nor to tighten label regulations. Instead, the use of artificial sweeteners was expanded, with official allowances extended for the curing of bacon and the coating of breakfast cereals, as well as for use in many new test-marketed food products.

The available supply of cyclamates in the United States increased from about 5 million pounds in 1963 to 15 million pounds in 1967, and was predicted to increase further.[29] It was estimated that about three quarters of the population consumed some non-nutritive sweeteners.

A group of prominent physicians in 1964 recommended a reappraisal of toxicological information concerning artificial sweeteners.[30] They stressed that studies were needed for the sick as well as for the healthy, for pregnant and lactating women, for the human fetus and for persons with chronic diseases.

Many studies, from diverse sources, began to give cause for concern. Professor Ryozo Tanaka, of the department of hygiene and public health in Iwate, Japan, studied the effects of artificial sweeteners on the fetus in pregnant mice. He found adverse effects from the cyclamates at a lower intake level than thalidomide. Dr. Tanaka found critical days during pregnancy when heavy quantities of the artificial sweeteners virtually killed the fetus. At reduced intake levels—those corresponding to amounts a woman might drink in two bottles of artificially sweetened soft drinks— there was only a 50 per cent chance that the young would be born alive. Dr. Tanaka's study has not yet been confirmed by other investigators.[31]

A laxative effect from high intake levels of cyclamate noted in humans has been produced in rats, dogs, and monkeys. Although the Food and Protection Committee's reports had noted data on the formation of soft or mushy stools with high intake levels of cyclamate, the Committee had dismissed this symptom as inconsequential. However, the persistent diarrhea observed in human subjects following intake of cyclamate was judged a "major effect" at a closed meeting held in 1968 by the Society of Toxicology.[32] Evidence indicates that the laxative effect is caused by osmotic action of unabsorbed cyclamate in the intestine.[33]

Chronic studies in several species of animals showed that a high dietary level of cyclamate (more than 1 per cent or daily doses above 1 gram per kilogram of body weight) inhibited the growth rate in rats, dogs, swine, and chickens.[34]

Pathologic changes were reported in the kidney, liver, intestinal tract, adrenal gland, and thyroid gland in studies of cyclamate involving numerous species of animals.[35]

Interference with the efficacy of drugs was also reported. There was one report of a change in certain blood-coagulation factors, with an indication that the cyclamate interacted with an anti-coagulant drug.[36] Cyclamate and saccharin were found to be bound to plasma proteins. Such binding processes may alter the activity of drugs and other chemicals taken into the body.[37] In another study, cyclamate was found to block the action of an antibiotic commonly used to control bacterial infection. The cyclamate interfered with the absorption of the antibiotic into the blood stream, and prevented it from reaching the infection site.[38]

Formerly, it was believed that cyclamate was not metabolized by the body, but simply excreted as cyclamate. More recently, it was found that about a third of those persons who consume cyclamate excrete a toxic breakdown product (cyclohexylamine). Dr. Marvin Legator, chief of the FDA's new cell-biology branch, reported that both in test tube and animal studies, cyclohexylamine, even in moderate amounts, caused "significant" chromosome breakage, which could result in genetic damage. (At present, there is no evidence that cyclamate damages human chromosomes.) The FDA was also concerned about another form of this breakdown product (dicyclohexylamine) which appears to be even more toxic than the original breakdown product.[39]

In late 1967, the FDA asked the NAS-NRC for a third review of the safety of artificial sweeteners for use in foods. In the report submitted in November 1968 the Committee concluded that "totally unrestricted use of the cyclamates is not warranted at this time."[40]

Although the FDA still doggedly continued to maintain that these artificial sweeteners posed no health hazard, by February 1969 the agency announced plans to remove cyclamates from the GRAS list (Generally Recognized As Safe).[41] A further shift of official position was made in April 1969, when the FDA proposed new labeling requirements.

By September 1969 it was apparent that further experiments conducted at the FDA's laboratories were raising new questions about the safety of cyclamate. Dr. Legator and his associates reported that in tests on rats a chemical related to the cyclamate had produced significant breaks in the chromosomes of cells that form sperm and in bone-marrow cells.[42]

For the next month the FDA was busily engaged in attempting to decide what official action should be taken. The Secretary of Health, Education, and Welfare assailed what he termed varying FDA assessments of possible health hazards associated with cyclamate use. He singled out for criticism an FDA experiment, widely reported, that demonstrated a 15 per cent incidence of birth defects after cyclamate was injected into chicken eggs.[43]

However, the data that led to official action were presented by one of the leading manufacturers of the cyclamates. This study showed that rats fed heavy doses of cyclamates during most of their life span developed bladder cancers. The information was reviewed by the National Cancer Institute and the Ad Hoc Sub-committee on cyclamate safety of the NAS-NRC. The Delaney clause makes it mandatory to remove any food additive if it has been shown to cause cancer when fed to man or animals. On Oct. 18, 1969, in a surprise move for the general public, if not to the cyclamate industry, Secretary Finch announced that cyclamates would be taken off the market for general use, and removed from the GRAS list.[44] In swift sequence, Dr. Herbert L. Ley of the FDA, who at the time was Commissioner, announced that his agency planned a thorough re-evaluation of all of the approximately 100 other items on the GRAS list. High on the list for re-examination is saccharin. Although it has been used widely for about fifty years, Ley noted that very little valid information was available on it.[45]

Removal of cyclamates from the GRAS list was called "arbitrary, unreasonable and capricious" by *Barron's*, the business and financial weekly.[46] A few scientists branded the Department of Health, Education, and Welfare's curb a sweeping decree after a "hurried meeting" and "on the basis of experiments employing only 12 rats." Seven consumers filed suit in a federal court to halt the ban.

THE NO-BAN BAN

A month after Secretary Finch's announced curb, he eased the blow to the multimillion dollar industry and other critics. By legal legerdemain, cyclamates were no longer classified as "additives" in foods, but became "drugs."[47] This maneuver circumvented the obstacle of the Delaney clause. Secretary Finch announced that cyclamates would now be regarded as over-the-counter nonprescriptive drugs and would be labeled as such. Cyclamates could be used in foods and as sugar substitutes in liquid or tablet form, as long as the label showed the cyclamate content of an average serving. The ban against the cyclamates in diet soft drinks and other beverages, effective Jan. 1, 1969, remained in effect.

The reclassification of cyclamates as drugs backfired. The FDA had issued orders permitting the marketing of cyclamate sweeteners and cyclamate-containing foods when sold as nonprescription drugs if companies filed "abbreviated" new drug applications with the agency, *without the usual safety and efficacy evidence*. Representative L. H. Fountain declared these orders "ill-advised" and "illegal," and he called for immediate action to rescind them.

Meanwhile, the FDA's Medical Advisory Group on Cyclamates had evaluated data and had concluded that the use of foods containing cyclamates was of little value in weight control. Actually, in 1969 experiments, male rats fed cyclamates in amounts equivalent to those normally consumed by man *gained* weight.

Since the evidence showed that cyclamates lacked value in weight-control programs, the FDA was forced to reimpose a total ban on cyclamates. This was issued on Aug. 14, 1970, to be effective on Sept. 1, 1970. A nationwide survey conducted during the month after the cut-off date revealed that half the stores were still selling food products containing the illegal cyclamates. The FDA took no vigorous action to enforce the order, but merely relied on voluntary compliance.

Was the original ban of cyclamates, as charged by opponents, "hysterical and unwarranted," because the dose to rats was 50 times as high as the recommended dose for man, and therefore it would be impossible for man to consume levels high enough to be dangerous? This reasoning is fallacious, said Dr. Umberto Saffiotti, associate scientific director for carcinogenesis at the National Cancer Institute. Researchers always use high levels of a chemical in order to detect the potential risk to man. In fact, said Dr. Saffiotti, a ratio of 50 times the human dose is actually a *low safety factor*. Usually researchers use 100 times the human dose to get significant results.[48]

Was the ban "on the basis of experiments employing only 12 rats"? The evidence of the bladder cancers in rats was *not* the only study showing that cyclamates and cyclamate compounds cause cancer. There were at least five studies demonstrating that these materials were carcinogenic. One study, conducted by the FDA, showed that bladder cancers were caused in rats at very low levels, only eight times more than dosages allowed for man.

One charge *was* true: it *is* difficult to judge with any degree of certainty the safety of materials for man, based on extrapolated results of animal tests. But there is irony in this charge. The very groups from industry that challenge the importance of adverse findings with test animals—whether it be cyclamates or other food additives, pesticides, drugs, or other consumer goods—are the very same groups that *rely* on similar animal tests to offer proof of safety in their products. How much protection is afforded consumers when the results of such tests *are* based on animals, and results *are* extrapolated to justify the use of substances by two hundred million or more people?

After the original curb on cyclamates was announced, pressures were renewed to weaken or repeal the Delaney clause. Secretary Finch admitted publicly that he would seek to have changes made in the Delaney clause. Dr. Saffiotti felt that the Delaney clause deserved to be strengthened, not weakened. In an interview he said, "I personally think we have too lenient a policy in that we apply the Delaney clause type of approach to a limited group of exposures."[49] He repeated what many leading cancerologists have said. Namely: a chemical that causes cancer at any level cannot be considered safe. There are numerous chemicals—in fact, the majority—that will not cause cancer when fed to animals, even at the highest tolerated dose. A chemical that is able to induce cancer when fed to animals is always potentially dangerous. Dr. Saffiotti considered this risk so serious that he advised people who had been taking large amounts of cyclamates daily—in grams, as some have—to have periodic urinary analysis of sediments for cancer cells.

"THE SYRUPY TIDE"

"Professional people who are trying to stem the syrupy tide are up against powerful forces. We are like hunters trying to stay elephants with air rifles," commented the well-known pediatrican Dr. Benjamin Spock. Part of the total excessive intake of sugar in the average diet comes from the syrupy sources.

Examine the bottles of waffle and pancake syrups that abound on the shelves in the grocery store. The labels are the fanciful creations of commercial artists, who depict farmers collecting sap from the maple sugarbush, using ox-drawn sleds, a rural kitchen scene, or some rustic cabin. Chances are, the syrup was never near a maple tree or farmhouse. Look closer, for the print under the picture may read: "Corn syrup, granulated sugar syrup, imitation maple flavor, caramel coloring, and salt."

Or, the syrup may be a mixture in which the presence of real maple syrup is so minute that it would scarcely be tasted. An example of this is a "buttered syrup," containing 2 per cent butter, and requiring no refrigeration. How much maple syrup is in this mixture? According to the label, the ingredients are:

sugar syrup 80 per cent, corn syrup 14 per cent, maple syrup 2 per cent, butter 2 per cent, water, algin derivative, salt, sodium citrate, citric acid, sodium benzoate 0.1 per cent as a preservative, artificial maple flavor, and coloring

The price, in this case, tells the story! This "original buttered syrup" which currently sells at 36 cents for three fourths of a pint offers quite a contrast to 100 per cent pure maple syrup that currently sells at $1.50 to $1.65 a pint. Convinced? Now look for real maple syrup.

HOW "PURE" IS 100 PER CENT PURE MAPLE SYRUP?

Traditionally, maple syrup has been sold as a pure unadulterated product. This was likely to have been true until 1962. In that year the FDA officially sanctioned use of a poisonous pellet (para-formaldehyde), which is placed in the taphole of maple trees. A tolerance for residue of this material was established. These pellets are long-lasting and slow-dissolving. They kill bacteria normally found in the tree, which, although harmless, slow down the flow of sap. Ostensibly, the pellets are used for "sanitizing."[50] But the real reason they are used is to keep the tapholes open longer, increase the sap flow, and reap more profits.[51]

Some experimenters have tapped as early as November, and then by adding a pellet, discovered that in the following April the taphole was still productive. In warm areas, others added a second pellet during midwinter and found that those trees also continued productive. Pellets make it possible to begin tapping in the north-east as early as January.

Although the pellet has been sanctioned by federal and state officials, it has not been greeted with enthusiasm everywhere. The maple-sugar industry in Canada is sizable. To date, the Canadian Food and Drug Directorate has resisted pressures to sanction the use of the pellet. Some U.S. producers, notably in Vermont, announced that they would not use the pellet. They said that maple syrup has always symbolized pure food, and this image should be maintained.[52]

Some producers, having tried the pellet, had unfavorable results. They found damage to trees below the tapholes,[53] and early runs have yielded syrup described as having a "leafy taste."

Use of the pellet may lower the quality of the syrup. There was wisdom in late tapping. If the sap is collected during a period when the chemistry of the tree changes from "sweet water" to substances used for tree growth, the sap becomes "buddy" and unfit for use in producing a table-grade syrup. With the wide-spread use of the pellet, the chance of producing "buddy" syrup is much greater than formerly. Even one or two trees in the "buddy" stage in a sugarbush can contaminate and downgrade the total flow from the area. To counteract this situation, a culture of bacteria (*Pseudomonas geniculata*) is added to the "buddy" syrup and allowed to ferment. The "buddy" flavor is disguised, making it possible to develop a syrup usable for commercial sales.[54]

There is no law that requires the producer to state on the label of maple syrup that he has used the pellet treatment. However, it is still possible to obtain 100 per cent pure *untreated* maple syrup. You must ask questions and make your desires known for syrup produced without pellet use.

Although flavorsome, even pure maple syrup is nutritionally limited. The long heating process has destroyed whatever food value was present originally in the sap. What remains is largely carbohydrate, an item already superabundant in the diet. Honey or unsulphured molasses (from cane or sorghum), with minerals, vitamins, and other nutrients, is a better choice.

HONEY—HOW GOOD?

Honey is relatively unadulterated. Bees are highly sensitive to pesticides. Exposed to sprays, they usually die before returning to the hive. Hence honey is one of the few foodstuffs low in pesticidal contamination. Honey is also free of artificial flavors or colors. Its supersweetness, and possibly the presence of an enzyme (inhibine), prevents honey from molding. Preservatives are unnecessary, and are not added.

The consumer has not been educated to accept the slight cloudiness and crystallized appearance of raw, unfiltered honey as a mark of quality. In a product that is clear, brilliant and easy-flowing the fine flavor may be lost.

The conscientious beekeeper can remove the honey from the comb with mild heat, not exceeding 120° F., and still retain nutrients in the product. But even with heat as low as 150° F., and by filtering out the "impurities," analysis shows losses:[55]

	Percentage of loss
thiamin	27–30
riboflavin	22–45
pantothenic acid	8–22
niacin	15–27
ascorbic acid	9–20

In addition, filtration removes valuable vitamin F and the Wulzen factor. Excessive heat makes ferments lose their character and destroys colloids and esters present in raw honey. Some countries, notably Germany, do not permit the importation of heated honey.

Even careful label reading fails to guarantee accurate information. To date, standards have not been established either by beekeepers, or formulated by the federal government, to differentiate between heated and unprocessed honey. According to beekeepers, some honey is sold as uncooked though it has been heated up to 200° F; or labeled "unpasteurized" and heated up to 160° F. Look for the label that reads "unheated," or "no heat used," or "raw and unfiltered."

A crystallized state of honey *should* indicate quality, but unfortunately this appearance does not guarantee that the product has not been subjected to excessive heat. The beekeeper may remove honey prematurely from the hive before it has ripened completely. Such green honey is high in moisture (often exceeding 20 per cent), accompanied by a biting, disagreeable flavor. If the honey is left in the hive longer, and permitted to ripen normally, the bees reduce the moisture to a lower percentage (less than 17 per cent), resulting in a smooth, mellow flavor.

Green honey will undergo some fermentation, which shortens its shelf life. To avoid this, the beekeeper may resort to heating the honey. Although the heating prevents fermentation, the honey still has an ability to crystallize.

To extract honey from the comb, beekeepers formerly used a simple bee-escape device to remove the bees, and brushed any stray bees off gently with a soft brush. Such practices are still in use among beekeepers who have only a few hives. At present, commercial beekeepers resort to poisonous materials which save time. These include carbolic acid, nitrous oxide, propionic anhydride, and more recently, benzaldehyde.[56] Repeated exposures to these substances may shorten the life span of bees.[57] No positive proof exists that these materials, reported to dissipate quickly, do not alter the honey or leave a residue.

Sulfa drugs and other antibiotics may be used to control bee diseases. These are fed to the bees in sugar syrup before or after a honey flow. In cases of severe disease conditions, the entire hive may be destroyed with hydrocyanic gas. Or beekeepers may use this poison in the autumn to kill bees before they winter, finding it easier to replace them with new stock the following spring. Sometimes empty combs are fumigated with moth balls (paradichlorobenzene) or methyl bromide; either material can contaminate and impair the flavor of honey. Concerned beekeepers, reluctant for their own safety as well as their bees' to use hazardous materials, find it possible to have healthy bees and quality honey without resorting to dangerous adjuncts.

"ENERGY-YIELD"

"Personally, I believe that candies should be given very sparingly to children, because of the tendency to decrease and debase the natural appetite, creating a longing for only sweet foods, which increase the danger of digestive disturbances," wrote Dr. Wiley.[58]

Sticky, tough sweets, retained for a long time in the mouth, or requiring continuous sucking, licking, or chewing, are especially notorious in encouraging dental decay. To overcome public distrust and boost sales even higher, the candy, chocolate, and confection trades created an institute to "educate" the public to "the many positive appeals" of their products. A spokesman reported: "Our industry has long felt the need for a program to communicate the taste appeal, nutritive values, and wholesomeness of our products."[59]

With this in mind, the group invests in promotional campaigns. Among them, "psychological benefits" have been gathered from diverse sources. Testimony was given in praise of the quick "energy-yield" of confections. These items were purported to prevent seasickness, inhibit alcoholism, and prepare the patient for surgery by increasing blood sugar without adding bulk or fat.[60] The National Safety Council suggested candy to counteract drowsiness at the wheel: "keep some in the glove compartment."[61] Similar safety features were intimated by military experts, who avowed that candy-eating fliers during World War II had a low accident rate. A few diet "experts" were located who suggested confections, ranging from sourballs to chocolate, to palliate the craving for rich desserts.[62] The Institute encountered some difficulty in locating dentists who would agree to enter into the spirit of the program and find "psychological benefits" in confections.

The annual per capita consumption of candy in the United

States by 1967 had reached 19.6 pounds.[63] This shows a 16 per cent rise since 1960, and means that the promotional campaigns of the industry have been effective. The current annual sum spent on candy in the United States, upward of $3 billion, is more than what is spent on dental care. Candy expenditures in England, equally staggering, caused a Ministry of Education official to comment that children "eat sweets so regularly that their teeth start rotting even before they go to school."[64]

Failing to get dental co-operation, the candy industry tried other tactics. A search was made for a child without cavities. After she was found, industry presented to her—accompanied by hoopla— an amount of candy equal to her own weight. Pictures and stories about the child were printed, and she appeared on television. The "psychological benefits" were apparent. An impression was created that 45½ pounds of candy could not possibly harm this child, or anyone else. Commenting on this promotional stunt, a dental journal branded it as "45½ pounds of cariogenesis" (generation of dental decay).[65]

Every opportunity is grasped to promote the sale of confections. St. Valentine's Day, Christmas, Easter, Mother's Day, Halloween, and birthdays are all familiar occasions for boosting confection sales. Parents and teachers use candy as a reward, and doting grandparents and neighbors bestow such items as symbols of their affection. Physicians give candy to brave little children, and the Lollipop Foundation of America donates lollipops to hospitals. This Foundation, begun by a philanthropic businessman, now supplies some U.S. hospitals with regular monthly shipments.[66]

Another popular campaign, encouraged by the confection industry, is to schedule candy-eating on the job. This is described by the Institute: "Secretaries, production workers, and the boss work better and are generally in a better mood because of the 'candy break.' The midafternoon snack usually does away with that four o'clock slump. Some of the larger factories and offices have instituted a new approach to the candy break and have one of their employees going through the plant à la cigarette girl, so that all employees might enjoy this delicious 'pep-up' food."[67]

Despite all the objectionable substances already permitted and likely to be found in candy (sugar, glucose, citric acid, glazes, artificial colors and flavors, etc.), industry now pressures for the inclusion of nonnutritive additives. For years candy has been singled out for special regulations because many purchasers, being young children, are considered unsophisticated shoppers. Also, certain chemicals, with no apparent adverse effects on adults, may be toxic to children.

The confectionery industry has smarted under these special regulations, considering them "discriminatory." In recent years industry has pressed for their repeal "to keep pace with scientific progress." Industry wants to use nonnutritive additives such as artificial sweeteners, emulsifiers, stabilizers, antioxidants, release agents, and preservatives, to extend the shelf life of candy. Passage of proposed legislation, according to a supporter, Representative Leo W. O'Brien, of New York, "will save the industry from enormous losses which come about as a result of stale candy."[68]

HAD YOUR BUTADIENESTYRENE RUBBER TODAY?

Chewing gum is defined legally as food and rightly so, for about two thirds of the stick of gum is actually swallowed. About 60 per cent of the total weight is sugar, which amounts to one half teaspoonful in each stick.[69] This high proportion of sugar is reason enough to avoid chewing gum. In studies, the chewing of a single stick of gum increased sugar in the saliva about 3,500 per cent, and the effect lasted about half an hour.[70]

Chewing gums have been touted as "aids to digestion." Not so. Experimentally, it was demonstrated that the chewing of gum by healthy people reduced acid in the stomach for an entire hour. This acid is the juice normally required for digestion.[71]

Chewing gum contains many questionable materials, some of which are known allergens, while others are suspected carcinogens. When chewed, they end up in the digestive tract.

Although the consumer supposedly has a legal right to know what ingredients are used in a foodstuff, the labeling of chewing gum serves as a classic example of the violation of this basic principle. This was pointed out by Consumers' Research,[72] when in 1939, a newly adopted amendment to the federal food laws was put into effect.[73] Chewing-gum manufacturers requested exemption for ingredient listing. Industry members pleaded "impracticability" in listing some 25 to 30 ingredients on a wrapper of chewing gum. Although the FDA denied exemption, great leniency was permitted. All "masticatory substances" could be collectively termed "gum base," a meaningless term to the consumer. Originally, the gums were natural materials from tropical trees. In recent years they have been largely supplanted by synthetic petroleum products, best avoided in the digestive tract.

The FDA also ruled that other ingredients in the chewing gum should be named individually. Dissatisfied with this decision, the gum manufacturers proposed to group another set of materials—which might include as many as 12 items—under an equally vague phrase: "modifying agents." The FDA consented to this request, and suggested that since the principal effect of these ingredients was as plasticizers, the term "softeners" would be satisfactory. Industry found this agreeable, but it became just one more meaningless term for the consumer.

In this new ruling, the FDA suggested an acceptable label that would list only two sweetening ingredients (sugar and corn syrup), despite the fact that most chewing gums include several other carbohydrates (dextrose, dextrin, starch, and maltose). This recommendation, offered by the FDA, is, in this author's opinion, an example of *how the agency not only sanctioned but encouraged flagrant evasion of the requirements of the federal Food, Drug, and Cosmetic Act.*

The FDA went further in its disregard of the law. From the very beginning, the agency has insisted that ingredients on labels be listed in the descending order of predominance, a practice which gives the consumer a modicum of information. But with chewing gum, the FDA advised manufacturers to list gum base *first* on the label, followed by sugars, even though sugars are present in greater amounts than gums.

The ingredients in chewing gum, both natural and synthetic, are best avoided. On occasion, shipments of chicle and some 15 other natural gum bases have been seized because they "contained insect and rodent filth,"[74] were "prepared under unsanitary conditions," or contained unapproved coal-tar colors. The synthetic materials (butyl or butadienestyrene rubber, paraffin, polyethylene, polyisobutylene, or polyvinyl acetate) are of questionable safety. In nearly all cases petroleum "cracking" products are strongly suspected as cancer-inciters.

The plasticizers (glycerine from petroleum) also are synthetics. Polyterpene resins from gum turpentine are permitted. The antioxidants (BHT, BHA, and propyl gallate), used to prevent staleness and brittleness in chewing gum, are derived from coal tars and petroleum. Other ingredients, including synthetic flavors[75] and colors, are found in chewing gum, and almost without exception, they are coal-tar, wood-tar, or petroleum derivatives.

How impractical is it to list these ingredients on the chewing-gum label? *Consumer Bulletin,* which has long championed the cause of adequate and accurate labeling, demonstrated that 25 or more ingredients *could* be listed clearly on the gum wrapper.[76] When the FDA granted the chewing-gum manufacturers the right to leave out most ingredients from the label listing, an official in the agency commented that some of the components were present in such *small* proportions that the FDA was unimpressed "with the importance to the consumer of a revelation of such ingredients."[77] The FDA seemed not to be overconcerned with its clear mandate to enforce the law strongly enough, which required the naming of *all* ingredients, without exception. Such decisions should not be made arbitrarily at the whims of the agency.

SOFT DRINKS: TOOTH DISSOLVERS

"I saw a pregnant woman in Guatemala who had become malnourished because her diet had consisted of soft drinks and tortillas. The same may happen in children, and we are beginning to see it in West Africa,"[78] reported a nutritionist, Dr. F. D. Sai, at an international nutritional conference.

"We have had cases," added another participant, Dr. Nevin S. Schrimshaw, "in which the mother has exchanged eggs for soft drinks and the baby has developed kwashiorkor"[79] (a disease of severe malnutrition in children). Nutritionists do not have to go to Guatemala or West Africa to see the ravaging effects of soft drinks in the diet. They can be seen in the United States as well.

The annual U.S. consumption of soft drinks amounts to 243 eight-ounce bottles for every man, woman, and child.[80] This represents a total of nearly $4 billion in yearly sales, which have more than doubled in the last decade, and doubtless will continue to mount. Introduction of the low-calorie soft drinks, the sales of which keep doubling year by year, accounts for part of this boom. Artificial sweeteners in the soft drinks, especially in the colas, created new markets; 17 per cent of these sales are to individuals who previously never drank cola, and nearly half of them to persons who never drank soft drinks of any kind.[81]

Nutritionally, soft drinks are low in value. Their food energy comes solely from refined sugar. Every element of nutritional importance, except calories, is zero.[82]

Soft drinks have much in common with hard liquor, claimed the codiscoverer of insulin, Dr. Charles Best. Used excessively, either may create protein deficiency by providing no nutrients and lessening the desire for nourishing foods. Among other effects, prolonged protein deficiency ultimately damages the liver. Cirrhosis of the liver has been found among teenagers who drink large quantities of soft drinks, as well as among chronic alcoholics.[83]

As with all empty foodstuffs, soft drinks may displace nourishing items in the diet. Nutritionists, writing in *Food for Life,* deplored that "Americans spend for soft drinks . . . [money] which could more wisely be spent for milk, vegetables, eggs, meat and cereals. Where the budget cannot afford both, malnutrition results; where it can afford both, the result is obesity."[84]

Soft drinks contain large amounts of refined sugar (or, until banned, artificial sweeteners). Soft-drink manufacturers are among the top commercial users of sugar. An eight-ounce bottle of a soft drink contains about five teaspoons of sugar.[85]

All soft drinks contain a sizable amount of acid, usually phosphoric or citric. Both erode tooth enamel, and impair the appetite as well as the digestive processes by creating excessive acidity in the stomach. Even mild acids from citrus fruits can erode tooth enamel,[86] and the stronger ones in soft drinks are far more destructive.[87] The problem is compounded by the high sugar content in the soft drink, which acts on bacteria present in the mouth, and forms additional acid to that already present in the beverage. Soft drinks are drunk frequently between meals, so the sugar remains in the mouth and is readily converted into acid. Frequently soft drinks are consumed repeatedly during the day, in which case the teeth are being subjected *constantly* to both the acids present in the drink and those formed in the mouth.

The harm of the phosphoric acid in soft drinks was dramatized in the work of nutritionist Dr. Clive M. McCay and his associates. During World War II, Dr. McCay noted that naval men spent a considerable portion of their food stipends on cola drinks. While studying the composition of these drinks, Dr. McCay was astonished by the high amounts of phosphoric acid present in all soft drinks, but especially in the colas. The strong acid taste is masked by the high sugar content.

Dr. McCay, working at the Naval Research Institute, placed extracted human teeth in cola drinks. Within two days the teeth became very soft, and the enamel surface lost much of its calcium.[88] Studies were continued from 1943 to 1950. Similar erosion was produced on the teeth of experimental rats, dogs, and monkeys when they were given cola drinks. One technician became so expert in judging the condition of the rats' molar teeth that she was able to tell which animals had had only single drinks of cola, amounting to two and one half teaspoonfuls. Rats, well fed but given nothing to drink except cola beverages, after six months *had their molar teeth dissolved down to the gum line.* Erosion was so severe that the rats could not eat normally, and experiments had to be discontinued.[89]

The significance of this study is clear. Many teenagers admit that they use soft drinks almost to the exclusion of water. Sadly enough, many of these young people are *not* so well fed as were the experimental rats.

A high intake of phosphorus, in any form, can upset the body's calcium-phosphorus balance. This is an especially important factor in children with rickets. There is also evidence that excessive phosphate prevents the absorption of iron, a mineral essential in the diet.[90]

Soft-drink processors may use many different colorings, flavorings, preservatives, antifoaming agents, emulsifiers, and fillers in their beverages. Both coal-tar colors of "certified dyes" approved by the federal government and "decertified" ones (which may still be used within the confines of certain states with impunity) offer unnecessary risks. Similarly, objections can be raised about the inclusion of artificial flavors and other additives, as well as the drug caffeine.

When Dr. McCay reported the rat experiments before the Delaney hearings on chemicals in foods, a lawmaker reminded him

that the soft-drink industry represented huge economic investments. He suggested that Dr. McCay's alarming findings be soft-
pedaled to avoid disrupting the industry and the economy as a
whole. Dr. McCay countered by stating that the health of the
nation's children might be as important as the welfare of the soft-
drink industry.[91]

The pressures to maintain a good public image for soft drinks
has been felt abroad as well as in the United States. Traditionally,
many European countries remained unenthusiastic about these
beverages. They were unwelcome in Italy. They are not sold in
Greece. The Belgian government has always required clear bold
lettering on cola bottles, warning of the caffeine content. Denmark
taxed these drinks out of existence. The French Parliament, recognizing the health hazards, especially of the cola drinks, banned
their sale in 1950. This move was interpreted as a grave threat to
the cola drinks, possibly to be followed by the closing of the entire
European market. The cola manufacturers, aided officially by our
federal government, exerted sufficient pressure to force the French
Legislature to repeal its law. As a result, the far-flung cola empires
today, with thousands of bottling plants, have succeeded in making the cola bottle a symbol recognized everywhere. Indeed, many
foreigners naïvely believe that the Statue of Liberty holds aloft a
cola bottle, not a torch!

SOFT DRINKS—WHAT'S IN THEM?

To date the consumer is largely uninformed regarding the ingredients used in soft drinks and colas. The soft-drink industry has had
a long record of resisting attempts to bring about informative
labeling. The 1938 amendment to the Food, Drug, and Cosmetic
Act granted temporary exemption of ingredient listings to certain
segments of the food industry, including soft drinks. Originally,
the exemption was granted for about two years. Finally, in 1961
the FDA served notice that label exemptions would end the
following year. A month prior to the end date the FDA granted
another year's extension to the soft-drink industry, presumably
because the trade association for this industry was busy formulating a standard of identity for its products. In 1963, the FDA

granted another extension. Repeatedly, similar expiration dates have been extended. At present no definite action is within sight. Soft drinks contain many additives, including caffeine. This drug is contained in *all* cola drinks without being stated on the label; it may be in other soft drinks if the label reads "with caffeine" or "caffeine added." Parents who may forbid their children to drink coffee or tea because these drinks contain caffeine may unwittingly be offering them the same drug in soft drinks. Experimentally, caffeine has produced genetic changes in bacteria, fruit flies, various plants, and in human cell cultures. Although the possible mutagenic effect on man is controversial, some researchers have said: "There is . . . a strong likelihood that caffeine may prove to be one of the most dangerous mutagens in man."[92]

Soft drinks contain other additives, about which the industry is vague. The soft-drink industry has requested a number of "optional" additives. Judging from past actions, if and when the standard of identity is established for these drinks, "optional ingredients" may not be required on the label.

More than half a century ago, Dr. Wiley wrote: "At least every parent having at heart the welfare of his child is entitled to know what that child drinks when he patronizes the soda fountain or the bottled beverages."[93] To date, this basic right has not been won.

SWEETS, ANYONE?

By eliminating processed foods, and eating mainly proteins, fruits, and vegetables, you can avoid most of the sweetening agents. Substitute raw, unfiltered honey or unsulphured molasses (from cane or sorghum) for any necessary sweetening. Limit the intake of these, since even they are bad for the teeth. Try to acquire a taste for foods in their natural, unsweetened state.

A "health snacks" plan was devised for kindergarten children by a school nurse eager to reduce sugary and starchy foods. She held conferences with parents, explaining the importance of nutritious snacks to help maintain children's appetites and sound teeth. Co-operating parents supervised foods taken to school by the children to eat and share with others. These snacks consisted of raw carrot or celery sticks, apple or orange wedges, and other fruits in season.

After eating the snacks, the children were urged to "swish and swallow" water, thereby cleansing their mouths. The children readily accepted the "health snacks," and newcomers to the group soon learned that sweets were not acceptable.[94]

Such habits can be established in the home for any age group. Fresh fruit satisfies a craving for sweetness, but keeps the craving within bounds. Also consider raw unsalted nuts, sunflower and pumpkin seeds, pieces of fresh coconut, wedges of natural cheese, cold cooked meat, chicken or turkey, and unsalted popcorn or roasted chestnuts. These snacks are nutritious, help maintain the blood sugar at a good level without creating havoc, and satisfy the appetite without developing abnormal desires for sweetness. Eliminate all soft drinks from the household. You will discover that water is the best no-calorie thirst quencher of them all.

PART IV

◆ ◆ ◆ ◆

SANE
ALTERNATIVES

15

What's to Be Done?

DURING THE 1969 Congressional Hearings by the Select Committee on Nutrition and Human Needs, Senator George McGovern, its chairman, noted a paradox. Despite our abundant production, our technological marvels of food processing, and our magnificent marketing systems, our population as a whole reflects disturbing dietary deficiencies. This affects not just the poor, but also our vast middle class and even the rich. This problem requires some critical examination, Senator McGovern admitted. He called into question our assumptions about the technological progress we seem to have accomplished. He called for "a serious inquiry into the general nutritional quality of foodstuffs now being marketed, the performance and nutritional standards of our industry, the performance of our governmental agencies charged with monitoring industry and maintaining nutrition standards, as well as the role of the scientific and medical community in setting and maintaining these standards."[1]

WE NEED A NEW FOOD REVOLUTION

When we come to realize that high nutritive food value is more important than any other quality, many changes will follow. A new food revolution should begin on the farm, with a shift of emphasis from quantity to quality; a restoration and maintenance of soil

353

fertility and balance; crop and livestock management for health and wholesomeness; and conversion from monoculture to mixed farming, intercropping, and diversification.

To do this, institutions and agencies responsible in formulating agricultural policy should reorient their viewpoint. Agricultural experiment stations and agricultural colleges need to develop and expand their work on safe and wise agricultural management. Federal and state agencies, in making recommendations for farm practices, should be guided by unbiased data drawn from numerous sciences, including agronomy, horticulture, entomology, plant pathology, ecology, biochemistry, and toxicology, as well as soil, plant, animal, and human nutrition. Policies must be abandoned that represent short-term expedients, in favor of long-range policies and recommendations wisely formulated so that health as well as a clean environment is a primary concern.

Federal and state agencies were advised as early as May 1963 in a White House report, *Use of Pesticides*,[2] to shift their emphasis from research on "broad spectrum" chemicals which are non-specific, to those which are selective and nonpersistent, as well as to develop nonchemical control methods. At that time, the USDA Secretary Orville L. Freeman admitted that his department's annual budget allotted less money for biological control of insect pests than the pesticide industry would spend to develop a single new pesticide.[3] Although some official work in biological controls has been initiated, federal and state government agencies still give the main emphasis to toxic chemicals. It is urgent that the USDA and state departments of agriculture expand their work with nontoxic measures and drastically reduce the toxic ones. An immediate ban should be placed by federal and state agencies on the use of *all* persistent pesticides and agricultural materials that are highly toxic, mutagenic, or carcinogenic.

Some officials have begun to consider such a change of direction. In April 1969, Health, Education, and Welfare Secretary Robert Finch stated: "I think it time to question the continued use of persistent pesticides . . . [and] to move forward to the use of more degradable chemicals and to stimulate research and production in the field of biological controls."[4] The appointment of an expert advisory committee to report on the extent of human health hazards created by pesticides would, he hoped, constrain the use of these chemicals and encourage industry and food producers to move toward other means of controlling insects. Again in 1969 the National Research Council, in its report on persistent pesticides, recommended to the USDA that support should be continued for work on nonchemical methods as alternatives.[5]

Both the agricultural fertilizer and the pesticide industries must revamp their materials for improved agricultural management. The nitrate problem, especially, will force changes in fertilizing practices. One chemical company abandoned its production of persistent pesticides as early as 1957, because it deemed these materials to be self-defeating over a long period of time.[6] Another company canceled its pesticide-research program—a move cited by a trade magazine as a "shadow of things to come."[7] Other pesticide companies have begun to explore the possibilities of producing low-toxicity materials directed against specific insect pests instead of "broad spectrum" materials. Others have considered the commercial production of nontoxic materials such as microbial disease organisms that are fatal to specific insect pests but presumed to be harmless to other life forms. The resources of these industries, with their vast technological skills and laboratory facilities, can be turned to harmless, ingenious approaches.

Food processors will assume a different role in the future food revolution. They will have a new conception of their responsibilities, and will recognize nutritional food values as the prime concern. Qualities such as attractive appearance and uniformity will become minor considerations, as they were in the past. Perhaps these stirrings have already begun. Witness *Food Technology:* "Most practicing food technologists have very little nutrition background. They little appreciate the impact of their efforts on the nutritive value of food and the nutritive well-being of consumers. If we do not pay proper attention to the nutritional problems associated with food technology, we run the risk of eventually producing an abundance of palatable, convenient staple foods that are not capable of meeting man's nutrient needs. We run the risk of undermining the nutritional well-being of our nation."[8]

This shifting of viewpoint by food processors to serve consumer interests better will require a rechanneling of energies already present. Just as it is a fact with the agricultural chemical industry, food processors also possess enormous technological skills and facilities, in addition to efficiency of operations. No drastic alterations are required to redirect present research efforts, so that the nutritional qualities in food would be stressed rather than an endless drive toward the further extension of shelf life and other features now being emphasized. Conceivably, the food processors could meet a challenge that, up to now, has been a dismal failure in the colleges and with federal and most state agencies, namely *basic research in nutrition, biochemistry, and toxicology.* The food industry could educate and train its researchers to have a scientific awareness of these important areas of concern, rather than to view food manipulation merely as a subject of physical and chemical technology.

Perhaps the food processors will meet this new challenge by allotting more funds for basic food research. As recently as 1966 they spent only $12 million for this subject, compared with $1.4 billion on advertisements and about $123 million on research into promotional devices such as package design.[9]

At a medical symposium in Atlanta, Georgia, sponsored in part by the Georgia Heart Association and the USPHS, the food industry was called upon to play a large, and perhaps crucial, role in making favorable alterations in the American diet.[10] A desirable trend of the times was noted at the meeting in the dairy industry's development and promotion of low-fat products, as well as in the meat industry's move to produce leaner meats.

The supermarket will also be revamped. Sellers of foods have always been responsive to consumer demands, and have adapted themselves to changing desires. Many food additives now deemed essential in food could be eliminated if refrigerators and freezers were used to a greater extent. Perhaps the future supermarket will consist mainly of long rows of refrigerator and freezer units, with only a very small area devoted to open shelves of packaged and canned items.

Recently, the USDA announced successful overseas shipping tests for frozen poultry.[11] If such techniques can be devised for long-distance boat shipments, surely American ingenuity can develop feasible methods for extended shipments within the country. The idea of refrigeration was suggested to help serve world food needs when a food scientist recommended the mobilization of large refrigerated facilities to store foods and retard their spoilage in tropical countries.[12]

The consumer, too, will play a vital role in the future food revolution. "When [the housewife] sees the inefficiency of foods that are causing body tissue breakdown, she will be quick to demand health-giving foods, with high nutrients, unprocessed and uncontaminated. When she demands and purchases living health-giving foods we shall soon have a bountiful supply," predicted Will Kinney, a grower of fine-quality foods.[13]

Meanwhile, until these changes take place, try to make wise selections under present conditions. Avoid foods that have had their basic chemistry altered by the removal of any element essential to human nutrition. Shun foods that have been artificially ripened. Eliminate foods so formulated as to keep for long periods at room temperature. Avoid, too, artificially processed, synthetic substitutes for natural foods, concentrated baby foods devoid of a basis for peristaltic action, and all foods artificially colored or flavored, as well as those artificially preserved.

What is left, you may ask, to put into your food basket? Choose, as far as possible, foods close to their natural state: fresh fruits and vegetables, meats, fish, fowl, eggs, nuts, grains, natural cheeses, butter, and crude vegetable oils. Try to find sources of food uncontaminated with chemicals. Nearly all of these are, in some way, unwholesome; many, as we have seen, represent a danger to health.

THE SEARCH FOR QUALITY FOODS

Repeatedly, statements are made by people in both government and industry that current methods of food production must be continued in order to feed a starving world. Although we should recognize our moral obligations toward hungry people everywhere, this problem must not be raised to divert us from a consideration of the problem of deterioration of quality in our own food supply.

Exports of processed foods, cola drinks, and candy bars will not save the starving world. Nor will intensive food production solve this problem, which basically is related to population control.

Experts have stated that far more promise is offered in developing new methods of fertility regulation and implementing programs of voluntary family planning than in trying to increase food and industrial production faster than population growth.

Changes in the choice of food crops will need to be made so that more high-protein foods become available. The demand is not solely for calories, but also for good-quality food.

The quest for adequate amounts of good-quality protein requires a new food revolution, in which conventional agricultural products will be handled in new ways, many unconventional sources explored, and feasible ones developed.[14] The sea yields many useful products, which have not been exploited adequately. The residues of processed oilseeds are now discarded completely in many areas, or at best used only as animal feed. Yet available amounts from this source alone *contain twice as much protein as the estimated world protein deficit.* Some protein foods of long standing are CSM, a corn-soy-milk food blend; Incaparina, corn and cottonseed flour; ProNutro, a mixture of protein materials available in South Africa. Additional ones have been developed, and more are being tested. Sesame and sunflower seeds, peanuts, coconuts, and nutritional yeasts are additional protein foods being considered. The production of a single-cell protein, using yeasts, bacteria, and algae, is being investigated. Research on leaf protein shows promise that this universally available material may be converted into an inexpensive protein to feed the world's malnourished.

To conserve valuable tillage land, the water weeds and plants growing in swamps and lake margins—which contribute little to human nutrition—can be collected and fed to land animals. By treating materials such as wood, cotton, flax, fur, wool, silk, and natural rubber, some scientists hope to create food proteins. Others have been attempting to convert petroleum into protein concentrate. Other unusual sources suggested include the use of wild herbivores.

Entirely new methods of food production may lead to a major and general means of increasing the world's food supply. For greater efficiency, expensive secondary foods like milk may gradually be abandoned in favor of primary ones of plant or sea origin. The nonessential foods must be eliminated if we are to use our food resources most efficiently. Highly processed and overrefined foods, offering little or no nourishment, must be viewed as wasting precious basic commodities. We need potatoes rather than potato chips, cherries as fruit rather than as maraschino decorations, fresh beef rather than frankfurters.

Another aspect of the problem of feeding the world is the need to conserve arable land, which is vanishing at an alarming rate. Land reclamation through better farming practices, restoration and maintenance of fertility and topsoil, greater control of erosion, and reforestation are all needed.

TIGHTER CONTROL OF FOOD SAFETY

Try to read a copy of the amended Food, Drug, and Cosmetic Act, even though it was formulated largely by skillful industry and government lawyers, and drafted so that a legal specialist's background is necessary to understand its provisions. The law affects the health and welfare of all. There has never been any complete, comprehensive digest in layman's language for consumers. This would be a worthwhile project for concerned constituents to suggest to Congressmen.

The amended act contains loopholes that benefit industry. For example, no provision is made for laboratory tests completely independent of direction and control by, and pressure from, any food manufacturer desirous of "proving" the safety of an additive he wishes to put into food. The folly of this omission was shown in the case of BHT and BHA.

The widely accepted test of repeated subcutaneous injections on experimental animals should once again be accepted as valid evidence of cancer-inciting properties of a substance. The Delaney clause should be supported and vigorously enforced.

The Delaney clause should be extended to include not only cancer-inciting substances, but also those that produce congenital deformities, mutations, and other chronic biological injury or damage. Such a proposal was introduced by Senator Gaylord Nelson on Dec. 22, 1970, in a food-additives-safety bill.

The present law does not set safe maximum levels for pesticide residues, but only provides that "the residue in or on the raw agricultural commodity shall have been removed *to the extent possible in good manufacturing practices* and the concentration of such residue in the processed food when ready to eat is not greater than the tolerance prescribed for the raw agricultural commodity."[15] (Emphasis mine.) Consumers must demand the reduction and elimination of residues, and try to rescind the present policy of raising tolerances of residues to meet agricultural practices.

The FDA is a political agency and subjected constantly to pressures from many directions. As a political entity it would like to perform its statutory duty without hurting anyone. But even with the best of intentions, its judgment is apparently affected by these pressures.

THE GRAS LIST—"THE NEVER-NEVER LAND OF NONREGULATION"

The original Generally Recognized As Safe (GRAS) list, established by the federal Food Additives Amendment in 1958, was drawn up by the FDA after polling 900 experts. Only 355 responded. From the replies, the FDA formulated the GRAS list, giving approval for the use of certain food additives for which safety tests were nonexistent. The shortcomings of this procedure have been demonstrated in the subsequent withdrawal of additives from the GRAS list. Meanwhile, the number of GRAS additives has multiplied through FDA's laxity. Winton B. Rankin, former Deputy FDA Commissioner, stated: "The manufacturer is entitled to reach his own conclusions, based on scientific evidence, that a substance is, in fact, generally recognized as safe, and he is not required to come to us and get the material added to the list."[16] Thus, if a manufacturer decides an additive is GRAS, he can start using it. If he has some doubt, he can go to the FDA and ask for a determination. This looseness of management was described by Senator George McGovern as "the never-never land of nonregulation." In order to remove a substance from the GRAS list, the FDA has to demonstrate the harmfulness of the additive. Instead, every food additive should be pretested before it is approved for use. A "proved as safe" list should be established, and GRAS should be eliminated.

The FDA has the power to make decisions that affect the welfare of over 200 million people. The agency may decide upon a safe amount of an additive not by known and reliable toxicological testing data that provide the greatest possible safeguards, but rather by what the agency deems "the opinion" of experts qualified by scientific training and experience to evaluate the safety "on the basis of animal experimental data." This policy leaves to the discretion of the Secretary of the Department of Health, Education, and Welfare (the parent body under which the FDA functions) a vital decision as to *which* opinion, among conflicting ones, is to be chosen, as well as *which* experts have the "right" training and experience. Such decisions must be based on scientific data, not on political expediency. No single individual in government service should be charged with such an awesome responsibility. Independent technical experts and trained scientists, free from pressures, should evaluate such matters.

PUBLIC EDUCATION AND PUBLIC EXPOSURE

As Consumers' Research pointed out in its *Bulletins*,[17] explaining the FDA's curious evasion of responsibility to the public, the agency's best weapons are left largely unused. These are public education and public exposure of wrongdoing. For instance, when the FDA knew that a certain food ingredient was potentially toxic but being used to enhance the appearance of baked goods, the agency failed to take the simple and obvious action of public warning and notification of the baking trade. When queried about its lack of action, the FDA retreated to a position that it could not proceed properly except when formal complaints were made through the courts, followed by legal trial—action it was not prepared to take.

Commenting on this incident, Consumers' Research noted: "Legal proceedings on such matters are a poor method of dealing with a problem that essentially involves *education* of manufacturers, retailers, and consumers. Where education fails, as it will in some cases, the practical, effective solution is *exposure by publication* of those who purvey questionable food materials or cheat in their choice and amount of ingredients or in labeling of their packages! The FDA needed in these and most other instances only to issue straightforward, non-propagandistic releases to the trade and general press to bring about correction of a situation unfavorable to consumers. It has the legal power to do this, and does do it occasionally, when it chooses to . . . [Most of the poor practices] in packaging and labeling could be corrected by a very inexpensive, quick-acting process of *calling them to public attention by name of manufacturer and brand,* without the delay and expense of legal action and trial in overcrowded courts."[18] (Emphasis supplied.)

THE 1966 FREEDOM OF INFORMATION ACT— PROGRESS OR STANDSTILL?

Under the amended Freedom of Information Act of 1966,[19] federal agencies are obliged to adopt new guidelines for publication and disclosures of information to the public. The FDA has managed to cling to its traditional policy. It states as its goal "full agency disclosures" for an informed public, combined with "protection of private and individual interests through proper application of the exemptions"[20] contained in the new law. Much of the information obtained from individual and private sources is still restricted as to disclosure, and the exemptions allow a wide latitude in keeping them restricted. There seems little cause for the alarm, raised by segments of industry, that the FDA or USDA would alter a policy of "maintaining the confidentiality" of materials submitted. On the contrary, there is justification for the concern expressed that "exemptions would be used and interpreted in such a way as to avoid full agency disclosure."[21] Court cases are now being litigated because an agency has refused to supply requested information required to be made available under the new Act.

"READ THE LABEL"

"Tell the truth on the label, and let the consumer judge for himself," advised Dr. Wiley[22] in the early days of food surveillance. This philosophy, given lip service repeatedly, has not yet been achieved. The late President Kennedy, in addressing Congress, said that "under our system, consumers have a right to expect that packages will carry reliable and readily usable information about the contents."[23] This statement was reaffirmed by former President Johnson,[24] and President Nixon,[25] and countless other officials. Publications, as well as spot announcements on radio by the FDA, emphasize that "labeling must tell the truth" and consumers should "read the label."[26]

Labeling inadequacies and untruthfulness are apparent to all who investigate. Although the amended Federal Food, Drug, and Cosmetic Act is clear and unequivocal in its requirements of label information, very loose and unsatisfactory practices continue to be tolerated.

Concerned consumers should demand action on any or all phases of the following labeling requirements, quoted from the federal law, but violated frequently and flagrantly:

> (Section 402,b,1) A substance recognized as being a valuable constituent of a food must not be omitted or abstracted in whole or in part . . .

If this were enforced, *refined flour, oil, and sugar would be unlawful.*

> (Section 402,b,2) . . . nor may any substance be substituted for the food in whole or in part.

This phrase negates the principle of "enrichment" and "fortification."

> (Section 402,b,3) Damage or inferiority in a food must not be concealed in any manner.

Officials sanction the practice of dyeing oranges to make them appear ripe. This principle could be applied to many other practices as well, such as the gassing of green tomatoes or the treatment of onions with sprout inhibitors so that the old ones appear new.

> (Section 402,b,4) No substance may be added to a food to increase its bulk or weight or make it appear of greater value than it is.

The addition of starch, breading, glucose, and sodium carboxymethylcellulose, to name a few, as cheap extenders and fillers

violates this section of the law. Also, many additives are used by
bakers to increase the bulk of bread, to make it appear of greater
value than it is.

(Section 403,f) Required label information must not only be
conspicuously displayed, but it must be in terms that the ordinary
consumer is likely to read and understand under ordinary conditions
of purchase and use.

The presence of peroxide bleach in cheese, printed on the
wrapper of the large round, is not made known to the customer
who purchases a small wedge of the product; fruit treated with
diphenyl bears no indication of this fumigation; nor do dates,
fumigated with methyl bromide. Terms such as "butylated hydroxytoluene" or "butylated hydroxyanisole," two examples from
many, are not understood by the average shopper. The solution is
not for the housewife to become an amateur chemist, but for the
FDA to limit and decrease the number of additives permitted in
foodstuffs.

(Section 403, h and l) The following statements must appear on the
label. . . . The common and usual name of each ingredient, except
foods for which identity standards have been promulgated, which
must make label declarations of ingredients in accordance with the
prescriptions of the standards.

"Moisture" on the label may be water. Optional ingredients in
most cases are *not* required to be listed on the label.

(Section 401) The ingredients should be listed in the order of their
predominance in the food.

This principle is violated, with the FDA's approval, on chewing-
gum labels.

(Section 403,k) Foods must bear labeling stating the presence of
any artificial flavoring, artificial coloring, or chemical preservative.

Butter, cheese, and ice cream are exempt in part from this label
declaration; for other foods it is not mandatory to list the specific
ones used. In the case of preservatives, the vague terms "preservative added" or "freshness preserver" or "antioxidant added" fail to
inform consumers. The specific preserver should be named, as well
as the amount used.

(Section 403,c) Imitations must be labeled as such.

Water-pumped ham and peanut butter with low percentages of peanuts are two examples of inferior products which *deserve* the term "imitation" but are not so labeled.

The food-label policies of another federal agency, the USDA, are not always in the best interests of the consumer. A small firm raised and sold quality beef produced without hormones or exposure to chemical pesticides. The producer attempted to put these facts on the label for the benefit of consumers who seek sources of such beef. But the USDA forbade such a label statement, branding it as a "negative label."

Although *more* adequate label information is in the interest of consumers, the FDA makes generous concessions for *less* informative labeling. Consumers should urge adoption of the following practices: Labels should give the actual amounts present of ingredients in a food product. A mere listing of items in the descending order of their presence falls short of today's needs. Foods for dogs and cats have ingredients listed by percentages, with statements of the exact amounts of water and mineral content in products. Labels on foods for human consumption should be at least as informative. *All additives should be required listing on the label.* Explicit technical names should be given, without recourse to vague nonidentifying expressions such as "shortening," "sweetening," "preservative," "antioxidant," and others. Specific additives should be named, so that persons who need or desire to avoid certain ones can do so. If such labeling results in long and disturbing listings, so much the better. Perhaps such a requirement would be an incentive for food processors to *reduce* the additives and return to simple, familiar ingredients.

Date labeling should be required on all packages of perishable food. This practice is finding favor abroad. Butter, bought at premium prices, doubled in sales at a food chain in West Germany after the date of manufacture was printed on the wrapper. Products still edible but sold beyond the expiration date are reduced in price.[27] Travelers in Yugoslavia report that the freshness of supermarket foods is controlled by the dating of all packages.[28] Some supermarket chains in America are attempting "quality control" by analyzing foods sold under their private labels, for components such as protein, fat, salt, sugar, and moisture, as well as weight, color, and acidity.[29] Consumers should urge food dating as an important component in quality control.

Many perishable items in supermarkets are coded with "packing dates" or "pull dates" for the benefit of the store manager. Some co-op stores now post such codes, with aids for deciphering them, to assist consumers who are interested in freshness as a quality of foodstuffs.[30]

MORE INFORMATION, NOT LESS!

In theory, the idea of establishing standards of identity for individual foods was to "promote honesty and fair dealings in the interests of consumers."[31] In actual practice, too often this original purpose has been perverted in ways unintended and unanticipated by its framers with results that work *against* consumer interests. Numerous instances have already been cited demonstrating that by the time standards are established, they are low and long overdue. Usually they are substandard, if judged by the quality of their home-prepared counterparts.

Once a food is standardized, the food processor needs to list only one or very few ingredients on the label. Thus, *the label of a standardized food is likely to be much less informative than that of a nonstandardized one.* The label may actually mislead the consumer. Consumers should urge both the FDA and food processors to list ingredients on standardized foods.

A good precedent was set by the Canadian Food and Drug Directorate which, in 1969, disclosed in its Trade Information Letter Number 310 to the food industry that it intended to require ingredient labeling of *all* food products, including standardized foods and those classes of nonstandardized foods now exempted from ingredient labeling requirements. The agency favored the listing of ingredients by "specific common names rather than functional or group names."[32]

Optional ingredients in standardized foods are not governed by the standards of identity, nor is there a consistent policy. Ingredients may or may not be required on the label, according to the whims of the FDA, which issues administrative orders. The current trend has been to omit, rather than include them on the label. Consumers should urge that *a listing of optional, as well as other ingredients, and their percentages, appear on the labels of all foodstuffs, whether standardized or not.* The FDA has the power to change its present policy of laxity toward optional ingredients. Consumer protests can help reverse this trend.

FOOD ADDITIVES—GOOD ONES CAN BE USED

If additives are used to prolong the shelf life of foodstuffs, consumers who use such items should urge processors to substitute safe for hazardous ones. Even if costs need to be higher, consumers would willingly pay for that margin of safety. Natural food flavors and colors can be used, but even these should be listed on labels. A rich supply of vitamin E in soy flour makes it an excellent natural antioxidant for bakery and confectionery products. Ascorbic acid reduces the curing time for meats, maintains a uniform color, and retains flavor during storage, distribution, and display of the product. In addition, vitamin C has demonstrated its value in keeping the natural flavor and color in frozen fruits and vegetables intact. Fresh fruit juice can be preserved better with vitamin K than with conventional preservatives. Soybean concentrate is a nutritious stretcher for meats, dehydrated foods, and baked goods. These are only a few examples, of many, which demonstrate that food additives need not be "badditives."

IMPROVING THE FDA

"There is a distinct tendency to put regulations and rules for the enforcement of the law into the hands of industries engaged in food and drug activities," wrote Dr. Wiley. He added: "I consider this one of the most pernicious threats to pure food and drugs. Business is making rapid strides in the control of all our affairs. When we permit business in general to regulate the quality and character of our food and drug supplies, we are treading upon very dangerous ground. It is always advisable to consult business men and take such advice as they give that is unbiased, because of the intimate knowledge they have of the processes involved. It is never advisable to surrender entirely food and drug control to business interests."[33]

The wisdom of Dr. Wiley's warning has been amply demonstrated in this book. The FDA consistently has followed a policy that former Representative Jerry Voorhis described as being more concerned about "singing in close harmony with industry than in prudent protection of the people."[34]

In recent years, the FDA has come under more attacks from individual critics, Congressmen, investigating committees, and the press than any other branch of federal government. At least seven Congressional committees have probed the activities of this agency. Invariably, the findings have charged that the FDA is too much regulated by the industries that it supposedly regulates. The agency has been accused of "administrative incompetence, shiftiness, and a preference for backstairs methods where honest, scrupulously impartial, and open dealing are peculiarly necessary, and finally a marked and growing indifference to the people's interests."[35]

A retired FDA inspector avowed publicly but anonymously:

> There appears to be a definite policy on the part of the Administration FDA to treat the big manufacturers of foods and drugs with care and to be much more severe with small manufacturers. Fear of consumer lawsuits and of adverse publicity acts as a much greater deterrent in preventing violation of the FDA laws than do the investigations and prosecutions of the FDA. The fines and sentences handed down . . . are too lenient to have much effect. . . . Too often the producer rather than the consumer is given the benefit of the doubt. There have been instances in which chemicals of proven harmfulness to man have not been immediately withdrawn, but have been allowed to be used until the manufacturers' supplies have been exhausted."[36]

The former FDA inspector also charged that promotions are "often based largely on the number of violations found by a particular inspector. This encourages the overly ambitious inspector to use his authority unscrupulously to further his own ends." The inspector added that the present agency policy toward inspectors seems to be "to reward mediocrity, apathy, and even on occasion, downright chicanery."[37]

An official committee appointed to study the functioning of the FDA reported that the widely used chemicals and dyes in foods and cosmetics, the greatly increasing use of pesticides, and the dangers from radiation all suggest that "many of the major problems of consumer protection lie in areas other than those of short weight, filth, or other matters over which legitimate concern was first expressed by the FDA years ago. Today, it is the new scientific discoveries and applications which pose the most complex and difficult problems in the protection of health."[38] But the FDA has failed to meet this challenge. Instead of becoming, as it should, "a scientific agency of high calibre," the writer Morton Mintz charged that the FDA became "a scientific backwater, prisoner of a glorious past that has become somewhat irrelevant."[39]

A more recent FDA study panel has concluded that the agency is not equipped to protect the American consumer from bad food, bad drugs, bad cosmetics, or faulty products. The panel concluded that the FDA "has been unable to develop the kind of concerted and co-ordinated efforts needed to deal adequately and simultaneously with problems of pesticide residues, food sanitation, chemical additives, microbiological contamination . . . medicated animal feeds, and myriad other problems."[40]

Shortly after the surprise official curb on cyclamates and the withdrawal of MSG from baby foods, President Nixon requested Secretary of Health, Education, and Welfare Finch to undertake a thorough re-examination of the FDA, which Nixon expected would "produce a number of important reforms in the agency's operations." Among the relevant questions to be answered in the review were: "Are laboratory findings communicated as promptly and fully as is desirable to high Administration officials and to the public? What should be the relationship of the FDA to other scientific arms of the Government? What methods can bring the greatest possible talent to bear on the critical questions the FDA considers?"[41]

Other critics have deplored the lack of original research within the FDA and its lack of contact with the scientific community. Some medical libraries of small pharmaceutical companies are better equipped than this agency. Suggestions were made that federal food and drug workers carry out research as they did in Wiley's time and again freely publish results, which they have not done since that era. Such publications should be issued promptly, and be free of control from pressure groups. In addition, the FDA needs current knowledge from other disciplines, as well as research performed in related areas here and abroad. Despite yearly budget increases, the FDA has continued to stress the legal and enforcement aspects of its work.[42] By so doing, it has neglected vital technical and scientific developments, and has been unable to attract top-quality personnel in these fields.

Nor has the FDA used its enforcement powers wisely. The agency has waged unrelenting warfare against alleged quackery. While everyone is as much against quackery as sin, murder, rape, or war, the groups prosecuted by the FDA all too often turn out to be harmless special dietary food stores which do a total yearly business of $1.5 million. Such stores specialize, among other things, in such items as fresh whole-grain flours, cereals, and breads, as well as produce grown poison-free on fertile soil. By persecuting those who promote natural foods, the FDA lends its support to some food refiners who, while choosing to ignore the shortcomings of their own products, cry quackery at others. The FDA claims that many low-income families are buying costly and often unnecessary food that they can ill afford when they seek natural foods. Such crocodile tears might be spared; such big-brother concern might be better directed toward the vast sums spent on candy, soft drinks, breakfast cereals, and hundreds of other overprocessed foods which not only account for staggering amounts of consumer expenditures, but present medically recognized health hazards.

Increased appropriations for the FDA will not, in themselves, assure better consumer protection. An official committee appointed to study the functioning of the FDA recommended: "The philosophy and leadership . . . should be reoriented." The committee found that the FDA was "oriented primarily to investigation and prosecution activities, as opposed to education and co-operation. In the long run consumers would be more confident in the FDA as custodian of the safety and nutritional integrity of our national food supply if the decisions were based on scientific data rather than on legal and regulatory judgments. It is doubtful whether the degree of secrecy now maintained is compatible with the public interest. The FDA should re-evaluate its priorities of work on foods, and should concentrate more on health hazards."[43]

The USPHS, which functions under the parent body of the Department of Health, Education, and Welfare, shares some responsibility for food safety. In a report on environmental health problems to the Surgeon General nearly a decade ago, a committee recommended "a five- to sixfold increase in the scope and intensity of both the intramural and extramural food-protection activities of the Public Health Service" for the next five years "to overcome the evident deficiencies and to keep pace with new developments in the food field."[44]

The report estimated "one million cases of food poisoning occur annually in the U.S. This estimate is probably too low, because scarcely any individual escapes an occasional intestinal upset. The number of reported outbreaks has approximately doubled since 1952, and the majority of these outbreaks are of undetermined etiology and scope. *Staphylococcal* food poisoning and *salmonella* infections are among the most commonly reported forms of gastro-enteritis, but investigation and reporting of foodborne illness are so grossly inadequate that a real evaluation of the impact of contaminated food on health cannot be made at the present time."[45]

The report continued, "Acute illnesses represent but one facet of the total problem. To this should be added other difficulties intro-duced through direct and indirect addition of chemicals which may have long-term effects on health. These may be introduced at different stages; e.g., during production (residues of insecticides, growth regulators in plants, hormones in animals, etc.), during processing (detergents or other contaminants of the water supply, dust and fumes from the air, and additives used in formulation), during storage (via leaching from containers) and during prepara-tion for serving (contact with faulty utensils, and residues of cleaners or sanitizing agents)."[46]

The committee admitted that study of the cumulative effects from repeated exposures to small amounts of food contaminants has only begun, and knowledge of the interrelationships between dietary factors and other elements of the environment is essentially lacking. The report recommended that "positive action is needed to stem the trend toward obsolescence of the food protection program in public health agencies, and thus keep pace with the developments in food science and technology. In contrast to the notable progress made in food sanitation during the first half of the 20th century, this area of government activity has now become the *weakest link in the protection of the Nation's food supply.*"[47] (Emphasis mine.)

"CONSUMERISM"

Traditionally, consumer legislation received little support among Congressmen. They found it difficult to balance brief sporadic flurries of complaints from unorganized John or Mary Doe against the year-round unrelenting pressures exerted by industry's professional lobbyists.

Times are changing. Congressional proposals to protect consumers from hazards extending from the superhighway to the supermarket now appear in the legislative hopper. As one lawmaker said of these bills: "They're 'butter' that doesn't cost anything."

"Consumerism" in recent years was given impetus by the late President Kennedy, who declared during campaigning that "the consumer is the only man in our economy without a high-powered lobbyist in Washington. I intend to be that lobbyist."[48] After assuming office, he sent a message to Congress on consumer protection. This was the first Presidential address ever devoted exclusively to the problem of protecting consumers. The message was formulated from ideas submitted by 34 different agencies in the federal government, invited by the President to make suggestions. This diffuse and unco-ordinated network of agencies, devoted partly or largely to other problems, has actually worked against real concern for consumers.

The essence of Kennedy's address, affirming the consumer's four basic rights—to safety, to be informed, to choose, and to be heard—still need implementation. A Consumers' Advisory Council was created and advised by Kennedy to be "functional, not ornamental" in alerting each and every department of government to consumer needs. Results have been disappointing. The Council has failed to have a voice that is "loud, clear, uncompromising and effective."[49] Even Congressmen have complained that the Council has "displayed excessive timidity and administrative ineptitude"[50] and have urged that it should "stiffen its spine or be abandoned."[51]

The Council fell far short of goals to co-ordinate all the activities of the many new consumer deputies involved in consumer protection. The establishment of a department of the consumer in the federal government has been suggested by others, but such an agency might be unwieldy and unworkable.

A new post, created during the Johnson administration, but invested with no power, was special assistant to the President for consumer affairs. Mrs. Esther Peterson, the first appointee, attempted to improvise power and succeeded in upsetting business and advertising interests. Her successors, Mrs. Betty Furness and Mrs. Virginia Knauer, have had to grapple with the same problem.

Consumer counsels at the state level have begun to spring up everywhere, to hear complaints of people who feel they are being treated unfairly by business. Such agencies deal mainly with fraud, deception, and oppressive contractual arrangements. They are apt to be pointed to with pride as "achievements" gained under certain political administrations.

SPURRING THE FOOD INDUSTRY TOWARD A NEW DEAL FOR THE CONSUMER

Food from Farmer to Consumer, an official investigation released in 1966, attempted to discover, among other things, why 59 cents of every food dollar goes to the marketer, and only 41 cents to the farmer.[52] Even before the report was released officially, it was condemned by the food industry as "outlandish" and "retrogressive."[53]

The report was highly critical of the food industry's advertising and sales promotion, and declared these practices to be "an important form of inefficiency." They were noted as "a significant reason for the substantial spread between farm and retail prices. In 1964, food corporations spent $2,172 million for advertising . . . and retailers spent $680 million for trading stamps. These amounts were added to processing and distribution costs and became part of the food bill."[54]

The report criticized the "cost devoted to selling efforts that yield little value to consumers" and "the difficulty they encounter in trying to buy so as to get the most for their money."[55] Here are some of its recommendations which, if implemented, would have far-reaching effects on the consumer:

The food industry should slash advertising and other selling costs in half to help reduce food prices.

Consumer grades should be developed and be required to appear on all foods for which such grades are feasible.

Where grading is not feasible, the label should disclose all ingredients in descending order of importance and the quantity of each in excess of 5 per cent of the total quantity.

Trading stamps and other similar gimmicks should be banned because of increased cost to the consumer.

Packaging and labeling should help consumers to gain an accurate impression of the contents, and to make price comparisons. Both the FDA and the FTC should devote more attention to the subjects of packaging and labeling in order to prevent deceptive practices. These agencies should be given additional power, if needed, for adequate control.

A centralized consumer agency should be established by statute in the executive branch of the government.

The main purpose of the proposals is "to provide consumers with the choices and unbiased information they need to get the most satisfaction for their money."[56]

In commenting on the proposals, Sylvia Porter, financial columnist, admitted that while most of these recommendations "are given virtually no chance to become law in the near future, they are even now spurring the food industry into a deep restudy of itself and of the consumers' real food wants. They are sure to bring demands by consumer protection agencies for stricter legislation to regulate the nation's biggest industry and to add the pressures from the 'inside' for self-policing."[57]

CONSUMER ACTION, ANYONE?

Despite the recent trend toward consumerism, in the last analysis, you, the individual, will need to raise your voice to improve your own welfare. Remember that in times when most citizens are inarticulate, the few who speak up can wield influence. This was demonstrated several years ago when Paul Hoffman faced confirmation as a government official. One of his Congressional friends frankly admitted that he could not support Hoffman because of a "groundswell" of opinion against him. When he was questioned, the "groundswell" turned out to be six letters written by constituents.[58]

"A lone consumer may feel helpless in facing up to a giant corporation," noted Vance Packard. "Actually, this lone consumer should know that this monolith tends to over-react to criticism of its product. One strong letter, neatly typed, addressed to the president, can create concern in the executive suite (even though the president himself is probably spared from seeing the letter). Two letters of protest will create panic. Three letters of protest will create pandemonium."[59] It is time for you, the individual consumer, to write to food processors, and express your desires for fresh, dated foodstuffs, without artificial colors, flavors, preservatives, and other economic short cuts benefiting the trade.

Write inquiring letters to manufacturers when label information is lacking, or protest letters when advertising claims are exaggerated. Commend food producers and processors who attempt to grow and sell quality items without resorting to additives. Such individuals need and deserve encouragement, as well as customers. When occasions demand action on a government level, write:

The Food and Drug Administration, Washington, D.C. 20204, about food safety, labeling, adulteration, misbranding, and other areas of concern.

The U.S. Department of Agriculture, Washington, D.C. 20250, about meat, poultry, and egg inspection, labeling and grading, as well as pesticide use on food crops.

The Federal Trade Commission, Washington, D.C., concerning false or exaggerated advertising.

Special Assistant to the President for Consumer Affairs, The White House, Washington, D.C. 20501.

If the agency you write to does not respond, or fails to deal effectively with your complaint, you may want to ask your Congressman to write in your behalf. Mail from Congressmen is handled promptly and with care.

To keep informed on subjects of consumer interest, read: *Consumer Bulletin,* published by Consumers' Research, Inc., Washington, N.J. 07882.

Consumer Reports, published by Consumers Union of U.S., Inc., Mount Vernon, N.Y. 10550.

The Federation of Homemakers, 922 North Stuart Street, Arlington, Va. 22203, is a national organization started by four housewives who were deeply concerned over the chemical treatment of foods, and the inadequacy of protection under the food laws. By means of newsletters, the Federation keeps other housewives informed and suggests appropriate action through letter writing. Although membership is mainly for women, interested men are invited to join.

Perhaps the best suggestion was offered by a woman from the Norwegian cabinet, who advised consumers concerned with the safety and quality of consumer goods "to return to their rightful role—that of being appropriate hell-raisers."

NOTES

◆ ◆ ◆ ◆

CHAPTER 1

1. John W. Vassos and Senator Harrison A. Williams, Jr., *testimony*. 89th Congress, 1st session, Hearings before a special subcommittee of the Committee on Labor & Public Welfare, U.S. Senate, to Amend Section 402 (d) of the Federal Food, Drug, & Cosmetic Act, Aug. 24, 1965, pp. 18, 25.
2. *U.S. Food Consumption, Sources of Data & Trends, 1909–1963*. USDA Statistical Bulletin 364. Washington, D.C.: Economic Research Service, USDA, June 1965, p. 12.
3. David Ogilvy, *Confessions of an Advertising Man*. New York: Atheneum, 1963, p. 88.
4. *Advertising Age*, Oct. 3, 1960.
5. Rosser Reeves, *Reality in Advertising*. New York: Knopf, 1961, p. 145.
6. *Advertising Age*, July 10, 1961.
7. *National Advertising Investments*. Chicago: Publishers' Information Bureau, Jan.–June, 1965, pp. 8–9.
8. *Advertising Age*, Dec. 8, 1969.
9. *Background on U.S. Agriculture*. USDA Leaflet 491. Washington, D.C.: USDA, June 1965, revised, p. 6 (unfolioed).
10. *This Week Magazine*, Sept. 10, 1961, pp. 16–22.
11. "How to Save $200 a Year at a Supermarket." *Consumer Reports*, Feb. 1961, pp. 64–67.
12. *Agricultural Marketing—Vital Link Between Farmer & Consumer*. USDA Bulletin 36. Washington, D.C.: Oct. 1965.
13. Prof. Irston R. Barnes, *testimony*. 88th Congress, 1st session, Hearings before the Subcommittee on Antitrust Monopoly of the Committee on the Judiciary, U.S. Senate, on Packaging and Labeling Legislation, Part 1, Mar. 1963, p. 373.

14. *Poultry Tribune,* Oct. 1964, p. 10.
15. *Co-Op Newsletter,* Beltsville (Md.), Dec. 1, 1965.
16. "Where Does Your Food Dollar Go?" *Consumer Reports,* Mar. 1956, pp. 139–42.
17. Vance Packard, *The Waste Makers.* New York: David McKay, 1960, p. 14.
18. "Automated Aerosols." Union Carbide's *Chemical Progress,* May 1963, p. 7.
19. Martin Mayer, *Madison Avenue, U.S.A.* New York: Pocket Books, 1959, pp. 245–46.
20. John Brooks, "The Little Ad That Isn't There." *Consumer Reports,* Jan. 1958, pp. 7–10.
21. Dr. Ernest Dichter, *Handbook of Consumer Motivation, the Psychology of the World of Objects.* New York: McGraw-Hill, 1964, p. 32.
22. *Ibid.,* p. 326.
23. *Ibid.,* pp. 59–60.
24. Consumers' Research, Inc., letter to author, Apr. 10, 1969.
25. "Quote Without Comment." *Consumer Reports,* May 1963, p. 206.
26. "Consumers Are Subsidizing Manufacturers' Advertising." *The Californian,* Feb. 1962.
27. "A Story For Our Times." *Consumer Reports,* Mar. 1965, p. 119.
28. *Packaging,* Aug. 1962.
29. Paul S. Willis, *address.* Annual meeting, Television Bureau of Advertising, New York, Nov. 16, 1962.
30. "An Outrageous and Shocking Speech." Editorial, *Sponsor,* Nov. 26, 1962.
31. Senator Philip A. Hart, "Don't Be Fooled by Deceptive Packaging." *Coronet,* Apr. 1965.
32. "Quote Without Comment." *Consumer Reports,* Jan. 1965, p. 6.
33. Packard, *op. cit.,* p. 189.
34. As in Note 16, above, p. 139.
35. *Co-Op Newsletter,* Beltsville (Md.), June 26, 1968.
36. Harriet Van Horne, "What's Cooking on TV?" *New York World Telegram & Sun,* Aug. 18, 1961.
37. Carla A. Williams, *address.* Economic panel, mid-winter conference, Advertising Federation of America, Washington, D.C., Feb. 7, 1962, pp. 2, 5–6 (script).

CHAPTER 2

1. *The Good in Your Food.* Proceedings, 23rd annual convention, Super Market Institute. Chicago: Super Market Institute, 1960, p. 1.

2. Eleanor Roosevelt and Quartermaster General Edmund B. Gregory, *broadcast*. WJZ, Dec. 9, 1942, New York.
3. "The Power of the $$$." *Family News,* Vol. 4, No. 3, St. Petersburg (Fla.): Page Foundation, Mar. 1957, pp. 1–3.
4. Sugar Research Foundation, *7th Annual Report*. New York: Sugar Research Foundation, 1950, p. 23.
5. Dr. Robert C. Hockett, "Research on Dental Caries." *The Sugar Molecule*, Vol. 3, No. 4, Oct. 1949, p. 3.
6. James H. Shaw and R. R. Sognnaes, "Relationship Between Nutrition & Dental Caries in Primates; Nutrition & Dental Caries." *Journal of the American Medical Association*, Vol. 166, pp. 633–37.
7. *Time*, Jan. 13, 1958.
8. *Life*, Oct. 11, 1968, pp. 100–1.
9. Ogden C. Johnson, Ph.D., "Nutrition Education—What Is the Goal?" *Nutrition Reviews*, Vol. 23, No. 12, Dec. 1965, p. 355.
10. "Quote Without Comment." *Consumer Reports*, Feb. 1951, p. 92.
11. "Objectionable Advertising of Foods and Beverages." *Consumer Bulletin*, Nov. 1963, p. 36.
12. Nutrition Foundation, *Annual Report, 1950, Concerning Food & Health, a Report to the Public on a Decade of Adventure in Science, 1942–1951*. New York: Nutrition Foundation, 1951.
13. "Calling 'Dr. Nutrition,' Dr. Fredrick J. Stare." *Medical Tribune*, Nov. 15, 1963, p. 4.
14. *Ibid.*, p. 4.
15. Carol Phillips, "A Doctor Explodes Some 'Health Food' Myths, an Interview with Dr. Fredrick Stare, M.D., Chairman of Harvard's Department of Nutrition." *Vogue*, June 1967, p. 174.
16. Fredrick J. Stare, M.D., "On Food & Your Health." *Manchester* (N.H.) *Union Leader*, May 18, 1961.
17. *Idem.*, "Bread, Potatoes, & Sugar, Fiend or Friend?" *McCall's*, Jan. 1956, p. 72.
18. *Idem.*, "Are There Poisons in Your Foods?" *Farm Journal*, Feb. 1961.
19. *Idem., Eating for Good Health*. New York: Doubleday, 1964, p. 194.
20. *Ibid.*, p. 194.
21. *Ibid.*, p. 42.
22. *Ibid.*, pp. 67, 42.
23. "Harvard Gets a Record Gift." *Boston Sunday Herald*, Feb. 14, 1960, p. 27.
24. Nutrition Foundation, *Annual Report, 1963–1964*. New York: Nutrition Foundation, 1964, pp. 26–28.
25. *Capital Times* (Madison, Wis.), Oct. 7, 1965, pp. 1, 6.

26. "The Intake of Too Much Vitamin D." *Consumer Bulletin*, Nov. 1965, p. 42.
27. Nutrition Foundation, *Annual Report of the Executive Director, 1961*. New York: Nutrition Foundation, 1961, p. 43.
28. *McCall's*, Jan. 1956, p. 72.
29. Muriel G. Wagner, "Dial-A-Dietician." *American Journal of Clinical Nutrition*, Vol. 18, Jan. 1966, p. 66.
30. Nutrition Foundation, *printed letter to librarians*, & enclosed reprints of book reviews by Dr. William J. Darby & Dr. Fredrick J. Stare; Manufacturing Chemists' Association reprint; & special insert, "What Consumers Should Know About Food Additives." May 1960.
31. Nutrition Foundation, *printed letter to professionals*, Jan. 1963.
32. Senator Abraham S. Ribicoff, *open letter* to Dr. Franklin M. Foote, Commissioner of Health, Hartford, Conn., May 20, 1965.
33. *Publications*. Washington, D.C.: Food & Nutrition Board, NAS-NRC, Jan. 1965, p. 6.
34. Hazel K. Stiebeling, "Food in Our Lives." USDA yearbook *Food*. Washington, D.C.: USGPO, 1959, p. 4.
35. Nutrition Foundation, *Annual Report of the Executive Director, 1963–1964*. New York: Nutrition Foundation, 1964, p. 53.
36. *Dietary Allowances, a Report of the Food & Nutrition Board*. Washington, D.C.: NAS-NRC, 1964, revised.
37. *Nutritional Data*. Pittsburgh: H. J. Heinz Co., 1960, 4th ed., p. 90.
38. Katherine H. Fisher and Raymond W. Swift, "Calories & Body Weight." As in Note 34, above, p. 101.
39. E. V. Askey, M.D., "American Public Wasting Millions on 'Vitamania.'" *Journal of the American Medical Association*, Vol. 174, 1960, p. 1332.
40. Agnes Fay Morgan and Lura M. Odland, "The Nutriture of People." As in Note 34, above, p. 187.
41. *Ibid.*, pp. 191–224.
42. *Federal Register*, Vol. 6, No. 227, Nov. 22, 1941, p. 5921; *ibid.*, amended, Vol. 22, No. 106, June 1, 1957, p. 3841.
43. Frank E. Egler, Ph.D., "Pesticides and the National Academy of Sciences." *Atlantic Naturalist*, Oct.–Dec. 1962, pp. 267–71.
44. "The Academy of Sciences Lays Another Thin-Shelled Egg." *National Audubon*, July 1969, p. 103.
45. *The Food & Drug Law Institute*. Washington, D.C.: The Food & Drug Law Institute, June 1, 1966, p. 6 (unfolioed).
46. *Ibid.*, p. 6.
47. Leonard Wickenden, *testimony*. 82nd Congress, 2nd session, Hear-

ings before the House Select Committee to Investigate the Use of Chemicals in Foods & Cosmetics, Part 3, 1952, p. 1083.

48. Walter Sullivan, "Heart-Diet Survey Will Cover 500,000." *The New York Times*, Aug. 31, 1961.

49. Quoted in *Bakers Weekly*, Nov. 29, 1965, pp. 23–27.

50. "Break Down of Pesticides in Processed Foods to be Studied." USDA release, July 18, 1968.

51. Elise Jerard, "Prudence, Profits & Environmental Cancer." *Modern Nutrition*, Vol. 14, No. 10, p. 6.

52. *Ibid.*, p. 6.

53. *Ibid.*, p. 8.

54. Quoted in *Consumer Bulletin*, Sept. 1957, p. 18.

CHAPTER 3

1. William Ogilvy Kermack and Philip Eggleton, *Stuff We're Made of, a Biochemical Survey of Life for the General Reader*. New York: Longmans Green, 1948, p. 226.

2. "Synthetic Caviar." *Soviet Life*, Oct. 1965, p. 19.

3. "Simulated Meat, 'Spun' Protein Is Planned for 1970's Suppers." *Food Field Reporter*, Dec. 11, 1961.

4. Carol Malstrom, *statement*. 88th Congress, 1st session, Hearings before the Subcommittee on Antitrust & Monopoly of the Committee on the Judiciary, U.S. Senate, Packaging & Labeling Legislation. Washington, D.C.: Federation of Homemakers, June 1961 (mimeographed reprint), p. 2.

5. *Report on Enforcement & Compliance*. Washington, D.C.: Food & Drug Administration, Apr. 1961, pp. 1–3, 10.

6. Ruth T. Robinson, *statement*. Hearings on Establishment of Definitions & Standards of Identity for Orange Juice & Orange Juice Products, FDA. Washington, D.C.: Federation of Homemakers, Mar. 17, 1961 (mimeographed reprint), p. 1.

7. "Those New 'Orange' Drinks." *Consumer Bulletin*, Aug. 1964, p. 38.

8. "For Citrus Juice Flavor Control." USDA *Agricultural Research*, Vol. 15, No. 5, Nov. 1966, p. 15.

9. Fredrick J. Stare, M.D., "Dr. Stare Answers Your Diet Questions." *McCall's*, Apr. 1959, p. 134.

10. *Advertising Age*, Mar. 8, 1965.

11. "Natural Vitamin C, Though Same as Synthetic, Has Advantages." *Nutrition Notes*, No. 30, Oct. 1963, p. 2.

12. S. E. Sadek, "Suspected Skeletal Scurvy in the Dog." *Veterinary*

Record, Vol. 74, 1962, p. 905, quoted in *Nutrition Notes*, as in Note 11, above, p. 2.

13. R. P. Nikolaev *et al.*, "Biological Value of Different Concentrates and Preparations of Vitamin C." *Biokhimiya* (U.S.S.R.), Vol. 18, 1953, pp. 169–74, quoted in *Nutrition Notes*, as in Note 11, above, p. 2.

14. H. Cotereau, M. Gabe, E. Géro, & J.-L. Parrot, "Influence of Vitamin P (Vitamin C_2) upon the Amount of Ascorbic Acid in the Organs of the Guinea Pig." *Nature*, Apr. 10, 1948, pp. 557–58.

15. Estelle E. Hawley, Ray G. Daggs, & Doran J. Stephens, "The Effect of the Administration of Acid and Alkaline Salts upon the Ascorbic Acid Content of Guinea Pig Tissues." *Journal of Nutrition*, Vol. 14, No. 1, 1937, pp. 1–8.

16. Claus W. Jungeblut, M.D., "A Further Contribution to Vitamin C Therapy in Experimental Poliomyelitis." *Journal of Experimental Medicine*, Vol. 70, 1939, p. 315, through H. von Bauer, *Helvet. med. acta*, Vol. 19, 1952, p. 470.

17. W. Becker, "Antiscorbutic Activity of Onions." *Deutsche medizinische Wochenschrift*, Vol. 76, 1951, pp. 615–16, quoted in *Nutrition Notes*, as in Note 11, above, p. 2.

18. Hans A. Schweigart, "Why Is Natural Vitamin C Superior to Synthetic Vitamin C?", *Hippokrates*, Vol. 5, 1955, pp. 151–52, quoted in *Nutrition Notes*, as in Note 11, above, p. 2.

19. Alf Elmby & Erik Warburg, "The Inadequacy of Synthetic Ascorbic Acid as an Antiscorbutic Agent." *The Lancet*, Vol. 233, Dec. 11, 1937, pp. 1363–65.

20. Emanuel Cheraskin, M.D., D.M.D., and Warren M. Ringsdorf, Jr., D.M.D., *paper.* "Diet and Nutrition in Oral Health and Disease," conference, University of Alabama Medical Center, Mar. 1965.

21. Theron G. Randolph, M.D., *Human Ecology and Susceptibility to the Chemical Environment.* Chicago: Charles C. Thomas, 1962, pp. 86–87.

22. "Risks of Synthetic Foods," leading article, *British Medical Journal*, No. 5470, Vol. 2, Nov. 6, 1965, pp. 1078–79.

23. "Gusher Gourmet?" *Newsweek*, Dec. 25, 1967, p. 56.

24. Quoted by F. J. Schlink, *testimony.* 81st Congress, 2nd session, Hearings before the House Select Committee to Investigate the Use of Chemicals in Food Products, 1950, p. 744.

25. Firman E. Bear, S. J. Toth, and A. L. Prince, "Regional Variations in the Mineral Composition of Vegetables." *The Land*, Vol. 7, No. 3, Autumn 1948.

26. Victor R. Boswell, "Farm Practices, Quality, and Cost." USDA yearbook, *Food.* Washington, D.C.: USGPO, 1959, pp. 401–2.

27. Werner Schuphan, *Nutritional Values in Crops & Plants, Problems for Producers & Consumers.* London: Faber & Faber, 1965, pp. 26, 51, 129–34.
28. *Consumers' Research Bulletin,* Mar. 1957, p. 3.
29. F. R. Theriault and C. R. Fellers, "Effect of Freezing & Canning in Glass & Tin on Available Iron Content of Foods." *Food Research,* Vol. 7, No. 6, Nov.–Dec. 1942, pp. 503–8.
30. Doris Howes Calloway and John J. McMullen, "Fecal Excretion of Iron & Tin by Men Fed Stored Canned Foods." *American Journal of Clinical Nutrition.* Vol. 18, No. 1, Jan. 1966, pp. 1–6.
31. "Hold That Salt!" *Consumer Bulletin,* Sept. 1959, p. 23.
32. Ruth M. Leverton, "Sodium, Potassium, & Magnesium." As in Note 26, above, p. 120.
33. "Food & Nutrition." *Consumer Bulletin Annual, 1960,* 1961, p. 150.
34. A. R. Patton, letter, *Nutrition Reviews,* Vol. 2, No. 5, May 1953, p. 159.
35. "Food Additives, Part 2." *Chemical & Engineering News,* Oct. 17, 1966, pp. 109–10.
36. Dr. Jean Mayer & T. George Harris, "Affluence: The Fifth Horseman of the Apocalypse." *Psychology Today,* Jan. 1970, p. 50.
37. "Makers of Baby Foods Curtail Use of Monosodium Glutamate." *The New York Times,* Oct. 25, 1969.
38. "Accent on Regulated Growth." Union Carbide's *Chemical Progress,* Aug. 1969, p. 7.
39. *It's What's Inside that Counts.* Washington, D.C.: Industrial Union Department, AFL–CIO, publication 52, no date, p. 9.
40. K. B. Norton, D. K. Tressler, and L. D. Farkas, "The Use of Monosodium Glutamate in Frozen Foods." *Food Technology,* Vol. 6, 1952, p. 405.
41. *Consumers' Research Bulletin,* July 1955, p. 4.
42. *Food Field Reporter,* Feb. 19, 1957.
43. P. C. Paul and K. Langworthy, "Acceptability of Msg in Frankfurters and Pork Sausage." *Journal of Home Economics,* Vol. 44, 1952, p. 284.
44. *Consumer Bulletin,* Sept. 1958, p. 35.
45. "Monosodium Glutamate Zips Flavor." *Rutland* (Vt.) *Daily Herald,* Sept. 28, 1965.
46. *FDA Definitions and Standards under Federal Food, Drug, and Cosmetic Act for Canned Vegetables and Vegetable Products; Dressings for Foods: Mayonnaise, French Dressing, Salad Dressing.* Washington, D.C.: USGPO, Sept. 1961, revised.
47. *Consumers' Research Bulletin,* Mar. 1955, p. 4.
48. Robert Ho Man Kwok, M.D., "Chinese Restaurant Syndrome."

New England Journal of Medicine, Vol. 278, No. 14, Apr. 4, 1968, p. 796.

49. "Post-Sino-Cibal Syndrome," editorial, and correspondence. *Ibid.,* Vol. 278, No. 20, May 16, 1968, pp. 1122–24; *ibid.,* Vol. 279, No. 2, July 11, 1968, pp. 105–6.

50. Earl C. Gottschalk, Jr., "Relief May Be in Sight for Those Who Suffer from Chinese Cooking." *Wall Street Journal,* July 11, 1968, p. 25; *idem,* "Flavoring Agent Tied to Strange Ailment from Chinese Food." *Ibid.,* Feb. 14, 1969.

51. *Wall Street Journal,* Feb. 14, 1969, *op. cit.*

52. "Questions and Answers." As in Note 26, above, p. 35.

53. John W. Olney, M.D., "Brain Lesions, Obesity, and Other Disturbances in Mice Treated with Monosodium Glutamate." *Science,* Vol. 164, May 9, 1969, pp. 719–21.

54. John W. Olney, M.D., & Lawrence G. Sharpe, "Brain Lesions in an Infant Rhesus Monkey Treated with Monosodium Glutamate." *Science,* Vol. 166, Oct. 17, 1969, pp. 386–88.

55. "Makers of Baby Foods Curtail Use of Monosodium Glutamate." *The New York Times,* Oct. 25, 1969.

56. *Consumer Bulletin,* Dec. 1961, p. 36.

57. *Consumer Reports,* Oct. 1965, pp. 492–93.

58. *Ibid.,* July 1964, pp. 326–28.

59. *Consumer Bulletin,* May 1957, p. 33.

60. *Consumer Reports,* Sept. 1963, p. 412.

61. *Ibid.,* Jan. 1959, pp. 16–17.

62. *Ibid.,* Mar. 1959, pp. 124–25; *ibid.,* Sept. 1965, pp. 434–36.

63. *Ibid.,* May 1963, pp. 225–27.

64. William Vogt, *People! Challenge to Survival.* New York: William Sloane, 1960, p. 65.

65. *The New York Times,* July 19, 1962.

66. "Gourmet Food Now TV Dinners." *Wall Street Journal,* May 5, 1967.

67. John Steinbeck, "In Quest of America." Part 2, *Holiday,* Dec. 1961, p. 63.

68. "What Batch Cooking Can Do for Vegetables." *The Modern Hospital,* Vol. 99, No. 3, Sept. 1962, p. 142.

69. Letter to author, 1968.

70. *American Automatic Merchandiser,* June 1964.

71. Quoted in *Health Bulletin,* Dec. 4, 1965, p. 1.

72. John Yudkin, "How to Fool Ourselves with Lots of Flavor but Little Nutrition." *Nutrition Notes,* No. 30, Oct. 1963, p. 3.

73. *Ibid.,* p. 3.

74. "Taste Is Not a Guide to Health." *Health Bulletin,* May 30, 1964, pp. 2–3.
75. "Nutritional Quality of Market Foods." *Report of the Committee on Environmental Health Problems to the Surgeon General.* U.S. Department of Health, Education, and Welfare, Public Health Service. Washington, D.C.: USGPO, 1962, p. 149.
76. Hazel K. Stiebeling, "Improved Use of Newer Nutritional Knowledge, Progress and Problems." *Journal of the American Dietetic Association,* Oct. 1964, p. 324.
77. *American Potato Journal,* Oct. 1961, p. 365.
78. *Nutrition Notes,* No. 46, May 1968, p. 4.
79. *Consumer Bulletin,* July 1964, p. 3.
80. As in Note 27, above, p. 74.
81. Philip L. White, Sc.D., "Let's Talk About Food." *Today's Health,* Vol. 41, No. 1, Jan. 1963, p. 14.
82. William Vogt, *op. cit.,* p. 64.
83. *Bakers Weekly,* Jan. 17, 1966, pp. 38–43.
84. "Tired of 'Tired' Lettuce?" *Co-Op Consumer,* Beltsville (Md.), Apr. 17, 1968.
85. "Freeze Drying." *Food Processing,* Nov. 1960.
86. *San Francisco Examiner,* Feb. 4, 1960.
87. *Boston Herald,* Feb. 9, 1963.
88. Dr. Edward S. Josephson, *address.* International conference on radiation research, laboratories of U.S. Army Materiel Command, Natick, Mass., 1963.
89. "Food Irradiation to be Tested Anew." *The New York Times,* Mar. 28, 1960.
90. Om P. Malhotra, Elwood F. Reber, and Horace W. Norton, "Effect of Methionine & Vitamin K_3 on Hemorrhages Induced by Feeding a Ration Containing Irradiated Beef." *Toxicology & Applied Pharmacology,* Vol. 7, No. 3, 1965, pp. 402–8.
91. M. S. Mameesh, V. C. Metta, P. B. Rama Rao, and B. Connor Johnson, "On the Cause of Vitamin K Deficiency in Male Rats Fed Irradiated Beef & the Production of Vitamin K Deficiency Using an Amino Acid Synthetic Diet." *Journal of Nutrition,* Vol. 77, No. 2, June 1962, pp. 165–70.
92. Norb Leinen, "Million Dollar Blunder." *Food Processing,* Dec. 1959, pp. 21–22.
93. "Radiation Reappraisal by Food Industry Research Experts." *Ibid.,* Jan. 1960, pp. 34–35, 37, 39.
94. "Smoked Mullet." *Orlando* (Fla.) *Sentinel,* Feb. 17, 1960.
95. "Army Wants to Irradiate More Meat." *Health Bulletin,* Apr. 4, 1964, p. 2.

96. *Gamma Radiation of Vegetables to Extend Market Life.* USDA
    Marketing Research Report 703. Washington, D.C.: USGPO, Oct.
    1965; *Gamma Radiation of Fruits to Extend Market Life.* USDA
    Marketing Research Report 717. Washington, D.C.: USGPO, Nov.
    1965.
97. "They Still Decay Away." USDA *Service,* No. 25, Jan. 1966, p. 1.
98. Z. Z. Ziporin, H. F. Kraybill, and H. J. Thach, "Vitamin Content
    of Foods Exposed to Ionizing Radiations." *Journal of Nutrition,*
    Vol. 63, No. 2, Oct. 10, 1957, pp. 201–9.
99. Dr. H. F. Kraybill, "Effect of Irradiation of Food on Amino Acids."
    Journal of Clinical Physiology, Vol. 1, No. 3, winter 1959, p. 51.
100. W. S. Tsien and B. C. Johnson, "The Effect of Radiation Steriliza-
     tion on the Nutritive Value of Foods, Part 4." *Journal of Nutri-
     tion,* Vol. 68, July 1959, p. 4149.
101. "Dangers Are Cited in Irradiated Food." *The New York Times,*
     Jan. 15, 1960.
102. William C. Summers, "A Model of Tumor Growth in Irradiated
     Hosts." *Nature,* Vol. 200, Jan. 23, 1965, p. 414.
103. Franklin Bicknell, M.D., *Chemicals in Food & in Farm Produce:
     Their Harmful Effects.* London: Faber & Faber, 1960, p. 55.
104. R. S. Hannon, *Scientific & Technological Problems Involved in
     Using Ionizing Radiations for the Preservation of Food.* London:
     HMSO, 1955, p. 1 ff.
105. *Monthly Supply Letter.* Washington, D.C.: United Fresh Fruit &
     Vegetable Association, Oct. 1964, p. 1.
106. *Food, Drug & Cosmetic Law Reports.* Washington, D.C.: Food &
     Drug Law Institute, Mar. 18, 1965.
107. "USDA Withdraws Permission for Radiation Treatment of Bacon."
     USDA release, July 2, 1969.
108. Dr. R. D. Holsten, Dr. M. Sugii, and Professor F. C. Steward,
     "Direct & Indirect Effects of Radiation on Plant Cells: Their Rela-
     tion to Growth & Growth Induction. *Nature,* Vol. 208, Nov. 27,
     1965, pp. 850–56.
109. "Irradiated Sugar Can Harm Human Cells." *Science Journal,*
     Vol. 2, No. 12, Dec. 1966, p. 4.
110. David Sanford, "Radio-Inactive Food." *New Republic,* June 15,
     1968, pp. 15–17.
111. "FDA Rejects Irradiated Canned Ham; Other Programs Jeopar-
     dized." *Health Bulletin,* June 8, 1968, pp. 1–2.
112. *Ibid.,* p. 2.
113. *Ibid.,* p. 2.
114. *Farm Journal,* Sept. 1967, p. 12.

115. *Joint FAO/WHO Committee on the Technical Basis for Legislation on Irradiated Food.* WHO Technical Report Series 316. Geneva: WHO, United Nations, 1966.

CHAPTER 4

1. "Chemicals No Menace." *Rutland* (Vt.) *Daily Herald,* Feb. 14, 1961.
2. Dr. Theodore R. van Dellen, "Better Foods Through Additives." *Caledonia Record* (St. Johnsbury, Vt.), Dec. 18, 1963.
3. "Food Additives Aid Nutrition." *Boston Herald,* Dec. 18, 1962.
4. Victor J. Hillery, "Food Additives: Despite Furor, Most Are Safe, Necessary & Beneficial." *Wall Street Journal,* Oct. 1, 1962.
5. Dr. William J. Darby and Gwen Lam, *Food & Science, Today* & *Tomorrow.* Public Affairs Pamphlet 320. New York: Public Affairs Committee, Nov. 1961, p. 7.
6. Sir Edward Mellanby, M.D., "The Chemical Manipulation of Foods." *British Medical Journal,* Oct. 13, 1951, p. 864.
7. William E. Smith, M.D., *letter* to Representative James J. Delaney, Jan. 28, 1957. Read by Delaney in House of Representatives, Extension of Remarks, Feb. 21, 1957.
8. William E. Smith, M.D., *address,* "Food Additives Legislation." Little Rock, Ark., Feb. 16, 1957.
9. Dr. Roy Newton, *letter.* 82nd Congress, 2nd session, Hearings before the House Select Committee to Investigate the Use of Chemicals in Foods & Cosmetics, Part 3, 1952, p. 1408.
10. *Ibid.,* p. 1409.
11. *Ibid.,* p. 1409.
12. *Ibid.,* p. 1409.
13. *What Consumers Should Know About Food Additives.* Publication 10. U.S. Department of Health, Education, and Welfare, FDA, Feb. 1963, revised, pp. 2–13.
14. "Food Additives." *Chemical & Engineering News,* Oct. 10, 1966, pp. 106–7.
15. "Food Additive Testing Is Inadequate, Says Goddard." *Health Bulletin,* Jan. 7, 1967, p. 4.
16. Dr. H. F. Kraybill, "Carcinogenesis Associated with Foods, Food Additives, Food Degradation Products, and Related Dietary Factors." Symposium on Chemical Carcinogenesis. *Clinical Pharmacology & Therapeutics.* Vol. 4, No. 1, Jan.–Feb. 1963, pp. 73–87.
17. "Enzymes—the Effective Agents." Ralph W. Gerard, M.D., ed., *Food for Life.* Chicago: University of Chicago, 1952, pp. 144–56.

18. R. A. Holman, M.D., "The Answer to Cancer." *Journal of the Soil Association*, Vol. 11, No. 4, Oct. 1960, p. 371.
19. Commissioner George P. Larrick, "The Consumer Looks at Chemicals in Our Food." *Food, Drug, and Cosmetic Law Journal*, Vol. 12, No. 6, June 1957, p. 345.
20. Deputy Commissioner John L. Harvey, *statement*. FDA release, Nov. 22, 1960.
21. *Chemical Week*, Dec. 3, 1960, p. 35.
22. "Food Chemicals in Relation to Cancer." *Consumer Bulletin Annual*, 1962–1963, p. 14.
23. "Food Additives." *Chemical & Engineering News*, Oct. 17, 1966, p. 124.
24. Wilhelm C. Hueper, M.D., "Carcinogens in the Human Environment." *Archives of Pathology, American Medical Association*, Vol. 71, Apr. 1961, p. 357.
25. *Idem., ibid.*, Vol. 71, Mar. 1961, p. 261.
26. *Evaluation of the Carcinogenic Hazards of Food Additives*. Technical Report 220, 5th Report of the Joint FAO/WHO Expert Committee on Food Additives. Geneva: WHO, 1961, p. 6.
27. Dr. Arnold J. Lehman, "Procedures for the Appraisal of Toxicity of Chemicals in Foods." *Food, Drug and Law Quarterly*, Vol. 4, 1959, p. 73.
28. Irving Selikoff, M.D., "Second Sunday." NBC program, Mar. 9, 1969, p. 15 (of printed script).
29. Wilhelm C. Hueper, M.D., and W. D. Conway, *Chemical Carcinogenesis and Cancers*. Chicago: Charles Thomas, 1964, pp. 73–74.
30. Wilhelm C. Hueper, M.D., "Potential Role of Non-Nutritive Additives and Contaminants as Environmental Carcinogens." Symposium on Potential Cancer Hazards from Chemical Additives. *Archives of Pathology, American Medical Association*, Vol. 62, 1956, p. 220.
31. Prof. Hermann J. Muller, *address*. The Great Issues of Conscience in Modern Medicine, Dartmouth Convocation, Hanover, N.H., Sept. 9, 1960.
32. *Science News Letter*, Nov. 18, 1960.
33. as in Note 30, above, p. 219.
34. *Tenox, 2, Eastman Antioxidant for Animal Fats*, Bulletin 1, 1952; *Tenox, Eastman Food-Grade Antioxidants*, Bulletin 6, 1953; *Tenox R, Key to Feed Markets for Animal Fats*, 1954; *Tenox Antioxidants for Edible Animal Fats*, Bulletin G-105, 1958. Kingsport (Tenn.): Tennessee Eastman Co.
35. *Antioxidant AC-3, Food Grade BHT*. New York: Catalin Corporation of America (no date).

36. "The Mystery of the Butylated Twins." *Consumer Bulletin,* Oct. 1961, pp. 18–20; "The 'Butylated Twins' in Foods." *Ibid.,* Aug. 1962, pp. 28–29.
37. W. B. Deichmann, J. J. Clemmer, R. Rakoczyk, and J. Bianchine, "Toxicity of Ditertiarybutylmethylphenol." *Archives of Industrial Health, American Medical Association,* Vol. 11, 1955, pp. 93–101.
38. J. C. Dacre and F. A. Denz, "The Metabolism of Butylated Hydroxytoluene in the Rabbit." *Biochemical Journal,* Vol. 64, No. 4, 1956, pp. 777–82; J. C. Dacre, "The Metabolism of 3:5-Di-tert.-butyl-4-hydroxytoluene and 3:5-Di-tert.-butyl-4-hydroxybenzoic Acid in the Rabbit." *Ibid.,* Vol. 78, 1961, pp. 758–66; W. D. Brown, A. R. Johnson and M. W. O'Halloran, "The Effect of the Level of Dietary Fat on the Toxicity of Phenolic Antioxidants." *Australian Journal of Experimental Biology and Medical Science,* Vol. 37, 1959, pp. 533–47; A. J. Day, A. R. Johnson, M. W. O'Halloran, and C. J. Schwartz, "The Effect of the Antioxidant Butylated Hydroxytoluene on Serum Lipid and Glycoprotein Levels in the Rat." *Ibid.,* Vol. 37, 1959, pp. 295–306; Susan M. Milner, "Effect of the Food Additive Butylated Hydroxytoluene on Monolayer Cultures of Primate Cells." *Nature,* Vol. 216, Nov. 11, 1967, pp. 557–60.
39. I. A. Karplyuk, "Toxicological Characteristics of Phenolic Antioxidants of Edible Fats." *Voprosy Pitaniya* (Romania), Vol. 18, No. 4, 1959, p. 24; Brown, Johnson & O'Halloran, *op. cit.,* pp. 533–47.
40. Brown, Johnson & O'Halloran, *op. cit.,* pp. 533–47.
41. Karplyuk, *op. cit.,* p. 24; Brown, Johnson & O'Halloran, *op. cit.,* pp. 533–47; D. Gilbert and L. Goldberg, "Liver Weight and Microsomal Processing Enzymes in Rats Treated with Butylated Hydroxyanisole or Butylated Hydroxytoluene." *Proceedings of the Biochemical Society* (England), Vol. 97, No. 3, Dec. 1965, pp. 28–29.
42. Brown, Johnson & O'Halloran, *op. cit.,* pp. 533–47.
43. Day, Johnson, O'Halloran, & Schwartz, *op. cit.,* pp. 295–306; A. R. Johnson and F. R. Hewgill, "The Effect of the Antioxidants, Butylated Hydroxyanisole, Butylated Hydroxytoluene and Propyl Gallate on Growth, Liver and Serum Lipids and Serum Sodium Levels of the Rat." *Australian Journal of Experimental Biology and Medical Science,* Vol. 39, 1961, pp. 353–60.
44. Brown, Johnson & O'Halloran, *op. cit.,* pp. 533–47.
45. *Ibid.,* pp. 533–47.
46. Karplyuk, *op. cit.,* p. 24.
47. Brown, Johnson & O'Halloran, *op. cit.,* pp. 533–47.

48. Dr. George H. Akau, *letter* to Hearing Clerk, Department of Health, Education, and Welfare, Sept. 3, 1966.

49. Mrs. X, letters to author, 1963–65; allergist of Mrs. X, letters to author, 1963–65.

50. Mrs. Z, letters to author, 1964–66.

51. Mellanby, *op. cit.*, p. 869.

52. James L. Trawick, "Protecting Quality." USDA yearbook, *Consumers All.* Washington, D.C.: USGPO, 1965, p. 430.

53. *Specifications for the Identity and Purity of Food Additives and Their Toxicological Evaluation: Food Colors and Some Antimicrobials and Antioxidants.* Technical Report 309, 8th Report, Joint FAO/WHO Expert Committee on Food Additives. Geneva: WHO, 1965, pp. 15–20, 25.

54. *Report on Antioxidants in Foods.* Food Standards Committee, Ministry of Agriculture, Fisheries, and Food. London: HMSO, 1963.

55. *Proposals for Revised Regulations on Antioxidants in Food.* As in Note 54, Sept. 13, 1965.

56. *Food Chemical News*, Dec. 4, 1967, p. 13.

57. H. C. Grice, G. Becking, and T. Goodman, "Toxic Properties of Nordihydroguaiaretic Acid." *Food and Cosmetics Toxicology*, Vol. 6, 1968, pp. 155–61.

58. Canadian Food & Drug Directorate, *Trade Information Letter*, Sept. 20, 1967.

59. "FDA Studies Antioxidant," *Health Bulletin*, Dec. 9, 1967, p. 2.

60. "NDGA Dropped from Generally Recognized As Safe List." *Ibid.*, May 4, 1968, p. 3.

61. *Federal Register*, Nov. 22, 1967.

62. *Ibid.*, Apr. 11, 1968.

63. Office of the Assistant Commissioner for Education & Information, FDA, letter to author, June 13, 1968.

64. "USDA Bars Use of Chemical NDGA in Most Meat Food Products." USDA release, Sept. 18, 1968.

65. Quoted by Dr. Thomas Carney, *testimony.* 86th Congress, 2nd session, Hearings before the Committee on Interstate and Foreign Commerce, House of Representatives, on Color Additives, 1960, p. 276.

66. Delaney Amendment, section 706 (b) (5) (B) of H.R. 7624 to the Federal Food, Drug, & Cosmetic Act, and a corresponding clause in the Food Additives Act of 1958.

67. As in Note 65, above, p. 275.

68. *Problems in the Evaluation of Carcinogenic Hazard from Use of Food Additives.* Food Protection Committee, Food and Nutrition

Board, Publication 749. Washington, D.C.: NAS-NRC, Dec. 1959, p. 27.

69. As in Note 29, above, p. 517.

70. Wilhelm C. Hueper, M.D., "Symposium: Environmental & Occupational Cancer Hazards, Part 1." *Clinical Pharmacology & Therapeutics.* Vol. 3, No. 6, 1963, pp. 776–813.

71. *Ibid.,* p. 783.

72. Dr. H. E. Cox, *address.* Food, Agriculture & Fine Chemical Groups of the Society of Chemical Industries. *British Medical Journal,* Oct. 13, 1951.

73. *Bulletin of the Association of Food & Drug Officials of the United States,* July 1950, p. 85.

74. Connecticut Agricultural Station, *54th Report on Food Products,* Apr. 1951.

75. Dr. Edward Eagle, *testimony.* 81st Congress, 1st session, Hearings before the House Select Committee to Investigate the Use of Chemicals in Food Products, 1950, pp. 297–305.

76. C. E. Poling *et al.,* "Effects of Feeding Polyoxyethylene Preparations to Rats and Hamsters." *Food Research,* Vol. 21, 1956, p. 337.

77. *Consumer Reports,* Mar. 1953, p. 96.

78. *The Safety of Polyoxyethylene (8) Stearate for Use in Foods.* Food Protection Committee, Food & Nutrition Board, Publication 646. Washington, D.C.: NAS-NRC, Dec. 1958, pp. 8–9.

79. Wilhelm C. Hueper, M.D., *address.* Seminar for science writers, American Cancer Society, 1960.

80. Helen Goldhammer and W. R. McManus, "Effect of Non-Ionic Surfactants Upon Animal Tissues. *Nature,* Apr. 1960, pp. 317–18.

81. "Nutritional Quality of Market Foods." *Report of the Committee on Environmental Health Problems to the Surgeon General.* U.S. Department of Health, Education, and Welfare, Public Health Service. Washington, D.C.: USGPO, 1962, pp. 149–50.

82. *The Merck Index,* 7th ed., Rahway (N.J.): Merck, 1960, p. 948.

83. W. E. Stehbens, M.D., and M. D. Silver, "Arterial Lesions—Induced by Methyl Cellulose?" *American Journal of Pathology,* Mar. 1966, p. 483.

84. Margaret G. Kelly, Roger W. O'Gara, Sidney T. Yancey, Kumidini Gadekar, Constance Botkin, & Vincent T. Oliverio, "Comparative Carcinogenicity of N-Isopropyl-α-(2-Methylhydrazino)-p-Toluamide HCL (Procarbazine Hydrochloride), Its Degradation Products, Other Hydrazines, & Isonicotinic Acid Hydrazide." *Journal of the National Cancer Institute,* Vol. 42, No. 2, Feb. 1969, pp. 337–44.

85. As in Note 30, above, pp. 218–49.

CHAPTER 5

1. Representative Leo W. O'Brien, *statement*. 86th Congress, 2nd session, Hearings before the Committee on Interstate and Foreign Commerce, House of Representatives, on Color Additives, 1960, p. 388.
2. *American Agriculturist*, May 1965, pp. 14, 27.
3. Don Neff, "Eastern-fed Beef Loses Its Meaning." *Los Angeles Times Outlook*, Aug. 20, 1961.
4. "Feeding Habits of Beef Cattle Reported and Explained by USDA Scientists." USDA release, Mar. 23, 1966.
5. Quoted in *Compassion in World Farming* (England), Apr.–May 1968, p. 7.
6. "No One Wants Fats." *Modern Nutrition*, Vol. 13, No. 8., Aug. 1960, p. 13.
7. "Rough Stuff." *American Agriculturist*, Jan. 1970, p. 7.
8. "Yes, There Will Be Meat Tomorrow." USDA *Service*, No. 55, Aug. 1968, p. 3.
9. American Chemical Society release, Sept. 12, 1968.
10. USPHS release, June 1968.
11. "Sodium Chlorite Treatment." *Agricultural Research*, Vol. 16, No. 12, June 1968, p. 15.
12. Dr. Rudolf Hauschka, *Nutrition*. London: Stuart & Watkins, 1967, p. 123.
13. "First Calf Born from Synthetic Diet." *Agricultural Research*, Vol. 13, No. 10, Apr. 1965, p. 9.
14. Secretary of Health, Education, and Welfare Arthur S. Flemming, *testimony*. As in Note 1, above, p. 70.
15. "Stilbestrol-fed Cattle: How They're Selling Now." *Farm Journal*, Aug. 1955, p. 16.
16. "Feed Additives for Beef Cattle." *American Agriculturist*, Mar. 1962, p. 30.
17. W. J. Hadlow, Edward F. Grimes and George E. Jay, Jr., "Stilbestrol-Contaminated Feed and Reproductive Disturbances in Mice." *Science*, Vol. 122, No. 3171, Oct. 7, 1955, pp. 643–44.
18. Granville F. Knight, M.D., W. Coda Martin, M.D., Rigoberto Iglesias, M.D., and William E. Smith, M.D., "Possible Cancer Hazards Presented by Feeding Diethylstilbestrol to Cattle." *Symposium on Medicated Feeds*. New York: Medical Encyclopedia, 1956, p. 168.

19. Quoted in "Drugs in Animals Affect Human Growth." *Health Bulletin,* Nov. 6, 1965, p. 6.
20. Knight, Martin, Iglesias, & Smith, *op. cit.,* p. 168.
21. M. Gawienowski, H. W. Knoche, and Herbert C. Moser, *paper.* 138th national meeting, Division of Biological Chemistry, American Chemical Society, New York, Sept. 14, 1960.
22. "Antibiotics in Food Held Bad for Heart." *The New York Times,* Aug. 13, 1961.
23. C. D. Van Houweling, D.V.M., "Drugs in Animal Feed? A Question Without an Answer." *FDA Papers,* Vol. 1, No. 7, Sept. 1967, pp. 11–15.
24. "Salmonella in Meat." *British Medical Journal, Nov.* 21, 1964, p. 1281.
25. "Drugs in Meat Among Problems of Food Industry." *Health Bulletin,* Dec. 3, 1966. p. 4.
26. "Widespread Use of Antibiotics Poses New Threat." *Ibid.,* Aug. 13, 1966, p. 4.
27. *Federal Register,* Apr. 11, 1968.
28. Alvin Shuster, "Britain to Curb Antibiotic Feed." *The New York Times,* Nov. 21, 1969, p. 17.
29. Lawrence K. Altman, "Drug Use in Feed Arouses Concern." *The New York Times,* Nov. 23, 1969, p. 81.
30. "Is the Next Step Cortisone for Leaner Beef?" *Western Livestock Journal,* Apr. 1964.
31. "Will Tranquilizers Find Use in Animal Feed?" *Chemical Week,* Aug. 31, 1957, pp. 44–48.
32. "Tranquilizers Aid Beef Gains." *Farmers' Weekly,* Mar. 27, 1959.
33. "Israeli Studies May Lead to Increased Milk Production." *Agricultural Research,* Vol. 16, No. 12, June 1968, p. 11.
34. J. F. Sykes, J. W. Thomas, J. Bitman, and C. F. Winchester, "Antibiotics, Hormones, and Tranquilizers in Animals." *The Nature and Fate of Chemicals Applied to Soils, Plants, and Animals.* Symposium, USDA Agricultural Research Service, Sept. 1960, pp. 218–19.
35. Franklin Bicknell, M.D., *Chemicals in Food and in Farm Produce: Their Harmful Effects.* London: Faber & Faber, 1960, p. 75.
36. "Feed Additives." Editorial, *Journal of Clinical Physiology,* Vol. 3, No. 4, Spring 1962, p. 10.
37. John A. Rohlf, "It's Here: Timed Breeding for Livestock." *Farm Journal,* July 1965, p. 39.
38. "Artificial Breeding." *New England Homestead.* Oct. 1964, p. 7.
39. *Arkansas Farm Research,* Spring 1955.
40. As in Note 37, above, p. 24.

41. "Breeding Control." *American Agriculturist,* Nov. 1965, p. 8.
42. *Health Bulletin,* Sept. 16, 1967, p. 1.
43. "Two Lamb Crops a Year." *Agricultural Research,* Vol. 17, No. 1, July 1968, p. 10.
44. "How Do Implanted Spirals Stop Animal Reproduction?" *Ibid.,* Vol. 14, No. 7, Jan. 1966, pp. 4–5.
45. *Farm Journal,* July 1964, p. 24.
46. *Ibid.,* p. 24.
47. "USDA Reports on Urea Fed to Cattle on Feed." USDA release, Jan. 23, 1969.
48. "Trimming Feet." *American Agriculturist,* Nov. 1965, p. 10.
49. "Swift Injects Enzymes to Tenderize Its Cattle." *The New York Times,* May 11, 1960.
50. "USDA Alters Procedures for Testing Enzyme-Treated Meats." USDA release, Nov. 9, 1965.
51. R. D. Radeleff and R. C. Bushland, "The Toxicity of Pesticides for Livestock," as in Note 34, above, p. 141.
52. "Charcoal Called Antipoison in Cattle." *The New York Times,* Sept. 5, 1968.
53. Representative James J. Delaney, "Perils on Your Food Shelf." *American Magazine,* July 1951, p. 114.
54. "Fences Go Down as Farms Raise Cattle Indoors." *The New York Times,* Nov. 1, 1966.
55. "The Farm Becomes the Factory." *Business Week,* Aug. 19, 1967, pp. 68–70.
56. "New Look in the Livestock Business." *Farm Progress,* Vol. 3, No. 5, Sept.–Oct. 1965, p. 5.
57. "Solving the Problem of Calf Pneumonia." *The Times* (London), Nov. 30, 1964, p. 14.
58. Ruth Harrison, *Animal Machines: The New Factory Farming—A Pictorial Summary.* London: Vincent Stuart, 1964, pp. 62–88.
59. "Should We Outlaw Garbage Feeding?" *Farm Journal,* Apr. 1965, p. 46.
60. *Successful Farming,* Dec. 1962.
61. *Farm Journal,* as in Note 59, above, p. 46.
62. "Nutrition." *Health Bulletin,* Dec. 21, 1963, p. 6.
63. "Antibiotics in Animal Husbandry." *Journal of the Soil Association,* Vol. 7, No. 2, Apr. 1953, p. 41.
64. "Poor Pork Costs Everybody Money." *Ag Business Journal,* July–Aug. 1969, p. 9.
65. "Hogs—A Crop at a Time." *Agricultural Research,* Vol. 14, No. 3, Sept. 1965, pp. 3–4.

66. "New Heat Synch Drug May Boost Al." *Farm Journal,* Jan. 1965, p. 34.
67. As in Note 58 above, pp. 95–96.
68. *Ibid.,* p. 96.
69. *Ibid.,* p. 96.
70. "Gets Attention." *American Agriculturist,* Nov. 1965.
71. Dr. Virgil W. Hayes, *address.* Pfizer Research Conference, swine nutritional research (1964), Chicago, 1965.
72. "Humane Slaughter with Carbon Dioxide." *Food Processing,* Sept. 1960.
73. "Preslaughter Treatment for Quality Pork." *Feed Management,* Sept. 1965, p. 44.
74. "Anesthesia Before Slaughter Means Better Pork." *What's New in Farm Science?* annual report, part 2, University of Wisconsin Agricultural Experiment Station Bulletin 580, Fall 1965, pp. 16–17, 19.
75. Quoted by William Longgood, *The Poisons in Your Food.* New York: Simon & Schuster, 1960, p. 159.
76. "Shearing Sheep with Chemicals." *Agricultural Research,* Vol. 17, No. 4, Oct. 1968, pp. 8–9.
77. Dr. William A. Albrecht, *address.* International symposium, Man's Role in Changing the Face of the Earth, Wenner-Gren Foundation, Chicago, 1956.
78. FDA Commissioner George P. Larrick, *address.* Livestock conference, annual meeting of American Farm Bureau Federation, Chicago, Dec. 14, 1959.
79. *Summary of Activities 1950–1959.* Meat Inspection Division, USDA, 1960.
80. S. Perry Abraham, M.D., "A New Zealand Doctor Gives Views on Nutrition." *Modern Nutrition,* Vol. 14, No. 1, Jan. 1961, p. 17.
81. "Will Tranquilizers Find Use in Cattle Feed? Agricultural Research May Find the Answer." *Chemical Week,* Aug. 31, 1957, p. 46.
82. "Beef Sold off Cancerous Cattle." *Detroit News,* Feb. 9, 1970.
83. "Needles in Meat." *Health Bulletin,* May 18, 1963, p. 2.
84. "Cattlemen Strive for Higher Quality Beef." *Health Bulletin,* Aug. 7, 1965, p. 3.
85. A. R. Miller, "To Assure Good, Clean Meat." USDA yearbook, *Food.* Washington, D.C.: USGPO, 1959, p. 340.
86. *A Consumer's Guide to USDA Services.* Washington, D.C.: USDA Miscellaneous Publication No. 959, Mar. 1964, p. 5.
87. A. V. Nordquist and C. H. Pals, "Economic Losses from Animal Diseases and Parasites." USDA yearbook, *Animal Diseases.* Washington, D.C.: USGPO, 1956, p. 11.

88. *Ibid.*, p. 12.
89. Animal Health Division, Agricultural Research Service, USDA, Hyattsville, Md., letter to author, Jan. 12, 1966.
90. *Ibid.*, Jan. 27, 1966.
91. David Weinman, M.D., and Anne H. Chandler, "Toxoplasmosis in Man & Swine—an Investigation of the Possible Relationship." *Journal of the American Medical Association,* Vol. 161, No. 3, May 19, 1956, pp. 229–32.
92. "Toxoplasmosis & Undercooked Pork." *Consumer Reports,* June 1957, p. 298.
93. "Pork Sold in Butcher Shops." *Consumer Bulletin,* Sept. 1961, p. 4.
94. "Trichinosis Detection Test Is Efficient and Effective." USDA release, Apr. 17, 1969.
95. Harvey W. Wiley, M.D., *The History of a Crime Against the Food Law.* Washington, D.C.: Harvey W. Wiley, M.D. (publisher), 1929, p. 63.
96. *Idem., 1001 Tests.* New York: Hearst's International Library, 1914, p. 149.
97. Dr. M. R. Clarkson, *A Review of Certain Aspects of State and Federal Meat Inspection Services and Procedures.* Washington, D.C.: Agricultural Research Service, USDA, Jan. 1963, pp. 3–4.
98. Ralph Nader, "We're Still in the Jungle." *New Republic,* July 15, 1967, p. 11.
99. "Is 'Protecting Consumers' a Better Campaign Tactic than Kissing Babies?" *Consumer Bulletin,* Oct. 1968, pp. 25–26.
100. "The Wholesome Meat Act—a Quick, Quiet, and Confidential Project?" *Ibid.*, Aug. 1968, p. 17.
101. Dr. Oscar Sussman, "Health Expert Reveals New Law's Dangerous Deceit." *Nation's Business,* May 1968, p. 35.
102. *Ibid.*, p. 36.
103. "Meat Grading Is Threatened." *Consumer Reports,* Aug. 1959, p. 437.
104. "Canned Hams—Pig in a Tin-Plated Poke." *Consumer Reports,* Aug. 1962, p. 390.
105. "Canned Hams." *Consumer Bulletin,* Aug. 1965, pp. 36, 43.
106. "Bacon: a Broad Definition," letter to editor. *Consumer Reports,* July 1962, p. 314.
107. Representative Charles A. Vanik, *remarks. Congressional Record,* Mar. 3, 1966, p. 4811.
108. "What Price Bacon?" *Consumer Reports,* Jan. 1964, p. 18.
109. "Sausages for Breakfast?" *Ibid.*, Aug. 1968, p. 410.
110. "Ham." *Consumer Bulletin,* Mar. 1963, p. 4.

111. "The Great Ham Robbery." *Consumer Reports,* Mar. 1961, pp. 120–25.
112. *National Hog Farmer,* Oct. 1960.
113. Editorial, *The National Provisioner,* Aug. 1960.
114. "Armour & Co. Asks Court for Green Light on Wet Ham." *Co-Op Newsletter,* Beltsville (Md.), Nov. 15, 1961, p. 1.
115. *Federal Register,* Dec. 30, 1960.
116. As in Note 111, above, p. 122.
117. *Ibid.,* p. 122.
118. "USDA to Reopen Ham Study." USDA release, Mar. 17, 1961.
119. "Hearings on Watered Ham." *Consumer Reports,* July 1961, p. 427.
120. "U.S. Loses a Test on Watered Hams." *The New York Times,* Feb. 9, 1962.
121. "When You Buy Hamburger." *Consumer Reports,* Sept. 1960, p. 480.
122. Howard J. Sanders, "Chemical Mutagens, The Road to Genetic Disaster?" *Chemical & Engineering News,* May 19, 1969, p. 61.
123. "The Docket." *Consumer Reports,* June 1964, p. 303.
124. "Chopped Beef." *Consumer Bulletin,* July 1963, p. 37.
125. "Ground Meat." *Ibid.,* Mar. 1962, p. 3.
126. "Luncheon Meats, Sausage, Frankfurters, Hamburger." *Ibid.,* June 1966, p. 26.
127. "City Accuses Butchers of Selling Hamburger Containing 90% Fat." *The New York Times,* Feb. 7, 1962.
128. As in Note 121, above, p. 478.
129. "The Docket." *Consumer Reports,* May 1965, p. 248.
130. As in Note 121, above, p. 478.
131. "The Docket." *Consumer Reports,* Oct. 1963, p. 487.
132. "Tainted Meat Scandal Prompts Nationwide Investigation." *Health Bulletin,* May 29, 1965, p. 1.
133. As in Note 121, above, p. 479.
134. "Seeing Red." Letter to editor, *Consumer Reports,* Jan. 1963, p. 45.
135. Olin Mathieson Chemical Corp., U.S. Patent 3,041,184, issued June 26, 1962.
136. *Consumer Bulletin,* Mar. 1958, p. 35.
137. "The Anatomy of a Hot Dog." *Consumer Reports,* Sept. 1958, p. 467.
138. "Frankfurters." *Ibid.,* Sept. 1964, p. 430.
139. *Federal Register,* Sept. 23, 1969.
140. "Hot Dog Additive Banned by FDA." *U.S. News & World Report,* Dec. 5, 1960, p. 14.
141. New York *Herald Tribune,* Dec. 7, 1962.

CHAPTER 6

1. Douglas Gordon Campbell, M.D., interviewed by Colin Edwards, "Gambling with Public Health." Canadian Broadcasting Company, Dec. 1962, pp. 5–6 (printed script).
2. "Complete Automation Adapted to Poultry Feeding Operation." USDA release, May 24, 1960.
3. *Feed Age,* July 1965, p. 17.
4. N. R. Ellis, R. E. Davis, and C. A. Denton, "Use of Antibiotics, Hormones, Tranquilizers, and Other Chemicals in Animal Production." *The Nature and Fate of Chemicals Applied to Soils, Plants, and Animals.* Symposium, USDA Agricultural Research Service, Sept. 1960, p. 45.
5. *Everybody's Poultry Magazine,* Mar. 1960.
6. "Arsenic in Chicken Livers?" reply to letter to editor, *Consumer Reports,* Feb. 1965, p. 50.
7. Secretary of Health, Education, and Welfare Arthur S. Flemming, *testimony.* 86th Congress, 2nd session, Hearings before the Committee on Interstate and Foreign Commerce, House of Representatives, on Color Additives, 1960, p. 218.
8. Manuel Schreiber, *address.* Annual meeting, Federation of American Societies for Experimental Biology, Chicago, Apr. 1965.
9. *Farmers Weekly* (England), Sept. 29, 1961.
10. Franklin Bicknell, M.D., *Chemicals in Food and in Farm Produce: Their Harmful Effects.* London, Faber & Faber, 1960, p. 74.
11. William A. Randall, "Antibiotic Residues," *paper. Proceedings,* 1st international conference on antibiotics in agriculture. Washington, D.C.: NAS-NRC, 1956, p. 261.
12. "Drugs Fed to Animals Worry Health Researchers." *Health Bulletin,* June 5, 1965, p. 2.
13. As in Note 4, above, p. 44.
14. Consumer and Marketing Service, USDA, Washington, D.C., letter to author, Feb. 2, 1966.
15. *Food Technology,* Vol. 15, 1961, pp. 361–64; *ibid.,* Vol. 18, June 1964, pp. 102–7.
16. "Antibiotics in Poultry." *Consumers' Research Bulletin,* Nov. 1956, p. 34.
17. "Controls Likely Against Antibiotic Residues." *Health Bulletin,* Aug. 27, 1966, p. 2.
18. As in Note 10, above, p. 75.
19. *Feed Age,* July 1965, p. 51.

20. "Aspirin." *Health Bulletin,* Dec. 7, 1963, p. 5.
21. *World's Poultry Science Journal,* Vol. 21, 1965, pp. 12–22.
22. *Poultry Tribune,* Aug. 1965, p. 13.
23. As in Note 4, above, p. 44.
24. Dr. Robert K. Enders, *testimony.* 82nd Congress, 1st session, Hearings before the House Select Committee to Investigate the Use of Chemicals in Food Products, 1951, p. 432.
25. *Ibid.,* p. 435.
26. Josephine Ripley, "Flemming Curbs Capon Sales." *Christian Science Monitor,* Dec. 11, 1959.
27. "Banned Poultry Is Seized in City." *The New York Times,* Feb. 10, 1962.
28. "Injected Chickens Seized in Market." *The New York Times,* Feb. 27, 1962.
29. "Condemned Chickens Reprieved." *Modern Nutrition,* Vol. 13, No. 8, Aug. 1960, p. 17.
30. Mattox & Moore, Inc., U.S. Patent 3,042,525, issued July 3, 1962.
31. Ruth Desmond, *statement.* Hearing before Subcommittee on Health and Safety on House of Representatives 7247, Animal Drug Amendments of 1963, 1963. Federation of Homemakers release, p. 2 (unfolioed).
32. "Official FDA Tolerances, Complete Through Dec. 31, 1968." *National Agricultural Chemicals News & Pesticide Review,* Vol. 27, No. 3, Jan.–Feb. 1969, p. 23.
33. *Florida Poultryman,* Sept. 1963.
34. *USDA Food Processing/Marketing Report.* Washington, D.C.: USGPO, 1965.
35. *Farm Journal,* July 1964.
36. "Red Lights for Cannibalism Control." *Poultry Tribune,* Jan. 1965, p. 14.
37. "Cannibalism Still a Problem." *Ibid.,* Nov. 1964, p. 12.
38. "Watch How You Debeak." *Ibid.,* Oct. 1964, p. 8.
39. Ruth Harrison, *Animal Machines: The New Factory Farming—A Pictorial Summary.* London: Vincent Stuart, 1964, picture 8 (unfolioed).
40. Everett E. Wehr and Marion M. Farr, "Coccidiosis of Chickens and Turkeys." USDA yearbook, *Animal Diseases.* Washington, D.C.: USGPO, 1956, pp. 439–40.
41. R. L. Miller, "Coccidiosis." *American Agriculturist,* Oct. 1965, pp. 18, 21.
42. *Drug Trade News,* Nov. 30, 1959.
43. *New England Homestead,* Apr. 1965, p. 12.
44. "Handy Dead Bird Disposal." *Poultry Tribune,* Feb. 1965, p. 66.

45. "Dead Bird Disposal." *American Agriculturist,* Mar. 1966, p. 2.
46. *Feed Age,* July 1965.
47. "Chicken Doesn't Have That Tasty Flavor of Earlier Days." *Consumer Bulletin,* Nov. 1964, p. 41.
48. "Flavor Injection for Poultry." *Science News Letter,* Vol. 87, No. 1, Jan. 2, 1965, p. 14.
49. "Frozen Chickens." *Consumer Bulletin,* Feb. 1966, p. 41.
50. "U.S. Poultry." *Ibid.,* Feb. 1964, p. 42.
51. "Poultry." *Health Bulletin,* May 18, 1963, p. 7.
52. "Frozen Food." *Ibid.,* May 4, 1963, p. 6.
53. "Additives Threaten U.S. Poultry Exports." *Ibid.,* Apr. 6, 1963, pp. 4–5.
54. Roy W. Lennartson, "What Grades Mean." USDA yearbook, *Food.* Washington, D.C.: USGPO, 1959, pp. 349–51. 349–51.
55. *Poultry Slaughtered Under Federal Inspection and Poultry Used in Canning & Other Processed Foods.* Feb. 1960, USDA Agricultural Marketing Service, released Apr. 4, 1960, p. 1.
56. "A Sick Chick Goes to Market." *Consumer Reports,* Mar. 1955, pp. 143–44.
57. *National Report of Animal Diseases, Jan. through Dec. 1964.* USDA Agricultural Research Service, Animal Disease Eradication Division.
58. "Government Check Finds Poultry Unfit to Eat." *Health Bulletin,* Feb. 24, 1968, p. 3.
59. Dr. Oscar Sussman, "Health Expert Reveals New Law's Dangerous Deceit." *Nation's Business,* May 1968, p. 36.
60. "Turkeys Found Tainted with Pesticide; None May Be in Markets." *Wall Street Journal,* Nov. 10, 1969.
61. "Pesticide in Turkeys Is Linked to Chigger Control." *The New York Times,* Nov. 12, 1969, p. 28.
62. Tom Herman, "Chicken Cancer Called Widespread Enough to Pose 'Nightmare' for Poultry Industry." *Wall Street Journal,* Feb. 10, 1970, p. 6.
63. "U.S. Panel Backs Sale of Chickens with Cancer Virus." *The New York Times,* Jan. 26, 1970.
64. *Ibid.*
65. "Beef Sold off Cancerous Cattle." *Detroit News,* Feb. 9, 1970.
66. "When You Buy a Turkey." *Consumer Reports,* Nov. 1960, pp. 617–20.
67. *Consumer Bulletin,* Jan. 1958, p. 3.
68. As in Note 66, above, p. 620.
69. "Stuffed Frozen Turkeys." *Consumer Bulletin,* Nov. 1964, p. 4.
70. "Step Right Up and Guess the Weight of the Turkey—U.S. De-

partment of Agriculture Style, That Is!" *Consumer Bulletin,* Jan. 1968, p. 33.

71. "Labeling and Grading: Improvements Needed." *Consumer Reports,* Nov. 1967, p. 571.
72. As in Note 70, above, p. 34.
73. *Ibid.,* p. 34.
74. *Ibid.,* p. 34.
75. As in Note 66, above, p. 620.
76. *Farm Quarterly,* Spring 1962.
77. "Egg Costs Cut with Environmental Housing." *Poultry Tribune,* Feb. 1965, p. 16.
78. John B. Randall, Jr., "A New Look at New England's Egg Business." *Ibid.,* Jan. 1965, pp. 48–50.
79. D. D. Bragg, "How Much Does Improved Environment Pay?" *Ibid.,* Mar. 1965, pp. 18–19.
80. As in Note 39, above, pp. 37–61.
81. "The Pressures of Efficiency." Editorial, *Poultry Tribune,* Feb. 1964, p. 94.
82. "Financing Arrangements for Feed and Pullets." *Ibid.,* Feb. 1965, p. 14.
83. William A. Junnila, "What to Do About Those Laying House Ventilation Problems." *Ibid.,* Jan. 1965, p. 22.
84. "News from the Southwest." *Ibid.,* Feb. 1965, p. 15.
85. *Compassion in World Farming* (England), Apr.–May 1968, p. 7.
86. "Electronic Egg Recorder Automates USDA Poultry Research." USDA release, Feb. 28, 1966.
87. Richard E. Phillips, "How Lights Increase Egg Production." *Poultry Tribune,* Oct. 1964, p. 43.
88. "Replacement Pullets—Their Feeding, Management and Rearing." *Feed Age,* July 1965, pp. 22–29.
89. D. M. Cooper, "Artificial Insemination in Poultry." *World's Poultry Science Journal,* Vol. 21, 1965, pp. 12–22.
90. "Vineland Gets New Patent on Egg Dipping Procedure." *Poultry Tribune,* Oct. 1964, p. 74.
91. "Airtight Idea Cuts Poultry Hatch Out Losses." *Ibid.,* Oct. 1964, p. 46.
92. "Force Molting, Is It a Sound Practice?" *Poultry Tribune,* Dec. 1964, pp. 24–25.
93. *Farm & Stockbreeder* (England) Apr. 28, 1964.
94. Milton R. Dunk, "Disposal of Fowl an Increasing Problem." Editorial, *Poultry Tribune,* Mar. 1965, p. 80.
95. "High Mortality in Multiple Cages." *Journal of Poultry Science,* Vol. 43, 1964, pp. 801–5.

96. "Constant Battle Against Diseases." *Poultry Tribune,* Feb. 1965, p. 94.

97. Quoted in "Contamination in Eggs." *Modern Nutrition,* Vol. 14, No. 10, Oct. 1961, p. 17.

98. As in Note 10, above, p. 74.

99. "How to Keep Pesticides Out of Eggs." *Farm Journal,* Sept. 1964, p. 51.

100. *Journal of Poultry Science,* Vol. 31, 1952, p. 388.

101. "Fumigating Eggs." *American Agriculturist,* Mar. 1962.

102. "University of Georgia Gets USDA Contract to Study Elimination of DDT Residue From Poultry." USDA release, July 6, 1966.

103. *Poultry Tribune,* Aug. 1965, p. 33.

104. *Farm Journal,* Feb. 1965, p. 56.

105. *Poultry Tribune,* Aug. 1965, p. 29.

106. R. S. Harris and H. W. Loesecke (eds.), *Nutritional Evaluation of Food Processing.* New York: Wiley, 1960, p. 31.

107. *Poultry Tribune,* Sept. 1964, p. 97.

108. "Spotting Deception in Food Processing Gets More Difficult." *Health Bulletin,* Feb. 27, 1965, p. 3.

109. "Egg Contract Based on Case Weight & Whole Egg Color." *Poultry Tribune,* Aug. 1965, p. 12.

110. As in Note 10, above, p. 120.

111. *Consumers' Research Bulletin,* Oct. 1956, p. 4.

112. Sam Ridlen and Hugh Johnson, "What Causes Mottled Yolks?" *Poultry Tribune,* Jan. 1965, p. 36.

113. Robert C. Baker, "When Eggs Have Bloodspots." *American Agriculturist,* Mar. 1960.

114. *Feed Age,* July 1965, p. 12.

115. "Stronger Shells." *Wisconsin State Journal,* Apr. 10, 1966.

116. Dr. Joseph Riboulleau, *Substances hormonales dans l'Oeuf et l'embryon des oiseaux.* Paris: Vigot Frères, 1939.

117. "Nutritional Values of Eggs Vary." *Modern Nutrition,* Vol. 14, No. 6, June 1961, p. 14.

118. Michael J. Walsh, Sc.D., "Answers to Your Questions on Foods and Nutrition." *Ibid.,* Vol. 17, No. 2, Feb. 1964, p. 18.

119. *Cleveland Plain Dealer,* Dec. 20, 1966.

120. *Poultry Tribune,* Nov. 1964, p. 34.

121. *American Agriculturist,* June 4, 1960, p. 28.

122. *Poultry Tribune,* Sept. 1964, p. 59.

123. As in Note 106, above, p. 31.

124. "Aluminum Eggshells." *Modern Nutrition,* Vol. 13, No. 5, May 1960, p. 23.

125. "Keep Eggs Fresh—At Least Two Years!" *Farm Journal,* Dec. 1964, p. 20.

126. *Poultry Tribune,* Nov. 1964, p. 77.

127. "Are the Eggs You Buy Making the Grade?" *Consumer Reports,* Feb. 1966, pp. 62–66.

128. "Quality Eggs? You're Kidding!" *Farm Journal,* July 1964, p. 34.

129. As in Note 127, above, p. 64.

130. "Eggs." *Consumer Bulletin,* May 1965, p. 4.

131. "Is the Floor Egg Problem Increasing?" *Poultry Tribune,* Sept. 1964, pp. 66, 82.

132. "The Docket." *Consumer Reports,* May 1963, p. 209.

133. "Salmonella, the Ubiquitous Bug." *FDA Papers,* Vol. 1, No. 1, Feb. 1967, pp. 13–19.

134. *Ibid.,* p. 14.

135. "Salmonella Food Poisoning Laid to Eggs." *Health Bulletin,* June 15, 1963, p. 4.

136. *Ibid.,* p. 4.

137. "Face Up to the Salmonella Problem." *Poultry Tribune,* Nov. 1964, p. 70.

138. "Pasteurizing Egg White." *Agricultural Research,* Vol. 14, No. 3, Sept. 1965, p. 10.

CHAPTER 7

1. Hal Higdon, "Obituary for DDT (in Michigan)." *The New York Times Magazine,* July 6, 1969, p. 35.

2. George J. Wallace, "Insecticides and Birds." *Address.* 54th annual convention, National Audubon Society, New York, 1958, p. 8 (script).

3. F. P. Ide, "Effect of Forest Spraying with DDT on Aquatic Insects of Salmon Streams." *Transactions.* American Fisheries Society, Vol. 89, 1957, pp. 208–19.

4. *"Effects of Pesticides on Fish & Wildlife in 1960.* Bureau of Sport Fisheries & Wildlife, Fish & Wildlife Service, U.S. Department of the Interior Circular 143, 1962, pp. 20–24; *Pesticide—Wildlife Studies, a Review of Fish & Wildlife Service Investigations During 1961 and 1962. Ibid.,* Circular 167, June 1963, pp. 11–42.

5. "Pesticide Fatal to Fish Is Traced." *The New York Times* (Sunday), Apr. 5, 1964, p. 70.

6. "Government Says Fish Containing Endrin Is 'Safe to Eat.' " *Health Bulletin,* Apr. 11, 1964, p. 1.

7. *Ibid.,* p. 1.

8. Alan Edmonds, "Death of a Great Lake." *Maclean's* (Canada), Nov. 1, 1965, pp. 28–29, 42–46.

9. "F.D.A. Sets Limits for DDT in Fish Shipped Interstate." *The New York Times*, Apr. 23, 1969.

10. "Pesticides Must Be Controlled." Editorial, *Plain Dealer*, Apr. 1, 1969.

11. As in Note 9, above.

12. Julie Morris, "State May Pull Chubs from Grocery Shelves." *Detroit Free Press*, Dec. 22, 1969.

13. "Wide Curb on DDT Scheduled by U.S. in Next 2 Years." *The New York Times*, Nov. 13, 1969, p. 1.

14. Harold M. Schmeck, Jr., "Strict Ban on DDT Is Sought in Suits." *The New York Times*, Dec. 30, 1969, p. 14.

15. "Pesticides Seen Disaster Cause." *The Evening' News* (Newark, N.J.), July 10, 1969.

16. "Search for Food Purity Focuses on Fish and Shellfish." *Health Bulletin*, Apr. 8, 1967, p. 1.

17. Robert L. Dow, "Watch Those Pesticides." *Farm Journal*, Nov. 1967, p. 12.

18. *Idem.*, "Pesticide Residue Trends in Lobster." *Maine Environmental Bulletin*, Natural Resources Council of Maine, Jan. 1969, pp. 1–2.

19. "Clams." *Health Bulletin*, Feb. 22, 1964, p. 6.

20. John G. Rogers, "Champion of Oyster Steps Up War on its Foes." New York *Herald Tribune*, Apr. 17, 1961.

21. "Pollution of Shellfish Worries Health Officials." *Health Bulletin*, Oct. 2, 1965, p. 4.

22. Robert W. Risebrough, Daniel B. Menzel, D. James Martin, Jr., and Harold S. Olcott, "DDT Residues in Pacific Sea Birds: A Persistent Insecticide in Marine Food Chains." *Nature*, Vol. 216, Nov. 11, 1967, pp. 589–90.

23. *Industrial Radioactive Waste Disposal.* 86th Congress, 1st session, Hearings before the Special Subcommittee on Radiation of the Joint Committee on Atomic Energy, Vol. 2, 1959, p. 1028.

24. E. M. Wood, Ph.D., M.D., and Charles P. Larson, M.D., "Hepatic Carcinoma in Rainbow Trout." *Archives of Pathology*, American Medical Association, Vol. 71, No. 5, May 1961, pp. 478–79.

25. Wilhelm C. Hueper, M.D., and W. D. Conway, *Chemical Carcinogenesis and Cancers.* Chicago: Charles Thomas, 1964, p. 17.

26. "Trout Liver Study Held Cancer Clue." *The New York Times*, July 18, 1961.

27. Wilhelm C. Hueper, M.D., and W. W. Payne, "Observations on the Occurrence of Hepatomas in Rainbow Trout." *Journal of the National Cancer Institute*, Vol. 27, 1961, pp. 1123–43.

28. *Ibid.*, p. 1123.
29. "Frozen Food." Letter to editor, *Consumer Reports*, July 1952, p. 310.
30. "Frozen Fish Fillets." *Ibid.*, Jan. 1963, p. 31.
31. "Frozen Fillets." *Ibid.*, Jan. 1952, pp. 19–20; "Fish on Ice." *Ibid.*, Feb. 1958, pp. 94–95.
32. Quoted in *Consumer Bulletin*, June 1957, p. 31.
33. "Frozen Fried Fish Sticks." *Consumer Reports*, Feb. 1961, pp. 80–83; "The Record of Shrimp." *Ibid.*, Sept. 1961, pp. 506–10.
34. "Frozen Shrimp." *Ibid.*, Oct. 1952, pp. 461–62; "Frozen Shrimp." *Ibid.*, Feb. 1957, pp. 71–72.
35. *U.S. Standards for Grades of Frozen Raw Headless Shrimp*, U.S. Department of the Interior, Sept. 1960.
36. "The Record of Shrimp." As in Note 33 above, p. 506.
37. *Ibid.*, p. 506.
38. "Government Official Says Some Frozen Fish Inedible." *Health Bulletin*, May 8, 1965, p. 1.
39. "The Record of Shrimp." As in Note 33 above, p. 508.
40. "Big Shrimp." *Consumer Bulletin*, Feb. 1962, p. 3.
41. "Frozen Fish Sticks." As in Note 33 above, p. 63.
42. As in Note 33, above, p. 80.
43. *Ibid.*, p. 80.
44. "Frozen Breaded Fish Portions." *Consumer Reports*, May 1965, p. 235.
45. As in Note 38 above, p. 1.
46. *Ibid.*, p. 1.
47. *Consumer Bulletin*, Apr. 1958, p. 36.
48. *The Fish Boat*, Aug. 1959.
49. "Tuna Fish, the Favorite Canned Seafood." *Consumer Reports*, Feb. 1964, p. 82.
50. *Ibid.*, p. 82.
51. "The Mystery of the Botulism-Poisoned Fish." *Ibid.*, Feb. 1964, p. 84.
52. Harold J. Humphrey, "Potentialities of Industry in Preparing Protein-Rich Foods," *address*. The Nutrition Society & the Society of the Chemical Industry, London, Nov. 30, 1960, p. 5 (script).
53. *Fish Protein Concentrate*. Bureau of Commercial Fisheries, Fish & Wildlife Service, U.S. Department of the Interior, Sept. 1962, pp. 1–6.
54. *Federal Register*, Sept. 15, 1961.
55. William B. Bradley, letter to editor, *Bakers Weekly*, Jan. 24, 1966, p. 48.
56. *Ibid.*, p. 48.

57. Dr. Paul B. Pearson, statement, *ibid.,* p. 48.
58. "Whole Fish Flour Is Barred for U.S." *The New York Times,* Jan. 25, 1962.
59. *Federal Register,* Jan. 25, 1962.
60. "U.S. Lifts Ban on Fish Flour." *Boston Herald,* Jan. 31, 1967.
61. Martin Skala, "Consumer Sales Near, Food-from-Fish Process Readied." *Christian Science Monitor,* Sept. 16, 1969, p. 13.
62. FDA release, Mar. 2, 1968.
63. Franklin Bicknell, M.D., *Chemicals in Food and in Farm Produce: Their Harmful Effects.* London: Faber & Faber, 1960, p. 54.

CHAPTER 8

1. "Food and Nutrition." *Consumer Bulletin Annual,* 1962–1963, p. 20.
2. *Ibid.,* 1960–61, p. 144.
3. "Refrigeration Eliminated." *Health Bulletin,* Apr. 3, 1965, p. 5.
4. "Peanut Industry Jittery Over Cancer-Mold Scare." *Ibid.,* May 30, 1964, p. 4.
5. "FDA to Study Mold Contaminants in Light of Liver Cancer Reports." *Ibid.,* Apr. 11, 1964, p. 3.
6. *Ibid.,* p. 3.
7. Dr. R. Allcroft, H. Rogers, and G. Lewis, "Metabolism of Aflatoxin in Sheep: Excretion of the 'Milk Toxin.'" *Nature,* Vol. 209, Jan. 8, 1966, pp. 154–55.
8. "Dying Bears Focus Attention on Toxic Mold." *Health Bulletin,* Mar. 20, 1965, p. 5.
9. "Quiet Search On in California for Suspect Peanut Butter." *Ibid.,* Dec. 19, 1964, p. 2.
10. "Canadians Doubt That All U.S. Peanuts Are Safe to Eat." *Ibid.,* Jan. 22, 1966, p. 1.
11. *Journal of the Association of Official Agricultural Chemists,* Dec. 1964.
12. A. J. Zuckerman and F. Fulton, "What Mold Poisons Do to Liver Cells." *New Scientist,* Vol. 31, No. 505, July 21, 1966, pp. 146–47.
13. As in Note 5, above, p. 3.
14. As in Note 4, above, p. 4.
15. *Ibid.,* p. 4.
16. As in Note 9, above, p. 2.
17. *Ibid.,* pp. 1–2.
18. "Food Standards." *Health Bulletin,* Oct. 30, 1965, p. 6.
19. *Federal Register,* Nov. 28, 1961.
20. Letter from food processor to author, Nov. 26, 1965.

21. "Sec. Freeman Asks Reconsideration of Court Decision on Watered Hams." USDA release, Feb. 9, 1962 (definition of "imitation" food).
22. *Federal Register,* Nov. 10, 1964.
23. Theron G. Randolph, M.D., letter to Commissioner of FDA George P. Larrick, Feb. 2, 1965.
24. "Consumers Voice Opinions on Ingredients in Peanut Butter." *Health Bulletin,* Feb. 13, 1965, p. 1.
25. *Federal Register,* July 8, 1965.
26. "Battle Continues over Ingredients in Peanut Butter." *Health Bulletin,* Dec. 18, 1965, p. 2.
27. "Harvard Nutritionist Testifies for Peanut Butter Industry." *Ibid.,* Jan. 8, 1966, p. 2.
28. *Ibid.,* p. 2.
29. *Federal Register,* Dec. 6, 1967.
30. "Peanut Butter Wrangle May Get Court Hearing." *Wall Street Journal,* July 25, 1968.
31. "That Long Awaited Peanut Butter Definition." *Consumer Bulletin,* Mar. 1969, p. 6.
32. Ruth Desmond, *statement.* Hearings before the Subcommittee on Labor and Health, Education and Welfare Approporiations of the House Appropriations Committee, Mar. 24, 1965. Washington, D.C.: Federation of Homemakers Newsletter, Apr.–May 1965, p. 3.

CHAPTER 9

1. Quoted in "Food and Nutrition." *Consumer Bulletin Annual,* 1965, p. 43.
2. "Top Medical Body of American Heart Association Recommends Changes of Fat Consumption to Prevent Heart Attack and Strokes." American Heart Association release, Dec. 10, 1960.
3. *Consumer Bulletin,* July 1957, p. 26.
4. Leading article, *The Lancet,* 1956, Vol. 2, p. 557.
5. R. S. Harris and H. W. Loesecke (eds.), *Nutritional Evaluation of Food Processing.* New York: Wiley, 1960, p. 250.
6. *Ibid.,* p. 250.
7. Franklin Bicknell, M.D., *Chemicals in Food and in Farm Produce: Their Harmful Effects.* London: Faber & Faber, 1960, pp. 69–70.
8. Dr. Hugh Sinclair, "Sees Essential Fatty Acid Lack Causing Degenerative Disease." *Drug Trade News,* Vol. 32, No. 13, July 1, 1957, pp. 33, 50.
9. Ancel Keys, "Blood Lipids in Man—A Brief Review." *Journal of the American Dietetic Association,* Vol. 51, No. 6, p. 510.

10. Henry A. Schroeder, M.D., "Is Atherosclerosis a Conditioned Pyridoxal Deficiency?" *Journal of Chronic Diseases*, Vol. 2, No. 1, July 1955, p. 36.
11. *Consumer Bulletin*, Dec. 1957, p. 26.
12. *Federal Register*, June 7, 1941; amended July 23, 1963; amended Feb. 12, 1964; amended July 27, 1965.
13. *Consumer Reports*, Oct. 1953, pp. 440–41.
14. Dr. Ernest Dichter, *Handbook of Consumer Motivation, the Psychology of the World of Objects*. New York: McGraw-Hill, 1964, p. 51.
15. "Margarine Output Outpaces Creamery Butter." *Chemical Week*, Apr. 19, 1958, p. 112.
16. *Wall Street Journal*, Oct. 19, 1960.
17. "Margarines." *Consumer Reports*, May 1963, p. 234.
18. As in Note 7, above, p. 127.
19. As in Note 5, above, p. 245.
20. P. R. Peacock, "The Carcinogenic Action of Heated Fats and Lipoids." *British Medical Bulletin*, 1947, Vol. 4, p. 364.
21. As in Note 5, above, p. 242.
22. *Ibid.*, p. 246.
23. *Ibid.*, p. 247.
24. *Ibid.*, pp. 248–49.
25. Quoted by Paul Keene, *The Story of Oils*. Penns Creek, Pennsylvania: Walnut Acres, 1961, p. 1.
26. R. W. O'Gara, L. Stewart, J. Brown, and W. C. Hueper, "Carcinogenicity of Heated Fats and Fat Fractions." *Journal of the National Cancer Institute*, Vol. 42, No. 2, Feb. 1969, pp. 275–84.
27. "Food and Nutrition." *Consumer Bulletin Annual*, 1962–1963, pp. 20–21.
28. *Ibid.*, p. 20.

CHAPTER 10

1. "Death Due to Penicillin Anaphylactic Reaction." *The Lancet*, Vol. 1, 1956, No. 12, Mar. 24, 1956, p. 339.
2. Richard W. Brown, "Residues in Milk from Antibiotics Used in Mastitis Treatment." *The Nature and Fate of Chemicals Applied to Soils, Plants, and Animals*. Symposium, USDA Agricultural Research Service, Sept. 1960, p. 189.
3. Franklin Bicknell, M.D., *Chemicals in Food and in Farm Produce: Their Harmful Effects*. London: Faber & Faber, 1960, p. 72.
4. FDA release, Feb. 22, 1956.

5. "Proceedings: Joint Conference on Chemical Additives in Foods." *Food, Drug & Cosmetic Law Journal*, Vol. 12, 1957, p. 451.
6. Director M. R. Stephens, *A Report from the FDA, California Creamery Operations Association, Lake Tahoe, California.* Bureau of Enforcement, FDA, June 16, 1960.
7. As in Note 3, above, p. 76.
8. Brian Inglis, *Drugs, Doctors, and Disease.* London: André Deutsch, 1965, p. 128.
9. Howard J. Sanders, "Chemical Mutagens, The Road to Genetic Disaster?" *Chemical & Engineering News*, June 2, 1969, p. 65.
10. Dr. Georges Valensin, *The Question of Fertility.* Garden City: Doubleday, 1960, pp. 80–81.
11. "Detergents at Large." Annotation, *The Lancet*, Vol. 2, No. 6902, Dec. 10, 1955, p. 1233.
12. E. F. Stula, R. H. Benson, and L. R. Glazier, "Antibiotic and Pesticide Residues in Market Milk" (detergents), *Farm-Home 4-H Extension Reports*, College of Agriculture, University of Connecticut, No. 59 (undated).
13. Hans L. Falk, Paul Kotin, and Adele Miller, "Milk as an Eluant of Polycyclic Aromatic Hydrocarbons Added to Wax." *Nature*, Vol. 183, Apr. 25, 1959, pp. 1184–85.
14. Wilhelm C. Hueper, M.D., "Symposium: Environmental & Occupational Cancer Hazards, Part 1." *Clinical Pharmacology & Therapeutics*, Vol. 3, No. 6, 1963, p. 786.
15. E. H. Marth and B. E. Ellickson, "Insecticide Residues in Milk from Treatment of Dairy Cows and Barns." *Journal of Milk and Food Technology*, Vol. 22, 1959, pp. 145–49, 179–82.
16. "DDT in Milk, Heir to the Cranberry Mess?" *California Farmer*, Aug. 18, 1962.
17. Seminar on Pesticides, American Chemical Society, New York, 1963.
18. John L. Harvey, *address.* Milk Industry Foundation, 1961.
19. M. R. Stephens, *address.* Dairy industry conference, Cornell University, Jan. 5, 1960.
20. Henry Heineman, *address.* As in Note 17, above.
21. "Effects, Uses, Control, and Research of Agricultural Pesticides." *A Report by the Surveys and Investigations Staff, USDA.* Presented at Hearings before a Subcommittee on Appropriations, 89th Congress, 1st session, House of Representatives, Department of Agriculture Appropriations for 1966, Part 1, p. 174.
22. "They Told Us: Dump Your Milk." *Farm Journal*, July 1964, pp. 24, 37.

23. "Economic Impact on the Milk Industry." *A Report by the Surveys and Investigations Staff, USDA.* As in Note 21, above, p. 181.

24. "Insecticide-Tainted Milk Put to Use." *Health Bulletin,* Sept. 5, 1964, p. 4.

25. *Report on "No Residue" and "Zero Tolerance."* Washington, D.C.: NAS-NRC, Pesticide Residues Committee, 1965, p. 6.

26. *Ibid.,* pp. 10–11.

27. *Federal Register,* Nov. 16, 1965.

28. "The Milk All of Us Drink—and Fallout." *Consumer Reports,* Mar. 1959, p. 103.

29. "Radioactive Contamination of the Environment: Public Health Action." *A Report to the Surgeon General Prepared by the National Advisory Committee on Radiation.* U.S. Department of Health, Education and Welfare, Public Health Service, May 1962, p. 9.

30. "Fallout and the U.S. Diet." *Consumer Reports,* Mar. 1962, p. 143.

31. H. D. Cremer *et al.,* "Dental Caries and Growth in Rats Fed Whole-Milk Powder with Increasing Lysine Deterioration." *Journal of Nutrition.* Vol. 70, 1960, pp. 533–36.

32. "Vitamin D Poisoning." Annotations, No. 6965, *The Lancet,* Vol. 1, Feb. 23, 1957, No. 8, p. 416.

33. "Salmonella, the Ubiquitous Bug." *FDA Papers,* Vol. 1, No. 1, Feb. 1967, p. 14.

34. Quoted by Dr. E. E. Pfeiffer, "Milk, a Special Fluid." *Modern Nutrition,* Vol. 15, No. 4, Apr. 1962, p. 21.

35. *Wall Street Journal,* Feb. 9, 1965.

36. Harvey W. Wiley, M.D., *Principles and Practice of Agricultural Analysis,* Vol. 3. New York: Chemical Publishing Co., 1914, p. 563.

37. "Chronic Pyridoxine Deficiency in the Rat." *Nutrition Reviews,* Vol. 13, No. 4, Apr. 1955, p. 19.

38. R. B. Davidov, "The Content and Loss of Vitamins in Evaporated Milk." *Chemical Abstracts,* Vol. 52, No. 7, Apr. 10, 1958, p. 5688.

39. *Milk and Cream, Definitions & Standards Under the Federal Food, Drug & Cosmetic Act.* FDA, revised July 1962, p. 3.

40. *Ibid.,* p. 4.

41. Francis M. Pottenger, Jr., M.D., "The Effect of Heat-Processed Foods and Metabolized Vitamin D Milk on the Dentofacial Structures of Experimental Animals." *American Journal of Orthodontics & Oral Surgery,* Vol. 32, No. 8, Aug. 1946, pp. 484–85.

42. David Sanford, "Unmilk, Cowing the Consumer." *New Republic,* Aug. 10, 1968, p. 11.

43. Elaine R. Monsen and Lieve Adriaenssens, "Fatty Acid Composition

and Total Lipid of Cream and Cream Substitutes." *American Journal of Clinical Nutrition,* Vol. 22, No. 4, Apr. 1969, pp. 458–63.

44. M. F. Brinks, Marie Balsley, and E. W. Speckman, "Nutritional Value of Milk Compared with Filled & Imitation Milks." *American Journal of Clinical Nutrition,* Vol. 22, No. 2, Feb. 1969, p. 179.

45. Milton E. Rubini, M.D., "Filled Milk & Artificial Milk Substitutes." *Ibid.,* pp. 163–67.
    pp. 163–67.

46. As in Note 42, above, p. 12.

47. Weston A. Price, D.D.S., "A New Vitamin-Like Activator." *Nutrition and Physical Degeneration.* Los Angeles: American Academy of Applied Nutrition, 1950 (5th printing), pp. 437–59.

48. Wilhelm C. Hueper, M.D., "Carcinogens in the Human Environment." *Archives of Pathology, American Medical Association,* Vol. 71, Apr. 1961, p. 358.

49. *Federal Register,* Feb. 5, 1960; *ibid.,* July 2, 1960; *Docket No. FDC 69,* June 24, 1961.

50. *Cheese and Cheese Products, Definitions & Standards Under the Federal Food, Drug & Cosmetic Act.* FDA, Part 19, Title 21, Code of Federal Regulations, reprinted Nov. 1959 with appendixes, p. 2.1.

51. F. S. Thatcher and W. Simon, "The Resistance of Staphylococci and Streptococci Isolated from Cheese to Various Antibiotics." *Canadian Journal of Public Health.* Vol. 46, 1955, p. 407.

52. "Cheese Situation in Utah." *A Report by the Surveys & Investigations Staff, USDA,* as in Note 21, above, pp. 183–85.

53. *Deseret News* (Salt Lake City), Feb. 26, 1964.

54. "Economic Impact on the Milk Industry." *A Report by the Surveys & Investigations Staff, USDA,* as in Note 21, above, p. 181.

55. Peter Millones, "U.S. Impounding Pesticide-Tainted Cheese Imports." *The New York Times,* Sept. 12, 1969.

56. W. H. Martin, V. D. Foltz, and W. D. Rutz, "A Survey of Cottage Cheese Quality." *Journal of Milk and Food Technology,* Vol. 23, No. 10, Oct. 1960, p. 306.

57. "Urges Amending Standards for Cottage Cheese." *Food Processing.* Nov. 1960, p. 16.

58. "Adhesive Maker Asks to Add Chemical to Cottage Cheese." *Health Bulletin,* Aug. 10, 1965, p. 5.

59. Federation of Homemakers, *Newsletter,* Aug. 4, 1960, p. 3.

60. "A Sorry Tale of Cottage Cheese." *Consumer Reports,* Oct. 1964, pp. 485–87.

61. F. J. Schlink, *Eat, Drink, and Be Wary.* New York: Covici Friede, 1935, p. 294.

62. Vivienne Marquis and Patricia Haskell, *The Cheese Book.* New York: Simon & Schuster, 1965, p. 197.

63. *Cheese and Cheese Products, Definitions & Standards . . . op. cit.,* Part 19, Cheese Standards, paragraph 19.750, p. 27.

64. *Frozen Desserts, Definitions & Standards Under the Federal Food, Drug & Cosmetic Act.* Part 20, Title 21, Dec. 1964, paragraph 20.1 Ice cream; identity; label statement of optional ingredients.

65. "Ice Cream, What Is It?" *Consumer Bulletin,* July 1962, p. 13.

66. As in Note 64, above, paragraph 20.1, (9) (c), p. 2.

67. "Agar-Agar, Algin, and Carrageenan, And That's What Ice Cream's Made of." *National Observer,* Jan. 20, 1969.

68. As in Note 64, above, Finding of Facts, No. 15, p. 5.

69. *Ibid.,* No. 2, p. 1.

70. *Ibid.,* No. 7, p. 3.

71. *Ibid.,* No. 32, p. 9.

72. "Ice Cream, What's In It?" As in Note 65, p. 14.

73. Harvey W. Wiley, M.D., *1001 Tests.* New York: Hearst's International Library, 1914, p. 167.

74. As in Note 64, above, Finding of Facts, No. 27, p. 8.

75. *Ibid.,* No. 41, p. 13.

76. Joseph Merory, *Food Flavorings: Composition, Manufacture and Use.* Westport: Avi Publishing Co., 1960, p. 170.

77. *Ibid.,* p. 186.

78. Wilhelm C. Hueper, M.D., "Potential Role of Non-Nutritive Food Additives and Contaminants as Environmental Carcinogens." Symposium on Potential Cancer Hazards from Chemical Additives. *Archives of Pathology, American Medical Association,* Vol. 62, 1956, pp. 235–37.

CHAPTER 11

1. Congressman Morgan M. Moulder, *question.* 86th Congress, 2nd session, Hearings before the Committee on Interstate and Foreign Commerce, House of Representatives, on Color Additives, 1960, pp. 376.

2. M. R. Clarkson, *statement. Ibid.,* pp. 376–77.

3. As in Note 1, above.

4. Robert C. Ruark, "Please Don't Pass Any of Those Strawberries." *Cleveland Press,* Apr. 22, 1965.

5. "Annual General Meeting Royal Horticultural Society 1959." *The Times* (London), Feb. 25, 1959.

6. "It Couldn't Be Done!" USDA *Service,* No. 47, Nov. 1967, p. 3.

7. "Tomorrow's World." *Ibid.*, No. 53, June 1968, p. 2.
8. "Tomatoes." *Consumer Bulletin,* Oct. 1968, p. 42.
9. Dr. William A. Albrecht, "Managing Nitrogen to Increase the Protein in Grains." *Victory Farm Forum,* Chilean Nitrate Educational Bureau, Dec. 1951.
10. *Idem., address.* "Physical, Chemical & Biochemical Changes in the Soil Community." International symposium, Wenner-Gren Foundation, Chicago, 1956.
11. R. J. Block and D. Bolling, "The Concept of Balanced Protein." R. S. Harris and H. W. Loesecke (eds.), *Nutritional Evaluation of Food Processing.* New York: Wiley, 1960, pp. 510–12.
12. Susan Abraham, "Studies in Spontaneous and Induced Mutations." *Cytologia,* 1965, pp. 155–72.
13. Dr. Werner Schuphan, *Nutritional Values in Crops and Plants, Problems for Producers and Consumers.* London: Faber & Faber, 1965, p. 108.
14. *Ibid.,* p. 50.
15. *Ibid.,* p. 108.
16. Dr. R. F. Milton, "Trace Elements in Soil, Plant and Animal." Sanderson-Wells Lecture, Middlesex Hospital (England), May 21, 1957.
17. Quoted by Dr. H. H. Koepf, "Nitrate, An Ailing Organism Calls for Healing." *Biodynamics.* No. 73, Winter 1965, p. 1.
18. "Foods Gaining Ability to Eat Through Cans." *Health Bulletin,* Jan. 22, 1966, p. 2.
19. J. K. Wilson, "Nitrate in Foods and Its Relation to Health." *Agronomy Journal,* Jan. 1949, pp. 20–22.
20. Prof. Barry Commoner, "The Balance of Nature." *Journal of the Soil Association,* Vol. 15, No. 2, Apr. 1968, pp. 76–77.
21. *New England Weekly,* Mar. 29, 1945.
22. Burt Schorr, "Pesticide Amounts in Food May Be Higher Than U.S. Tests Hint, 2 Incidents Suggest." *Wall Street Journal,* Nov. 28, 1969, p. 4.
23. "German Pesticide Law May Pose Problems for U.S. Farm Trade." *National Agricultural Chemicals Association News & Pesticide Review,* Vol. 25, No. 5, June 1967, p. 13.
24. "FDA and USDA Move to Cut Pesticide Residues." *Health Bulletin,* Feb. 17, 1968, p. 3.
25. Dr. O. W. Grussendorf, "Removing Pesticide Residues from Food." *Biodynamics,* No. 76, Fall 1965, pp. 28–29.
26. Bernice K. Watt, Annabel L. Merrill, *et al., Composition of Foods, Agricultural Handbook 8.* Consumer and Food Economics Research

Division, Agricultural Research Service, USDA, Dec. 1963 (revised), p. 176.

27. Samuel S. Epstein, J. Andrea, H. Jaffe, S. Joshi, H. Falk, and N. Mantel, "Carcinogenicity of the Herbicide Maleic Hydrazide." *Nature*, Vol. 215, No. 5108, Sept. 23, 1967, pp. 1388–90.

28. F. Dickens and H. E. H. Jones, "Further Studies on the Carcinogenic Action of Certain Lactones & Related Substances in the Rat & Mouse." *British Journal of Cancer*, Vol. 19, No. 2, 1965, pp. 393, 399–400; also C. D. Darlington and J. McLeish, "Action of Maleic Hydrazide on the Cell." *Nature*, Vol. 167, No. 4245, Mar. 10, 1951, pp. 407–8.

29. Dr. J. M. Barnes, Dr. P. N. Magee, Prof. E. Boyland, Prof. A. Haddow, Prof. R. D. Passey, Prof. W. S. Bullough. Dr. C. N. D. Cruickshank, Dr. M. H. Salaman, and Prof. R. T. Williams, "The Non-Toxicity of Maleic Hydrazide for Mammalian Tissues." *Nature*, Vol. 180, July 13, 1957, pp. 62–64.

30. Epstein *et al.*, as in Note 27, p. 1390.

31. Samuel S. Epstein, "Chemical Hazards in the Human Environment." *Paper*, 11th science writers seminar of the American Cancer Society, New Orleans, Mar. 28–Apr. 2, 1969, pp. 3–4 (script).

32. *Hartford Times*, Jan. 31, 1962.

33. "How to Spot Untreated Onions." *Farm Journal*, Feb., 1965, p. 56.

34. *Wall Street Journal*, Feb. 15, 1968.

35. Quoted by Thomas Whiteside, "Defoliation." *The New Yorker*, Feb. 7, 1960, p. 33.

36. Robert M. Smith, "U.S. Curbs Use of Weed Killer That Produces Rat Deformities." *The New York Times*, Oct. 30, 1969.

37. Sam Pope Brewer, "Defoliants Used in South Vietnam Are Linked to Birth Defects." *The New York Times* (Sunday), Dec. 7, 1969, p. 7.

38. As in Note 36, above.

39. As in Note 35, above, pp. 62–69.

40. L. P. De Wolf, letter to author, Feb. 2, 1966.

41. A. Levan and J. H. Tjio, "Induction of Chromosome Fragmentation by Phenols." *Hereditas*. Vol. 34, 1948, pp. 453–84.

42. As in Note 13, above, p. 171.

43. Quoted in *Consumer Bulletin*, Nov. 1957, p. 33.

44. "Growers Say FDA Produce Proposal Not Satisfactory." *Food Field Reporter*, Dec. 9, 1957.

45. "Three States Object to FDA Proposal on Citrus Labeling; Would Eliminate Need to Identify Chemicals Used After Harvesting." *Food Field Reporter*, June 9, 1958.

46. Food Advisory Branch, Division of Industry Advice, Bureau of Education and Voluntary Compliance, FDA, letter to author, Jan. 19, 1966.

47. "Food Laws." *Health Bulletin,* Oct. 3, 1964, p. 6.

48. *Federal Register,* Mar. 12, 1964.

49. Wilhelm C. Hueper, M.D., "Carcinogens in the Human Environment." *Archives of Pathology, American Medical Association,* Vol. 71, Apr. 1961, p. 357.

50. "Mineral Oil." *Consumer Bulletin,* Dec. 1966, p. 42.

51. Theron G. Randolph, M.D., *Human Ecology and Susceptibility to the Chemical Environment.* Chicago: Charles Thomas, 1962, p. 77.

52. Hans L. Falk, Paul Kotin, and Adele Miller, "Milk as an Eluant of Polycyclic Aromatic Hydrocarbons Added to Wax." *Nature,* Vol. 183, Apr. 25, 1959, pp. 1184–85.

53. *This Week in Public Health.* Massachusetts Department of Health, Sept. 12, 1966.

54. R. S. Harris and H. W. Loesecke (eds.), *Nutritional Evaluation of Food Processing,* New York: Wiley, 1960, p. 145.

55. F. J. Schlink, *Eat, Drink, and Be Wary.* New York: Covici Friede, 1935, pp. 131–32.

56. *Federal Register,* Nov. 16, 1955, Finding of Facts: Red No. 32, color certification, p. 8494.

57. M. B. Folsom, FDA, delisting, Nov. 10, 1955. *Ibid.,* p. 8494.

58. Finding of Facts. *Ibid.,* p. 8494.

59. Dr. Clive M. McCay, *testimony.* 81st Congress, 2nd session, Hearings before the House Select Committee to Investigate the Use of Chemicals in Food Products, 1950, p. 86.

60. L. P. De Wolf, as in Note 40, above.

61. Advisory Opinions Branch, Division of Industry Advice, Bureau of Education and Voluntary Compliance, FDA, letter to author, Mar. 17, 1964.

62. *Federal Register,* June 21, 1968.

63. Harvey W. Wiley, M.D., *The History of a Crime Against the Food Law.* Washington, D.C.: Harvey W. Wiley, M.D. (publisher), 1929, pp. 80–81.

64. Oscar E. Anderson, Jr., *The Health of a Nation.* Chicago: University of Chicago Press, 1958, pp. 206–8.

65. As in Note 63, above, p. 63.

66. Arthur Kallet and F. J. Schlink, *100,000,000 Guinea Pigs, Dangers in Everyday Foods, Drugs and Cosmetics.* New York: Vanguard, 1933, pp. 27–28.

67. *Ibid.,* pp. 29–30.

68. Vincent A. Kleinfeld, *interrogation of witness.* 82nd Congress, 1st

session, Hearings before the House Select Committee to Investigate the Use of Chemicals in Food Products, Part 1, 1951, p. 27.

69. As in Note 66, above, pp. 243–44.

70. *Ibid.*, p. 243.

71. Division of Consumer Education, Bureau of Education and Voluntary Compliance, FDA, letter to author, June 13, 1966.

72. "Malathion-Treated Drying Trays Protect Raisins form Insects, USDA Reports." USDA release, Oct. 9, 1967.

73. As in Note 51, above, p. 69.

74. Fred R. Ingram, "Methyl Bromide Fumigation & Control in the Date-Packing Industry." *Archives of Industrial Hygiene & Occupational Medicine, American Medical Association,* Sept. 1951, Vol. 4, No. 3, pp. 193–98.

75. R. E. Duggan, "Pesticide-Residues in Total-Diet Samples: Bromine Content." *Science,* Vol. 152, No. 3729, June 17, 1966, p. 1645.

76. Mary E. Eheart, "Effect of Microwave vs. Water-Blanching on Nutrients in Broccoli." *Journal of the American Dietetic Association,* Vol. 50, No. 3, Mar. 1967, p. 207.

77. *USDA Food Processing/Marketing Report.* Washington, D.C.: USGPO, Mar. 1966.

78. *Know Your Canned Foods.* Washington, D.C.: National Canners Association, Mar. 1963, p. 8.

79. "Chemical Peeling Process Saves Time and Vegetables." *Canadian Food Industry,* Feb. 1952.

80. "Food Peeling Concentrate." *Agricultural & Food Chemistry,* Mar. 1959.

81. *Canned Vegetables & Vegetable Products, Definitions & Standards Under the Federal Food, Drug & Cosmetic Act.* Washington, D.C.: FDA, 1964, p. 3.

82. "Question, Please." USDA yearbook, *Consumers All.* Washington, D.C.: USGPO, 1965, p. 411.

83. As in Note 13, above, p. 178.

84. *Ibid.*, p. 177.

85. *Ibid.*, pp. 177–79.

86. *Ibid.*, p. 178.

87. *Ibid.*, p. 178.

88. Kyuzo Oda, "Polarigraphic Studies on Canned Foods, No. 8, Solubility of Tin in Orange Juice in the Container." *Brenseki Kaguku lo.* Kawaguchi (Japan): Oriental Canning Institute, 1961, pp. 882–86.

89. Harvey W. Wiley, M.D., *1001 Tests.* New York: Hearst's International Library, 1914, pp. 43–44.

90. As in Note 82, above, p. 411.

91. As in Note 78, above, p. 8.
92. Peter von Marquardt, "Nahrungsmittelzusatzstoffe, ihre Toxizitaet und ihre Bedeutung fuer die menschliche Ernaehrung." *Hippokrates,* Vol. 36, No. 14, July 31, 1965, pp. 541–42.
93. "Canned Foods & Cancer." Leading article, *British Medical Journal,* No. 5248, Aug. 5, 1961, pp. 362–63.

CHAPTER 12

1. John Jelly, *Daily Mail* (England), July 14, 1960.
2. Quoted in "Bread." *Consumer Bulletin Annual,* 1965–1966, p. 7.
3. Quoted by FDA Commissioner Paul B. Dunbar, "Chemical Additives in Foods." *Food, Drug & Cosmetic Law Journal,* Vol. 6, No. 6, June 1951, p. 436.
4. William Connor, "Cassandra" (column), *The Daily Mirror* (England), Aug. 1958, quoted in *Journal of the Soil Association,* Vol. 10, No. 4, Oct. 1958, p. 348.
5. Editorial, *Bakers Review,* Aug. 15, 1958.
6. R. A. McCance and E. M. Widdowson, *Breads White and Brown.* Philadelphia: Lippincott, 1956, p. 46.
7. A. M. Copping, "The Nutritive Value of Wheaten Flour and Bread." *Nutritional Abstracts, Review,* Vol. 8, 1939, p. 555.
8. Eleanor Baker and D. S. Lepkovsky, *Bread & the War Food Problem.* Riverside: College of Agriculture, University of California, June 1943.
9. *Ibid.*
10. "Minerals Are Missing in White Bread." *Health Bulletin.* July 25, 1964, p. 1.
11. As in Note 8, above.
12. "Bread Standards." Annotation, *The Lancet,* 1911, Vol. 1, p. 316.
13. Sir Robert McCarrison, M.D., *Studies in Deficiency Disease.* London: Henry Frowde, Hodder & Stoughton, 1921.
14. *Report on the Physiological Bases of Nutrition. The Problem of Nutrition,* Vol. 11, No. A12(a) II B. Geneva: League of Nations, 1939.
15. Hazel K. Stiebeling and Callie Mae Coons, "Present-Day Diets in the United States." USDA yearbook *Food and Life.* Washington, D.C.: USGPO, 1939, pp. 304–5.
16. Dr. I. M. Rabinowitch, "Man and His Diet." *The McGill News* (Canada), June 1932.
17. R. A. McCance and E. M. Widdowson, "Mineral Metabolism of

Healthy Adults on White and Brown Bread Dietaries." *Journal of Physiology.* Vol. 101, No. 1, June 1942, pp. 44–85.

18. E. F. Ladd and R. E. Stallings, *Bleaching of Flour.* Bulletin 72. Fargo: North Dakota Agricultural College Experiment Station, Nov. 1906, p. 233.

19. Oscar E. Anderson, Jr., *The Health of a Nation.* Chicago: University of Chicago Press, 1958, pp. 269–70.

20. *Ministry of Health: Report of the Departmental Committee on the Treatment of Flour with Chemical Substances.* London: HMSO, 1927.

21. Sir Edward Mellanby, M.D., "Diet & Canine Hysteria Experimentally Produced by Treated Flour. Preliminary Report." *British Medical Journal,* Vol. 2, 1946, Dec. 14, 1946, pp. 885–93.

22. "Flour Bleachers and Improvers." Leading article, *British Medical Journal,* No. 5252, Sept. 2, 1961, pp. 631–32.

23. B. S. Platt, "Fourth International Congress of Nutrition, Paris." *The Lancet,* Vol. 2, 1957, p. 288.

24. "Flour Improvers." Editorial, *British Medical Journal,* No. 5268, Dec. 23, 1961, p. 1695.

25. Franklin Bicknell, M.D., *Chemicals in Food & in Farm Produce: Their Harmful Effects.* London: Faber & Faber, 1960, p. 66.

26. *Lockwood's Technical Manual: Flour Milling.* London: Crosby Lockwood, 1948.

27. Dr. Anton Julius Carlson, *statement,* 81st Congress, 2nd session, Hearings before the House Select Committee to Investigate the Use of Chemicals in Food Products, 1950, p. 8.

28. Sir Edward Mellanby, M.D., *broadcast.* BBC, Jan. 27, 1950. Reprint, *The Farmer,* Spring 1955.

29. I. M. Sharman and Pamela J. Richards, "Commercial Breads as Sources of Vitamin E for Rats Determined by the Hemolysis Test." *British Journal of Nutrition,* Vol. 14, 1960, p. 85.

30. Dr. Hugh M. Sinclair, "Deficiency of E.F.A. & Atherosclerosis." *The Lancet,* Vol. 1, 1956, p. 381.

31. T. Moran *et al.,* "Interaction of Chlorine Dioxide with Flour: Certain Chemical Aspects." *Nature,* Vol. 171, 1953, p. 103.

32. As in Note 20, above.

33. S. G. Impey and T. Moore, Sc.D., "Nutritive Value of Bread Made from Flour Treated with Chlorine Dioxide. *British Medical Journal,* No. 5251, Aug. 26, 1961, p. 556.

34. As in Note 25, above, p. 67.

35. Sir Edward Mellanby, M.D., "The Chemical Manipulation of Foods." *British Medical Journal,* Oct. 13, 1951, p. 869.

36. *Bakery Products, Definitions & Standards Under the Federal Food, Drug & Cosmetic Act.* Washington, D.C.: FDA, Sept. 1963, reissued, FDC regulations, Part 17, amended Aug. 27, 1965.
37. Dr. A. J. Shukis, "Current Status: The Federal Standards of Identity for Bread & Rolls." *Bakers Weekly*, Nov. 22, 1965, p. 40.
38. Mark Levin, "FDA Regulations of Petroleum Products." *Bakers Review*, Dec. 1965, pp. 17–18.
39. Advertisement, *Bakers Review*, Nov. 1958, p. 61.
40. "Products Review." *Bakers Weekly*, Dec. 20, 1965, p. 113.
41. *Ibid.*, pp. 115–16.
42. "The Docket." *Consumer Reports*, May 1964, p. 236.
43. "Bakers Snap Long Decline in Profits." *Bakers Weekly*, Jan. 17, 1966.
44. *Sweeteners Used by the Baking Industry.* Agricultural Economic Report No. 32, Economic Research Service, USDA. Washington, D.C.: USGPO, May 1963, p. iii.
45. *Food Additives, What They Are/How They Are Used*, Washington, D.C.: Manufacturing Chemists' Association, 1961, p. 15.
46. *What Consumers Should Know About Food Additives.* FDA Publication 10. Washington, D.C.: USGPO, Feb. 1963, revised, p. 7.
47. S. C. Werch, M.D., letter to editor. *Journal of the American Medical Association.* Vol. 187, No. 11, Mar. 14, 1964, p. 872.
48. Advertisement, *Bakers Review*, May 1950, p. 63.
49. *Ibid.*, p. 21.
50. Advertisement, *Bakers Weekly*, Jan. 17, 1966, p. 51.
51. Quoted by Fred D. Miller, D.D.S., *Open Door to Health.* New York: Devin-Adair, 1959, p. 133.
52. R. S. Harris and H. W. Loesecke (eds.), *Nutritional Evaluation of Food Processing.* New York: Wiley, 1960, pp. 214–15.
53. *Ibid.*, pp. 208–9.
54. Richard Carter, "The Unappetizing Truth About Dry Cereals." *Pageant*, Dec. 1957.
55. Advertisement, *Good Housekeeping*, June 1921.
56. Agnes Fay Morgan and Florance B. King, "Changes in Biological Value of Cereal Proteins Due to Heat Treatment." *Proceedings of the Society of Experimental Biology & Medicine*, Vol. 23, No. 5, Feb. 1926, pp. 353–55; also Agnes Fay Morgan, Florance B. King, Ruth E. Boyden, and V. Ann Petro, "The Effect of Heat upon the Biological Value of Cereal Proteins and Casein." *Journal of Biological Chemistry*, Vol. 90, 1931, pp. 771–92.
57. "Breakfast Cereals." *Consumer Bulletin Annual*, 1965–1966, p. 7.
58. Quoted in "Breakfast Cereals." *Consumer Reports*, May 1961, p. 238.

59. "Quote Without Comment." *Consumer Reports,* June 1965, p. 274.

60. "Breakfast Cereals." As in Note 58, above, p. 238.

61. "Breakfast Cereals, Part 2." *Consumer Bulletin,* Feb. 1962, p. 32.

62. Dr. L. Emmett Holt, Jr., "Protein Economy in the Growing Child." *Postgraduate Medicine,* Vol. 27, No. 6, June 1960, p. 797.

63. *Nutritional Data.* Pittsburgh: H. J. Heinz Co., 1960, 4th ed., pp. 98–99.

64. Louise Page and Eloise Cofer, "Your Money's Worth." USDA yearbook, *Food.* Washington, D.C.: USGPO, 1959, p. 571.

65. *Ibid.,* p. 571.

66. Quoted in "Breakfast Cereals, Part 2." As in Note 61, above, p. 31.

67. Marguerite A. Constant, H. William Sievert, Paul H. Philips, and C. A. Elvehjem, "Dental Caries in the Cotton Rat." *Journal of Nutrition,* Vol. 53, May 1954, pp. 26–27.

68. Bob Barnes, "The Better Half" (cartoon), Register & Tribune Syndicate, 1965.

69. Dr. Ernest Dichter, *Handbook of Consumer Motivation, the Psychology of the World of Objects.* New York: McGraw-Hill, 1964, p. 25.

70. Dr. Aaron Altshul, *address.* American Association for the Advancement of Science. Dec. 27, 1966.

CHAPTER 13

1. Harvey W. Wiley, M.D., *1001 Tests.* New York: Hearst's International Library, 1914, p. 48.

2. Harold Aaron, M.D., "Infant Formulas." *Consumer Reports,* Oct. 1952, p. 483.

3. Bernice K. Watt, Annabel L. Merrill, *et al., Composition of Foods, Agricultural Handbook 8.* Consumer and Food Economics Research Division, Agricultural Research Service, USDA, Dec. 1963 (revised), p. 96.

4. "Coca-Cola Now Used in Baby Formulas." *Wall Street Journal,* Aug. 19, 1966.

5. J. G. Weart, "New 'Blue Baby' Disease." *Science News Letter,* Vol. 53, No. 18, 1948, pp. 275–76.

6. Anita A. Jarvis, M.D., and John R. Brown, Ph.D., "Strontium 90 Levels in Three Infant 'Formula' Foods." *Canadian Medical Association Journal,* Vol. 86, 1962, pp. 73–75.

7. Paul A. Harper, M.D., *Preventive Pediatrics.* New York: Appleton-Century-Crofts, 1963.

8. Quoted by Dr. Nelles Silverthorne, "My Most Unforgettable Character." *Reader's Digest*, Apr. 1962, p. 129.

9. *National Advertising Investments.* Chicago: Publishers' Information Bureau, Inc., Jan.–June, 1965, pp. 8–9.

10. As in Note 2, above, p. 483.

11. Dr. Martha W. Dicks-Bushell and Karen C. Davis, "Vitamin E Content in Infant Feeding Formulas and Cereals." *American Journal of Clinical Nutrition*, Vol. 20, No. 3, Mar. 1967, pp. 262–69.

12. Sandra Blakeslee, "Makers of Baby Foods Curtail Use of Monosodium Glutamate." *The New York Times*, Oct. 25, 1969.

13. Lewis K. Dahl, Martha Heine, and Lorraine Tassinari, "High Salt Content of Western Infant's Diet: Possible Relationship to Hypertension in the Adult." *Nature*, Vol. 198, June 22, 1963, pp. 1204–5.

14. *Ibid.*, p. 1204.

15. Helen A. Guthrie, Ph.D., "Infant Feeding Practices—A Predisposing Factor in Hypertension?" *American Journal of Clinical Nutrition*, Vol. 21, No. 8, Aug. 1968, pp. 866–67.

16. *Evaluation of the Toxicity of a Number of Antimicrobials & Antioxidants.* 6th Report, Joint FAO/WHO Expert Committee on Food Additives, Technical Report 228. Geneva: WHO, United Nations, 1961.

17. Reported in "Additives in Baby Foods." *Health Bulletin*, Jan. 21, 1967, p. 6.

18. Dr. L. G. Cox, *testimony.* 82nd Congress, 2nd session, Hearings before the House Select Committee to Investigate the Use of Chemicals in Foods & Cosmetics, Part 3, 1952, p. 1387.

19. *Ibid.*, pp. 1391–92.

20. *Ibid.*, p. 1390.

21. Harvey W. Wiley, M.D., "League for Longer Life." *Good Housekeeping*, Sept. 1920.

CHAPTER 14

1. "The Improvement of Human Nutrition." Ralph W. Gerard, M.D. (ed.), *Food for Life.* Chicago: University of Chicago Press, 1952, p. 270.

2. *Nutritional Data.* Pittsburgh: H. J. Heinz Co., 1960, 4th ed., pp. 108–9.

3. W. C. Hueper, M.D., "Are Sugars Carcinogens? An Experimental Study." *Cancer Research*, Vol. 25, No. 4, May 1965, p. 442.

4. *The Composition of Cane Juice & Cane Final Molasses.* New York: Sugar Research Foundation, 1953.

5. M. A. Antar, M. A. Ohlson, and R. E. Hodges, "Changes in Retail Market Food Supplies." *American Journal of Clinical Nutrition,* Vol. 14, Mar. 1964, pp. 169–78.
6. Quoted in *Consumer Bulletin Annual, 1961,* 1962, pp. 180–81.
7. Michael J. Walsh, D.Sc., *paper.* Sugar symposium, an appraisal. *Journal of Southern California Dental Association,* Vol. 17, Dec. 1950, pp. 18–24.
8. *Food Field Reporter,* June 22, 1959.
9. E. M. Abrahamson and A. W. Pezet, *Body, Mind and Sugar.* New York: Holt, 1951.
10. Quoted by C. M. McEachern, D.D.S., "Sugar." *Family News,* Vol. 5, No. 4, St. Petersburg (Fla.): Page Foundation, Mar. 1958, p. 1.
11. "Sugar Fortified with Vitamins Can Be Sold, Appeals Court Says." *Health Bulletin,* July 18, 1964, p. 1.
12. Pete Weitzel, "Sugar Is Sweet and Vitaminized, Judge Declares." *Miami Herald,* Mar. 1, 1963.
13. Harvey W. Wiley, M.D., *The History of a Crime Against the Food Law,* Washington, D.C.: Harvey W. Wiley, M.D. (publisher), 1929, p. 320.
14. John James Rickard McLeod, *Physiology & Biochemistry in Modern Medicine.* St. Louis: C. V. Mosby, 1918.
15. As in Note 13, above, p. 317.
16. *Ibid.,* p. 317.
17. Oscar E. Anderson, Jr., *The Health of a Nation.* Chicago: University of Chicago Press, 1958, p. 205.
18. *Ibid.,* p. 206.
19. Harvey W. Wiley, M.D., *An Autobiography.* New York: Bobbs Merrill, 1930, p. 270.
20. F. C. Dohan and F. D. W. Lukens, "Experimental Diabetes Produced by the Administration of Glucose." *Endocrinology,* Vol. 42, 1948, p. 244.
21. Harvey W. Wiley, M.D., "Bitter-Sweet, the Story of the Fight Against the Use of Saccharin in Foods." *Good Housekeeping,* Nov. 1913.
22. As in Note 13, above, pp. 162–66, 191–92.
23. *The Safety of Artificial Sweeteners for Use in Foods.* A Report by the Food Protection Committee of the Food and Nutrition Board, Publication 386. Washington, D.C.: NAS-NRC, Aug. 1955, p. 1.
24. *Ibid.,* p. 7.
25. *Ibid.,* p. 8.
26. *Fruit Butters, Jellies, Preserves, Definitions & Standards Under the Federal Food, Drug & Cosmetic Act.* FDA, F.D.C. Regulations, Part 29, revised Feb. 1961, p. 20, paragraph 29.5.

27. "The Boom in Artifical Sweeteners." *Consumer Reports,* Oct. 1964, p. 471.
28. *Ibid.,* pp. 469–70.
29. The Ad Hoc Committee on Nonnutritive Sweeteners, *Summary & Conclusions from an Interim Report to the U.S. Food & Drug Administration.* Washington, D.C.: Food Protection Committee, NAS-NRC, Nov. 1968, p. 1.
30. Harold Aaron, M.D., *editorial. Medical Letter,* Sept. 11, 1964.
31. As in Note 29, above, p. 3.
32. "Committee to Study Artificial Sweeteners." *Health Bulletin,* Mar. 23, 1968, p. 1.
33. As in Note 23, above, p. 7.
34. As in Note 29, above, p. 3.
35. *Ibid.,* p. 3.
36. *Ibid.,* p. 5.
37. *Ibid.,* p. 5.
38. "Artificial Sweeteners Impair Usefulness of Anti-Infection Antibiotic." *Health Bulletin,* Nov. 30, 1968, p. 1.
39. As in Note 29, above, pp. 5–6.
40. *Ibid.,* p. 8.
41. "Cyclamates to be Taken off 'Generally Recognized As Safe' List." *Health Bulletin,* Feb. 22, 1969, p. 2.
42. Richard R. Leger, "FDA Experiments with Cyclamate Raise New Questions Over Safety of Sweetener." *Wall Street Journal,* Sept. 15, 1969, p. 12.
43. "Finch Assails FDA on Cyclamate Views." *The New York Times,* Oct. 8, 1969, p. 29.
44. "Finch Is Reported Ready to Ban Cyclamates Used in Diet Drinks." *The New York Times,* Oct. 18, 1969, p. 1.
45. Harold M. Schmeck, Jr., "FDA to Restudy Four Substances." *The New York Times,* Oct. 23, 1969, p. 35.
46. "Sweetness and Light? The Ban on Cyclamates Is a Triumph of Pseudo-Science." Editorial, *Barron's,* Nov. 17, 1969, p. 1.
47. "U.S. Now Classifies Cyclamate as Drug." *The New York Times,* Nov. 23, 1969, p. 23.
48. Sen. Warren G. Magnuson and Jean Carper, "Consumer Protection: Those Cyclamates." *Newark Sunday News,* Jan. 4, 1969.
49. "Is Your Food Safe?" *U.S. News & World Report,* Dec. 15, 1969, p. 47.
50. "Pellet Payoff." *American Agriculturist,* Oct. 1965, p. 43.
51. C. O. Willitz, *Maple Sirup Producers Manual.* Agricultural Handbook 134. Washington, D.C.: USGPO, June 1965 (revised), pp. 11–12.

52. "Maple Syrup." *Consumer Bulletin,* Sept. 1962, p. 42.
53. As in Note 50, above, p. 43.
54. Fred E. Winch, Jr., "New Vigor for an Old Industry." *American Agriculturist,* Feb. 1966, pp. 30–31.
55. M. H. Haydak, "Nutritional Value of Honey." *American Bee Journal,* Vol. 95, 1955, p. 185.
56. "A Good Bee Repellent." *American Agriculturist,* Apr. 1965, p. 35.
57. "Bee Smoke." *Ibid.,* Dec. 1965, p. 33.
58. Harvey W. Wiley, M.D., *1001 Tests.* New York: Hearst's International Library, 1914, p. 34.
59. "Candy." *The New Yorker,* June 3, 1961, p. 24.
60. *Ibid.,* pp. 24–25.
61. *Ibid.,* p. 25.
62. *Ibid.,* p. 25.
63. *Food Field Reporter,* June 6, 1961.
64. Quoted in *Modern Nutrition,* Vol. 15, No. 11, Nov. 1962, p. 5.
65. Quoted in "Sugar, Enemy of Good Nutrition." *Consumer Bulletin,* Feb. 1961, pp. 10–11.
66. "Lollipops Donated to Hospitals." *Evening Herald* (Dublin), Apr. 5, 1968.
67. As in Note 59, above, p. 26.
68. *Food Chemical News,* June 14, 1965.
69. "Sugar, Enemy of Good Nutrition, Part 2." *Consumer Bulletin,* Mar. 1961, p. 41.
70. D. A. Dowell, M.D., "Chewing Gum and Dental Caries." In "Queries & Minor Notes," *Journal of the American Medical Association.* Vol. 148, No. 13, Mar. 29, 1952, p. 1167.
71. Clayton S. Smith, M.D., Helen L. Wikoff, M.D., and Martha E. Southard, "Some Effects of Gum Chewing on Gastric Acidity in Healthy Individuals." *American Journal of Digestive Diseases.* Aug. 1946, pp. 245–47.
72. "What Goes into Modern Chewing Gums?" *Consumer Bulletin,* Oct. 1962, pp. 30–32.
73. *Federal Register,* Sept. 28, 1962.
74. "Chewing Gum." *Consumer Bulletin,* Aug. 1961, p. 31.
75. R. Heggie, R. C. Bucher, F. T. De Angelis, E. L. Fenimore, J. L. Scanlan, John Staley, R. S. Towne, J. I. Weeks, and F. Witzel, "Flavoring Substances Used in Chewing Gum." *Food Technology,* Vol. 19, 1965, p. 960.
76. As in Note 72, above, p. 31.
77. *Ibid.,* p. 32.
78. Anne Burgess and R. F. A. Dean (eds.), *Malnutrition & Food Habits.* International & Interprofessional Congress on Malnutrition &

Food Habits, Cuernavaca, 1960. New York: Macmillan, pp. 39–40.
79. *Ibid.*, p. 40.
80. "Soft Drinks Sales Soar." *Modern Nutrition,* Vol. 18, No. 11, Nov. 1965, p. 22.
81. "Sales of 'Syntha-Colas' Are Booming." *Health Bulletin,* July 25, 1964, p. 1.
82. Bernice K. Watt, Annabel L. Merrill, *et al., Composition of Foods, Agricultural Handbook 8.* Consumer and Food Economics Research Division, Agricultural Research Service, USDA, Dec. 1963 (revised), p. 16.
83. "Soft Drinks and Their Labeling." *Consumer Bulletin Annual,* 1965–1966, p. 10.
84. As in Note 1, above, p. 271.
85. As in Note 69, above, p. 41.
86. "Food Acids and Caries." Lead article, *Journal of the American Medical Association,* Vol. 145, No. 5, Feb. 3, 1951, pp. 321–22.
87. D. Carey Miller, "Enamel Erosive Properties of Fruits and Various Beverages." *Journal of the American Dietetic Association,* Vol. 28, No. 4, Apr. 1952, pp. 319–24.
88. Clive M. McCay, Ph.D., *testimony.* 81st Congress, 1st session, Hearings before the House Select Committee to Investigate the Use of Chemicals in Food Products, 1950, pp. 90–91.
89. *Ibid.*, pp. 99–109.
90. "Phosphates and Phosphoric Acid." *Consumer Bulletin Annual,* Sept. 1956, pp. 73–74.
91. As in Note 88, above, p. 92.
92. Howard J. Sanders, "Chemical Mutagens, The Road to Genetic Disaster?" *Chemical & Engineering News,* June 2, 1969, pp. 60–61.
93. As in Note 58, above, p. 21.
94. Mary Cantrell, P.H.N., "Health Snacks at School." *Journal of School Health,* Vol. 29, No. 10, Dec. 1959, pp. 386–87.

CHAPTER 15

1. Sen. George McGovern, "Private Industry and Nutrition." Senate Floor Speech, July 14, 1969, *release,* p. 2.
2. *Use of Pesticides: A Report of the President's Science Advisory Committee.* Washington, D.C.: USGPO, May 15, 1963, pp. 20–21.
3. U.S. Secretary of Agriculture Orville S. Freeman, *broadcast,* CBS, Apr. 3, 1963.

4. "Health Hazards Due to Pesticides to Get Study by Newly Formed Panel of Experts." *Wall Street Journal,* Apr. 22, 1969.

5. *Report of Committee on Persistent Pesticides to Administrator, Agricultural Research Service, USDA.* Washington, D.C.: NRC-NAS, National Academy of Engineering, May 27, 1969, p. 28.

6. "Important Notice, Subject: Agricultural Insecticides." Thompson Chemicals Corporation release, May 1, 1957.

7. *Crop Life,* Nov. 1967.

8. George F. Stewart, "Nutrition and the Food Technologist." Editorial, *Food Technology,* Vol. 18, No. 9, Oct. 1964.

9. *New York Post,* July 16, 1969.

10. Ancel Keys, M.D., "Some Notes for Cholesterol Watchers." University of Minnesota School of Public Health release, June 24, 1969.

11. "USDA Makes Overseas Shipping Tests with Frozen Poultry." USDA release, May 10, 1966.

12. Dr. Georg Bergstrom, *address.* Food science symposium, Michigan State University, 1967.

13. Will Kinney, *Food-Dollars Can Revolutionize Food Industries.* Vista (Calif.): Will Kinney, 1957 (reprint).

14. N. W. Pirie, "Orthodox & Unorthodox Methods of Meeting World Food Needs." *Scientific American,* Vol. 216, No. 2, Feb. 1967, pp. 27–35.

15. "The 1958 Amendment to the Food & Drug Act." *Consumer Bulletin,* Nov. 1958, p. 11.

16. "Food Safety and the FDA." *San Francisco Chronicle,* Nov. 10, 1969.

17. "The Thumb on the Scale." *Consumer Bulletin,* June 1968, pp. 39–40.

18. *Ibid.,* p. 40.

19. Public Law 89–487, effective July 4, 1967. Regulations: *Federal Register,* June 30, 1967.

20. Joseph M. Mamana, "FDA's Obligations Under the 1966 Public Information Act." *FDA Papers,* Vol. 1, No. 7, Sept. 1967, p. 16.

21. *Ibid.,* p. 16.

22. Quoted by S. H. Holbrook, *The Golden Age of Quackery.* New York: Macmillan, 1959, p. 27.

23. President John F. Kennedy, "Special Message on Protecting the Consumer Interest," *address.* Congress of the U.S., Washington, D.C., Mar. 15, 1962, p. 10 (script).

24. "Clearer Labels Coming on Food Packages." *Health Bulletin,* July 25, 1964, p. 4.

25. "Text of President Nixon's Message to Congress on Proposals to Help Consumers." *The New York Times*, Oct. 31, 1969, p. 22.
26. *Read the Label.* U.S. Department of Health, Education and Welfare, FDA, Washington, D.C., 1964.
27. "Date Labeling." *Consumer Bulletin*, Aug. 1965, p. 41.
28. "Dating." Letter to editor, *Consumer Reports*, Sept. 1962, p. 418.
29. "Consumer Protection." *Health Bulletin*, May 16, 1964, p. 5.
30. "Co-op Freshness Codes." *Co-op Consumer*, Silver Spring, Md., Nov. 5, 1969, p. 1.
31. *What Consumers Should Know About Food Standards.* Food & Drug Administration Publication No. 8. Washington, D.C.: USGPO, 1961, p. 1.
32. *Food Chemical News*, Apr. 7, 1969.
33. Quoted by Morton Mintz, *By Prescription Only*. Boston: Houghton Mifflin, 1967 (2nd ed. revised & updated), p. 130.
34. Elise Jerard, "Consumers' Lobby, You Are Invited!" *Modern Nutrition*, Vol. 14, No. 6, June 1961, p. 19.
35. Arthur Kallet and F. J. Schlink, *100,000,000 Guinea Pigs, Dangers in Everyday Foods, Drugs, and Cosmetics*. New York: Vanguard, 1933, pp. 195–96.
36. "Letter from a Retired Drug Inspector." *Saturday Review*, Feb. 4, 1961, p. 43.
37. *Ibid.*, p. 43.
38. *Report of the Second Citizens Advisory Committee on the Food & Drug Administration.* Washington, D.C.: USGPO, Oct. 1962, p. 7.
39. As in Note 33, above, p. 53.
40. Harold M. Schmeck, Jr., "Food-Drug Panel Criticizes Agency." *The New York Times*, Aug. 8, 1969.
41. As in Note 25, above, p. 22.
42. "A Consumer's View of Food Controls." *Consumer Bulletin*, July 1966, p. 6.
43. As in Note 38, above, pp. 15–16.
44. "Milk and Food." *Report of the Committee on Environmental Health Problems to the Surgeon General.* U.S. Department of Health, Education and Welfare, Public Health Service. Washington, D.C.: USGPO, 1962, p. 136.
45. *Ibid.*, p. 140.
46. *Ibid.*, pp. 141–42.
47. *Ibid.*, p. 142.
48. Quoted in "An Official Consumer Voice in Washington." *Consumer Reports*, Sept. 1962, p. 463.
49. "A New Era in Consumer Affairs." *Consumer Reports*, Mar. 1964, p. 144.

50. *Ibid.*, p. 144.
51. *Ibid.*, p. 144.
52. *Food from Farmer to Consumer,* Report of the National Commission on Food Marketing, USDA. Washington, D.C.: USGPO, June 1966, pp. 11–19.
53. Sylvia Porter, "Food Marketing Proposals." *New York Post,* June 3, 1966 (magazine section) p. 2.
54. As in Note 52, above, p. 92.
55. *Ibid.*, p. 101.
56. *Ibid.*, p. 101.
57. As in Note 53, above, p. 2.
58. Quoted by William J. Lederer, *A Nation of Sheep.* New York: Norton, 1961, p. 175.
59. Vance Packard, *The Waste Makers.* New York: David McKay, 1960, p. 253.

SUGGESTED READING

Franklin Bicknell, M.D., *Chemicals in Food & in Farm Produce: Their Harmful Effects.* London: Faber & Faber, 1960; also, New York: Emerson, 1960.

R. S. Harris and H. W. Loesecke (eds.), *Nutritional Evaluation of Food Processing.* New York: Wiley, 1960.

Ruth Harrison, *Animal Machines: The New Factory Farming—A Pictorial Summary.* London: Vincent Stuart, 1964; also in paperback, New York: Ballantine, 1966.

Wilhelm C. Hueper, M.D., and W. D. Conway, *Chemical Carcinogenesis and Cancers.* Chicago: Charles Thomas, 1964.

Theron G. Randolph, M.D., *Human Ecology and Susceptibility to the Chemical Environment.* Chicago: Charles Thomas, 1962.

Werner Schuphan, *Nutritional Values in Crops and Plants, Problems for Producers and Consumers.* London: Faber & Faber, 1965.

Hearings before the House Select Committee to Investigate the Use of Chemicals in Foods & Cosmetics. 81st Congress, 1st session, 1950; 82nd Congress, 1st session, Parts 1 & 2, 1951; and Hearings before a Subcommittee of the Committee on Interstate & Foreign Commerce, on Food Additives. 85th Congress, 1957–58, Parts 1, 2, & 3.

Hearings before the Committee on Interstate and Foreign Commerce, House of Representatives, on Color Additives. 86th Congress, 2nd session, 1960.

Hearings before the Subcommittee on Reorganization and International Organizations of the Committee on Government Operations, United States Senate, Interagency Co-ordination in Environmental Hazards (Pesticides). Parts 1–7, 1963, Part 8, 1964; and Appendix 1–6 to Part 1.

Hearings before the Subcommittee on Antitrust & Monopoly of the Committee on the Judiciary, United States Senate, on Packaging & Labeling Legislation. 88th Congress, 1st session, Parts 1–3, 1963–64.

Hearings before a Special Subcommittee of the Committee on Labor & Welfare, United States Senate, to Amend Section 402(d) of the

Federal Food, Drug, & Cosmetic Act. 89th Congress, 1st session, 1965 (additives in candy).

Report of the Secretary's Commission on Pesticides and Their Relationship to Environmental Health, Parts I and II, U.S. Department of Health, Education, and Welfare, Dec. 1969.

INDEX

◆ ◆ ◆ ◆

About the Author

BEATRICE TRUM HUNTER, a native New Yorker, lives on 150 acres of woodland, meadows and beaver pond in the foothills of New Hampshire's White Mountains. With her husband, John F. Hunter, she runs a small guest house. In addition to doing all the cooking, she also prepares all grains for cereal, bread, and muffins in her own stone-grinding mill. She writes for *Land Fellowship* (Canada), *Journal of the Soil Association* (England), and other publications both in the United States and abroad in the fields of food, gardening, and nutrition. Well known throughout New England for her demonstrations of whole-grain bread baking, she has also lectured all over the United States. She is a past vice-president of the American Academy of Applied Nutrition and honorary member of the Board of the Federation of Homemakers. Mrs. Hunter holds a B.A. from Brooklyn College and a master's degree from Columbia University. She has also done graduate work at State Teachers College, Buffalo, N.Y., Harvard University, and other institutions.

SORBIC ACID - MOLD RETARDER
CALCIUM SULFATE - STABILIZER